Exploring Archaeoastronomy

Exploring Archaeoastronomy

A History of its Relationship with Archaeology and Esotericism

Liz Henty

Oxford & Philadelphia

Published in the United Kingdom in 2022 by
OXBOW BOOKS
The Old Music Hall, 106–108 Cowley Road, Oxford, OX4 1JE

and in the United States by
OXBOW BOOKS
1950 Lawrence Road, Havertown, PA 19083

© Oxbow Books and Liz Henty 2022

Paperback Edition: ISBN 978-1-78925-786-1
Digital Edition: ISBN 978-1-78925-787-8

A CIP record for this book is available from the British Library

Library of Congress Control Number: 2021951953

All rights reserved. No part of this book may be reproduced or transmitted in any form or by any means, electronic or mechanical including photocopying, recording or by any information storage and retrieval system, without permission from the publisher in writing.

Printed in the United Kingdom by Short Run Press

Typeset in India by Lapiz Digital Services, Chennai.

For a complete list of Oxbow titles, please contact:

UNITED KINGDOM	UNITED STATES OF AMERICA
Oxbow Books	Oxbow Books
Telephone (01865) 241249	Telephone (610) 853-9131, Fax (610) 853-9146
Email: oxbow@oxbowbooks.com	Email: queries@casemateacademic.com
www.oxbowbooks.com	www.casemateacademic.com/oxbow

Oxbow Books is part of the Casemate Group

Front cover: Two circles stones at Loanhead of Daviot Recumbent Stone Circle, Aberdeenshire (photo by author), superimposed on a simulated panoramic skyscape showing archaeolines for the sun and the moon, created with Stellarium software program v.0.21.1 (Licensed under GNU GPL version 2).

Contents

List of figures viii
Acknowledgements x

1. Introduction: contesting the past 1
   Contested space 2
   Historiography 7
   Exploring archaeoastronomy 9

2. Antiquarianism: the *longue durée* 11
   The intellectual background 15
   Esotericism 18
   Antiquarian societies 21
   The legacy of antiquarianism 25

3. The emergence of archaeoastronomical thought 26
   Antiquarian practice 29
   Astronomical methodology 32
   Astronomical theories 37
   19th century contestations 46
   The implications for archaeoastronomy 48

4. 'The great subject of orientation' 50
   Lockyer and his contemporaries 50
   Orientation practice 53
   Archaeology 60
   Esoteric archaeology 64
   The language gap 65
   The implications for archaeoastronomy 67

5. Lines in the landscape 71
   Landscape lines 72
   The romance of the historic landscape 74
   Hybrid studies 79
   Esotericism and metrology 81
   The implications for archaeoastronomy 84

6. 'God in the machine' 87
   Astro-archaeology 88
   Solving the mysteries of Stonehenge 93
   The New Age 95
   The implications for archaeoastronomy 98

7. Megalithic science 101
   The Thom paradigm 103
   New Age appropriations 110
   The never-ending language gap 112
   Megalithic science – the debate 115
   The implications for archaeoastronomy 119

8. New World archaeoastronomy 123
   Archaeoastronomy 125
   Ethnoastronomy 128
   Communities 130
   Debates and divides 140
   The implications for archaeoastronomy 145

9. A turning point for British archaeoastronomy 147
   1985: a milestone year 147
   Archaeoastronomy: new name, new practices 149
   A turning point for archaeology 152
   Archaeoastronomy: advancing but lagging behind 155
   Esotericism 159
   Learning resources 161
   The implications for archaeoastronomy 164

10. Archaeoastronomy and cultural astronomy in Europe 168
    Michael Hoskin 169
    European studies 173
    Cultural Astronomy 182
    Communities 184
    The implications for archaeoastronomy 188

11. Archaeoastronomy in the 21st century 191
    Re-invigorating archaeoastronomy 192
    The ontological turn 194
    Skyscapes and skyscape archaeology 197
    Esotericism 202
    Disseminating archaeoastronomy 203

  Learning resources 206
  Towards convergence 208
  The implications for archaeoastronomy 211

12. Final thoughts 215
  The archaeologists 216
  The archaeoastronomers 219
  Current attitudes and steps towards the future 223

Bibliography 227
Glossary 263
Index 275

List of figures

Figure 1. Sir Walter Scott, image by Auguste Edouart (1830). 12
Figure 2. Drawing of Kits Coty house, by William Stukeley on 15 October 1722. 14
Figure 3. The Spalding Gentlemen's Society Meeting Room. 23
Figure 4. William Stukeley's drawing of *A View at Stanton Drew*. 28
Figure 5. Stonehenge as depicted in Godfrey Higgins' *The Celtic Druids* (1827). 36
Figure 6. Edward Duke's 'grand astronomical scheme' 1846. 41
Figure 7. Drawings of Hue's combined compass and clinometer (top) and a surveyor's rotating Y level with telescope (bottom) as portrayed in Sir Norman Lockyer's *Surveying for Archaeologists*. 54
Figure 8. Alfred Devoir's diagram of the alignments at Le Menéc. 57
Figure 9. Section of Boyle Somerville's plan of Callenish (now Calanais) showing the northern moon limit. 58
Figure 10. Diagram of some of the solar alignments found by Henry Hudson. 73
Figure 11. Dowsing along an ancient trackway at Petit-Ménec, Carnac. 76
Figure 12. Grahame Gardner (President of the British Society of Dowsers 2008–2014) dowsing at Aboyne Stone Circle, Aberdeenshire in 2014. 83
Figure 13. Gerald Hawkins 1969. 89
Figure 14. IBM 7090 computer as used in 1965. 92
Figure 15. Radiation monitoring at the King Stone, part of the Rollright Stones complex. 97
Figure 16. Alexander Thom's meticulous card index and one of the many notebooks he used in the field. 102
Figure 17. Alexander Thom's diagram showing the degree of precision (within 1°) he found for lunar sightlines. 105
Figure 18. Alexander Thom's plan of the recumbent stone circle at Aquorthies, Kingausie in northeast Scotland. 107
Figure 19. The Nazca ceremonial site Cahuachi in Peru, 2017. 124
Figure 20. Anthony Aveni surveying at Castillo de Teayo in the state of Veracruz, Mexico beside a Huastec carved relief, January 1979. 127
Figure 21. John B. Carlson at the Second International Conference on Archaeoastronomy held in Merida, Yucatan, Mexico in January 1986. 131
Figure 22. First Inter-American School of Astronomy in Culture, in the Facultad de Ciencias Astronómicas y Geofísicas, Universidad Nacional de La Plata, Argentina, 2012. 133
Figure 23. Clive Ruggles at the European Society for Astronomy in Culture (SEAC) conference in 2010. 150

List of figures   ix

Figure 24. Looking from the centre of Stonehenge towards the west.   152
Figure 25. At the Newgrange passage tomb the standing stone GC-1 casts
    a moving shadow over the highly decorated central kerbstone.   158
Figure 26. Lionel Sims presenting at the Theoretical Archaeology Group
    Conference, December 2017.   163
Figure 27. The Naveta d'Es Tudons, a megalithic chamber tomb in Menorca.   171
Figure 28. The precinct of Torralba d'en Salort in Menorca with its
    distinctive stone taula.   172
Figure 29. The reconstructed wooden poles at Magdalenenberg, October, 2014. 178
Figure 30. The 18th meeting of the European Society for Astronomy in
    Culture (SEAC) at Gilching, Germany, September 2010.   185
Figure 31. Fabio Silva and Liz Henty opening the Visualising Skyscapes
    session at the Theoretical Archaeology Group conference in
    Southampton, 2016.   199
Figure 32. Table-top planetarium demonstration with Daniel Brown (left)
    and Frank Prendergast (right) at the National Astronomy Meeting
    in Llandudno, July 2015.   200
Figure 33. Learning how to use a theodolite for the UWTSD
    archaeoastronomy module with Bernadette Brady (left)
    Fabio Silva (centre) and Nicholas Campion (right).   207
Figure G1. Annotated panorama of Sunhoney Recumbent Stone Circle
    showing how altitude can be measured using photographs.   266
Figure G2. Schematic representation of the Celestial Sphere.   266
Figure G3. Passage of the sun and the moon at Tomnaverie Recumbent Stone
    Circle showing both celestial and horizon crossovers for 2580 BC.   267
Figure G4. Diagrams of a solar eclipse (a) and a lunar eclipse (b).   267
Figure G5. Schematic representation of where the sun's solstices, the sun's
    cross quarter days and the moon's major and minor lunar standstills
    appear on the horizon in Britain.   270
Figure G6. Measuring the azimuths of two stones at Loanhead of Daviot
    recumbent stone circle.   271
Figure G7. The moon's monthly cycle showing its different phases.   273

Acknowledgements

In this book I point out the importance of communities and certainly without the help of my colleagues and friends from the wider circles of archaeoastronomy and archaeology this volume would not have been possible. Many thanks to those of you who supplied me with images, read chapters, gave feedback, shared insights on some aspects of this history and encouraged me throughout. A special shout-out to Fabio Silva who has been my constant sounding board during this journey. I would also like to thank Stellarium for allowing me to use the panoramic image of the sky for my cover, generated by using their software program v.0.21.1. Finally I would like to acknowledge a grant from the Sophia Centre Press and the Sophia Centre for the Study of Cosmology in Culture at the University of Wales Trinity Saint David which helped towards the cost of indexing.

Chapter 1

Introduction: contesting the past

Archaeoastronomy and archaeology are two distinct fields of study which examine the cultural aspect of societies, yet from different perspectives. They share the aim of studying the past through its material remains in order to shed light on the cultures responsible. Archaeology's investigations are informed by a ground-based methodology, which primarily involves the excavation of sites, the scientific analysis of various forms of artefacts and their interpretation according to which archaeology theory is currently in vogue. Archaeoastronomy seeks to discover the impact of astronomy on culture, whether this is intentionally incorporated in sites of archaeological interest by precision alignment, orientation, or in symbolism derived from the sky. This field, unlike archaeology which has an unbroken lineage from the late 19th century, has been called various different names in its history, such as alignment studies; orientation theory; astro-archaeology; megalithic science; archaeotopography; archaeoastronomy, cultural astronomy and skyscape archaeology: names which depict variants of its methods and theory, sometimes in tandem with those of archaeology and sometimes in opposition. While archaeoastronomy is one of these variants, it also serves as a term to describe the others in general. By exploring the astronomical properties of the sites, archaeoastronomy, through the use of a sky-based methodology, seeks to add another layer of meaning, which is unrecoverable through traditional archaeological techniques alone. For example, Britain is home to a legacy of megalithic constructions which date to the Neolithic and Bronze Ages (*c.* 4000–1000 BC). It is the monuments from these critical millennia, when astronomy might have had a bearing on how they were constructed, that have provided the focus for archaeoastronomy in Britain. On the other hand, British archaeologists not only study the entire span of prehistory which ranges from the Palaeolithic to the end of the Iron Age (*c.* 2,600,000 BC–AD 50) in a comprehensive way that includes economics, technology, culture and domestic settlement as well as monuments, but also the entire historical period up to the present day. Consequently only a small number of these archaeologists study prehistory but references to the sky and the use to which it was put by past cultures are virtually non-existent in archaeological text-books. Despite their common aim, the two fields, because of their different histories, have unequal positions today: archaeology is recognised in the academy while archaeoastronomy sits on the sidelines with little academic presence.

This begs the question of what in their particular histories has caused this inequality. Clearly history matters: its survivals and legacy live on in colouring our actions and views of archaeoastronomy and archaeology today. This is because, academic disciplines 'are products of a particular past' (Dyson 1999, 103). In other words, a discipline's history may influence what is deemed useful today and what has to be discarded. Although this can provide positive ways forward, it also gives rise to limitations and restrictions when past habits are not sufficiently questioned (Dyson 1999, 103). By examining the history of disciplines, insights are gained about 'the points of discontinuity or departure from obsolete practices' (Krishnan 2009, 31). While it may be more comfortable for a discipline to continue treading the inherited path, new discoveries, more robust methods or theoretical insights make change inevitable. These changes have to be studied in perspective because a change in one discipline may have an impact on other closely related fields. Archaeoastronomy methods and approaches have certainly changed over the years as have those of archaeology, but both retain remnants of their pasts and memories of earlier controversies. Consequently, because of their similar study areas pertaining to prehistory, the development of archaeoastronomy has to be understood in the context of the history of archaeology to find how their histories have impacted their relationship.

While archaeology and archaeoastronomy provide the main narratives, on the periphery esotericists and geomancers throw earth forces and sacred numbers into the mix. Esotericism, as used here, represents those epistemologies, characterised by superstitious, spiritual or magical beliefs, which are at odds with rational explanations. These include several strands of esoteric thought found in antiquarianism, such as 17th century Hermeticism, 18th century Romanticism and the search for ancient wisdom in the 19th century Occult Revival. Alternative theories such as these have proliferated over time and never more so than in the New Age, being variously described as esoteric, fringe or pseudoscientific. Unfortunately archaeoastronomy has often been tarred with the same brush and its theories dismissed accordingly, so its apparent relationship with esotericism also needs to be explored to see whether this misunderstanding has affected its academic status.

Contested space

What fuels the study of megalithic remains is our incessant curiosity about the past and what meaning the past has for us. This has led to the growth of a large heritage sector whereby some special monuments have been restored or reconfigured, with no heed paid to the archaeological consequences, for the purpose of creating national monuments (see for example, Harvey 2008, 29). Signboards and displayed information give a politicised and sanitised version of prehistory which is palatable to the public imagination. As Barbara Bender (1998, 110) argued, what we are being sold is 'a particular sort of experience, a particular interpretation of the past'. The question then arises as to who speaks for the past. Undoubtedly this is the domain of the archaeologists or is it? Archaeoastronomers also study prehistoric monuments but, as their aims and questions differ from those of archaeology, they come up with different answers. Yet, although both archaeology and archaeoastronomy are influenced by theories imported from other disciplines, such as social science, anthropology, psychology and statistics, and have some common approaches, what is certain is that both disciplines have competing claims to and about the past.

Archaeology brings a range of specialisms to survey, excavate, record, date and interpret the prehistoric monuments and sites. However there are 'silences and gaps' in archaeological explanations which determine which sites or artefacts are 'privileged in the legitimising of expert archaeological knowledges' (Rowlands 1997, 141). While archaeology's resulting narrative can therefore only be partial, archaeologists, because of the rigour of their investigations and historical monopoly in academia, are able to justify their reconstructions of the past. Yet, we respond to ancient places which we encounter by chance through our own sensibilities and through visiting them we not only own them but create our own vision of them, our personal engagement with the past, whether we are long-dead antiquarians, artists, tourists, archaeologists, archaeoastronomers or sacred geographers. This idea of democratic ownership is belied by the reality of the power-play between the competing claims of archaeology and archaeoastronomy; the former part of the mainstream while the latter is relegated to the margin. So deep-rooted are our cultural preferences that flaws and omissions are unconsciously pervasive. Because prehistory is 'a kind of empty space, a land that's ripe for colonisation' (Stout 2008, 1), it gives rise to conflicts or becomes 'a battleground of rival attachments' (Lowenthal 1994, 302). These ideas can be seen playing out in Bender's (1992) assessment of Stonehenge, where she introduced the idea of contested space to examine the various claims that different factions, such as archaeologists, heritage bodies, tourists and New Agers, make about this iconic British prehistoric monument. As Murray (2000, 116) observed, 'intellectual warfare depends first on defining a disputed territory, preferably an area about which we know very little, but which has high emotional appeal'. Prehistory is such a territory.

In Bender's analysis of contested space, New Agers were identified as interested parties but archaeoastronomy is conspicuous by its absence, despite her view that landscape is something which is constantly open to renegotiation. As archaeoastronomy tries to interpret the prehistorical material record, using a specialised methodology that bears little relation to the methods of archaeology, the net result is that the relationship between archaeology and archaeoastronomy has become a complex politicised issue with contestation at its heart; an issue which plays out in the arena of academia. This is because the focus of contestation in this instance is not that there are differing accounts of the past, indeed archaeology has provided several, but rather hinges around the issue of who has the more socially and academically entitled voice. Not only that, but the strength of a dominant discourse is not because it is nearer to the truth, and anyway claims about the past can only be best guesses, but because its exponents have more power than its critics. This brings us back to the question of who speaks for the past: whilst everyone is free to take part in the creative process, some voices carry more weight than others (Stout 2008, 3). As will be shown, in the academy it is the archaeologists' voices that are the most powerful.

With around 30 British universities having dedicated faculties or schools of archaeology which teach elements of the mainstream view of prehistory it is no surprise that archaeology feels entitled. Yet, while archaeological knowledge can only ever be partial and subjective, despite aiming for comprehensiveness and objectivity, then the obvious question is why not look at all the evidence available? There may even be benefits in doing so because contestation between disciplines fosters an awareness of approaching a problem from multiple points of view (Blair 2008, 577–578). Without interdisciplinary collaboration we have 'a series of contending fabrications, which pit interest to power, [and] meaning to experience' (Bond and Gilliam 1997, 17). This implies that the different narratives about the past cannot be neutral so must therefore be written with an eye for power, or at least authority. It is this authority that intellectuals achieve variously as teachers, conference presenters or peer-reviewed authors that adds them to the collective powerbase and allows them to sideline other contradictory voices. Stout (2008, 17–18) agreed that power was the motivation behind the development of archaeology as a discipline, saying it was 'the power to pronounce with authority upon the past, to control all aspects of the archaeological record, from excavation to interpretation; and to marginalise those whose ideas were incompatible with their own'. To paraphrase Bourdieu (1988, 36), archaeologists occupy 'a temporally dominant position in the field', which distinguishes them from 'the less institutionalized and more heretical sectors of the field', i.e. the archaeoastronomers and esotericists. However, while insights such as these can be gained from looking at the politics of knowledge, it does not necessarily follow that power is either actively sought or aimed for, to the detriment of other voices. In the relationship between archaeology and archaeoastronomy, while both fields study the same material remains but contest each other's narratives, the reason seems less about power-play but rather the historical circumstances that led to the establishment of archaeology as a discipline towards the end of the 19th century at a time when interest in archaeoastronomy declined, as this history aims to explore.

The success of archaeology today can be judged by its position within institutional spaces such as universities, council archaeology and planning departments, as well as by its intellectual output in books, journals and conferences. In the public arena the approval of archaeology and its accessibility may also play a part as funding is crucial; only those projects which attract funding can be undertaken. It follows that authority rests with those who control the narrative and status is conferred through authorship. Not only that, but we are culturally conditioned to believe the professional over and above the amateur or hobbyist. It is a story of success breeding success. For example, Talcott Parsons (2007, 424) described academic beliefs and cultural norms as a process of 'internalization' which becomes 'institutionalized' in order to maintain the system. This institutionalisation is accompanied by what Hobsbawm (2012) called 'invented tradition'; a set of practices, governed by accepted rules which through repetition imply continuity with a discipline's past. However, the standoff between archaeology and archaeoastronomy benefits no-one because the more details and interpretive options available, the greater the likelihood of arriving at an account which takes all convergent data into account. This might in practice be difficult to administer where different conceptual approaches often reflect the traditions and prejudices of the participants; where traditions can be handed down through the generations. Not only does the dominant discipline have power over the narrative but its student may unconsciously assimilate the views expressed and then propagate them. The lack of reference to the sky in archaeological accounts of prehistory is an example of where an archaeologist may be unaware that anything is missing so continues writing similar narratives. This is not to say that archaeology or any other discipline remains static: just as there are changing fashions in everyday life, so too are there changing fashions in how the past is presented.

On the other hand, sidelined fields can, as Bourdieu (1988, 61) observed, reach 'the winning-post by cross-country routes', as they have more freedom to experiment, innovate and try out new methodology and ideas than those in established disciplines whose praxis is dictated by those in authority and learned by rote. In this context praxis refers to both theory and methodology which are not only inextricably linked but are contained in a semiotic language system which provides the sets of values and specialised terms that define a particular academic discourse. In any sphere of enquiry when these factors are combined they either produce new understandings or confirm existing knowledge within the confines of their own disciplinary arena. There is no ordering to this process: for example, theory may determine what data is to be examined and by what methodology or alternatively data may be discovered which demands different theories and/or new methodologies to turn it into a knowledge claim. Certainly, exponents of subjects excluded from the academic curriculum struggle to make themselves heard because the dominant fields can determine whether or not to admit a new unorthodox view into the mainstream or ignore it altogether. The sidelined and subordinate field has no power to do this by itself. A further problem can be where there is a language gap so that members of different disciplines cannot speak the others' language or understand their terms and concepts. Take the example of archaeological and archaeoastronomical terms found in two books published in 2016. The following terms, ten from each publication, have been picked to demonstrate that these can only be understood 'from the native's point of view', as Geertz (1974) expressed it.

> Archaeology: revetment, socket, fragment, scatter, sherd, spall, transect, ploughsoil, penannular, cordon. (Bradley and Nimura 2016)
>
> Archaeoastronomy: zenith, altitude, azimuth, declination, elevation, precession, equinox, solstice, amplitude, alignment. (Magli 2016)

Archaeology and archaeoastronomy have their own distinguishing terms and even commonly used words such as 'scatter' or 'alignment', included in the above lists, mean something slightly different when put in their related context. This can lead to difficult relations between groups through a simple lack of understanding one another's terms. Because of all these multiple factors which come into play when examining contestation, the relationship between archaeology and archaeoastronomy has ebbed and flowed for over a century, often divided but sometimes coming together as this history will show.

Yet while discussing what makes one discipline mainstream and another marginalised, some consideration has to be given to both tradition and mythology. The archaeological narrative is disseminated widely, particularly through academic and popular literature and seeps into our ideas of heritage, which are bound up with subjective ideas of what sites and objects are worthy of preservation, often at the cost of seemingly inferior remains. These in turn merge with ideals of national pride where the past provides a safe haven to retreat from the present, as epitomised by the Romantic and nationalist notions of William Blake's 'green and pleasant land', penned in 1804. Whether the narrative is ground-centred or sky-based, archaeology and archaeoastronomy fulfil this need and have so since their very beginnings. There is certainly continuity between the modern discipline of archaeology and antiquarianism but, at some point, archaeology assumed control of the narrative, built its theory, established its faculties and achieved recognition and in so doing separated itself from the narrative of archaeoastronomy. Of course archaeology today is very different from its early beginnings so continuity may not be entirely seamless. Nevertheless the idea of it being traditional, appeals to a social and cultural requirement which verges on being nationalistic, as suggested earlier. Although this history will maintain that archaeoastronomy has had a similar unbroken lineage from antiquarianism, its ideas and methodology were dispersed in several directions so it never had the direct disciplinary continuity of archaeology. Additionally, there is a suggestion that the fierce hold that archaeologists have on prehistory today may well be explained by a battle that they won a long time ago in their successful transformation from their antiquarian beginnings.

While theories relating to contested space and the politics of knowledge are useful in showing the dynamics between two similar but sparring disciplines that are both concerned with the same space, they only hint at the relationship between archaeology and archaeoastronomy and the reasons why archaeology produces the dominant narrative on prehistory, while archaeoastronomy's accounts are mainly ignored. Archaeoastronomers were not intending to set themselves against archaeology; they simply had a different vision, which could have, if accepted, illuminated the archaeological narrative of prehistory. It was never meant to be a competition. Naturally any discipline seeks to defend its orthodoxy in the face of encroachment from another discipline; the nearer the contesting disciplines are to one another the fiercer the battle to maintain power and recognition. At its simplest, the debate between archaeology and archaeoastronomy represents different views of the past. As this history will show, the archaeological narrative seeps into our ideas of heritage, space and nationalism as Bender (1998) suggested in her narrative on Stonehenge; a pervading ideology of who we are and where we have come from. This volume is not meant to be an endorsement of either archaeology or archaeoastronomy; it attempts to set the record straight so readers can judge for themselves. This is perhaps a bold claim given the following difficulties encountered when compiling a history.

Historiography

The idea that you can write an accurate history is illusory. The historian Richard Evans (2000, 219) observed that increasingly historiographers note that there is no such thing 'as historical truth or objectivity', adding that no historians believe in '*absolute* truth', only '*probable* truth'. That is because historians, like prehistorians, have to work with only a partial record. For example, the British Isles is home to a vast range of differing prehistoric sites but these remains cannot possibly encompass the entire material record that would have been in existence at the time of their building. With the development of agriculture, many sites have been ploughed over and destroyed and throughout history the needs of an increasing population led to the robbing of monuments for building materials. Add to this the sites we simply do not know about; the ones awaiting discovery. Thus, in terms of material evidence, any account of prehistory can only be incomplete. Historians face the same problem: it is difficult to judge what written sources are important, let alone access them. Similarly many foreign texts lack a suitable translation, so references to them are often simply omitted. Histories are therefore fragmentary and provisional and anyway, 'the sheer bulk of the past precludes total history' (Jenkins 2003, 14). Histories are also time-specific in that the very writing of historical narrative adds a certain flavour to the facts presented, because language carries its own cultural and value-laden meanings which change over time.

History then becomes an invention in which narrators search for patterns amidst the chaos of data, creating links between events that may only be creditworthy through this necessarily selective hindsight. Swathes of time can be reduced to chapters which presume a rationality that is by no means obvious from the evidence alone. Perhaps it would be useful to follow E. H. Carr's advice (1973, 23), 'Study the historian before you begin to study the facts', because written histories reflect the mindsets of their authors, however objective they try to be. Michael Oakeshott (1933, 93) was kinder to historians through taking the view that their 'business is not to discover, to recapture, or even to interpret; it is to create and to construct'.

Indeed he went on to say that history is the historian's experience, a subjective view based on ideas about objective data so that, in the final analysis, supposed facts and events are inferential judgments. Various authors have recommended reflexivity as a cure-all. It has been described by Kim Etherington (2005, 19) as the 'need to be *aware* of our personal responses and to be able to make choices about how to use them', adding that we must 'also be aware of the personal, social and cultural contexts in which we live and work and to understand how these impact on the ways we interpret our world'. It was Ian Hodder (2003, 58) who introduced the need for reflexivity when writing up archaeological projects, counselling 'a critique of one's own taken-for-granted assumptions'; in other words, taking a fresh, impartial and unbiased look at the material under consideration. His advice is also relevant here.

Rowlands (1997, 134) took the view that historical writings 'are equally mythological and are simply desirable or undesirable at any particular moment in time'. This is of course reminiscent of Jacquetta Hawkes' famous dictum about Stonehenge – that each age 'has the Stonehenge it deserves – or desires' (Hawkes 1967, 27). Here we encounter another problem in historiography, that of diminishing the entirety through selection. We can only work on the past with what we have in the present and this is undoubtedly partial evidence, as already mentioned. Each discovery requires either a revision or a consolidation of what we already know. An example of this is Mike Parker Pearson's *Stonehenge* (2013), the cover of which claims that the story of Stonehenge has been retold through 'years of excavation, cutting-edge technology and sophisticated analysis'. On the other hand, some theoretical advances require a complete overhaul of existing narratives: for instance, landscape archaeology tends to link sites, once regarded as disparate and unconnected, to create entirely new cultural histories. This reappraisal of prehistory is widespread and continuous. At worst it can be manipulative in its selection: the disadvantage of dealing with heterogeneous material vying with a competing desire for a narrative overview.

Generally histories are selective, especially if the author is concentrating on a particular theme rather than an all-encompassing narrative. This is particularly true when histories attempt to answer questions about what the history of a certain theme means in the present. For example, recent commentaries touching on archaeoastronomy have been driven by other enquiries: Nicholas Goodrick-Clarke (2011) looked for the emergence of esoteric theory in antiquarian writings about ancient monuments; Ronald Hutton (2009a) researched the history of the druids; Nicholas Campion (2008) sought the origins of astrology and Nigel Pennick and Paul Devereux (1989) looked at orientation studies to find early instances of the alignments of ancient sites across the landscape. What these examples show is the importance of the chosen context and how it is presented to different audiences. It then follows that if the backgrounds and choices differ from one historian to another, we may expect to see different versions of any history.

Given these inevitable problems with historiography, it is necessary to state my own position relative to this exploration of the history of archaeoastronomy and explain its aims. I had been researching the archaeoastronomy of the recumbent stone circles in northeast Aberdeenshire for many years before being encouraged to apply for a PhD to take these studies further. I approached a senior lecturer in archaeology at a well-known university who, having listened to my proposal, turned it down saying, 'I must warn you I am very sceptical of archaeo-astronomical alignments and prehistoric architecture'. Nevertheless he thought that a worthwhile project would be to study the under-researched Neolithic four-poster monuments. It was *archaeoastronomy* that was in question not my *ability*. This reaction caused me to change my plans because the immediate questions that sprang to mind were, why is archaeoastronomy sidelined, what is its place in the academy and what is its relationship with archaeology? Unwittingly I had raised the research topics which have become the focus of this book. In it, it is important to place the history of archaeoastronomy side by side with that of archaeology because they both draw on the same primary sources, yet come to different conclusions. Also, I was interested to see whether this particular archaeologist's opinion of archaeoastronomy concurred with that of his peers as well as wondering how long-standing this negativity was and why. So alongside the history of archaeoastronomy I will examine the history of archaeology and the relationship between archaeologists and archaeoastronomers over time, because the developments in the one surely have had an impact on the other. The roots of prejudice can be difficult to pin down but as archaeoastronomy has often been bracketed with and even dismissed as esotericism or pseudoscience, this perceived connection may also be the source of residual disdain and needs to be examined in this light.

Exploring archaeoastronomy

As the title of this book suggests, I am exploring the history of archaeoastronomy and its relationship with archaeology and esotericism to write *a* history, based on many years of reading on and about the subjects and conversing with their practitioners. Facts and dates reported are in themselves neutral, being only the pillars around which the narrative is woven. Although there are brief nods to archaeoastronomy's history in many of its books, there is only one volume which is devoted to it: John Michell's *A Little History of Astro-archaeology*, as archaeoastronomy was briefly called, first published in 1977 (1989). Michell is regarded as one of the leading protagonists of the New Age and he wrote his history from this perspective, clearly at odds with the archaeological mainstream. My own exploration began from a similar dismissive view of archaeoastronomy but by contrast weighs up the field's many failings as it disappeared down unproductive rabbit holes against its considerable successes, while at the same time suggesting that one or more versions can be utilised by archaeologists to provide a less one-sided narrative on prehistory.

Within the literature, the origins of archaeoastronomy are perceived differently by several authors who stress not only the relative importance of different personalities, but give alternative time-scales the credit for its beginnings. Among its generally recognised founding fathers are the antiquarian William Stukeley, the early 20th century archaeologist F. C. Penrose and the astronomer Sir Norman Lockyer, followed in the 1960s by Gerald Hawkins and Alexander Thom, as the following authors declare:

> The history of archaeoastronomy … dates back to William Stukeley (Campion 2002, 202);
>
> Modern archaeoastronomy began with a discovery by F. C. Penrose, in 1893 (Kelley and Milone 2005, 1);
>
> Lockyer can still rightly be considered as the "father of Archaeoastronomy" (Polcaro and Polcaro 2009, 224);
>
> Archaeoastronomy … had its beginnings in the 1960s (Aveni 2008, 1);
>
> [Archaeoastronomy] was established in the 1970s and 1980s, on a wave of excitement created by pioneering works of the 1960s. (Hutton 2013)

These conflicting opinions seem to beg for an encompassing history of archaeoastronomy to show its origins, which actually date even further back than Stukeley's 18th century antiquarian research, in the accounts by Diodorus and Pliny the Elder in the 1st century AD. The three-century long period of antiquarianism which began with enthusiastic enquiries, culminated in serious scholarship with the formation of many university disciplines that are ongoing today.

Chapter 2 focuses on antiquarianism in order to understand the intellectual atmosphere which created these advances. The following chapters in turn describe the history of archaeoastronomy under its many guises and, as its study and methods largely came into existence and were developed by British scholars, the emphasis will inevitably be on archaeoastronomy in Britain; how, when and why it changed through the efforts of its key personalities. However British archaeoastronomy does not exist in a vacuum so there are separate chapters, one for the Americas and one for Europe which will show how it progressed there in different ways. The penultimate chapter will bring archaeoastronomy's history up to date by looking at developments and innovations in the 21st century. Over the course of its history, archaeoastronomy has been called by many different names with the latest suggestion being skyscape archaeology, so the book closes with my thoughts on archaeoastronomy's future and whether it is ever likely to be incorporated into the archaeology mainstream. To read this book, it is not necessary to have a detailed knowledge of astronomy or archaeoastronomy's methodology, though of course references to it are frequent but, rather than obscure the text with detailed explanations of unfamiliar terms and technical concepts, an illustrated Glossary is placed at the end of the volume. It is hoped that the extensive bibliography will be useful to those wishing to pursue further studies.

Chapter 2

Antiquarianism: the *longue durée*

The study of archaeological heritage, including the findings that some monuments seemed to reference the sky in their construction and alignments, has a long history. Although there is some evidence of astronomical connections being suggested in early historical writings, the innovative methodologies of archaeoastronomy and archaeology were established during a three century period roughly from the beginning of the 1600s to the end of the 1800s. As this foundational work dictated the tone of early 20th century studies relating to archaeoastronomy and archaeology, it is helpful to understand the intellectual climate which fostered it. Antiquarianism is the umbrella term which covers the vast output relating to antiquities for this three century period. With respect to the history of ideas, the term *longue durée* was coined by Fernand Braudel (1958). It has come to represent a theory which looks at long-term continuities, 'that other, submerged, history, almost silent and always discreet … which is little touched by the obstinate erosion of time', that underlie a historical period which is otherwise punctuated by short-term 'crises' (Braudel 1995, 16, 101). It is a useful model to examine the continuities of antiquarianism and how that continuity was challenged by major intellectual changes which occurred in the first half of the 19th century.

In Britain and Europe, antiquarianism broadly covered the collection of items of interest, from musical scores, early texts, folklore and coins to old weapons and ancient tools. It led to the publication of many tracts describing these artefacts and theorising on their ages and origins and many included descriptions and records of sites of historical interest, not just from preliterate society but from Classical times to the then relatively modern times of the Middle Ages. In short, antiquarianism was the study of a miscellany of mismatched collections of objects and facts which were of recommendation because they belonged to ages past. The accounts of the antiquarians were more encyclopaedic than interpretive or critical and generally lacked an analytical narrative, but without their efforts much of the material they collected would have been lost for all time. The antiquarians were famous enough for Sir Walter Scott (1771–1832) to pen *The Antiquary*, which can be read as a light-hearted satire on the antiquarianism of the day. It is not clear when the term antiquarianism was first used though it was in evidence by the 1893 edition of *The Antiquary*, first published in 1816. In his introduction to this later edition, Andrew Lang (1893) mentioned antiquarianism as being the hobby of Sandy Gordon, a Scottish antiquary who was the author of the 1726 publication, *Itinerarium Septentrionale* and on whom, according to Scott, his character Jonathan Oldbuck was based. Scott himself, besides being a prolific author, was an avid collector who also dabbled in archaeology and took part in excavations of vitrified forts; factors which give *The Antiquary* a certain air of credibility (Fig. 1).

Figure 1. Sir Walter Scott, image by Auguste Edouart (1830). © The Metropolitan Museum of Art Collection, Open Access.

Scott's novel refers to the last ten years of the 18th century when the pastime was both well-known and popular and when there were many antiquarian societies which had come into existence from the 17th century onwards. Scott's antiquaries, Sir Arthur Wardour and his friend Mr Jonathan Oldbuck were drawn in part from Scott's acquaintance with such hobbyists. As portrayed by Scott, antiquarians came from the upper echelons of society and had enough money and leisure time to pursue their interests:

> He, had, however, the usual resources, the company of the clergyman, and of the doctor when he chose to request it, and also his own pursuits and pleasures, being in correspondence with most of the virtuosi of his time, who, like himself, measured decayed entrenchments, made plans of ruined castles, read illegible inscriptions, and wrote essays on medals in the proportion of twelve pages to each letter of the legend. (Scott 1816, 19)

Scott makes much of an incident where a supposed Roman Praetorium turned out to be of modern construction. This fiction actually happened to the antiquary Sir John Clerk of Penicuik who showed the distinguished English antiquarian Roger Gale a small hillock near the centre of a Roman camp which he confidently described as the Praetorium. A shepherd who had been listening to their learned conversation immediately declared 'Praetorium here, Praetorium there, I made the bourock myself with a flaughter-spade' (Scott 1816, 61). A similar fictional and mocking account of antiquarians, entitled *Bouvard and Pécuchet*, was published in France by Gustave Flaubert in 1881, a year after his death. Scott and Flaubert's descriptions of archetypal antiquarians resonate with a description of a real-life American antiquarian, Thomas Robbins from Connecticut, who was described by his contemporary Dr Henry R. Stiles, as amassing 'old portraits, old chairs and chests out of the Mayflower, Captain Miles Standish's dinner pot, Indian relics, worm-eaten manuscripts, old battle flags … and scraps of ancient costume' (Dicuiri 2010, 565–566).

When trying to categorise antiquarians it is difficult to get rid of Scott's image of the well-meaning antiquary who trampled the countryside, digging up barrows and other archaeological sites indiscriminately to add a little bit of knowledge or material evidence to his collection. While Scott and Flaubert's antiquaries were of course caricatures, antiquarians were, according to Bann (1987, 27), associated with a kind of failure to achieve the level of 'true, "scientific" historiography', being enthusiasts 'liable to be led astray by absurd and fanciful conjectures'. This was partly because they were generally concerned with details, often in disembodied isolation, rather than interpreting them. However, despite their untrained forays into the past, they left a legacy of pioneering data, theories, plans and drawings which helped shape the conventions of modern archaeology (see for example Fig. 2). In Britain, loosely bound together by the mores of societies such as the Society of Antiquaries, founded in 1717, the antiquarians produced a large number of pamphlets, books and letters which provided the basis for later archaeoastronomical and archaeological studies.

14 · *Exploring Archaeoastronomy*

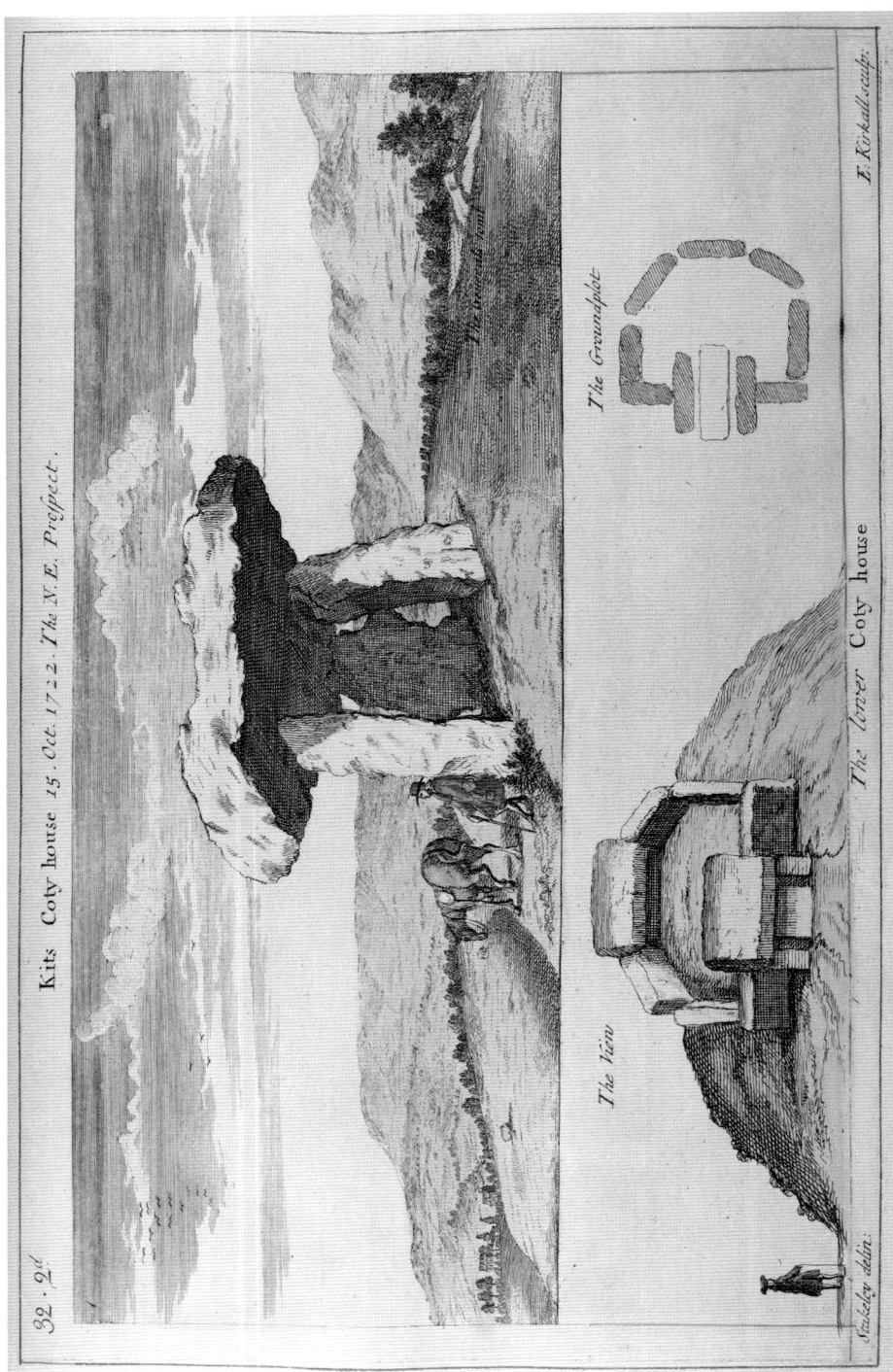

Figure 2. *Drawing of Kits Coty house, by William Stukeley on 15 October 1722. Taken from Stukeley's Itinerarium Curiosum published in 1776. With permission from The Spalding Gentlemen's Society.*

Antiquarianism was not just confined to Britain, France and America as mentioned, it was a world-wide phenomenon (see for example Schnapp 2014). Indeed the antiquarian was a figure common to all literate cultures with much of their work, particularly in Europe, central to its political and social history (Schnapp 2014, 1–2). Of course, antiquarians from different countries had dissimilar ideas: generally Europeans concentrated on monuments such as stone circles, standing stones, mounds and barrows, while in the Americas, in the 18th century, according to Achim (2014, 27), there was a focus on documenting artefacts such as those gathered on antiquarian expeditions to places like Palenque in Yukátan, Mexico. Notable publications included an account of Antonio del Rio's 1787 visit to Palenque, in *Description of the Ruins of an Ancient City*, published in 1822 and Lord Kingsborough's *Mexican Antiquities*, published in several volumes (1830–1848). However, during the 19th century, the emphasis turned to the origins of the Americans and the various Amerindian cultures, because various theories suggested that the civilised monument builders of the past had degenerated into the 'barbarian' Indians of the present (Achim 2014, 28). In this respect American antiquarianism differed from its European counterpart because, as the Americas were populated by a variety of local indigenous cultures as well as the European conquerors who overcame them, their studies focused on origin and race.

The intellectual background

The widespread incidence of antiquarianism is not surprising because the Scientific Revolution and the Age of Enlightenment that accompanied it acted together as motivating forces for new intellectual achievements. While Nicolaus Copernicus (1473–1543) is generally credited with being the father of the new scientific turn with his 1543 publication *De revolutionibus orbium coelestium* (*On the Revolutions of the Heavenly Spheres*), Sir Isaac Newton (1642–1726) brought it to culmination with his grand oeuvre *Philosophiæ Naturalis Principia Mathematica* (*Mathematical Principles of Natural Philosophy*), which was published in 1687. Other famous philosophers in the Age of Enlightenment included François-Marie Arouet Voltaire (1694–1778), Jean-Jacques Rousseau (1712–1778) and Immanuel Kant (1724–1804), to name but a few. Their attainments are all the more remarkable considering Michel Foucault's more recent description of the western cultural *episteme* of 16th century 'man' as being 'a complex of kinship, resemblances, and affinities', though he argued that this period of 'superstitious or magical beliefs' was generally superseded by 'rationalism' in the 17th century (Foucault 2002, 60).

This mixture of esotericism and rationalism is nowhere more evident than in the writings of some early British antiquarians who documented and analysed many of the monumental remains present in their countryside. For example, Loomis (1930, 400) found that it was not until the 19th century that Geoffrey of Monmouth's (*c.* 1095–1115) narrative associating Merlin, an Arthurian legendary figure, with Stonehenge was understood to be fiction: a confirmation that the intellectual shift from mythology towards more scientific fact-based narratives did not take place quickly. Similarly, French (1987, 188) noted that, from the 16th century histories, some scholars 'often accepted historical legends without verification; on the other hand, some men were using antiquities to determine the true facts about history'. It was William Camden's *Britannia: a chorographica descriptio*, first published in 1586 and subsequently republished in several editions, that was the stimulus for this factual approach (Butler 1998, 718). At that time chorography was a term used to refer to studies of topography, place, community, history and memory (Shanks 2017). Thus, the perpetuation of legends derived from Geoffrey co-existed with the factual chorography of William Camden (1551–1623) and John Leland (1503–1552). There were few attempts to analyse the history that was being reported because of 'the inadequacy of existing philosophical histories to account for the raw materials the past had left behind' (Goode 2003, 61). In his critical essay, *The Use and Abuse of History*, Nietzsche summed up the attitudes to historiography in 1873 by formulating three approaches to history: the monumental, the antiquarian and the critical. Thus, monumentalism glorifies the past and has a political motivation, antiquarianism reveres the past and wants to preserve it, whereas the critical approach seeks to learn from the past and transcend it.

The legacy of antiquarianism has been pored over by many scholars and one of the conclusions is that from the differing strands of antiquarianism a modern historical discipline grew up in which 'systematic research has become indivisible from the task of representing the past in narrative' (Phillips 1996, 298). Similarly, Lynch and Lynch (1968, 33) agreed that the foundations for the systematic study of prehistoric sites had already been laid by 1800. They also found evidence in antiquarian writings of a distinction between historical sites and those remains which antedated written sources with studies including not only pre-Roman Britain but discourses on stone tools. These tools inform the study of technological and cultural evolution and they were first recognised as human artefacts in the 17th century. Before that time Goodrum said that they were collected by naturalists and classified as 'fossils' and as they were thought to have been produced when lightning hit the ground they became known as 'ceraunia' or 'thunderbolts' (Goodrum 2002, 255–256).

While antiquarianism was satirised in its own time and has been robustly critiqued ever since, at the time a certain degree of royal and aristocratic support enhanced the reputation of antiquarian studies. For example, the interest in European heritage was encouraged by royal patronage: in Britain, John Leland was appointed as Henry VIII's King's Antiquary from 1534–1542 and James I and Charles II extended this patronage to Inigo Jones (1573–1652) and John Aubrey (1626–1697) respectively, while in France, Antoine Galland (1646–1715) was a royal antiquary of Louis XIV. Despite there being a greater interest in the antiquities of Classical Greece and Rome, Richard Gough (1735–1809), author of *British Topography* (1768), a gazetteer of topographical writings for the whole of the British Isles, was one of the growing number of antiquaries, including William Stukeley (1687–1765), who believed that the study of national antiquities should take preference because they played an essential part in the continuum of British history (Sweet 2001, 186–187). At the same time the research of many European antiquarians was aimed at glorifying the national tradition in their respective countries (Wang 2008, 514). In this vein, Bann (1987, 37) suggested that the embodiment of antiquarianism was the '*amor vetustatis*', the love of antiquity, which sought to rehabilitate all ancient finds to a place of honour. Not all antiquarians confined their research to physical objects: the French author Charles François Dupuis examined ancient myths from many countries to suggest there was a common origin for their astronomical and religious opinions in his study *Origine de toutes les Cultes ou la Réligion Universelle* (1794) (Iwaniszewski 2008, 255). He is usually credited with being one of the founders of astralism; that branch of research which focused on the astronomical component found in religions and myths.

It is generally agreed that antiquarian discoveries shaped nearly every facet of British culture. Their wide sphere of influence included Church chronicles about the arrival and spread of Christianity in Britain and linguistic studies of the Anglo-Saxon roots of English and its impact on British heritage (Butler 1998). Indeed Butler suggested that the revival of the past could be seen in literature as well, such as Ben Jonson's masques for King James and King Charles, one of which, *The Fortunate Isles and Their Union*, played on the idea of British national pride. Milton's history of Britain and Shakespeare's use in his plays of the legends of early British kings can all be read as attempts to revive the past (Butler 1998). Also local studies such as Sampson Erdeswicke's *A Survey of Staffordshire* (1717) were as much a feature of antiquarian literature as the more comprehensive national studies which included Thomas Cox's *Magna Britannia Antiqua & Nova* (1738) and Nathaniel Salmon's *A New Survey of England* (1731) (Kebbell 2009, 92).

With their abiding interest in ancient material remains, the antiquarians formed a nascent heritage movement, though the 19th century saw several major changes which had a bearing on how the past was interpreted. First, through the efforts of the local antiquarian societies many county maps had been published but by the end of the 1790s there was still no accurate national map of Britain or surveys on which it could be based. In 1791 Charles Lennox, the 3rd Duke of Richmond, then Master General of the Board of Ordnance, purchased a theodolite and gradually commissioned Ordnance Survey maps for the whole of Britain. Because of the antiquarian interest William Mudge, then Superintendent of the Survey, sent a memorandum in 1816 to the surveyors instructing them that 'all remains of ancient Fortifications, druidical monuments, vitrified forts and all Tumuli or Barrows shall be noticed in the Plans wherever they occur' (Owen and Pilbeam 1992, 64). In such a way, the association between the druids and the heritage of the ancient remains became irretrievably linked for the entire 19th century. Major Henry James had been appointed as Superintendant of the Ordnance Survey in 1854 and it was under his direction that 'Descriptive Remarks of such Objects of Antiquity' were published. Surveyors were instructed to use literary sources before nominating 'new' antiquities and written authority was required before they could be put on a map (Owen and Pilbeam 1992,

64). To qualify as an antiquity a site had to have been in existence before 1688, the end of James II's reign. The archaeological survey work was complementary to the mapping survey and each Ordnance Survey region had its own specialist team of archaeological surveyors. Despite the guidelines laid down by the Survey, the recording of antiquities depended on the personal interest of the surveyor (Seymour 1980, 64). There was obviously collaboration between the antiquaries, the local societies and the Ordnance surveyors. Similarly, in Scotland in 1855, the Society of Antiquaries of Scotland requested that 'all remains such as barrows, pillars, circles and ecclesiastical and other ruins' should be noted' (Seymour 1980, 174). Owen and Pilbeam record that because of the Highland clearances, many monuments were partially destroyed but all the ruins were recorded by surveyors from a special office set up for the purpose in Edinburgh (Owen and Pilbeam 1992, 153).

Esotericism

While the methods the antiquarians established became more formalised and scientific over this long period, many of their theories have not stood the test of time because of their unconscious mixture of esotericism and rationalism. In his study of Western esotericism, Hanegraaff (2013, 13–14) argued that it is a field which generally emphasises the inner world, but is also characterised by being 'set apart' from mainstream religious and intellectual culture with its epistemologies being at odds with normative post-Enlightenment culture. In antiquarianism, several strands of esoteric thought, found in 17th century Hermeticism, 18th century Romanticism and the search for ancient wisdom in the 19th century Occult Revival, permeated antiquarian intellectual life. This continuous theme of esotericism can be examined as an example of Braudel's submerged history; a long-term continuity of ideas which flavoured even the most objective accounts.

The 15th century Latin translation by Marsilio Ficino of the *Corpus Hermeticum*, a body of writings attributed to Hermes Trismegistus (*c.* AD 100–200), laid down the foundations of western esotericism (Campion 2008, 188). That some antiquarians were familiar with the texts which were translated within ten years of the 1611 publication of the King James Bible, is evidenced by their mention in John Douglas' *A Dissertation on the Antiquity of the Earth* (1785, vi–vii). With 'The Sun is the father and the Moon the mother', Hermeticism's main axiom is 'That which is below is like that which is above and that which is above is like that which is below'. Often shortened to 'as above, so below', where the microcosm reflects the macrocosm, this maxim of the Emerald Tablet of the *Hermetica* reveals a type of sympathetic magic or correspondence in which the celestial realm influences events on earth (Faivre and Voss 1995, 60). The mixture of primitive animistic thinking identified by anthropologists such as Edward Burnett Tylor (1832–1917) and Max Müller (1823–1900) together with Foucault's complex *episteme*, mentioned earlier, had its counterpart in an esoteric view where correspondence was one of the fundamental elements. Allied to these ideas was the

Pythagorean vision which Campion (2008, 144) described as 'a coherent picture of a harmonious cosmos based on soul and number'. In 1619, this concept was visited by Johannes Kepler in *Harmonices Mundi* (*The Harmony of the World*; Kepler 1939) in which he sought and found harmonies in the solar system, a notion that re-occurred in some of the astronomical theories relating to monuments, which will be detailed later. By contrast, John Douglas acerbically noted that the ideas of Hermes Trismegistus 'would have little weight in a plain relation of discoveries in the fossil kingdom' (Douglas 1785, vii).

In a similar vein, the 18th century Romantics 'were driven by nostalgia for a lost paradise in which humanity and cosmos were one' (Campion 2009, 199). This is particularly evident in the romantic poetry of the time with William Blake's notion of a 'green and pleasant land' being an underlying but recurrent theme in the verses of Wordsworth, Keats, Byron and the like. Romanticism glorified both the past and nature and attempted to find what Johnson (2010, 151) described as 'a more authentic and less alienated way of life'. An illustration of this idea can be found in a play written by John Dryden in 1672 (Dryden 1672) which contained the lines,

> I am as free as nature first made man
> Ere the base laws of servitude began
> When wild in woods the noble savage ran.

Evidence of the longevity of this association between nature and simplicity can be found in Scott's *A Legend of Montrose* (1819) where Dryden's lines are cited. Piggott (1974a, 727) believed that the antiquarians were 'caught up in the net of the growing enthusiasm for the picturesque, the romantic, and the vaguely religious quest for the Noble Savage in antiquity'. As will be shown later the 'noble savage' was one of three portrayals of prehistoric humankind.

Freemasonry or Masonry became popular in Britain during the 18th century and many of the members of its Lodges were the same antiquarians who also held memberships in the Royal Society and the Society of Antiquaries of London. Elliot and Daniels (2006, 222) suggested that there was the belief that, as initiation and advancement to Freemasonry provided the keys to the secrets of Masonic texts and rituals, a similar study of antiquities and druidic temples would reveal the sophistication of ancient mathematics, geometry and astronomy. Naturally the thought of being able to recover ancient secrets was appealing to antiquarians. Not only that but the Masonic belief in a mathematical deity, compatible with the Newtonian conception of the universe, with its grand mathematician or architect at the centre, affirmed their cosmological beliefs. Stukeley (1740, 35) stated that it was this 'curiosity' that led him to be 'initiated into the mysteries of masonry, suspecting them to be the remains of the mysteries of the ancients'. The Masonic connection can be demonstrated in Stukeley's description of Stonehenge where he appeared convinced that the alignment of the temple to the midsummer sunrise was done 'in imitation of the Mosaic tabernacle'. The corresponding part of Masonic ritual is the affirmation, 'As the sun rises in the East and opens the day, so the Master stands in the East ... to open the Lodge' (Kebbell 2009, 3). Fellow Mason John Wood (1747, 62) believed he had rediscovered the 'exquisite rules of the Ancients' relating to proportion at the 'druidical works' which inspired his design of Bath's Royal Crescent. Similarly, a letter written by the poet Goronwy Owen in 1754 says his decision to join a Freemason's Lodge was because he believed that Freemasonry was 'a branch of the craft of my ancient ancestors, the Druids of old' (Kebbell 2009, 117).

Because of evidence such as this, Kebbell has underlined the importance of 18th century Freemasonry by saying that:

> To ignore its existence in social and cultural histories of Britain since the early eighteenth century ensures that a significant element of our understanding of that history is lacking. (Kebbell 2009, 3)

Part of its impact was that druidry and Freemasonry became intrinsically linked in the eyes of popular culture and the Masonry literature of the time was infused with solar symbolism, either where the sun was seen to be an emblem of God's wisdom or as the creator of earth (see for example, Mackey 1860). The then contemporary view, as stated by J. M. Anderson in his 1734 history of Masonry, was that God, 'the great architect of the Universe', created the world according to geometry. Anderson's idea was that these geometrical principles were handed down to Adam and subsequent generations so that monuments erected by the 'Ancient *Britains*', exhibited the '*Remains of good Masonry ... raised by the original Skill that the first Colonies brought with them*' (Anderson 1734, 27). That the Freemasons' cosmological beliefs were informed by their knowledge of astronomy is supported by evidence that lectures on astronomy were sponsored by Bristol Freemasons in 1789 (Elliot and Daniels 2006, 216).

There were indeed two antiquarian viewpoints which vie with one another: one that the past could be understood and recovered 'scientifically' through the empiricism of antiquarian scholars, versus the esoteric idea that there was a secret history, a continuum of ancient knowledge passed on through time. This pursuit for ancient wisdom took a new twist in the 19th century when, as argued by Morrisson (2008) there was a distinction between individual esoteric quests and those of exoteric literature and social communities, such as Rosicrucianism, the order of the Golden Dawn and the Theosophical Society. Associated publications included John Wilson's *The Lost Solar System of the Ancients Discovered* (1856) and John O'Neill's two volume treatise, *The Night of the Gods: an inquiry into cosmic and cosmogonic mythology and symbolism* (1893; 1897). W. Winwood Reade's *The Veil of Isis or Mysteries of the Druids* (1861) may have been an inspiration for H. P. Blavatsky's *Isis Unveiled*, published in 1877, which cited both Wilson and Reade. These examples, which attempted to unlock the beliefs of the ancient druids, are far removed from the empirical attempts to understand monumental culture, but the mixture of romantic and esoteric thought can be seen as a sub-text in many antiquarian writings about British monuments.

Antiquarian societies

Today, archaeology and archaeoastronomy have their own specialised terms and language but initially during antiquarianism there were few specialised terms to comprehend. From references mentioned in antiquarian literature, such as Stukeley's citation of Strabo and Caesar or the reference to Macrobius by Edward Duke (1779–1852) (1846, 4ff.), it is clear that before interests became necessarily restricted through the emergence of specialisms, many antiquarians were polymaths. Nowadays most scholarly research is conducted in compartmentalised disciplinary departments and only published after scrutiny but as the antiquarians had no rules or traditions to follow they were able to express their innovative ideas freely. This is not to say that they were isolated because they communicated with one another by letter, courtesy of the cheap one penny post and, because printing was also inexpensive, they were able to disseminate their pamphlets and research papers between themselves. Throughout Britain these industrious antiquarians built up their private collections, published tracts about them and showed them to their fellow scholars at the newly formed local societies which took over the role of the mid-17th century coffee houses as the places to meet and exchange ideas.

To what extent the antiquarians were known to one another is unclear, though the beginnings of these societies are evidenced from the formation of a society of antiquaries in Elizabeth I's reign, so called following its usage when Leland was appointed King's Antiquary. Also the Royal Society, then called The Royal Society of London for Improving Natural Knowledge, was founded in 1662 under the patronage of Charles II and its publication *Philosophical Transactions* established the principle of peer review. It catered for the new interest in natural history which owed much to the scientific legacy of Francis Bacon (1561–1626) who had set out a new approach for understanding the natural world. The focus of The Royal Society was quite specific but the antiquarians had a choice of many other societies to which they could belong; for instance, the Society of Antiquaries of London, which evolved from a group interested in history and antiquities, met in London taverns from 1707. Maurice Johnson (1688–1755) played a part in its refounding in 1717 when Stukeley became its secretary. Not just a meeting place for the exchange of ideas, the society also published *Archaeologia* which Lynch and Lynch (1968) believed was the richest source of writings on prehistory for the entire early period. They noted that, from 1772 until 1800, each volume contained at least one or two major articles dealing entirely with British prehistory, in addition to a number of lesser references to megaliths, encampments or stone and bronze implements thought to date back to pre-Roman antiquity. Examples from both the start and the end of this period include John Watson's (1773) 'Druidical remains in or near the Parish of Halifax in Yorkshire' and William George Maton's (1800) 'Account of the fall of some of the stones of Stonehenge'.

The Society of Antiquaries and the Royal Society were complemented by regional societies such as The Society of Antiquaries of Newcastle upon Tyne, founded in 1813;

the Bannatyne Club, inaugurated in 1823 by Walter Scott; the Peterborough Society and The Spalding Gentlemen's Society (Fig. 3). The latter, founded in 1710 by Maurice Johnson 'for the supporting of mutual benevolence, and their improvement in the liberal sciences and in polite learning', included Isaac Newton and William Stukeley amongst its members (The Spalding Gentlemen's Society 2013). Its publication, the *Gentleman's Magazine*, frequently included antiquarian articles, an increasing number of which, especially toward the end of the 18th century, treated prehistoric subject matter. John Stuart, author of *Sculptured Stones of Scotland* in two volumes (1856 and 1867), belonged to the three Spalding Clubs in Aberdeen, while Glasgow hosted its own archaeological society founded in 1856. Goodrum (2002, 259) was of the opinion that, in the 17th and 18th centuries, antiquarian and scientific studies were closely related as memberships in such institutions as the Royal Society and the Society of Antiquaries frequently overlapped. There was a further link between these societies and Freemasonry with many of their prominent members also being members of Masonic lodges.

Apart from the above regional societies in Aberdeen and Glasgow, the Scottish antiquarian culture was more broadly served by the Society of Antiquaries of Scotland which was founded by the Earl of Buchan in 1780 and incorporated by Royal Charter in 1783. The Society's purpose was 'the Study of the Antiquities and History of Scotland, more especially by means of archaeological research' and the first volume of the Transactions of the Society, *Archaeologia Scotica*, was published in 1792. After a short break in publication it resumed with the 72nd Session, 1851–52 published under the editorship of David Laing and Daniel Wilson (1816–1892). In the subsequent anniversary address, the Hon. Lord Murray declared that 'we are entering, indeed upon a new era in the history of archaeological investigation' (Murray 1852–4, 98). The Society's initial purpose was continually re-affirmed and 77 years after its incorporation the number of Fellows had grown to 249. The proceedings show that the antiquarians were not just interested in local Scottish finds although reports of these dominated but in the first volume there were accounts of cromlechs found in Bengal and stone coffins and obelisks in India. While these societies undoubtedly played their part in validating antiquarian studies, Sayer (2014, 57) further suggested that they moved archaeology away from its hobbyist pursuit towards professionalisation.

The developing knowledge about prehistory was forged from the links that membership of the antiquarian societies encouraged, which led to authors regularly cross-referencing their work with other opinions or data: for example, in his work on Stonehenge, Stukeley referred to previous interpretations by Inigo Jones, John Webb, John Toland and John Aubrey, and Duke in turn referred to Stukeley's plans of Avebury and Richard Colt Hoare's measurements of Silbury. As part of the antiquarian tradition, the holders of all these ideas about monumental culture shared common attitudes, common standards and patterns of behaviour and operated as an informal community.

2. Antiquarianism: the longue durée

Figure 3. The Spalding Gentlemen's Society Meeting Room. From William Moore, The Gentlemen's Society at Spalding: Its Origin and Progress (1871, 60–61). With permission from The Spalding Gentlemen's Society.

The local societies aided continuity yet their publications chart changing attitudes to antiquity and in particular how some antiquarians began to see their subject matter as archaeological. Henry Rowlands had conferred a name on the study in 1723, first by subtitling his book *Mona Antique Restaurata*, 'An Archaeological Discourse' and secondly by declaring that 'Archaeology' was 'an Account of the Origin of Nations after the Universal Deluge'. His contemporary Sandy Gordon claimed that the discoveries of what he called 'archiology' would reveal 'True History distinguish'd from Falsehood and Imposture' (Gordon 1726). Archaeology as a term passed into general use as evidenced by the first book on archaeology, *Encyclopaedia of Antiquities, and Elements of Archaeology, Classical and Medieval* by Thomas Dudley Fosbrook, published in two volumes in 1822. Archaeology's popularity, in Scotland at least, can be gleaned from the fact that by 1860 the associated publications relating to Scottish archaeology amounted to some 300 quarto volumes (Simpson 1860–2, 15). The Royal Archaeological Institute began to play an important role in this developing field: founded in London in 1844 and gaining its royal charter some three years later, it has published *The Archaeologcal Journal* ever since (Royal Archaeological Institute 2017).

Similar antiquarian societies were founded in Europe and beyond. For example, the Société des Antiquaires de France was established in Paris in 1804 and in Denmark, La Société Royale des Antiquaires du Nord was launched in Copenhagen in 1825. The American Philosophical Society was founded in 1743 and The American Antiquarian Society was later inaugurated in 1812 and both, like the English and Scottish Societies of Antiquaries, are still active today. While most societies tended to be somewhat parochial in vision, in the mid-19th century there was an attempt to coordinate their activities and research. For example, the *Congrès International d'Anthropologie et d'Archéologie Préhistoriques* was proposed in Italy in 1866 with the first meeting taking place in Paris in 1867 (Goodrum 2009, 29). After that it met a further nine times at locations which included London, Copenhagen, Budapest and Moscow, before the Paris meeting of 1900.

With the activities of these societies and their respective publications, what had begun as a hobbyist endeavour became the foundation of the burgeoning academic discipline, archaeology. A small number of the antiquarians left their mark on what would be later called archaeoastronomical studies. Additionally, because the antiquarians were indiscriminate collectors of anything from the past, many of their collections were later housed in the new museums founded during the period. For example, Elias Ashmole desired that his collection of curiosities and antiquities were placed in a museum and the Ashmolean Museum, which he later gifted to Oxford University, opened in Oxford in 1683 (Ashmolean Museum 2014). In London, Sir Hans Sloane's immense collection of ancient British artefacts became the foundation for the British Museum's collection of prehistoric antiquities (Goodrum 2002, 260). Regional museums followed, such as the one in Manchester, opened by The Manchester Natural History Society in 1838 and taken over by Manchester University in 1867 (White

2017, 38). It was Daniel Wilson who proposed the National Archaeological Museum for Scotland in order to:

> secure the advancement of Archaeological Science, to promote popular education, and to excite a national interest in the preservation of the monuments of early art and ancient civilisation and to excite a national interest in the preservation of the monuments of early art and ancient civilisation. (Wilson 1851–2, 3)

He described the collections as 'merely the fruits of private zeal', which bears testament to the popularity of antiquarianism in Scotland. Another avid collector was General Pitt Rivers (1827–1900), an archaeologist who was the first Inspector of Ancient Monuments, and it was his donation of some 25,000 objects that led to the foundation of the Pitt Rivers Museum in Oxford in 1884.

The legacy of antiquarianism

It is clear that antiquarianism embodied a new way of looking at the past but while the antiquarians' records were based on empirical observation their texts were often intertwined with fanciful speculations on origins and purpose. As Fussner (2010, 71) observed, antiquarians contented themselves with asking 'what happened' rather than 'why' and 'how' and while they 'amassed facts ... never attempted to reconstruct a past age'. While this appears true for early antiquarianism, later accounts became more enquiring and disciplined. For example, Cosmo Innes (1857–9, 6) advocated that 'research and comparison of antiquities are our proper functions as antiquaries'. Certainly, without their efforts much of the material they collected and housed in museums would no longer exist for a variety of reasons, including adverse weather, erosion or indeed through farming, industrialisation or urbanisation which led to the destruction of innumerable sites because they were more important for national economies. Additionally, antiquarian descriptions and plans of prehistorical sites still have value today, particularly where they have since been destroyed or altered. Importantly, many of the antiquarian ideas and methodologies relating to prehistoric archaeology and astronomy fed into later narratives and paradigms, as will be shown in the following chapter. With the advent of specialisms in the late 19th century, what began as a communal interest in the remains of the past developed into two different strands in the *long durée* of antiquarianism. One became the named field of archaeology while the other, as yet unnamed, concentrated on recovering connections between monuments and the heavens.

Chapter 3

The emergence of archaeoastronomical thought

Erecting a monument is a deliberate act, whether now or in the past. Throughout Europe there is a vast legacy of ancient monumental remains, including menhirs, stone circles, standing stones, barrows and so on, but little knowledge of why or when they were placed there or by whom. The antiquarians took up the task of answering these very basic questions. There were two main strands of enquiry which developed beyond the initial empirical act of observing, measuring and recording the monuments. The first strand attempted to answer the question of why they had been specifically located where they were and not somewhere else in the landscape, as well as examining the use to which they were put. In this regard, while the term archaeoastronomy was not coined until 1971, some antiquarian authors devised its basic methodology to find alignments between the material remains in the landscape and the heavenly celestial bodies above (see Glossary: alignment). The second strand revolved around finding out who the monument builders were, what skills they possessed and when the monuments had been built.

Taking their cue from some early Graeco-Roman texts which first expressed ideas about the relationship between these monuments and the sky, some antiquarians began to see the same type of connections that Diodorus of Sicily recognised in the 1st century AD. His was the earliest commentary that associated astronomy with a British monument:

> They say, moreover, that the moon in this island seems as if it were near to the earth ... And that Apollo once in nineteen years comes into the island; in which space of time the stars perform their courses, and return to the same point; and therefore the Greeks call the revolution of nineteen years the Great Year. At this time of his appearance (they say) that he plays upon the harps, and sings and dances all the night, from the vernal equinox to the rising of the Pleiades, solacing himself with the praises of his own successful adventures. (Diodorus, book ii, xiii)

Diodorus described a temple 'of a round form' found on the island of Hyperborea where the 19 year cycle of the moon was observed. Henry Rowlands, writing in 1773, suggested that Hyperborea was most likely to be the Isle of Mona (Anglesey) which he thought was the original seat of the druids (Rowlands 1723, 77-82). More recently, the temple that Diodorus described has been associated with either Calanais on the Scottish Isle of Lewis, by Aubrey Burl (1993) or Stonehenge, by John North (1996).

It is unclear whether Diodorus was perhaps referring to the 19 year metonic cycle (see Glossary: metonic cycle) when the moon returns to the phase and position it occupied at the beginning of the cycle or, alternatively, his reference could relate to the lunar node cycle during which the moon reaches its furthest geocentric extreme every 18.6 years (see Glossary: moon). Similarly, Pliny the Elder (AD 23–79), found a link between druidical ritual and moon cycles, believing that the priests collected mistletoe,

> particularly on the sixth day of the moon (which for these tribes constitutes the beginning of the months and the years) and after every thirty years of a new generation, because it is then rising in strength and not one half of its full size. (Pliny the Elder, book xvi, chapter xcv)

Nothing more was heard about the subject until Hector Boece (1465–1536) authored the first British account to make an association between monuments and astronomy. Like Diodorus and Pliny, Boece found a link between stone circles and the lunar cycle in his *Historia Gentis Scotorum (History of the Scottish People)*, first published in 1527. One of Boece's legendary kings, Mainus 'commanded that huge stones be set up in circles at various places … with the largest stone set at the south of the circle to be employed as an altar, where burnt-offerings might be offered to the gods' (Boece 1575, book ii, 11). At this 'altar' stone *'the peopill maid their adoratioun to the new mone'*. According to Boece the druids, who were given the island of Mona as their headquarters, were in charge of all religion.

There is no concrete evidence that the antiquarians were aware of Boece's early 16th century work, though Rowland's reference to Mona may provide a clue. However they were certainly familiar with Graeco-Roman writings; some of them including Toland (1726 [1815]), Stukeley (1740) and Duke (1846) making frequent references to them in their texts, and they may have indirectly prompted their own research. The texts of Diodorus, Pliny and Boece focused on the importance of the moon and, nearly two centuries after Boece, John Wood's 1747 thesis proposed a lunar explanation for the Heel stone at Stonehenge. Tying in with this idea was his belief that 'the Number of Years in Meton's cycle' appeared in the stones found in the inner circle of Stonehenge. He also suggested that like Stonehenge, 'the temple of the moon at Stantondrue [Stanton Drew, Somerset]' (Fig. 4) was similarly laid out to indicate a phase of the new moon (Wood 1747, 80–81).

Interest in the sun was first mentioned by Robert Plot in his *Natural History of Staffordshire*, written in 1686, where he noted that, from a certain point in Leek churchyard in Staffordshire, the path of the summer solstice sunset could be observed cutting the edge of a hill called the Cloud (Plot 1686, 2; see Glossary: solstice). Thoughts about the influence of the sun and the moon were combined in the early 18th century when some stone circles became designated as being either solar or lunar temples. For example, in Stukeley's 1722 plan of Avebury, the two double concentric circles

Figure 4. William Stukeley's drawing of A View at Stanton Drew, in Itinerarium Curiosum published (1776). With permission from The Spalding Gentlemen's Society.

within the main circle were called respectively 'The Lunar Temple' and 'The Solar Temple' (Piggott 1935, 27).

Antiquarian practice

To satisfy their interest in material remains, regardless of type, the antiquarians had to devise their own methodology as they went along. While their investigations included textual analysis, the main basis for their research was fieldwork. This approach was prescribed by Richard Gough who believed that this was the basis of all antiquarian study, as history required 'a regular and elaborate inquiry into every ancient record and proof, that can elucidate and establish them' (Gough 1770, ii). He effectively set down the rules for antiquarian study but, prior to Gough, this enquiry had already started and from Leland, Aubrey and others grew a routine of fieldwork which included the recording of site details, drawing plans and pictures as well as grouping monuments into similar types. At Stonehenge for instance, Aubrey was the first to make any sort of objective empirical survey and in his planned *Monumenta Britannica* he noted a series of depressions, now known as the Aubrey Holes. Avebury did not receive as much attention as Stonehenge but nevertheless it was an important site and in 1663 Aubrey made rough sketches of the circle and the approach avenues, with his plans also showing the ditch and rampart surrounding the circle. Aubrey's work was never published in full but extracts of his chapter entitled *Templa Druidum* were published by Edmund Gibson in his 1695 edition of Camden's *Britannia* (Goodrick-Clarke 2011, 156).

Hearing of Aubrey's work, Stukeley went on to survey Avebury himself and although accuracy was sometimes sacrificed for the sake of his druidical theories, Stukeley's sketches have been particularly important for modern archaeologists (Lynch and Lynch 1968, 41). Another exponent of meticulous method was William Roy who, in 1775, drew up a map of Roman antiquities in Scotland which, apparently was not completely superseded until 1928. Not only was Roy attempting to be objective but he was a pioneer in the search for 'the more vestigial features of field archaeology and in the mapping of his results' (Seymour 1980, 63).

Along with surveying and recording, other archaeological methods developed. Camden had recognised that differential crop growths marked the presence of buried features, so to obtain more thorough knowledge than that gleaned from fieldwork alone the practice of excavation was added to the methodology (Schofield *et al.* 2011, 26). John Conyers (1633–1694) was probably the first antiquarian to take notice of layers or strata in the soil which either occur naturally or are man-made (Lynch and Lynch 1968, 45). Accordingly, at Stonehenge, Stukeley introduced the technique of cross-sectional excavations, supplemented by profile drawings. Stukeley's friend, the Earl of Pembroke, is reported to have opened mounds specifically to discover the orientation of the skeletons but it is unclear whether this was an astronomic interest (see Glossary: orientations). As cited by Piggott (1950, 106), Colonel Heneage Finch,

Earl of Winchelsea may have been the first antiquarian to record the dimensions and orientation of a barrow, reporting:

> I have been at Julaber's Grave, which I formerly measured only by my paces but I have now taken it with my measuring chain, and have all its dimensions very right; and I took its bearings with my compass, and from the top of it I have drawn out a prospect of the country.

Until the end of the 18th century, barrows were the only type of prehistoric site undergoing systematic excavation and John Milner's description of those carried out in Dorset in 1790 is typical of the reports of that time (Milner 1790). A letter from John Frere (1800), which detailed stratigraphy of the excavation at Hoxne in Suffolk, showed how these techniques advanced. Another innovation was a form of typology which Stukeley devised to classify stone circles: the round ones he called simply temples; those such as Avebury with 'the form of snake annext' were serpentine circles and those with 'the form of wings annext', were winged temples (Stukeley 1743, 9).

As methods became more advanced, field notes became more detailed as did the categories of evidence: there was a clear idea of what was important in a site and what should be preserved and recorded (Lynch and Lynch 1968, 50). Although Renfrew and Bahn (1991, 29–30) credited archaeologists such as General Pitt Rivers (1827–1900) and Sir William Flinders Petrie (1853–1942) as instrumental in developing the techniques of field methods in use today, they were building on practices established in early antiquarianism. This foundational methodology, as described above, which included empirical fieldwork and the recording of written site details such as size, position and composition, was supplemented by plans and pictures, comparative typology and excavation, both cross-sectional and open. Little by little, by trial and error, archaeology was beginning to take a modern form. Yet despite this, the various accounts found in Society proceedings show that the spirit and enthusiasm of antiquarianism had not immediately been replaced by scientific endeavour. The over-riding interest was in the recovery of artefacts to add to the national collection rather than the preservation or interpretation of the monuments themselves.

To complement this study, the antiquarians needed to have an understanding of chronology. Through studying the scriptures, Archbishop Ussher pronounced in 1636 that the date of creation was 4004 BC. In the light of the lack of evidence, most 17th and 18th century antiquarians believed that the Bible was the ultimate authority and therefore, as humankind was thought to be descended from Noah, all human history was post-diluvian. The use of Biblical history gleaned from the book of Genesis persisted, as evidenced by Henry Rowlands' (1723, vii) opinion that archaeology was 'an Account of the Origin of Nations after the Universal Deluge'. All new material had to be fitted into the prevailing Biblical history in which metal was associated with the earliest people, not stone tools. According to Goodrum (2002, 264), a fiction was fabricated suggesting that the consequences of the Deluge meant that people had to rely on the most primitive of tools to exist as no metal survived the Flood. Consequently, towards the latter half of the 18th century, studies included stone tools which were recognised as humanly manufactured artefacts rather than natural occurrences.

Any evidence which threatened to overturn existing views on chronology could be regarded as not only revolutionary but as crises which threatened the underlying continuities of antiquarianism, as suggested by Braudel (see Chapter 2). The first major challenge came from geologists, particularly James Hutton (1726–1797) and Charles Lyell (1797–1875), who found that the stratification of rocks indicated that the earth was much older than Ussher's 4004 BC. Lyell (1835, 224) demonstrated the successive development of animal and vegetable life by comparing the type of fossils in each layer and was able to agree with his fellow geologists that 'man is of comparatively recent origin'. Similarly in France, Jacques Boucher de Perthes (1788–1868) found human artefacts with extinct fauna thought to be older than the prevailing history (Renfrew and Bahn 1991, 22). It was the rapid growth of geology and palaeontology in the late 18th and early 19th centuries that radically transformed the study of the past (Goodrum 2002, 267). This new line of enquiry was fostered by The Geological Society of London, founded in 1807. Geology was closely linked to archaeology; for example William Boyd Dawkins (1837–1929), archaeologist and geologist, belonged to the geological societies of London and Manchester, the Society of Antiquaries and the Somerset Archaeological and Natural History Society at one and the same time (White 2017, 43).

A further dating revolution occurred around the same time when the Three Age classification system was proposed. The chronological order of Stone, Bronze and Iron Ages was originally formulated by the Danish archaeologist Christian Jurgensen Thomsen (1788–1865) in the 1820s and 1830s and later modified by Jens Jacob Asmussen Worsaae (1821–85). These distinctions were made on the basis of the different types of tools and weapons and their utilisation. John Lubbock (1834–1913) continued by dividing the Stone Age into two parts before adding further divisions into the Old, Middle and New Stone Ages, which represented the Palaeolithic, Mesolithic and Neolithic ages (Lubbock 1865; 1870). He showed how the Palaeolithic hunter-gatherers 'progressed' to farmers in the Neolithic Stone Age. This system 'provided a powerful new framework' for interpreting artefacts and all subsequent archaeological research was divided according to this basic chronology (Goodrum 2002, 256). This new approach to material culture led to a hypothesis about typology, different from that suggested by Stukeley. By grouping objects of the same type together, distinctions could be made between different technologies and materials and some understanding could be gleaned about their probable origins or ages. For example stone tools belonging to the Stone Age could be distinguished from Bronze Age artefacts, as noted by Greenwell (1894). Typologies of this sort became an established part of archaeological practice which eventually evolved into a more structured scientific approach to the past by the end of the 19th century. The rejection of the Biblical version of history and the uptake of the Three Age system were major paradigm changes.

These revolutions gave rise to a new conceptual model of the past, unlike anything that had gone before. Archaeology required new terminology and the named ages stood as tokens of different stages and artefacts in prehistoric culture. It was Daniel Wilson (1816–1892) who first used the term 'prehistory' to cover the earliest period of history in his 1851 book, *The Archaeology and Prehistoric Annals of Scotland*. In a letter to Sir Charles Lyell, now housed in the library of the University of Edinburgh, Wilson claimed that he coined the word 'prehistoric' for his book. However, he did not use prehistory to cover the entire prehistoric period as conceived of today because he was constrained by the order of the Three Age system. Accordingly he ordered his book into parts on 'The Primeval or Stone Period', 'The Archaic or Bronze Period', 'The Teutonic or Iron period' and 'The Christian Period' up to the Middle Ages. Welfare (2008, 12) has suggested that Wilson's book marked the watershed between the old chorographical/topographical tradition and the new 'scientific' archaeology of the late 19th century. However, changes of this magnitude took time to implement and vestiges of the Biblical version of history appeared in the mid-19th century when in 1856 the Scottish antiquarian Henry Callender agreed with Scott's description, found in his novel *The Pirate*, of 'these phantom forms of antediluvian giants'.

Astronomical methodology

At the same time as antiquarian practice was becoming more refined some antiquarians turned towards astronomy to understand the monumental remains. Astronomical research in this context, whether esoteric or proto-scientific in retrospect, required specialised knowledge of horizon and positional astronomy in order to find relationships between celestial events and the ways monuments were aligned (see Glossary: horizon; positional astronomy; surveying for alignments). This method had been pioneered by Plot when he found the summer solstice sunset alignment by using horizon astronomy. He brought his knowledge of astronomy to the task in hand by noting that the declination of the sun was at its greatest at the solstice before diminishing as the days advanced (Plot 1686, 3–4; see Glossary: declination). Plot was not only aware of azimuth and the different limbs of the sun but also how atmospheric refraction affects observation. His research came just after astronomy had been endorsed by royal patronage with The Royal Observatory at Greenwich being founded in 1675. Most astronomy was taught in the school of natural philosophy, according to Russell (1974, 123), and it is difficult to chart when it emerged as a separate discipline, though Cambridge University's observatory was completed in 1832. Dr Johnson's *Dictionary* of 1755 had defined an observatory as 'a place built for astronomical observations' and Ruis-Castell (2011, 532) suggested that 19th century cosmological narratives, 'thematising the place of man in the universe', were crafted from these observations. This interest is evident in some of the antiquarian narratives, which anachronistically described stone circles as observatories.

Observations of the type made by Plot were needed before any interpretation could be suggested and at stone circles this included measuring the size, position and number of stones as well as their orientations. John Smith of Boscombe (1747–1807) put his measurements at Stonehenge to good use to propose that it represented an early calendar of 360 days (Smith 1771, 63). In his complex astronomical explanation, he divided the circle into 360 parts, which was the multiple of the 30 stones of the outer sarsen circle and the 12 signs of the zodiac. Similarly, Alexander Lawson (1817, 424) noted that, at a circle in Fife, the number of stones in the outer circle 'corresponds exactly with the number of points in the compass', whereas the inner circle had half that number, but in both rings, 'a stone larger than the rest is placed at each of the cardinal points'. This does not quite tie up with his plan which shows 33 stones in the larger circle and 16 in the inner ring. Lawson did not appear to notice this discrepancy and continued with his astronomic argument, citing Huddleston's appendix to John Toland's (1814), *History of the Druids*:

> The Druids seem to have paid much attention to the numbers of erect stones which they placed in their circles ... and it is supposed ... from the circles consisting of seven, twelve or nineteen erect stones, that they had their respective astronomical references to the number of days in the week, the signs in the zodiac, or the cycle of the moon. (Lawson 1817, 427)

These ideas were long-lived and can be seen in Godfrey Higgins' observations on Stonehenge, which declared that the number of stones in the 'Druidical circles' were in agreement with 'the ancient astronomical cycles' such as the metonic cycles of the moon (Higgins 1827, 239). Similarly at Calanais, Callender (1856, 382) found that a single line of stones pointed to cardinal directions and that these must have been 'laid down from astronomical observation'. The circles at Calanais were also believed to be druidical but Callender also noted that the Gaelic term on the Ordnance Survey map was *Tursachan* which, roughly translated, meant mourners, confirming the then current view that the circles were sepulchral.

A couple of years earlier, John Stuart (1853) described the remains of 'druidical' circles found in Aberdeenshire and Banffshire, noting that one had an opening to it through the south or southeast and another had the 'altar stone' on the south side. The altar stone was the name given to the recumbent stone in a particular type of stone circle found in this region. Stuart concluded that this was the only trace we had of the knowledge of the druids who watched the motions of the heavenly bodies and marked their directions in lines of stone. But it was not just the circles that were regarded as druidical, stone vessels found in their vicinity were called 'Druidical Pateræ' (Wilson 1853). On the other hand J. Y. Simpson (1860–2, 30–31) was concerned by the misclassification which had led to Celtic rings and bosses being described as druidical astronomical instruments because they strengthened the case for believing that the druids were astronomers. Indeed, he thought the monuments were pagan as opposed to druidical and described them as 'our Megalithic Circles and Monoliths'. When using the term pagan, Simpson may have been referring to evidence of 'a former Baal Worship in Scotland' as suggested by Christine MacLagan in her (1881) book, *Chips from Old Stones*. Her sun worship theory had come about because many of the so-called altar stones were on the south side of the circles though MacLagan believed there were too many exceptions to this rule for the theory to be viable. Many of the texts reference solar alignments though, apart from MacLagan, they do not go as far as suggesting a solar religion. However Dupuis (1798), mentioned earlier in Chapter 2, was convinced that all myths and religions, including Christianity, were disguised versions of a universal solar religion. In a parallel vein Grensted (1892, 464) thought that there was a likeness between the solar-oriented rituals of the Zuñis in New Mexico with those orientations of the Greek Temples, the Pyramids and Stonehenge; a similarity caused by their similar scientific knowledge and development.

The archaeological ground-based methodologies and the astronomical techniques that were being established during antiquarianism did not run counter to one another and it is evident that the methodological cultures were overlapping. An example which shows how these methods were combined can be found in Stukeley's description of Stonehenge:

> And the works at Stonehenge generally vary to the right hand, from cardinal points, and that to the quantity of 6 or 7 degrees. The principal diameter or groundline of *Stonehenge*, leading from the entrance, up the middle of the temple, to the high altar, (from which line the whole work is form'd) varies about that quantity southward of the north east point. The intent of the founders of *Stonehenge*, was to set the entrance full north east, being the point where the sun rises, or nearly, at the summer solstice. (Stukeley 1740, 56)

The solar alignment at Stonehenge was a methodological discovery but it became part of Stukeley's hypothesis when he inferred intentionality. The intentional incorporation of an alignment within a monument is crucial for an astronomical argument because any other alignments, discovered through the research, may have occurred purely by chance.

A compass can be used to measure the entire panoramic horizon of 360° so the relative position of a stone in a circle, for example, can be measured in degrees. This measurement has to be compared to the position on the horizon at which celestial bodies rise or set for a particular location (latitude) to judge whether the stone is aligned to any of them. Stukeley's report shows that he was familiar with this methodology, that he understood not only the combined effect of latitude and the obliquity of the ecliptic (see Glossary: ecliptic) but was also aware of the necessity of correcting for magnetic variation, which is the difference between true north and magnetic compass north (see Glossary: magnetic north; true north). He drew up a list of dates from 1550 to 1740 showing this degree of variation in England, yet while his table showed nearly 16° west for 1740, his own estimation for Stonehenge was 6 or 7° (Stukeley 1740, 64–65). This inconsistency throws doubt on the compass readings of the antiquarians and even less clear is whether they regularly calibrated their magnetic compass readings to represent true astronomical readings. Nevertheless it became the norm, in Scotland particularly, to record directions, especially those referring to the orientation of bodies found in cists. For example, Alexander Robertson (1853) described four of these cists found in Banffshire by their orientations, adding that the directions of all of them varied by only a few degrees.

In addition to horizon astronomy the antiquarians needed to comprehend the main celestial cycles. Sir William Herschel's (1738–1822) observations led him to discover the planet Uranus in 1781 and in 1846 Neptune was charted. However, the planets noted in antiquarian accounts remained based on the old celestial system, found in Ptolemy's *Planetary Hypotheses* (c. AD 150), which was composed of the visible inner planets (see Glossary: planets). While most texts related to the sun and the moon, some planets were also considered. For example, Duke (1846, 81), in addition to looking for solar connections, thought alignments to Venus, such as at the stone circle at 'Winterbu[o]rne Basset', would have been based on the planet's position as an evening star, more readily observable than as a morning star. Higgins (1827, 158) demonstrated his understanding of astronomy when he dated Stonehenge to 4003 BC by associating it with the sun's entry into the first degree of Taurus from using calculations of the precession of the equinoxes (see Glossary: sun). His belief that the druids were interested in these 'Oriental cycles' led him to classify it as a druid monument (Fig. 5). This appears to be the first time that astronomy was used for dating purposes. For those antiquarians who lacked sufficient astronomical knowledge to interpret their surveys, a specialist could be employed, as was the case with Duke who asked an astronomer, the Rev. L. Tomlinson, to test some of the angles at Stonehenge.

Astronomical methodologies can be gleaned from snippets such as these: there were no rule books and the work was experimental. The most explicit example of the method of correlating material monuments with celestial positions was that of John Smith of Boscombe in his (1771) publication *Choir Gaur: the Grand Orrery of the Ancient Druids, Commonly Called Stonehenge, on Salisbury Plain Astronomically Explained and, proved to be a Temple for Observing the, Motions of the Heavenly Bodies*, as follows:

> From many, and repeated visits, I conceived it to be an Astronomical temple; and from what I could recollect to have read of it, no author had as yet investigated its uses. Without, an instrument, or any assistance whatever, but White's Ephemeris, I began my Survey. I suspected the Stone, called The Friar's Heel, to be the index that would disclose the uses of this Structure; nor was I deceived. This stone stands in a right line with the centre of the Temple, pointing to the north-east. I first drew a circle round the vallum of the ditch and divided it into 360 equal parts; and then a right line through the body of the Temple to the Friar's Heel; at the Intersection of these lines I reckoned the Sun's greatest amplitude at the summer Solstice, in this latitude, to be about forty degrees, and fixed the eastern point accordingly. (Smith 1771, v–vi)

Figure 5. Stonehenge as depicted in Godfrey Higgins' The Celtic Druids *(1827, pl. 4).*

In Newall's *Stonehenge Wiltshire (Official Guidebook)* (1955), Smith is credited as being the first to propose that the Heel stone was the solstitial sunrise indicator, overturning Wood's earlier lunar theory.

When calculating the possibility of alignments today, the altitude of the horizon is taken into account to note prominent features to which architecture may have been aligned. This methodology is nascent in antiquarianism in Smith's account and he may have been the first to mention the possibility of a distant target when he described sunrise in relation to a hill behind Durrington Field on the northeast horizon (Smith 1771, 64). Wansey (1796, 68) took the importance of the horizon a step further by suggesting that, as Stonehenge stood in such a good position for viewing the entire horizon, trees could have been planted on the distant hills 'to have measured any number of degrees of a circle, so as to calculate the right ascension or declination of a star or planet' (see Glossary: right ascension). Similarly, Knighton Barrow, the long barrow between Casterley Camp and Stonehenge, is a high mound which Duke (1846, 111) thought had been used as a gnomon from which the 'astronomical observer of yore' took his sighting of the summer solstice sunrise. A different method was proposed by William Chapple who was reported to have suggested in 1778 that the stones were designed for ancient astronomical and surveying purposes, by using the measurement of the shadows cast by the stones (Michell 1989, 14). There was also an attempt to by C. W. Dymond to draw inferences from interlinked or intervisible sites at the Stanton Drew complex, by suggesting that,

> it is noticeable that the centre of the south-west circle, the centre of the large circle, and the quoit, are nearly in one straight line; and that the centre of the north-east circle, the centre of the large circle, and the centre of the Cove, are still more nearly in another straight line. (Dymond 1877, 299)

From these examples six different methodologies based on astronomy can be extracted: horizon astronomy; the use of artificial horizon targets; the use of a gnomon; light and shadow effects; dating; and, lastly, intervisibility. Combined with the use of a magnetic compass with readings adjusted for true north, the antiquarians discovered basic methods which were foundational for the archaeoastronomy of the future. Yet at the same time, both types of methodology, the archaeological and the astronomical, were being developed and practised in tandem, often by the same scholars.

Astronomical theories

From the studies of monumental culture which took astronomy into account, two dominant suppositions emerged. The first was that in some way the monument builders observed the celestial cycles and incorporated them into their monuments intentionally, while the second related to the builders themselves, their origins and the extent of their knowledge. Though interdependent, these strands can be examined separately.

The monuments

The earliest British historical writings of the 12th century began what has been an enduring interest in archaeological remains and Stonehenge was singled out as being the most iconic of all. For example, Henry of Huntingdon (1088–1157) referred to Stonehenge with its 'hanging stones' as one of the four wonders of England, though added that no one could work out why it was there. Similarly, Geoffrey of Monmouth, noted earlier in Chapter 2, published his work *Historia Regum Britanniae* (*The History of the Kings of Britain*) in 1136 and although he did not name Stonehenge he recorded that Merlin counselled the importation of a ring of stones from Ireland, stones which had been taken there originally from Africa, so that once reconstructed 'in the way in which they are erected over there, they will stand forever' (1966 [1136], 196). Little else was discovered about these monuments until Boece suggested that the stone circles in Scotland had been constructed under the orders of the Scottish king Mainus (290 BC–AD 61).

The astronomical texts about the monuments show evidence of the longevity of dual theories which gave equal weight to the sun and the moon. Although Stukeley cited Diodorus, it is unclear to what extent antiquarian lunar theories were drawn from the earlier writings of Diodorus, Pliny or Boece. However, the moon certainly played a role in some antiquarian suppositions regarding the functions for which the monuments were constructed. Writing at the time of Stukeley, John Wood's (1704–1754) *Description of Stanton Drew and Stonehenge* and *Choir Gaure* were respectively published in 1740 and 1747. He proposed a lunar explanation for both the northeasterly orientation of the heel stone at Stonehenge and the 'altar' at Stanton Drew: 'and in each work a phase of the new moon is pointed out' (Wood 1747, 84–85). Additionally he attempted to relate the number of sarsen uprights to alternating lunar months of 29 and 30 days (see Glossary: synodic lunar month). On the other hand, Stukeley described both lunar and solar circles at Stonehenge and 100 years later Duke also believed that the early circle at Stonehenge was a sun temple, despite associating its 19 stones with the metonic cycle of the moon (Duke 1846). Also at Stonehenge, as stated above, Smith had used the outer circle stones for his solar calendar theory but he also believed the 30 bluestones of the inner circle stood for the 29 days and 12 hours of the lunar month (Smith 1771, 65). Similarly, in antiquarian writings about Orkney, the Ring of Brodgar was known as 'the Temple o' the Sun', with the Standing Stones of Stenness being called 'the Temple o' the Moon'. Yet by contrast, folklore dictated that marrying couples repaired to the northeast stone at Stenness, the direction of the midsummer solstice sun, according to F. W. Thomas (1851, 113). One of the earliest accounts linking these stones with the sun and the moon was by Martin Martin who recorded in 1716 that 'Several of the Inhabitants have a Tradition that the Sun was worshipped in the larger, and the Moon in the lesser Circle' (Martin 1716, 365); another example of the sun/moon dualism.

Yet while solar and lunar theories abounded, only at Orkney was there a reference to a temple of stars when Thomas (1851) referred to the Ring O' Bookan to the northwest of Brodgar as 'the Temple of Stars'. He related that Pocock, Bishop of Ossory, found 'a very minute astronomical description of the motions of the sun, moon and planets' in the stones composing the circle and semicircle but Thomas (1851, 115) dismissed these as fancies. This omission of the stars is surprising given Caesar's reference to the druids' knowledge of them:

> They likewise discuss and impart to the youth many things respecting the stars and their motion, respecting the extent of the world and of our earth, respecting the nature of things, respecting the power and the majesty of the immortal gods. (Caesar, *Gallic Wars* 6.14)

A different picture emerges from Egyptian studies where it was astronomers not antiquarians who made the case for considering the stars when interpreting monuments. Jean Baptiste Biot (1774–1862) found stellar alignments there and also suggested that the Great Pyramid served as an immense gnomon for determining the equinoxes (Lancaster Brown 1976, 270). Similarly, Charles Piazzi Smyth (1819–1900), an astronomer as well as an Egyptologist, examined the astronomy of the Pyramids and found 'order, method and regularity, with a close attention to the leading facts of astronomy, conjoined with an appreciation of geometrical excellence and mechanical exactitude' (Smyth 1868, 35). In his book *Our Inheritance in the Great Pyramid*, he concluded that the Great Pyramid was intentionally aligned to the 'Polar star', which Sir John Herschel had earlier identified as Thuban. Lancaster Brown (1976, 270) thought that all later cults for megalithic stellar alignments could be traced to Biot's and Herschel's ideas. Stars were also considered in Australian research into Aboriginal mythological culture. Here, connections were made between stars and the seasons, so that the appearance of certain stars heralded the start of the kangaroo hunt, for example, and likenesses were found between objects in the sky and those on the ground so it was thought that the boomerang represented the stars of the Northern Crown, now known as Corona Borealis (MacPherson 1881).

These astronomical propositions relating to the sun, moon and the stars, were mainly formulated from empirical observations at single sites but there was another system of ideas that attempted to imbue the wider monumental landscape with cosmological significance. The distinction between the proto-scientific methodology of the former with its own formulaic language and the wild theorising of the latter is very clear. For example, John Wood believed the seven hills of Bath were dedicated to the heavenly bodies and he drew a planetary model overlaid onto plans of the monuments near Stonehenge so, that for him, Silbury was the hill of Mars and Stonehenge was an oracular lunar temple of the moon (Michell 1989, 12). These imaginings which had no methodological foundation were esoteric in the extreme. Similarly, Duke in his (1846) publication, *The Druid Temples of the County of Wilts*, suggested that some stone circles portrayed, despite his acknowledged anachronism, a planetarium or stationary 'orrery', constructed on a meridional line 32 miles (51 km) long over the Wiltshire Downs. Stukeley had earlier described Avebury as serpentine and this so-called serpent was, in Duke's eyes, the path of the ecliptic: 'the ancients did designate the ecliptic, or winding path of the Sun, under the similitude of a Serpent' (Duke 1846, 44). For his part, Duke associated the stones with the days of the month and the months of the year using archaic material from Macrobius, a 1st century Roman author, who divided the year into three seasons, not four, an idea previously used by Smith, to explain a triangle of stones.

Duke believed Avebury was aligned to the winter solstice sun and Stonehenge to the midsummer solstice sun. Accordingly he suggested that Stonehenge was a sun temple, that the Avebury complex contained both sun and moon temples and declared that there were temples to Mercury and to Venus. Although Duke mentioned some suspect ethnographical material, the main reason for his categorisation was how the distance between them mirrored the distance between the planets. For Duke, Silbury represented the Earth, Walker's Hill, a Temple of Mercury, and the tumulus called Hatfield Barrow at Marden, Mars. He drew on the connections between them, found earlier by Richard Colt Hoare (1812), and used them for his own 'grand astronomical scheme', suggesting that the builders had a full understanding of cosmology and included the entire panoply of the sky into their monuments, whether stone or earthen. He therefore saw Silbury Hill as being the centre of the universe and therefore the centre of his planetarium which included associating nearby monuments with the visible planets in respect of the distances between them and Silbury. Three miles (c. 5 km) from Hatfield Barrow is Casterley Camp which he suggested was the temple of Jupiter. Duke did think that the early circle at Stonehenge was a sun temple, despite his ideas about the lunar cycle, but under his new rationalising system, Stonehenge, being the furthest from Silbury, changed to being a 'temple of Saturn'. This was because Duke believed its 30 stones represented the years of the Saturn cycle; a change made apparently when the builders had acquired 'a more advanced state of art and science' (Duke 1846, 130). His meridional line linked several places including Avebury, Silbury Hill and Stonehenge and he fitted this alignment into a diagram which equated the orbits of the planets with the distances between the monuments on the ground in a 'grand astronomical scheme' (Fig. 6). Both circles and barrows were all part of this 'mundane system'. Furthermore, Duke described the landscape alignments as 'meridional', further linking astronomy to the horizon alignments. Both circles and barrows were all part of this grand vision and his intentions were clear when he concluded,

> Thus have I brought the portions of this, as yet partial system of astronomy, into one harmonious and concordant whole, and thus, I trust, ere my work is brought to a close so to combine it with the other planetary temples as to shew forth one entire mundane system. (Duke 1846, 36)

Essentially Duke believed that the monuments were all built by the druids and he included quotations from Caesar and Pomponius Mela (a 1st century Roman geographer) to show that their astronomical knowledge was well-known. While Duke's scheme differed from Wood's earlier conjectures about the Bath landscape,

3. The emergence of archaeoastronomical thought

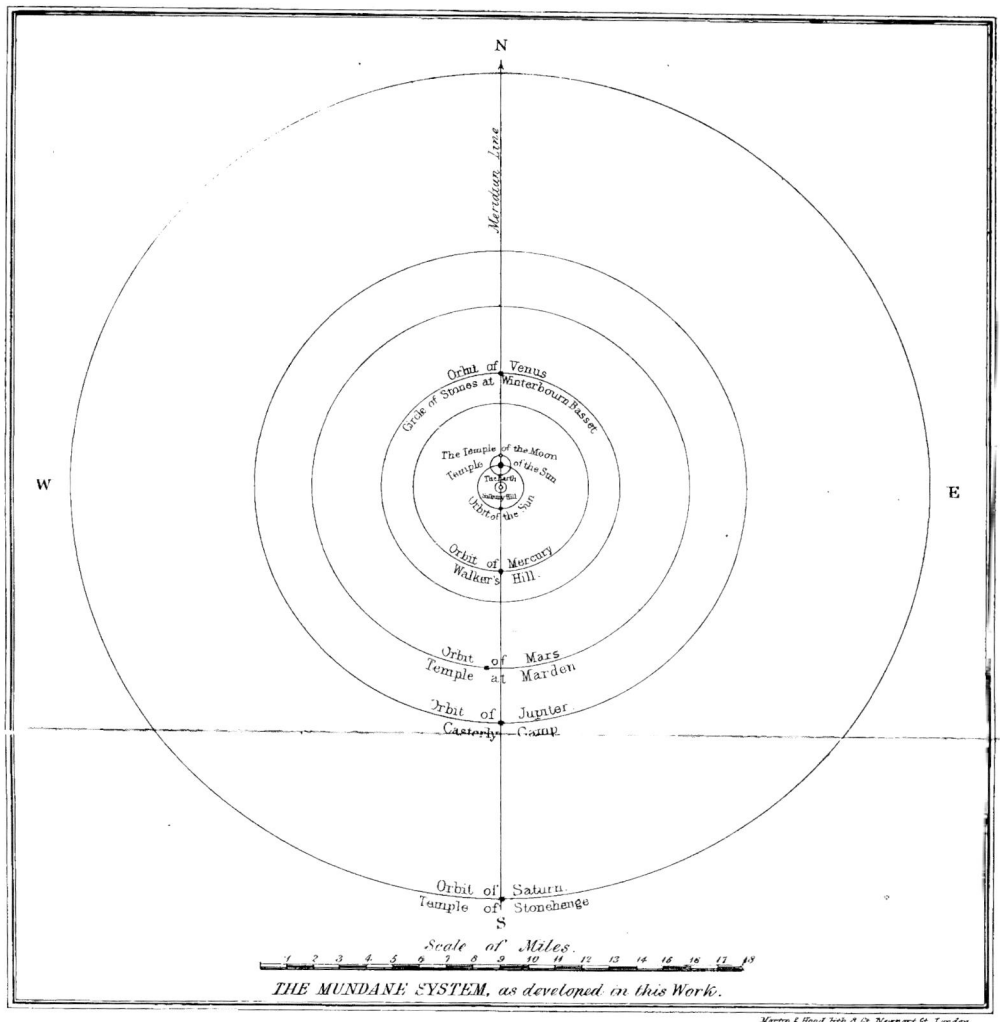

Figure 6. Edward Duke's 'grand astronomical scheme'. From The Druidical Temples of the County of Wilts *(1846, 6-7).*

his projected ratios between the monuments and the planets were surely inspired by Kepler's planetary harmonies and both schemes lay out the 'as above, so below theme' which was the central pillar of hermetic thought, as described earlier in Chapter 2.

Following Duke's thesis, a number of authors looked at monuments in their landscape settings and this line of enquiry continued for over 50 years. They included the claims made by William Henry Black in 1871 for 'grand geometrical lines' that could be detected in old boundaries and landmarks (Black 1871, 270-271).

Similarly, Joseph Houghton Spencer, in a paper entitled 'Ancient trackways in England', published in *The Antiquary* in 1889, found tracks at Corfe in Somerset that included an alignment to midsummer sunset while others in Dorset he referred to as long-distance signals. He also found another system of drives radiating from a wood higher than the surrounding landscape near Evershot in Dorset. Spencer proposed that the system was admirably adapted for astronomical observations and identified one of the drives as being aligned to the northeast and the rising summer sun. He designated the whole system of drives an 'observatory', 'more adapted for the observations and calculations connected with the movements of heavenly bodies ... of this great and far-reaching system' (Spencer 1889, 99). Other samples of this body of work include William Simpson's 'The orientation or direction of temples' (1897) and Magnus Spence's (1894) monograph, entitled *Standing Stones and Maeshowe of Stenness*, which detailed landscape alignments between the major Orkney monuments in terms of astronomy. As late as 1904, F. J. Bennett drew on Duke's work to show that the Kentish megaliths followed the same meridional line as discovered by Duke in Wiltshire (Ruggles 1999a, 225). While there were many standing stones and stone rows extant in the landscape they were not given particular attention except in France where Gaillard's (1888) paper suggested that the Carnac stone rows in Brittany were oriented to solar risings and settings at the solstices and equinoxes. He followed this up with a general treatise on prehistoric astronomy, *L'Astronomie préhistorique*, in 1897 (Gaillard 1897). Certainly during the 19th century there was an interest in both landscape and astronomical alignments and this interest was widespread over many locations.

The most important feature of antiquarian astronomical theory was the forging of an association between monuments and the heavens, not just to horizon events but to the entire planetary sphere, through a mixture of scientific methodology and speculation about cosmology. Two lines of enquiry emerged, one relating to individual sites and the other involving a number of sites, considered together in their wider landscape setting. For example, Wood's 18th century planetary scheme was contemporaneous with Stukeley's site investigations, but generally the landscape themes belonged to the 19th century, for which there is only sparse evidence for continued research into site-specific astronomical alignments.

The monument builders
Apart from the interest in the astronomical aspects of the monuments, the antiquarians had many theories relating to the monument builders themselves, embellished from what they gleaned from ancient texts. Diodorus had peopled his Hyperborean temple with Apollo's priests who Julius Caesar had earlier called druids: that order of men who 'are engaged in things sacred, conduct the public and the private sacrifices, and interpret all matters of religion' (Caesar, *Gallic Wars*, 6.12). Pliny had also associated the monuments with the druids but the reason did not become clear until Boece explained that the Scottish word for religious leaders was *durcerglii* but so that this

'foreign word might acquire a Latin flavour, Roman writers called these priests Druids' (Boece 1575, 29). That contrasts with Rowlands' later view that the term druid came from the Celtic word 'Derw' which also means oak, a tree sacred to the druids, whose first temples were built in oak groves (Rowlands 1723, 55, 237–238).

Consequently, most antiquarians were of the opinion that the circles were druidical. Martin, in 1695, appears to be the first author to associate Calanais with the druids, saying that the Chief Druid addressed the people from the big stone in the centre. This transmission of ideas is further evidenced by Toland's (1726) history of the druids, which drew extensively on Roman authors, and from Aubrey we learn that druid rituals were conducted at the *Templa Druidum*. A further example can be found in John Ogilvie's poem *The Fane of the Druids*. Ogilvie (1733–1813) was minister of Midmar, Aberdeenshire and his 1789 verse described the recumbent stone circle there:

> Time-hallow'd pile by simple builders rear'd!
> Mysterious round, through distant times rever'd!
> Ordained with earth's revolving orb to last! (Ogilvie 1789)

Callender (1856, 382) concluded that the only traceable knowledge of the druids, who observed the motions of the heavenly bodies and marked their directions in lines of stone, came from the monuments themselves.

By contrast, John Douglas, in his (1793) book *Nenia Britannica* believed Stonehenge and similar monuments preceded the druids and were of Celtic origin. Drawing conclusions about origins from a comparison of barrows and tumuli with similar types in Europe, he suggested the use of analogy to make comparisons. Theorising about the widespread instances of sepulchral monuments, even as far away as Asia, he speculated on the diffusion of ideas which 'indicates a marked communication between the ideas and the customs of the people who formerly inhabited China, England, and Portugal' (Douglas 1793, 189). This departure marked the development of theory in archaeology concerning the transmission of cultural signatures, later termed diffusion theory.

Although the stone circles were generally believed to have been constructed by the druids there was still an attempt by some antiquarians to find the origins of the builders. Most of these questions were directed towards Stonehenge and the attempt to establish its chronology. King James I visited Stonehenge in 1620 and instructed the prominent architect Inigo Jones (1573–1652) to 'make a plan of the monument and furnish some account of its nature and origins' (Lynch and Lynch 1968, 39). Jones's work, *Stone-heng Restored: the most notable Antiquity of Great Britain, vulgarly called Stoneheng*, published posthumously in 1655 (Jones 1655), concluded that Stonehenge was not built by the ancient Britons but was, in fact, a Roman temple dedicated to the sky god Coelus. It is the first sky-related reference to Stonehenge but Jones probably used it to add weight to his theory that the monument was built in Roman times. There followed much debate: Walter Charleton in his *Chorea Gigantum* (1663) suggested that it was a 9th century Danish monument, yet John

Webb's (1665) *Vindication of Stone-Heng Restored* repatriated it to the Romans once again (Lancaster Brown 1976, 51–53).

Contrary to these ideas on origin, Stukeley believed that Avebury, like Stonehenge, was a druid temple: the words Solar and Lunar were later carefully scratched out from his plan as he regarded druidry as monotheistic. In this way druidry could be regarded as a proto-Christian religion, well removed from Jones's sky god Coelus or other Greek and Roman pagan deities, and this may be one of the reasons why the notion of druid temples persisted for so long. Yet, the idea that the circles were places of worship came directly from Diodorus and Caesar. It was almost taken for granted that they were ritual sites: James Garden's letter of 1692, though not read to the Society of Antiquaries until 1766, pronounced that, 'THE general tradition throughout this kingdom ... is, that they were places of worship and sacrifice in heathen times' (cited by Lewis 1888, 50–51). He even described that the purpose of certain hollows in the stones was for pouring 'their *libamina* or liquid sacrifices'.

If the monument builders were able to incorporate celestial alignments into their positioning of the stones, then it follows that the antiquarians believed they were in possession of certain skills. From his reading of Caesar and Pomponius Mela, Duke believed that 'astronomy as a science, took early precedence' and was practised by the druid monument builders, who he assumed were 'Pythagoreans, Sabaeans or worshippers of the wandering planets or starry host of Heaven' (Duke 1846, 113). He also suggested that the druids were aware of the precession of the equinoxes, the Platonic cycle and the great year of 25,920 years: Stonehenge being 'denotive of the cycle of cycles, the Platonic year'. Regarding both monuments and their builders, Stukeley (1740, 63) observed that there was 'a greater exactness in placing them, with regard to the quarters of the heavens, than one would expect, in works seemingly so rude; and in so remote an age'. From this he deduced that the druids were 'geometricians' though he did not believe the circles were formed using equilateral triangles, as did fellow antiquarian Webb. Methods of determining meridians and longitude which had been developed by Hipparchus (190–120 BC) would have been known to the antiquarians (see Glossary: longitude). Black took this into account in his assessment of the builders' knowledge: 'But the ancients made no mistakes in longitude, because their method was this: they covered their land with monuments, having a strict geometrical relation to each other' (Black 1871, 270–271). Similarly, Higgins (1827, 7–9), while confessing to a little 'aerial castle-building', focused on the druids' mathematical abilities, suggesting that they must have learned 'the four common rules of arithmetic and how to make a square, a right-angled triangle, a correct circle, and perhaps useful knowledge in those sciences'. Half a century later Reverend Gordon (1880, 433) noted that some of the circles were elliptical. What the above antiquarians have in common is the notion that the builders had sophisticated skills in astronomy, mathematics and geometry, a thesis that endured for over two centuries.

Metrology

Another skill attributed to the monument builders was metrology and several authors attempted to find the systems of measurement used in laying them out. Isaac Newton appears to be the first author to recognise this when he wrote:

> [at the] 'Temple or Sepulchre at Abydus' [now Abydos] which was built by Amenophis some time before '887 before Christ', they placed 'a Circle of 365 cubits in compass ..., and divided it into 365 equal parts, to represent all the days of the year; every part having the day of the year, and the Heliacal Risings and Settings of the Stars on that day, noted upon it. (Newton 1728, 30)

Newton's further theories on the *Sacred Cubit* were published in 1737 by John Greaves as part of a collection of his own work. Greaves had measured the Great Pyramid and concluded that without Newton's explanations the Pyramid could not be understood.

At Stonehenge, on the basis of his own measurements, Stukeley (1740, 11–12) not only inferred that the builders used a magnetic compass to lay out the circle stones but their measuring system was the same as the 'old *Hebrew*, *Phœnician* or *Egyptian* Cubit', which he went on to call the 'Druid cubit'. He may have been influenced by Newton's findings but the *druid* cubit was Stukeley's invention to explain what appeared to be a standard unit of measurement, at least at Stonehenge. The length of his cubit was 20.8 inches, while Newton's was 20.7 inches. One hundred years later, Duke considered Stukeley's measurements of Stonehenge and found that its circumference was 540 cubits. Duke surmised this to be an important number as it was the sacred and mystic four repeated 135 times: the number referred to by Pythagoras in his *Golden Verses* as being the 'Source of eternal nature and Almighty Power' (Duke 1846, 53). Stukeley's cubit was utilitarian but Duke's esoteric twist implied that a sacred geomantic code was embedded in the construction of Stonehenge; a code which he recovered at Avebury as well (Henty 2020a, 54).

In Egypt, Piazzi Smyth agreed that a measurement system was similarly used in the construction of the pyramids. Rather than cubits, he compared his measurements with British inches and found that what he termed the 'Pyramid inch' was only slightly larger by 'half a hair's breadth' (Smyth 1874, 35): the Egyptians used this measure because they must have learned it from the ancestors of the 'Anglo-Saxon race'. Smyth's contemporary, the archaeologist Sir William Flinders Petrie (1853–1942) also dabbled in metrology, publishing a book called *Inductive Metrology: the recovery of ancient measures from the monuments* in 1877. He attempted to retrieve the ancient systems by taking over 10,000 measurements, found in the monuments of Egypt, Britain, Europe, Asia and North America, to find commonality in the measures used. Petrie then subjected the measures which he had converted to inches to probability tests (Petrie 1877, 24–39; Henty 2020, 55). He concluded that their overall similarity over wide areas must have been down to diffusion emanating from the ancient Near East (Petrie 1877, 147–148). He discounted Stukeley's druid cubit because he thought that the unit used was approximately 4.7 inches. Petrie's empirical approach distanced him from the earlier antiquarian esoteric metrology.

19th century contestations

The idea that the monument builders were highly skilled 'geometricians' was a viewpoint that conflicted with another set of revolutionary ideas that were voiced from the mid-19th century onwards. In 1859 Charles Darwin (1809–1882) published *On the Origin of Species* (Darwin 1909) and in it he proposed that in the struggle for existence those species best adapted for 'the varying conditions of life' would thus be naturally selected. Herbert Spencer (1820–1903) applied Darwin's thesis to humankind and in *The Principles of Biology* dealt a further blow to the Biblical version of history when he wrote that it was necessary to choose between two hypotheses – 'the Hypothesis of Special Creation and the hypothesis of Evolution' (Spencer 1864, 331). Spencer's evolutionary theory stated that 'the survival of the fittest' and Darwin's 'natural selection' were 'almost self-evident truths' (Spencer 1864, 444–445). Social systems could then be compared to biological organisms which move from being simple to being complex.

These evolutionary ideas permeated social anthropology and progression theory, which claimed that the main tendency of humankind is to progress from savage to civilised state, and they became a common thread. They were an integral part of Lubbock's theses (1865; 1870) and are also found in Tylor's *Primitive Culture* (1871), Lewis H. Morgan's (1877) *Ancient Society or Researches in the Lines of Human Progress from Savagery through Barbarism to Civilization* about the upward 'career' of 'mankind' and Sven Nilsson's Swedish work, *The Primitive Inhabitants of Scandinavia*, translated by Lubbock (1868). Progression theory had a particular impact on archaeology, as demonstrated by Simpson (1862, 10–11) who, having researched 'the aboriginal inhabitants of Scotland', declared that they had traced 'the stratifications … of progress and civilization by which our primaeval ancestors successfully passed upwards through the varying eras and stages of advancement'. In 1869, Lubbock commissioned a series of paintings to depict early prehistoric life which included scenes of these 'primaeval' ancestors hunting mammoths, making spears and using stone tools (Burnham 2013). Through written works and paintings such as these came the image of prehistoric humans who bordered on savagery and were certainly far removed from Stukeley's knowledgeable race, capable of building monuments which incorporated astronomical alignments.

Geology, evolutionism and anthropology combined to give a solid affirmation of progress through the ages. They not only transformed archaeological research in the second half of the 19th century but gave it a scientific basis. However, the authors of astronomical narratives ethnocentrically assumed that their methods were the ones the builders used, thereby giving them intellectual capacities at odds with the archaeological narrative of 'primitive man'. At the same time a distance was created between those antiquarians who called themselves archaeologists and those who were primarily concerned with the astronomical features of the monuments. There was no argument or debate about the importance of the monumental culture, both sides were united on that, but their different stances on the examination and interpretation of this culture created an epistemological divide; the scientific versus the esoteric. For example, Duke (1846, 185) dedicated his book to various archaeological organisations and asked those archaeologists who believed that 'our heathen ancestry' knew nothing of astronomy, why not? He suggested that, as 'we cannot look into times long since past, times of which there exists no record', studies of the landscape and the sky may provide some idea of the past. This argument was to counter such critics as Samuel Rowe who, while acknowledging that the druids probably erected cromlechs for sacrificial or sepulchral purposes, questioned the use of astronomy saying that 'the theory which is built upon a foundation so fanciful will scarcely demand a serious refutation' (Rowe 1848, 34). Stuart (1859, 212) agreed that the stone circles 'have been without any foundation associated with the ancient Druids'. Simpson's opinion was that, 'We have not, for instance, a particle of direct evidence for the too common belief that our stone circles were temples which the Druids used for worship'. He added, 'It is this craving after the mysterious, this reprehensible irrationalism, that has brought, indeed, the whole subject of Druidism into much modern contempt with many archaeologists' (Simpson 1862, 31). Contemporaneously, his namesake Rev. James Simpson (1862, 448) felt that his English counterparts had continued to speculate about the druidical temples and had failed to progress information beyond the ideas of the 18th century Stukeley.

In the pre-paradigmatic stages of a discipline many theories and methodologies may be proposed before, when taken together, one becomes dominant through consensual agreement. That is not to say that all earlier theories are abolished: some may be in tune with the main theory and can therefore be progressed whereas others may be sidelined or subjugated. Implausible or weaker theories, such as Higgins' self-confessed 'aerial castle-building' on druidry, simply vanish from view. Generally interpretations linking astronomy with monuments disappeared in Britain in the second half of the 19th century, though they continued in Egyptian studies, Europe and the rest of the world.

By contrast archaeology had forged ahead. Although the term archaeology had been used before, Daniel Wilson's address in 1852 not only confirmed the name of this field of study but deemed it to be scientific. That archaeological science was different from earlier forms of antiquarianism with their esoteric overtones was evident. Such were the advances that, in 1874, Boyd Dawkins (1874, viii) also emphasised that 'archaeology, by the use of strictly inductive methods, has grown from a mere antiquarian speculation into a science'. Archaeology had academic and institutional recognition with the establishment, at Cambridge in 1851, of the first Chair of Archaeology, named the Disney chair after its first incumbent. This was followed by others at Oxford and elsewhere, and through this early institutionalisation it became the dominant narrative on prehistory (Schofield *et al.* 2011, 31). Archaeology's disciplining in the middle of the 19th century achieved two things at one and the same time: first it established itself as the orthodox view of prehistory and, secondly, by so doing it distanced itself from the alternative theories which drew on cosmology and astronomy to interpret the material remains. Though the astronomical methods could have been useful for finding alignments in monuments other than Stonehenge the archaeologists did not take them up and the divide became complete.

The implications for archaeoastronomy

Interest in the monuments could be classified during the first two centuries of antiquarianism as both archaeological or archaeoastronomical, as can be seen in the treatises on Stonehenge, Avebury and other monuments, because all data was treated equally and Stukeley and others combined both methodologies. Interest in Egyptology also drew professional astronomers into the mix. There seems to be little evidence of criticism of archaeoastronomical thought until the mid-19th century and from that time archaeology forged ahead while antiquarian astronomical theories were marginalised and relegated to the sidelines. Archaeology's development had been aided by discoveries from other disciplinary arenas, the impact of which were foundational for archaeology's progress. As already mentioned these included the geological discoveries which led to the proposal of the Three Age system. Darwin and Spencer's evolutionary theory coupled with Lubbock's progression theory melded all these ideas into a new way of looking at prehistory. Prior to this there had been two pictures of prehistoric humankind; the archaeoastronomers' highly skilled 'geometricians' and the Romantic notion of the noble savage. Lubbock's thesis of the primitive condition of humankind and Nilsson's description of the savage state, added another way of looking at prehistoric people: there they were not ennobled in Romantic terms but viewed simply as 'savages'. These different versions were incompatible, yet backed by such 'scientific' evidence, archaeology held sway over both astronomical and esoteric theories of prehistory.

The antiquarians were concerned with details, often in disembodied isolation, but the further away from the past we are, the details diminish in the broader perspectival view. This is why Braudel's model of the *longue durée* is so useful in representing the period of antiquarianism with its underlying continuity, punctuated only by short-term crises. Although antiquarian enquiries became more scientific and rigorous throughout the course of three centuries, continuity was maintained with the same signatures, tokens and mythologies appearing over and over again. In other words, by the end of antiquarianism, scientific enquiry into monumental heritage became more disciplined while esoteric theories were in decline. Lacking entry into the archaeology profession, those desirous of studying the relationship between monuments and the sky, remained amateurs. Foucault (1980, 82) suggested that theories which become marginalised tend to be 'naïve knowledges', beneath the required level of 'cognition or scientificity', thereby losing what he termed as the 'power of a discourse'. And so it was for archaeoastronomy.

Despite this, from the emergence of archaeoastronomical texts in the 1st century AD to those written during antiquarianism, many theories and methods, which later crystallised into key tenets of 20th century archaeoastronomy, were formulated. The most important of these were that the builders of the prehistoric monuments observed the cycles of the sun, the moon, the planets and the stars and in some way incorporated them into their monuments in an intentional way. The speculation that the monuments were built by the druids as sacred places and that their priests were well versed in astronomy, understood mathematics, geometry and equilateral triangles and used standard measures was a long-held belief throughout the antiquarian period. As the druids were 'known' to understand astronomy it followed that their architecture could shed light on the builders' beliefs and advanced skills. The researchers' ideas about ancient methods may have been ethnocentric but in addition to their suspect beliefs they also proposed that the prehistoric structures were erected with an appreciation of features in the landscape, aligned to celestial events occurring at certain features on the horizon and that their architects understood how to use a gnomon and shadow effects. Circles were also understood to have calendrical properties and ancient lines on the landscape were discovered by Black, Dymond and Spencer (see above). The concepts of compass direction, magnetic variation, geometry and metrology were nascent during antiquarianism: this is not just apparent from Stukeley's observations but in the works of the many antiquarians described here. Various astronomical terms were used in relation to the methodology of finding alignments and it was the juxtaposition of these that created a new archaeoastronomical language. There is also the beginning of the idea that sites were not individual entities to be studied in isolation but that they were situated in a landscape which itself had meaning: a forerunner of both archaeoastronomy and landscape archaeology. As the 20th century dawned, anyone desirous of studying Stonehenge could take his/her pick of several narratives which included it being a temple of the sun; a temple of Saturn; part of a planetarium or an astronomical model of the planets; a calendar for the measurement of the solar year, or a place of druid worship. These narratives which also covered many ancient monuments, not just Stonehenge, had a mixed origin: some were influenced by Freemasonry, Romanticism and Hermeticism, some incorporated elements of the 19th century Occult Revival, while yet others reflected the emergence of interest in scientific astronomy. The testing of these theories, not just at Stonehenge but also in the wider monumental landscape of Britain, helped to develop a foundational methodology to pass on to 20th century archaeoastronomers.

Chapter 4

'The great subject of orientation'

During antiquarianism, up until the mid-19th century, there were no disciplinary boundaries between scholars who looked at the relation of ancient monuments to celestial events and those archaeologists who studied their material remains. At the turn of the 20th century, archaeology, which was already established as a discipline, continued its development and began to establish itself as the principal author of the narrative of the past. At the same time astronomical studies had very little status, despite the fact that, together with archaeology, they both studied the same source material of archaeological heritage. Between 1900 and 1960 they developed in different directions and finally went their separate ways. In the scant literature on archaeoastronomy's history, Sir Norman Lockyer (1836–1920) and Vice-Admiral Boyle Somerville (1863–1936) stand out as solitary figures for this time: a brief flowering in the early years of the 20th century which was followed by a hiatus between the beginning of the 1930s and the re-emergence of interest in the 1960s. Here and in the following chapter it will be shown that, on further scrutiny, this does not appear to be the case: indeed, interest in astronomical approaches, whether scientific or esoteric, continued, though albeit less recognised, up until 1960.

Lockyer and his contemporaries

As the 20th century dawned, many of the antiquarian studies had been consigned to the past, though some papers such as 'Astronomical theories relative to Stonehenge' published by Washington Teasdale in the *Leeds Astronomical Society Journal c.* 1900, in which he proposed that the barrows and tumuli surrounding Stonehenge formed a planisphere, were similar to some of the 'bizarre nineteenth-century astronomical ideas' (Lancaster Brown 1976, 114). Yet as already shown, many of the methods and key concepts of astronomical studies were already in place when Sir Norman Lockyer heralded a new era for astronomical alignment studies which veered away from their archaeological base. Lockyer was, according to Polcaro and Polcaro (2009, 224), the 'father of Archaeoastronomy', with his methods being used as a model for the subsequent studies of the period. On the other hand, Kelley and Milone

(2005, 240) suggested that 'modern' archaeoastronomy began with a discovery by the archaeologist F. C. Penrose (1817–1903) that some of the public buildings in ancient Greece possibly showed significant astronomical alignments. Whilst their work has been seen as foundational for archaeoastronomy, innovative in many ways, modern critiques generally ignore the earlier antiquarian studies and focus solely on Lockyer and his work, missing the continuity between his and the build up and diffusion of earlier ideas, variously expressed in the previous centuries.

Lockyer was an amateur astronomer who rose to fame to become one of Britain's most prominent astronomers following his discovery of helium using spectrographic analysis. He pursued his interest in astrophysics to become Professor of Astronomical Physics in 1885 at the Royal College of Science. While there he established a small observatory in South Kensington which was later to become the basis of the Hill Observatory in Sidmouth (Meadows 2008). *Nature*, the scientific journal that Lockyer established in 1869, remains one of the most prestigious scientific journals published today. Already respected and established in the scientific world, he became interested in the history of astronomy in his later years. From that perspective he began to consider orientations found in ancient monuments. At that time, these studies which took astronomy into account had no identifying name, but Lockyer (1894, viii), musing about the idea that English churches generally faced the place of sunrise on patron saints' days, suggested that 'this direction towards the sunrising is the origin of the general use of the term *orientation*'. From that point, theory based on the empirical study of alignments to astronomical directions became known as 'orientation theory' (Lockyer 1906a, 34, 40–42) or, as described in an anonymous review in *Nature* (1908, 573), 'the great subject of orientation'. Lockyer's contemporary, Vice-Admiral Boyle Somerville (1912, 23), who described himself as an orientationist, summed up the aims of this new field by saying, 'The object of the orientationist is to show that this [monument building] cult, whatever else it was, was connected definitely with the heavenly bodies: sun, moon, and stars'. The terms orientation and alignment were used interchangeably in this period.

Earlier, Lockyer (1891) had made a general foray into the subject of orientation before turning his efforts to the alignments he found in the Egyptian temples, as Biot, Smyth and others had done before him. F. C. Penrose, in the paper referred to by Kelley and Milone (2005), also applied the methods developed by these Egyptologists to use the stars for dating some of the Greek temples as the title of his paper demonstrates:

> On the results of an examination of the orientation of a number of Greek temples, with a view to connect these angles with the amplitudes of certain stars at the time these temples were founded, and an endeavour to derive there from the dates of their foundation by consideration of the changes produced upon the Right Ascension and Declination of the stars arising from the precession of the equinoxes. (Penrose 1893, 805)

This title alone establishes two characteristics of the practice relating to the stars: that it was firmly based on astronomy and that it was scientific in attempting to test theory by empiricism. Penrose went on to publish several related orientation studies and such was the spirit of cooperation before disciplinary divides that Lockyer used Penrose's data and Penrose was also influenced by Lockyer (Hannah 2013, 424). They (Lockyer and Penrose 1902) even collaborated on a paper attempting to date Stonehenge by using astronomical alignments, referring to the earlier work by Higgins who, in 1827, had dated it to *c.* 4003 BC by using the precession of the equinoxes, as mentioned in Chapter 3. There was also a later attempt by the archaeologist E. H. Stone (1922, 117) to date Stonehenge through astronomy, giving it a date of 1840 BC, earlier than 1680 BC, which Lockyer and Penrose had suggested.

Lockyer published *The Dawn of Astronomy* in 1894 where the 'dawn' of the title referred to the dawn of the rising sun. Convinced that the temples in Egypt were built with a knowledge of astronomy for the purposes of the 'worship of the sun and stars at the time of rising and setting' (1894, 44) he attempted to date them from their orientation to high magnitude stars like Canopus. This was because he believed, like Penrose, that as the stars involved would shift over time due to the precession of the equinoxes, their position, relative to buildings, at any given time could be accurately dated (see Glossary: the stars' motions). He was also interested in the decrease in the obliquity of the ecliptic and how this could affect alignments to solar extrema. Had Lockyer been correct this would have been of importance to archaeologists whose only method of dating at that time was typology.

Edward Holden (1897, 849), Lockyer's contemporary, noted the importance of this work but suggested that 'one should be historian, ethnologist and astronomer in one' to be able to judge Lockyer's arguments. He also maintained that Lockyer's conclusion that some of the temples were oriented by the stars was arrived at independently by the German researcher Heinrich Nissen (1839–1912) in 1885 and Robert Hannah (2013, 424) has recently agreed with this assessment. Although Lockyer next turned his attention to British monuments, interest in Egypt continued. For example the idea of observing the meridian transit of a circumpolar star (see Glossary: circumpolar stars) was first suggested by Romieu at the beginning of the 20th century and followed up by Pogo in the 1930s (Belmonte 2001a). Alternatively Zinner proposed, in 1931, that the use of a gnomon to produce the shortest shadow could be used as another method; one which was also favoured by Chatley in 1948 (Belmonte 2001a, S2). On the other hand, in 1947, Edwards suggested using an artificial horizon to avoid the problems of extinction and refraction near the horizon (Belmonte 2001a, S3). Further alignment studies were carried out by Zaba in 1953.

Stellar alignments were also considered by two members of the Welsh Society for the Astronomical Study of Ancient Stone Monuments, that Lockyer belonged to: Lord Boston and E. N. Baynes reported orientations to the Pleiades, Capella and Arcturus at some Welsh monuments (Griffith 1908a, 295). However, nearly 30 years later the archaeologist W. F. Grimes examined the Welsh alignments saying that not only were 'they as mysterious today as they ever were' but that there was no feature that was common to all and that the stone circles were little better (Grimes 1936, 106). Yet,

Somerville (1912, 26) believed that the stars were important and he pre-empted the criticism of why some stars would have been picked out from a multitude by saying that the number of bright stars for any period was remarkably small. Nevertheless he fell into the same trap as Lockyer by trying to use the stars for dating purposes. Whilst the stars might have been important to the builders of prehistoric monuments in and of themselves, they also had another function in relation to their positions relative to the sun, such as when the stars' heliacal risings or settings predicted a solar event (see Glossary: heliacal risings and settings). Hannah (2013, 424) reported that, at temples in mainland and colonial Greece, Penrose found solar orientations where star positions forewarned these solar phenomena.

Stonehenge, the most iconic site in Britain and the subject of many antiquarian studies, was the focus of Lockyer's next book *Stonehenge and Other British Monuments Considered* in 1906. Flinders Petrie (1880, 31) had considered the possibility of astronomic alignments at Stonehenge, drawing the most accurate plan to date, yet found that only the alignment to the midsummer sunrise bore scientific scrutiny. So, on the one hand Petrie was following the antiquarians in their interest in astronomical alignments but, on the other, he belonged to the new generation of archaeologists who brought modern field techniques into play. Following Petrie's research it might be assumed that the study of astronomical alignments found in British monuments was now the purview of archaeologists and although Lockyer was one of astronomy's most prominent figures, when he turned his interest to Stonehenge he crossed a disciplinary line by encroaching on the domain of the archaeologists. However, in Germany, Lockyer's work was well received with Albrecht writing favourably about his ideas in *Das Weltall*, a German astronomical journal, between 1914 and 1915, while Father Joseph Leugering applied these speculations to sites in Westphalia in 1920 (Goodrick-Clark 2011, 168).

Orientation practice

In the early years of the 20th century, the rudiments of existing orientation practice were developed and formalised into clearly defined elements and by looking at each element in turn it is possible to chart how the practice progressed. The first element to consider is the horizon, which is at the heart of orientation studies because it is where celestial bodies are seen to rise and set. The visible horizon depends on the nature of the site so, for example, A. L. Lewis (1892, 142) proposed that in mountainous districts, if circles were situated amongst hills then the hilltops could take the place of stones for alignment purposes; a reiteration of antiquarian ideas on foresights. Somerville particularly mentioned the possibility of some boulders on the horizon being used as a 'fore-sight' and believed that, in the absence of anything conspicuous:

> The inference is that we must look beyond the terrestrial termination of the line for some celestial body; and if such, it must naturally be at that moment of its path when it is either rising or setting behind the horizon of the observer. (Somerville 1912, 25)

John Fraser's work in Orkney underlined the importance of the horizon: writing about the Stones of Via in Sandwick he suggested 'A full view of the setting sun can be obtained from the site, but the view of the sunrise is obstructed by the hill to the south-east' (Fraser 1924, 23). He also described the cromlech of Helya or Haly Kirk from which there would have been an unrestricted view of the rising sun.

Lockyer's approach to calculating rising and setting points along the horizon was more technical as it took the horizon altitude into account when determining the azimuth at which these events would occur and also noted that the latitude of the site needed to be taken into account (see Glossary: latitude). Some of his

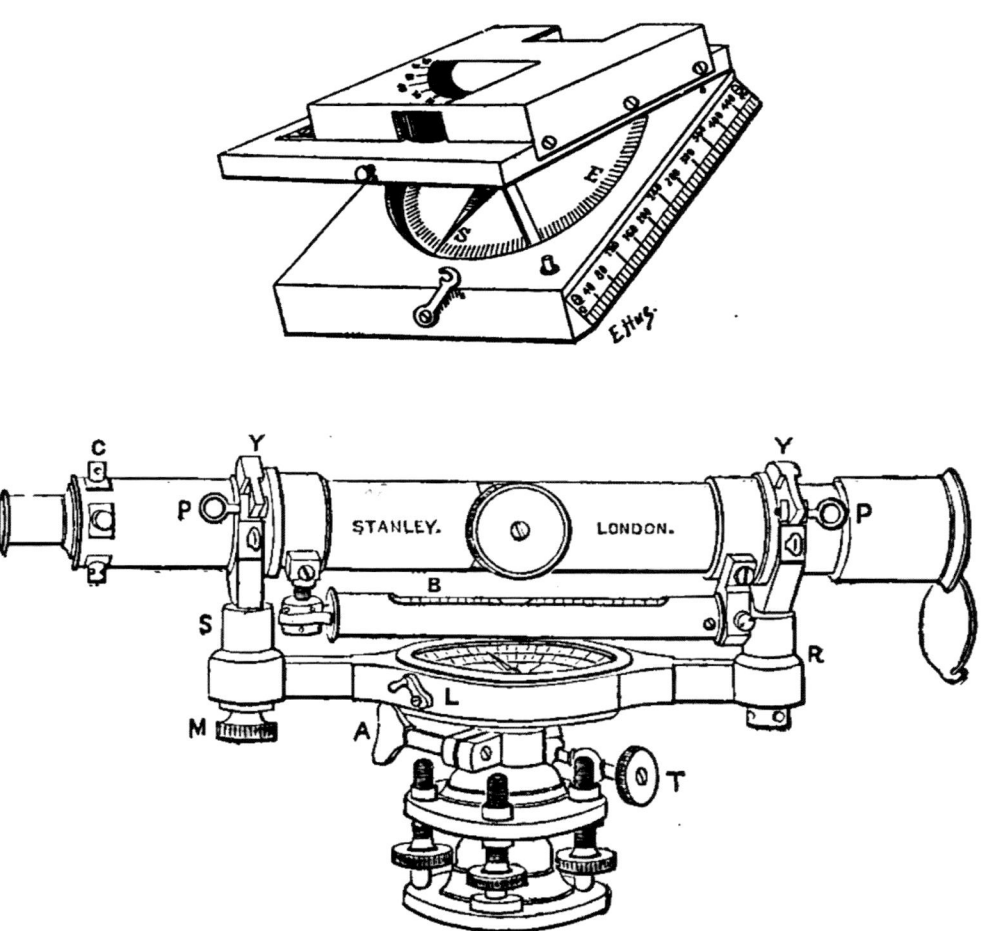

Figure 7. Drawings of Hue's combined compass and clinometer (top) and a surveyor's rotating Y level with telescope (bottom) as portrayed in Sir Norman Lockyer's Surveying for Archaeologists (1909, 27 (top), 24 (bottom)).

methodological refinements had been set out in his chapter 'Astronomical hints for archaeologists' in the *Stonehenge* volume, but in 1909 he published *Surveying for Archaeologists* which was a more detailed textbook and the first of its kind. In it, Lockyer pointed out the difference between true north and magnetic north, which archaeologists tended to use, a point that Somerville (1923, 193) reiterated later, together with giving instructions for calculating the angle of the horizon. Lockyer specified simple instruments such as a theodolite, clinometer and compass (Fig. 7) and his methodology was similar to that which any archaeoastronomer might use today, including how to determine the declination of a star from a measured azimuth. Lockyer emphasised the importance of horizon elevation, some angles of which could be determined from Ordnance Survey maps, and how refraction affected the calculations (see Glossary: atmospheric refraction). Additionally, he discussed what part of the solar or lunar disc was important: upper limb, centre (half orb), lower limb, or full disc.

While Lockyer set out a strict scientific methodology, he also advocated the inclusion of other approaches which included a thorough investigation of the sites, not just their archaeological or astronomical features, 'to see whether there are any concomitant phenomena, and, if there be any, to classify them and study the combined results' (Lockyer 1906a, 179). To this end he recommended the examination of folklore, traditions, holy trees, sacred wells and fires. The influence of the new anthropological discoveries about folklore and mysticism, as demonstrated in works by Tylor (1920 [1871]), Müller (1871) and J. G. Frazer's *The Golden Bough* (1995 [1890]), can be seen reflected in Lockyer's ideas.

Sun, moon and stars
The practice which looked at the stars as indicators of sun positions was applied to other sites, such as the investigation by Lewis (1900) of those 'sun and star' circles of Scotland, some of which in Aberdeenshire featured an 'altar-stone' (recumbent). In its attempts to classify circles according to typology his work was more archaeological than astronomical and he only looked for orientations with approximate azimuths. He did not argue for precision in the directions he found, later criticising Lockyer on a number of archaeological inaccuracies and over the precise observations needed for dating (Lewis 1910). At the same time the archaeologist Frederick Coles (1900) published the results of his survey of 23 recumbent stone circles in the northeast of Scotland, devoid of any archaeoastronomy. Welfare (2008, 13) reported that Coles went on to make further surveys, directing his conclusions, that there was nothing to justify astronomical speculations, at Lewis and Lockyer.

Applying the 'sun and star' theory of Lewis at the same type of circles in Aberdeenshire, Lockyer proposed that alignments were made to the 'direction of the rising sun or star by sighting across the circle at right angles to the length of the recumbent stone' (Lockyer 1908, 285). By determining the declinations from the azimuths of the stones, he found alignments to the summer solstice, the May quarter day sunrise and 'clock-star' observations between 5° and 30° (Lockyer 1908, 286). The term 'clock-star' in this context referred to the heliacal rising of stars such as the rising of the Pleiades at Stonehenge in May, an alignment Lockyer found at many monuments in Cornwall (Lockyer 1906a, 151–155). On the other hand, Müller (1871, 284) had also studied the Cornish monuments speculating that Men-an-tol was set up to record the autumnal equinox.

The idea of a prehistoric calendar had been muted by Smith in 1771 but the early 20th century usage appears to stem from Lewis (1910, 63) who wrote that the May-year was 'an indisputable fact'. On the other hand, Lockyer (1906a, 97–104) credited F. Gaillard's early work in Brittany for elements of his calendar, combining what he had learned from Gaillard with Alfred Devoir's later findings at Carnac (Fig. 8), to posit his version of the May-year calendar. Lockyer's year began on May 6th followed by quarterly divisions on August 8th, November 8th and February 4th. As noted above, certain stars heralded these dates, though Lockyer (1906b, 280) was more convinced by the idea of a solar calendar because certain stones marked key solar dates, the equivalent of Celtic festival days, especially in the four months he selected. Similarly, in Ireland, Windle (1913, 287, 301), who was assisted by Somerville for his surveys on the megalithic monuments around Lough Gur, found alignments to *Samhuin Sunset* at Rannach Cruim Duibh stone circle and midwinter sunrise at circles 'J' and 'K'.

With regard to the sun, theories became more complex and in this respect, Lockyer and Penrose (1902) jointly published a paper attempting to date Stonehenge, as referred to earlier. They cited Diodorus amongst the evidence they found for Stonehenge being a sun temple aligned to the midsummer solstice sunrise, using the change in the obliquity of the ecliptic as justification for their claim that Stonehenge was built in 1680 BC±200 years. Factors that they took into account included the difference between the lower limb of the sun's appearance and its semi-diameter; refraction and parallax; the altitude of the horizon and the azimuth. These important methodological qualifications effectively advanced astronomical studies from simple observations to highly technical surveys. Following an idea first proposed by Chapple in 1778, another theory relating to the sun was proposed by Dr McAldowie, who noted that the shadow cast by the sun at its zenith added to the relationship between certain stones by touching prominent points or edges (Anon 1912, 620). Later on, Stonehenge was also the subject of an anthropological enquiry by A. T. Hatto (1953, 103) who suggested, on the basis of similarities with other cultures, that the stones in its concentric circles represented male and female principals so that it was purpose built for fertility rites, with the 'penetration of the dawn ray of the midsummer sun an act of cosmic fertilization'.

Although the moon had featured in antiquarian accounts, knowledge of its cycle was limited. In 1912, Somerville made an important discovery when surveying the alignments at Calanais (then called Callenish), on the Isle of Lewis in the Outer Hebrides. He noted (1912, 29) that many of the stones were aligned to lunar risings which suggested a detailed prehistoric knowledge of the complex motion of the moon during its metonic cycle. Gerald and Margaret Ponting (1978, 20) believed that Somerville was the first person to suggest that megalithic astronomers understood the lunar extremes that Alexander Thom (1971) later called standstills (see Glossary: moon). Certainly, in Somerville's 1912, paper a direction on one of his diagrams is called 'Line of full moon rise – greatest northern declination (19 year cycle)' (see Fig. 9).

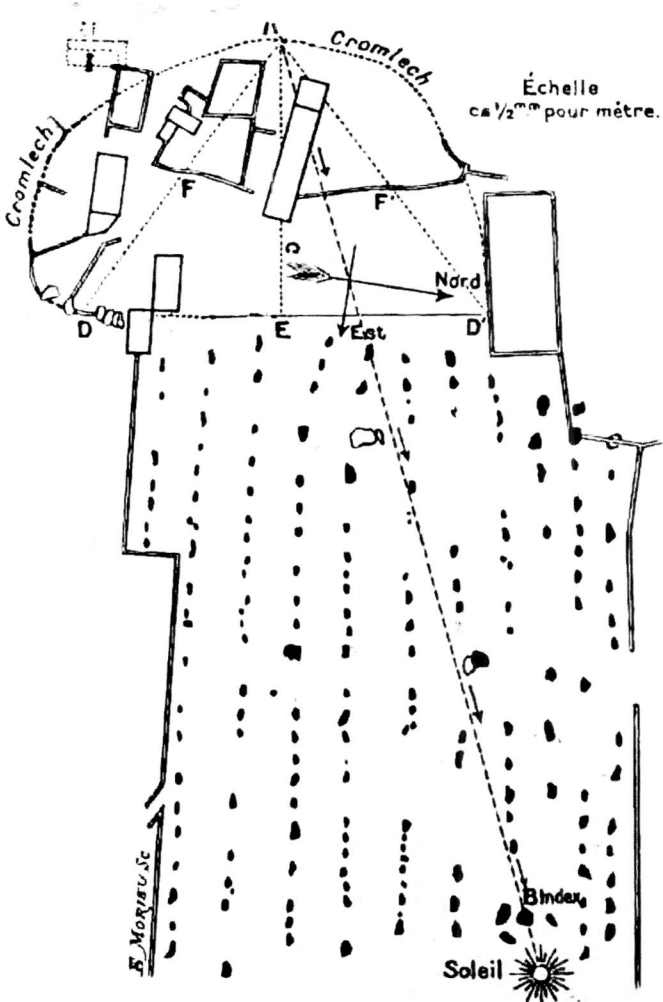

Figure 8. Alfred Devoir's diagram of the alignments at Le Menéc (one of the three groups of menhirs at Carnac, Brittany), adapted from Sir Norman Lockyer's Stonehenge and Other British Stone Monuments Astronomically Considered (1906a, 99).

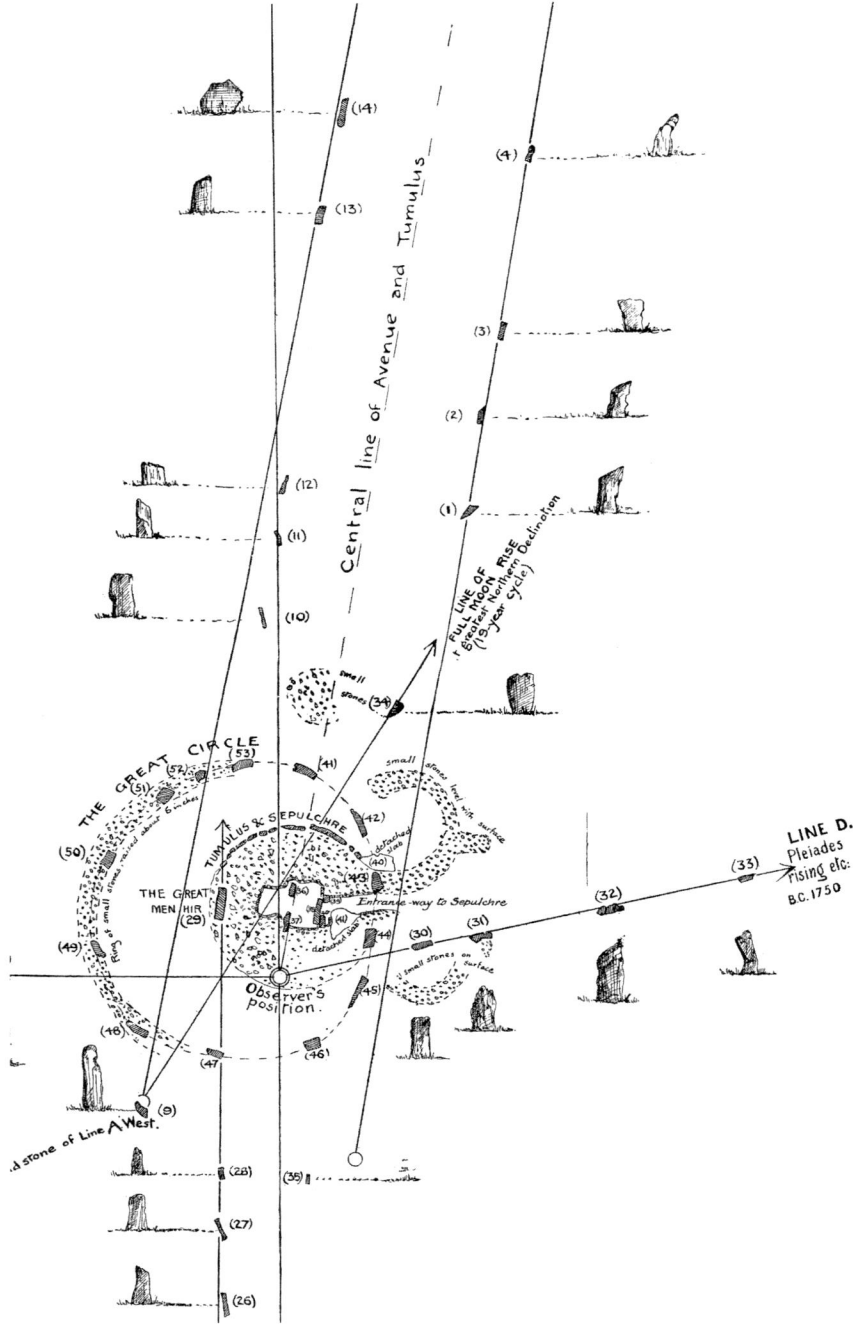

Figure 9. Section of Boyle Somerville's plan of Callenish (now Calanais) showing the northern moon limit. From his 1912 paper on the prehistoric monuments in the Outer Hebrides (fig. 2).

Yet Somerville (1912, 23) associated the Hebridean monuments with religious cults, saying that 'The object of the orientationist is to show that this cult, whatever else it was, was connected definitely with the heavenly bodies: sun, moon, and stars'. He pointed out that objects could be oriented in one of two ways, either to a natural feature such as a mountain or to a point on the horizon where a celestial body could be seen to rise or set (Somerville 1923, 194).

Lockyer's ethnocentric perspective placed astronomy as a motivating force for the monument builders while at the same time underlining the astronomical focus of orientation studies. Most of these studies concurred that the builders were skilled in astronomy and John Fraser (1923, 32), for example, like the earlier antiquarians, was of the opinion that the prehistoric inhabitants were not 'ignorant savage heathens' but that some 'possessed some practical knowledge of the sciences of Astronomy, Geometry, and Masonry'. Somerville agreed and his over-riding message on orientation is contained in the passage below,

> I have thus examined fifty-five separate megalithic objects in different parts of Ireland and Scotland, and in all this number there have only been six in which I could not find evidence of orientation. The ethnological importance of this is, of course, very great, arguing, as it does, the existence of a knowledge of the movements of the heavenly bodies, which implies an unexpected degree of culture among the inhabitants of these islands at an early date. (Somerville 1912, 51)

On the other hand, Herbert Hudson (1933) was opposed to the idea that the builders used astronomy for religious purposes and used his analysis of alignments to put forward his own ideas on prehistoric culture by explaining in economic terms why the sun became more important than the moon after the development of agriculture. His theory was that originally nomadic peoples paid more attention to the moon and that the influence of the sun was only required for the development of agriculture. Accordingly the builders marked out their alignments on the principle of sun dials to mark summer and winter. This was a more pragmatic solution than that proposed by other orientationists and more in line with the archaeological view on prehistoric culture.

International studies

Orientation studies were not just confined to Britain and Egypt: by the end of the period the field of study was represented in Europe and the Americas. In France, between 1912 and 1926, Baudouin (1912; 1913; 1917) studied the solar orientation of megalithic structures and suggested a technique for determining the orientation of the dolmens as well as theorising that there was prehistoric stellar knowledge. Devoir (1911; 1915–16), adding to his own early work which he had shared with Lockyer, continued with his research on the megalithic structures in Brittany. Devoir also conducted European surveys and in his paper of 1909 entitled 'Urzeitliche Astronomie in Westeuropa' ('Archaic astronomy in western Europe') he published diagrams of standing stones showing alignments to sunrise and sunset. Contemporaneously, Jacquot (1915) researched astral cults and Boule (1930) and Baschmakoff (1930) added to this body of work on orientations, with Lenoir publishing his ideas on megalithic mentality in 1956. The paintings in the Lascaux cave, which were thought to have astronomical significance, were discovered in France in 1940. Additionally, in Northern Ireland after the Second World War, at Beaghmore, A. McL. May found alignments at the stone circles there (Pilcher 1969).

Research in the Americas had a much broader base and was therefore of a quite different nature to the studies of European prehistoric monuments. The extant remains in the Americas belonged to diverse cultures in Mesoamerica, which included Mayan and pre-Columbian South America; those of indigenous North American Indians and those of the American Southwest, home to the antecedents of modern Pueblo peoples. The time periods covered by these studies included prehistory, the early historic period and the recent past. There is evidence of steady growth in Mayan studies (see for example Forstemann 1904; Ricketson 1928; Teeple 1931; Guthe 1932; Escalona Ramos 1940; Weitzel 1949; Andrews 1959). Other occasional studies delved into Zuni mythology and ceremonialism (Bunzel 1932; Benedict 1935); the Zapotec ruins at Monte Albán in Mexico (Caso 1932) and Berard Haile's *Starlore among the Navajo* (1947). Von del Chamberlain (1994) thought that Bill Miller's (1955) article in *Plateau*, which associated astronomy with two pictographs in Arizona, was the start of people looking at possible astronomical interpretations of Native American rock art. From these examples it is clear that there was a difference in the research questions and the methodologies used to answer them between the New and the Old Worlds.

The archaeoastronomy that developed in Britain and Europe from the early 20th century research related specifically to orientation or alignments to the sun, moon and the stars and the methodology used to recover them. It required special skills, so the researchers needed to understand astronomy and celestial mechanics (see Glossary: celestial mechanics; celestial sphere), as well as surveying. While the methods were clear, its theory still depended on the belief that the monuments builders were versed in astronomy, as it had been in antiquarianism. While there were different research themes in orientation studies, in practice much of the research was multi-faceted. For example, the work of the Rev. John Griffith, who had measured alignments with Lockyer in Anglesey and was secretary of the Welsh Society for the Astronomical Study of Ancient Stone Monuments, included studies of the orientation of earthworks, barrows and stone circles (Griffith 1909). Overall there were few practitioners apart from Lockyer, Penrose, Lewis and Somerville who all made major contributions in the first two decades of the 20th century, before being joined by Hudson in the 1930s.

Archaeology

By comparison, archaeology advanced in every way; it had academic presence in universities which ensured continuity; it was peopled by many prominent archaeologists; there were textbooks and written histories and many dedicated societies who published proceedings. Along with Flinders Petrie, the key figures who were instrumental in advancing archaeological methods in this period included General Pitt Rivers (1827–1900), O. G. S. Crawford (1886–1975) and Sir Mortimer Wheeler (1890–1976). Their combined changes were a mixture of innovations and refinements to existing methods. For example, excavation methodology was improved at the turn of the century by Pitt Rivers, who Christopher and Jacquetta Hawkes (1949, 172) described as 'the immediate inspiration of the scientific archaeology'. His methods, which were similar to those advocated by Petrie (1904) in his *Methods and Aims of Archaeology*, included 'total excavation' and the detailed recording of both stratigraphy and finds (Schofield *et al.* 2011, 32). Crawford brought new techniques to archaeology, developing aerial reconnaissance from its military importance in the First World War into an important source for the discovery of unknown sites from the identification of soil and crop-marks (Hauser 2009). Mortimer Wheeler advanced the field further by introducing the technique of excavating in grid squares, to provide more accurate data on the strata and context of the finds. Technical advances introduced the in 1950s, such as pollen analysis and 'resistivity surveying', revolutionised archaeology's practice (Hawkes 1951, 11; Clark 1958, 233). Another radical innovation was radiocarbon dating: when Childe turned his attention to Europe in his book *The Prehistory of European Society*, first published in 1958, he used the methods for Carbon 14 dating detailed in the 2nd edition of F. Libby's, *Radiocarbon Dating* (1955).

For archaeology to fully take its place as an academic discipline where the increased rigour of practices in the field was matched by its intellectual and academic development, it needed to have a presence in academic institutions. In addition to those departments established in the second half of the 19th century, the Edinburgh Abercromby Chair in Archaeology was established in 1927 and Durham University began teaching archaeology in 1931. Around the same time Cambridge University initiated its undergraduate archaeology programme, though this only became a full, stand-alone course after the Second World War (Schofield *et al.* 2011, 35). Although the Royal Archaeological Institute was already operating, the Institute of Archaeology added further academic weight. It was Sir Mortimer Wheeler who was instrumental in founding this new institute in 1934 (Stout 2008, 31). With the help of funds donated by Flinders Petrie, the Institute took up premises in Regents Park under the auspices of University College London in 1937. The Council of British Archaeology was formed a few years later in 1944. Additionally, the improvement in archaeological science was recognised when the Oxford laboratory was set up in 1955 to focus on magnetic dating in order to discover buried material through 'remanent magnetism' with the help of Geophysics (Clark 1958, 233).

The culture history approach
Some archaeologists, now having a sound methodology, turned their attention to developing theory as a way of providing a richer interpretation of the evidence. This

more critical approach to the study of prehistory was progressed by V. Gordon Childe (1892–1957) who believed that the correct way to study archaeology was through studying cultures, saying 'it is the cultures which should be classified chronologically rather than individual relics' (Childe 1935, 6). This is the idea that cultures are like organisms, so that the part is explained in terms of the whole (Johnson 2010, 80). Childe's new cultural-chronological framework was known as culture history, a theme which dominated archaeological theory in the period between the two world wars, with its proponents being Glyn Daniel, Christopher and Jacquetta Hawkes, Stuart Piggott, Graham Clark and Mortimer Wheeler (Trigger 1998, 696).

Childe, who was also an evolutionist who followed progression theory, did not believe the monument builders had advanced skills, as can be seen from his chapter headings in *What Happened in History* (1960 [1942]), which included 'Palaeolithic savagery', 'Neolithic barbarism' and 'Early Bronze Age civilization'; classifications that were mainly adopted from Tylor. Additionally, Childe (1973 [1925]; 1981 [1936]) tried to link progression theory to the Three Age system, the terminology of which implicitly suggests evolution. Early 20th century archaeology retained these antiquarian concepts of prehistory and the Three Age system; a scheme which imposed a disciplinary structure which was in tune with the overall restructuring of archaeology as a discipline. From Childe's simple evolutionary cultural sequence came the study of the complexity of cultures with classifications such as 'Beaker Cultures', 'Food-vessel Cultures', 'Passage-grave Cultures' and so on (Daniel 1962, 77). However Christopher Hawkes (1951, 9, 12) proposed a new system for classifying prehistory, breaking it down into five sub-sections starting with antehistoric and ending with protohistoric, though he agreed that there was 'a grading *in our degree of knowledge*'.

Although ideas on diffusion and the transmission of cultural signatures had been suggested by Douglas in 1793, Childe made these a central theme of his work and accounted for change only in terms of outside influence, migration or diffusion. This reworking of diffusionist ideas was formative for the early 20th century archaeological narrative when it became fully developed to account for similarities between cultures. Drawing on Marxist theories, Childe (1960 [1942], 10, 36) believed that the 'materialist concept of history' asserted that the economy determined the ideology, concluding that society organised itself around producing the necessities of life: when hunter-gathering gave way to food production then this 'suffices to distinguish barbarism from savagery'.

The combined evolutionary theory which linked cultural differences with chronology was epitomised by Christopher and Jacquetta Hawkes' opinion that the development of humankind was an evolutionary journey with 'no break in this procession of events', as set out in their book *Prehistoric Britain* (1949, 11). They presented their work as a chronicle in an attempt to convey a sense of continuity between the past, present and future of humanity. Their thesis (1949, 60) was that the 'dissemination of megaliths can be likened to that of a religion, accomplished by a comparatively small number of "missionaries" who made converts of, and came to dominate, the local populations of many lands'. While there is a view (Stout 2008, 236) that before the Second World War archaeology was under-theorised so that it was 'essentially a set of skills and processes', it was nevertheless characterised by these long-lasting theory changes.

Christopher Hawkes' seminal paper on the 'ladder of inference', which addressed the problems of understanding prehistory, was published in 1954. He theorised that it was from the comparison of archaeological phenomena that human activity could be inferred and enumerated four levels of inference whereby prehistory could be understood. Inferring to the first two, the *techniques* of producing archaeological phenomena and the economics of *subsistence-economies*, he deemed was relatively simple and straightforward. To infer to the *social/political institutions* was much more difficult and to infer to the *religious institutions and spiritual life* was 'the hardest inference of all' (Hawkes 1954, 162). Certainly archaeologists were concentrating on economic explanations almost to the exclusion of religion, which had only been covered in a 'piecemeal' way. Piggott, writing in 1959, with Hawkes' levels of inference in mind, concluded that due to the nature of archaeological evidence, rites 'must remain unknown' (Piggott 1959, 95, cited by Hayman 1997, 142). Unlike American archaeology which had an anthropological bias to inform it, British archaeologists like Piggott failed to marry economic progress with spiritual ideas in order to produce a holistic picture of the past and consequently paid little attention to the sky.

There were some exceptions to the rule and E. Herbert Stone set out the two purposes of Stonehenge to be considered by archaeologists in the mid-1920s: that it was set out for solar worship and the provision of a calendar or alternatively it was designed for sepulchral purposes connected with the adjacent barrows (Stone 1925, 69). Childe (1981[1936], 115) did mention the correlation between the flooding of the Nile, which determined the economic year in Egypt, with the heliacal rise of Sirius. He also recognised that cultivation required knowledge of the seasons, which together with Neolithic, 'magico-religious notions' emphasised 'the sun's role as ruler of the seasons' with its divinity thus guaranteed (Childe 1981 [1936], 91–92). Similarly, the Hawkeses (1949, 81) believed that the construction of such large monuments in Britain must have meant that there was a compelling power in religion, 'possibly one fostered and directed by a strong priesthood'. They suggested (1949, 77) that the shift to the principal architectural form of the 'open, sun-oriented temple' showed evidence of sun cults in the Early Bronze Age, speculating that the strong Indo-European element infused into the Beaker culture gave its religion 'this skyward trend'. They did not have a definitive answer and of Avebury they speculated (1949, 77) that 'the sun certainly played some part' and asked 'did it serve only to fix the time of the festivals, or was it the actual object of their worship?'. The Hawkeses also mentioned the solstitial alignment at Stonehenge and Woodhenge, but the stone carvings at Newgrange were simply described as 'magical'. From evidence such as this it can be concluded that some archaeologists believed that prehistoric builders had a simple understanding of celestial motions and that the sun was important to them, possibly for economic or religious reasons or both. However, there seems to be no evidence to suggest that alignment or orientation studies were given any detailed thought or that they experimented with the astronomical methods. Though Hudson's (1933) theory may have borrowed ideas from Childe, generally the orientationists contradicted the implications of progression theory. Also they tended to concentrate on individual sites and although they were interested in culture it was not in the comparative way that archaeologists modelled it. Another lasting difference between the two fields was the astronomers' belief in the cognitive skills of the monument builders or astronomer-priests. Accordingly, the economic explanations of archaeology generally displaced those ideas about ritual based on astronomical observation. Indeed, most archaeologists were seemingly unaware that the employment of orientation methods could contribute to their ideas on culture, despite Lockyer (1909, v) noting rather optimistically in the preface of his instructional text, *Surveying for Archaeologists*, that many archaeologists were taking up similar studies.

International conferences
British archaeology tended to operate in its own little bubble but as it became increasingly obvious from the diffusion debate that its questions could be informed by European studies, attention was turned towards international communities. As already mentioned, the first international meetings took place in the 19th century and this outreach continued at the beginning of the 20th century when some early meetings, organised by the Société Préhistorique Française took place in France between 1905 and 1913, resuming after the war in 1930 (Goodrum 2009, 30). Similar societies were formed in Switzerland, Austria, Spain and Germany around the same time and after the war Eastern European countries joined in by founding their own prehistoric societies. Not to be left behind, the American School of Prehistoric Research was founded at Harvard in 1921 (Goodrum 2009). This was shortly after an International Institute of Anthropology was founded in 1920, with central offices in Paris (Burkitt and Barnes 1921, 453). At its first congress in Lièges in 1921, anthropology was divided into eight sections, Human Palaeontology; Prehistory; Ethnography; Criminology; Eugenics; Religions, Later Archaeology and Folklore; Linguistic studies; and Sociology. Of these the Prehistoric Section was one of the most important, there being nearly 50 people, on an average, at their sessions. There were further international meetings: The International Congress of Pre- and Proto-Historic Sciences were held in 1932, 1936 and 1948 (Hawkes 1948, 234).

Esoteric archaeology

As with antiquarian studies, there was an esoteric component in many of the early 20th century reviews of monumental culture, particularly those which involved grand astronomical schemes, so that there remained many pockets of interest which lay outside the 'official' version of prehistory written by archaeologists. One of these was *Prehistoric London: its mounds and circles* by Elizabeth Oke Gordon (1914) of which the appendix describing astronomic alignments and elaborating Lockyer's methods with numerology was written by Reverend Griffith, mentioned earlier (Pennick and Devereux 1989, 38). Also by drawing on the 18th century antiquarian studies of Iolo Morganwg and the later 19th century work of Myvyr Morganwg, Griffith (1908b) concluded that stone circles had originally been set up to mark the quarter days while the solstitial stones were evidence of later use (Michell 1989, 36). These theories were also studied by Lewis Spence in his books, *The Mysteries of Britain* (1905) and *The Magic Arts in Celtic Britain* (1949). Spence wrote extensively about the druids and other arcane traditions during this period as well as two books on the mythical island of Atlantis.

Others were on the margins of archaeology: the Egyptologist Grafton Elliot Smith was a hyperdiffusionist whose belief in the sophistication of Egyptian culture led him to suppose that the pyramids were the prototypes of megalithic monuments found elsewhere, so anything similar had to be as a result of diffusion from Egypt (Daniel 1962, 83–88). Daniel added that in particular Smith found that symbols from different cultures represented underlying concepts whose universality added proof that they had spread from a single source. Smith published these alternative ideas in many books culminating in *The Diffusion of Culture* in 1933. Smith's disciple, the anthropologist W. J. Perry teamed up with experimental psychologist and anthropologist W. H. R. Rivers to examine the relationship between megalithic monuments and sun-cults in Indonesia where Perry found a correlation between the siting of megalithic monuments and mineral deposits, particularly gold (Stout 2008, 83). In his book *The Children of the Sun* (1923) Perry claimed that 'archaic civilisation' was diffused from these so-called children of the sun who were supreme at the beginning of the Fifth Dynasty in Egypt. Glyn Daniel (1962, 92), who became editor of *Antiquity* in 1958, suggested that Perry's volume and other similar works represented 'the rather large lunatic fringe of prehistory'. He accounted for this trend by saying that people were looking for a simplistic and easy solution to prehistory and pointed to, what was for him, the present day cult of Atlantis as an example of this type of wish.

The language gap

There were many differences between the language of archaeologists and that of the orientationists which led to mutual incomprehension. In his assessment of British prehistory, Christopher Hawkes decried the state of the archaeological literature which he thought was limited by its failure to systemise the subject. This was a preamble to his belief that what archaeology needed was improved documentation and 'a better terminology', while noting,

> Terminology is of two kinds: common or everyday, and learned or scientific. All learned studies or sciences carry a limited number of words of a common or everyday kind, which they share with, and use to explain themselves to, the common or everyday world. (Hawkes 1951, 2)

In the astronomical texts, because the methodology involved celestial mechanics, their common terminology was certainly not the everyday or common language described by Hawkes. The following passage from Lockyer illustrates this point:

> Take the mean of the times of transit as corresponding to the mean of the readings of the horizontal circle, and calculate as shown on the form. The formulae employed are: (1) Tan M = sec h tan δ, (2) Tan A = tan h cos M, cosec (φ M), where M is an auxiliary angle introduced for purposes of computation, and h, δ, A and φ have the significance given to them on p. 68. Of these, h is the local apparent time derived as shown in the form; δ (declination) is obtained from the Nautical, or Whitaker's, Almanac; A is the quantity we are seeking, and (latitude) may be read off from the one-inch Ordnance map of the locality. (Lockyer 1909, 69)

The language gap between the two fields was also emphasised by their different publications. For archaeology it became apparent that archaeologists were leaving antiquarianism and amateurism behind and their society proceedings and journals, such as the *Archaeological Journal*, reflected this by becoming the domain of the professional archaeologists. To underline this change, Crawford founded *Antiquity* in 1927, to 'attempt to summarise and criticise the work of those who are recreating the past'. In the opening editorial he wrote, 'Archaeology is a branch of science which achieves its results by means of excavation, fieldwork and comparative studies; it is founded upon the observation and record of facts', adding that the time was now right for interpretation and synthesis (Crawford 1927, 1). Recently, Stout (2008, 23) has recognised the importance of *Antiquity* in 'imposing a disciplinary yoke that had barely existed beforehand'. Apart from the journals the archaeologists had the textbooks of Petrie and Crawford to draw on, as well as the culture-histories of Childe and others.

Although Lockyer's *Surveying for Archaeologists* functioned as a textbook, his work on Stonehenge, published in book form, would have been the most accessible. Nissen's papers were published in German and the papers relating to astronomical orientations by Penrose, Lewis and others, such as the one published in Lockyer's journal *Nature* by Griffith, were scattered over several publications including anthropology and archaeology journals. For example, Lockyer chose the *Proceedings of the Royal Society of London* for his paper on the Aberdeenshire circles, while Lewis published in *The Journal of the Anthropological Institute of Great Britain and Ireland*. Consequently, there was no consistent publishing home for orientation studies so in simple terms of their different publication histories, the divide between the two fields was obvious.

It was a divide played out in their communities as well, though at the beginning of the 20th century the distinction between archaeology and astronomical studies was still not completely clear. For example, Griffith (1908c, 512) noted that there were three members of the Royal Commission on Welsh Monuments who were 'deeply interested in the astronomical enquiry'. Other archaeology societies that gave a home to orientation studies included the Wiltshire Archaeological Society, whose collaboration with the Royal Archaeological Institute in 1920, led to the publication of a handbook on Stonehenge which stated, 'The evidence seems to point irresistibly to the conclusion that it was planned and orientated in connection with the observation of the Sun, and consequently in all probability with its worship' (Stone 1925, 69). Similarly the North Staffordshire Field Society published the paper by McAldowie referred to earlier, on prehistoric time measurement, based on two years astronomical study (Anon. 1912). Despite *The Archaeological Journal* (1908) noting that there were at least 14 other local societies which were located across Britain from Derbyshire to Newcastle-upon-Tyne there were only a few communities specifically for orientation studies. These included the Leeds Astronomical Society and the Welsh Society, founded in 1907 with Griffith as its secretary. Lockyer was a member of the both the latter and the similar Cornish Society.

The Prehistoric Society of East Anglia was established in 1908, though it dropped 'East Anglia' from its title in 1935. W. Allen Sturge, reiterated the importance of community in his presidential address,

> It is high time that here in England we should begin to draw together ... those who are interesting themselves in the absorbing but difficult study of the early ages of the human race before the dawn of history. (Sturge 1911, 9)

His address was also a rallying cry for prehistoric research which Sturge believed had fallen behind European studies. As was evident during antiquarianism, these societies were vital in promoting community and the exchange of ideas.

The implications for archaeoastronomy

By the end of this period it is apparent that archaeology was the authoritative voice on prehistory while archaeoastronomy was relegated to the margins of intellectual life. To shed light on the possible reasons for this, we have to look at the relationship between archaeology and science for some clues. Although Daniel Wilson had declared archaeology to be a science in the mid-19th century, it was not until the 1890s that Lockyer urged the Royal Society to admit archaeologists (Meadows 2008, 227–228). Despite his intervention, the Society declared in 1901 that it would restrict membership to the natural sciences and it was this decree that led to the formation of a separate body, the British Academy for the Promotion of Historical, Philosophical and Philological Studies. This suggests that some archaeologists became wary of scientists in general some time before Lockyer published his astronomical theories on Stonehenge, despite Lockyer being quite outspoken in his opposition to this division. It is possible that this led to a residual antipathy towards astronomical science and may have contributed to the archaeologists' bias against interpretations based on astronomical orientations. Indeed, with regard to the dating of Stonehenge, A. H. Sayce (1914, 18) reported that astronomical explanations did not secure 'the suffrages of the archaeologist'. Similarly, G. L. Gomme, at the reading of Lewis' paper on 'sun and star' circles 'protested against' the premature adoption of astronomical interpretations of individual monuments (Anon. 1900, 530). Although some prehistorians had hinted at the importance of the sun in prehistoric rituals at a very primitive level, the disapproval of orientation studies was sustained: Arthur Evans, on evaluating the conclusions from Gowland's excavation report on Stonehenge which included astronomical arguments, agreed that, as applied to 'a rude stone monument', they had very little force (Gowland 1902, 22). Kendrick and A. F. Bennett took the criticism further, with Kendrick (2003 [1928], 190) saying that 'there is no ethnographical warrant that primitive man of the culture-level represented by the circles was capable of elaborate astronomical measurements of this kind'. Bennett (1933, 131) agreed by pointing out that only a minimum knowledge or skill would have been required to observe and mark the sun's extreme positions on the horizon. He added that there were differences of opinion not only as to the degree of astronomical knowledge that might reasonably be attributed to the prehistoric monument builders, but to the weight that should be attached to them or even to what purpose the orientations served. A further stinging critique was penned by George Engleheart (1930), counterposing the archaeological view of the capabilities of 'primitive people' with the advanced skills attributed to them by orientationists.

The archaeologists also found flaws in the astronomical inferences. For example, Engleheart, as reported by Somerville (1923, 224), questioned Lockyer's ideas on stellar alignments, reportedly saying 'It was a suspicious circumstance in Sir Norman Lockyer's system that when the sun did not explain the orientation of a stone circle, one star or another was adopted in its place'. Mortimer Wheeler (1925, 106) was more direct, saying that solar orientations had led to the 'waste of much time and ink upon the supposed astronomical properties of these circles', while Jacquetta Hawkes (1967, 174) later described Lockyer's work on Stonehenge as 'pseudo-scientific'. Nevertheless Bennett (1933, 132–135) proposed that archaeologists should read Lockyer, especially his chapters aimed at making astronomy easier for archaeologists, adding that discussions about the more speculative side of Lockyer's work should not obscure the real value of his contribution to the practice of astronomical surveys. Bennett also made the point that astronomical findings should not conflict with established archaeological facts and additionally made recommendations about how surveys could be carried out more accurately, though he felt it was a subject that naturally attracted the attention of astronomers rather than archaeologists.

Lockyer (1909, v) had perhaps foreseen the debate by recommending that archaeologists collect the preliminary data and pass the computation onto others. His view was that the descriptions astronomer and archaeologist were not 'as I think they should be, convertible terms', in the belief that astronomical studies should be taken into account in archaeological interpretations (Lockyer 1894, 416). Griffith (1909, 72) also made a case for uniting 'the spade and the theodolite' in archaeological research, but tempered this with a damning denouncement of the way archaeologists failed to note whether directions were to true or magnetic north, as undated magnetic bearings were useless. Somerville (1923, 193), following Griffith's lead, noted the same problem, adding that the archaeologists' imprecision had 'brought about indifference to the subject of orientation', and even 'complete disbelief in its occurrence in any megalithic structures'. Was this 'imprecision' due to a lack of interest or was it the result of the archaeologists not understanding astronomical science? While it is impossible to answer this question definitively, certainly conducting astronomical surveys required a requisite knowledge of astronomy and the mathematical expertise to make the calculations. In this connection, Dinsmoor (1939, 95–102), an archaeologist, suggested that the reason why orientation theory had become 'outmoded' was not through a fault in the theory but in the deduction of results from incomplete data, exacerbated by 'the niceties of modern astronomical calculation'. He explained the necessary astronomical calculations for Stonehenge in algebraic form, showing that he at least was capable of navigating the language, like Flinders Petrie and Penrose before him. Dinsmoor (1939, 173) concluded that it was possible to coordinate investigation of orientations and their archaeological, religious and calendar relationships.

Some 80 years since Duke had questioned why archaeologists did not consider astronomical explanations, the archaeologists were finally giving their reasons and these centred on their doubts about astronomical methodology and their very different beliefs about prehistoric humankind. The archaeologists' picture of the unskilled 'primitive man' was quite in opposition to that of the sophisticated accomplishments inferred by the astronomers: this seemed to be the very nub of the debate, as it had been in antiquarianism. However, while the practice of orientation studies might have been outside the experience of archaeologists and criticised by some, this is not to say that they were not willing to consider it within their domain. Contributors to the very first issue of *Antiquity* in March 1927 included Somerville and A. P. Trotter with papers entitled respectively, 'Orientation' (Somerville 1927) and 'Stonehenge as an astronomical implement' (Trotter 1927); the latter accepting a case for astronomical orientation, but not Lockyer's arguments for dating. Juxtaposed with these scientific astronomy papers was Clay's (1927) study of prehistoric trackways, at the opposite end of the spectrum. A year later, Somerville's (1928) paper on French dolmens also appeared in *Antiquity*. In this way, archaeoastronomy briefly entered the domain of archaeology, but the impetus was short-lived.

Beginning with the joint research of Lockyer and Penrose, it is clear that neither orientation studies nor archaeology could provide all the answers, but there appeared to be an open dialogue between the two which was not altogether unfavourable and more enquiring than contestatory. After all, their interests overlapped and they still frequented many of the same societies but, despite some blurring of the lines and attempts to unite the two fields, as the century advanced the two versions of prehistory became further apart. There is nothing unusual in two disciplines having completely separate theories, methods and language; what is unusual is that, from the same material data, archaeologists and archaeoastronomers proposed quite different interpretations. Stevens (1916, 66), making the point that is true for all times, noted that astronomers, archaeologists, geologists and anthropologists can each bring their knowledge to solving the problems of Stonehenge but that 'each also has the bias due to his own special science'. Although both fields were influenced by theories imported from other disciplines such as social science and anthropology and had some common approaches, they had competing claims about the past. To reiterate the points made in the introductory chapter, they were not contesting the material remains but the uses to which they were put. It was the archaeologists' institutionalised narrative that ultimately became the more desirable which rather impeded the progress of its rival.

Whereas most sparse accounts of the history of archaeoastronomy point out the importance of Lockyer to modern archaeoastronomy, not only did his work follow on from the traditions established in antiquarianism, but Nissen, Penrose and Lewis published detailed astronomical surveys before him. Modern critiques generally ignore these earlier studies and miss the continuity between Lockyer's and earlier ideas. This in no way should detract from the part played by Lockyer but serves to place his influential work into the correct historical context. Similarly, the received impression is that, after Lockyer, archaeoastronomy died out and lay forgotten for some sixty years before its rebirth in the 1960s: however, the evidence presented here shows that though it was less obvious in the following years, it had a small presence throughout. Importantly it was hampered by its lack of a consistent designation, being variously described as orientation studies, alignment studies or astronomical studies and had few key players. Another factor was that it had a mixture of methodologies and theories with some continuity but little consistency, leading to diverse astronomical narratives. Also unlike the pioneers of archaeology who were themselves archaeologists, archaeoastronomy did not have a common disciplinary pool to draw from: Penrose was an archaeologist; Lockyer an astrophysicist; Lewis an anthropologist and Somerville a trained naval surveyor. This concurs with Hutton's view (2013, 393) that archaeoastronomy's evolution was led by key personalities who acted 'as motive forces in human development'.

Chapter 5

Lines in the landscape

The enduring interest in British heritage was invigorated in the first half of the 20th century with an emphasis on conservation and preservation. The romanticised ideal of the 19th century, which viewed England as a 'green and pleasant land', became accompanied by a new anthem, *Land of Hope and Glory*, composed by Elgar in 1902. Heritage therefore became an idealised representation from a nationalist standpoint and various factors demonstrate the steps taken to restore 'national pride' (Harvey 2008). First the *Historic Buildings and Ancient Monuments Act* of 1953 extended *The Ancient Monuments Act* of 1882 by granting new powers and specifically providing for 'the preservation and acquisition of buildings of outstanding historic or architectural interest'. This enacted the concerns about heritage which had already been voiced in antiquarianism. For example, after surveying Stonehenge and Avebury, Stukeley (1743, iii), urged his readers 'to rescue [them] from oblivion, before it be too late'. Almost a century later, Henry Browne made protection a moral imperative, with this impassioned cry: 'Oh! Let not the rude and ignorant demolish what is still left of these venerable piles, these truly precious relics of antiquity ... (Browne 1823, 41).

Yet in the 20th century 'special' monuments such as Avebury were restored or reconfigured with no heed paid to the archaeological consequences, simply for the purpose of creating national monuments (Harvey 2008, 29). In addition, the heritage movement was enhanced by The National Trust, incorporated in 1907 and gaining further powers through a subsequent act in 1937. A press appeal in 1925, on its behalf, ultimately led to the purchase of 1400 acres (567 ha) around Stonehenge. The philanthropist and archaeologist Alexander Keiller bought Avebury and its surrounding land, later selling it to the National Trust in 1943. By 1945 the Trust had 7850 members. Another strand which reflected a changing attitude towards nature in post-war Britain was highlighted by Wilson (2014, 45–46) who theorised that 'conservationism morphed into environmentalism', following the 'militarisation of the landscape' for the WW2 preparations. As Lowenthal (1985, 348, 410) suggested, 'the past is always altered for motives that reflect present needs', because 'we require a heritage with which we continually interact, one which fuses the past with the present'. These developments may be linked to the popularisation of archaeology, as evidenced by Mortimer Wheeler's book *Still Digging: adventures in archaeology* (1955) and his numerous television appearances on shows such as *Animal, Vegetable and Mineral*, *Buried Treasure* and *Chronicle* between 1952 and 1966, with him becoming TV personality of the year in 1954. With its academic status and popular appeal, archaeology became embedded as a part of British culture. Against the horrors of the wars and the rapid advances brought about by scientific advances, the past and its material remains may have felt like a safe haven and an antidote to events in the then present.

Landscape lines

While Lockyer, Somerville and others were finding astronomical alignments at prehistoric monuments using the strict procedures that Lockyer had made mandatory, there was another line of enquiry; that of finding lines in the landscape. This followed a tradition laid down by the antiquarians Black, Dymond, Duke and Joseph Spencer as suggested earlier in Chapter 3. The land and the landscape had featured prominently in some of the antiquarian material and in the early 20th century some archaeologists considered it. For example, Crawford favoured a geographical approach to prehistory and according to Daniel it was Crawford's *Archaeology in the Field* (1953) which distinguished field archaeology (Daniel 1978, 305–306). As an adjunct to this, Cyril Fox pioneered landscape archaeology in his exploration of the Cambridge area, having achieved the distinction of being awarded the first British PhD in archaeology at Cambridge in 1922 (Fox, 1923; Collis 2013, 11). On the remote margins of archaeology, another type of study which attempted to find lines in the landscape combined elements of astronomy, archaeology and geography to form a hybrid field in Britain. These studies, in turn, led to a wider international focus, particularly where landscape lines stimulated interest elsewhere.

One of the earliest 20th century studies was by F.J. Bennett who, in 1904, showed that the Kentish megaliths followed the same meridional line discovered by Duke in Wiltshire. Similarly, Lockyer and Penrose (1902, 142) having measured the axis at Stonehenge, noted that it was on a line which ran from Silbury to the northeast and Grovely Castle to the southwest. This may have prompted Lockyer to include a chapter on the interrelation of monuments in his second edition of *Stonehenge* in 1909, where he also mentioned several landscape lines including another one passing through Stonehenge which connected to other notable sites such as Old Sarum and Salisbury Cathedral (Meadows 2008, 251). Lockyer investigated this line because, in the 1890s, Ordnance Survey director Colonel Duncan Johnston had found this alignment and pointed it out to him (Stout 2008, 178). Nearly 70 years later, in 1978, Paul Devereux and Ian Thomson studied this same line and extended it to Frankenbury Camp (Devereux, pers. comm.). Following the same theme, S.E. Dixon was inspired by Lockyer's findings to look for alignments in East Anglia. Dixon (1916, 172) drew a line from the earthwork at Broome Heath, aligned to the northeast, which continued by picking up other tumuli and stones, 'apparently in connection with the

5. Lines in the landscape

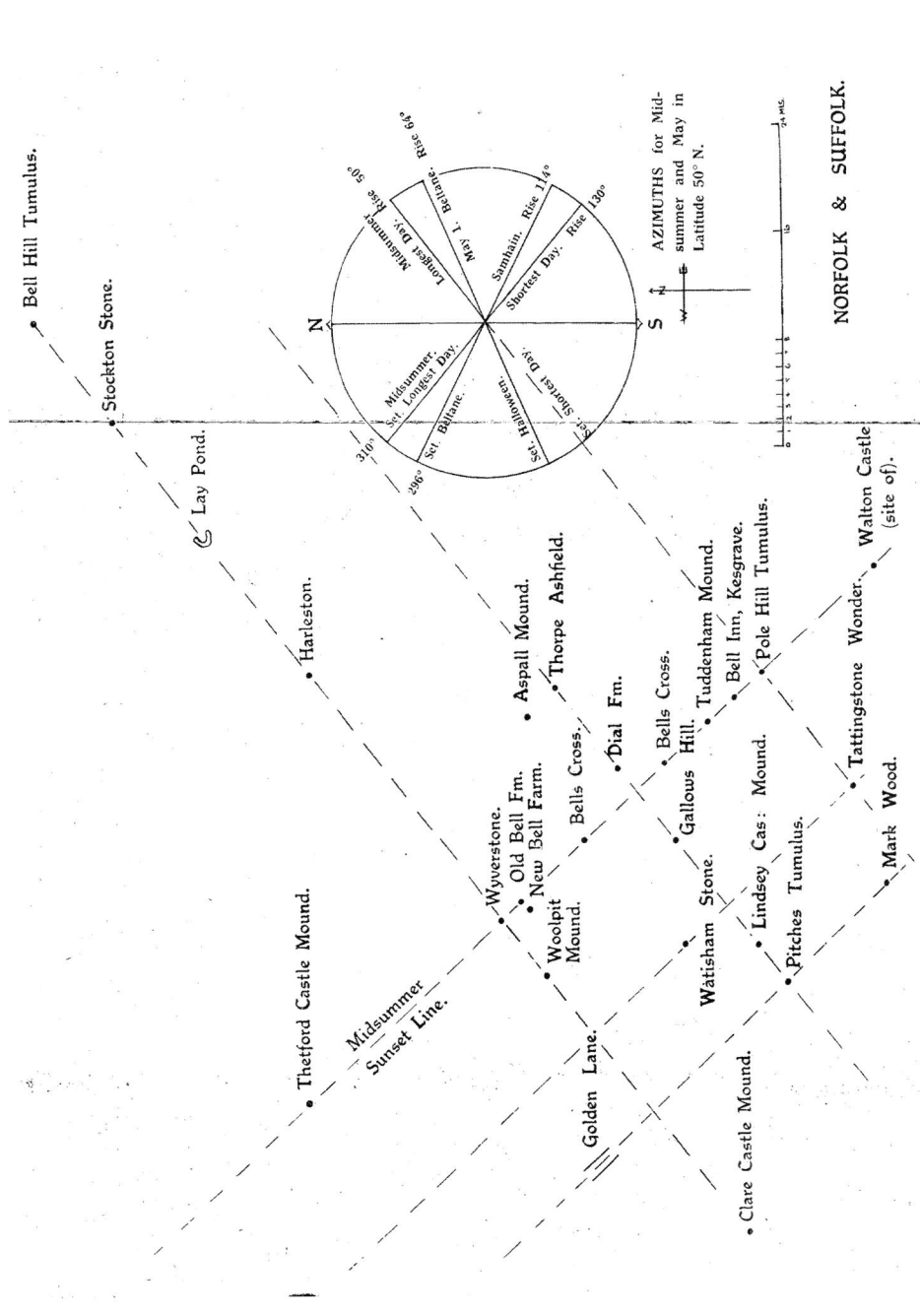

Figure 10. Diagram of some of the solar alignments found by Henry Hudson, adapted from his 1933 paper, 'Ancient sun alignments' (122–123).

alignment we are considering, or with subsidiary alignments'. He drew an analogy between Broome Heath and Stonehenge, noting that it had an outlier similar to the Heel stone, indicating a northeastern alignment.

Dixon belonged to a small East Anglian school of alignment studies which also generated two books by W.A. Dutt, *Standing Stones of East Anglia* (1921) and *Ancient Mark-Stones of East Anglia* (1926). These were apparently the basis for subsequent studies, such as Hudson's 1933 paper for the Suffolk Institute of Archaeology and Natural History, which found there were earthworks and mark stones all over Britain which bore names relating to the sun and which were linked by 'ancient solar alignments' (Fig. 10). In the face of this evidence, Hudson (1933, 130) suggested that if further research were carried out, the whole landscape of Great Britain would be found to be covered by a network of solar alignments. Similarly, in Orkney, Fraser published a paper that seems to show that he too was influenced by both Lockyer and ideas about the landscape. Writing about two standing stones in Harray Parish some 2840 feet (*c*. 865 m) apart, Fraser (1923, 32) noted that the line that joined the two was 42° east of north, the same bearing that existed between the Barn Stone and the centre of Maeshowe; an alignment that was believed to have marked the position of midsummer sunrise about 2000 BC.

A more comprehensive study was T. Arthur Matthews' research (1907; 1911) into Arbor Low stone circle which lies north of Stonehenge. He noted that a line through the landscape linked up with three high points in the distance, saying,

> if any three fixed points are in a straight line on plan they are so *by intention*, and that if any three fixed points are in the same horizontal line or gradient they are so *by intention*. (Matthews 1911, 88)

With landscape profiles showing lines of sight adjusted for refraction, Matthews' paper is both scientific and also theoretical with regard to the perceived intentionality of lines which demonstrated their 'sanctity' to the culture of the people who constructed their monuments with reference to the landscape. On the other hand it is interspersed with imaginative conjectures such as his suggestion that the outline of the largest dressed stone in the circle could be compared to the hawk-headed Egyptian sun god Ra. Taken together, these early findings detailing lines in the landscape have generally been neglected in the narrative because of the greater prominence of Alfred Watkins' leylines theory, detailed below.

The romance of the historic landscape

The poet Hilaire Belloc revived the idealised 18th century Romantic vision of a simpler life which glorified both nature and the past. In 1911, he published *The Old Road* in order to recover this past, because by doing so 'stuff and being are added to us' and 'the soul is fed' (1911, 9). The 'Road' was silent and humble, part of the historic landscape and by walking through it Belloc could step in the footsteps of the ancestors.

He followed this book up in 1913 with a monograph on the alignments of the ancient roads, entitled *The Stane Street* (Belloc 1913). Another volume in this vein followed in 1914 with *The Green Roads of England* by R. Hippisley Cox, in which he drew links between the prehistoric ridge roads, hill forts and earthworks of southern England.

At the time, astronomical studies were in the process of defining themselves into a distinct field but any progress towards acceptance was curtailed by the addition of another theory which took them in a different direction. Alfred Watkins' (1855–1935) *The Old Straight Track*, published in 1925 (1974), two years after Somerville's last extensive paper on British monuments, marked a turning point in orientation studies. Prior to this, theories on landscape orientations, as described earlier, had been accepted as part of astronomical studies, but Watkins' thesis was too different to subsume. Although it was a natural continuation of Cox's ideas, which Watkins found 'inspiring', he was continuing an antiquarian tradition of describing lines found in the landscape. Watkins' overall theory of leys was certainly novel, receiving popular acclaim and a band of followers, but it included methods that were completely new and not commensurable with the astronomical theories that preceded it.

Apparently Watkins had a deep and intimate knowledge of his home landscape but it was not until he was 66 years old that a 'flash of insight' led him to believe that all manner of markers in the landscape, from circular earthworks and standing stones, to trees and ponds, showed evidence of ancient trackways (Pennick and Devereux 1989, 17; Fig. 11). He believed these trackways were inevitably straight because they represented lines of sight, claiming that they were the remains of 'prehistoric antiquity'. The lines which were 'one or two to several miles in length' could be implied from the 'aligned placing of marker sites' (Pennick and Devereux 1989, 13). From a methodology of extensive fieldwork and the use of patterns discovered on Ordnance Survey maps, Watkins identified many examples of these tracks, for which his general term was leys. He was also interested in philology and found that many of the lines were linked by place-names which were variants of the word ley, therefore believing them to be evidence that the lines were constructed at the same time as the monuments were being built. As we have seen, Watkins was not the first person to have remarked on these ancient pathways and he also cited A. and G. Hubbard's 1907 volume on Neolithic dewponds and cattle-ways, which also discussed the astronomical significance of some earthworks and rings, according to Rolston (1908, 245). However, although the seed of Watkins' idea had been sewn earlier, it was the way in which Watkins combined Romantic notions and the esoteric quest for ancient wisdom with an empirical methodology for finding leys that made the study attractive to its followers.

Watkins' thesis fitted in with both the possibility of intervisibility and the interrelationship of sites, so although his theory of leys branched out in a different direction from the astronomical research which had preceded it, there were some similarities. It was the connections across the landscape that interested Watkins, as with Hippisley Cox before him who had suggested (1914, 82) that eight lines emanating

Figure 11. Dowsing along an ancient trackway at Petit-Ménec, Carnac. Photo: Grahame Gardner.

from Stonehenge might have been for observing the skies. By contrast, although Watkins noted on many occasions that alignments through mounds were across ridges, making the skyline important, he did not think the majority of them were to celestial events, despite citing Lockyer's theory about an avenue of sun-worship in Boroughbridge in Yorkshire (Watkins 1974 [1925], 132). Although astronomy was not at the heart of his thesis, nevertheless one of his four procedures for initialling a ley was 'sighting over or from a fixed point to a heavenly body' (Watkins 1974 [1925], 57). His ideas about orientation differed from those that characterised the setting out of a ley, believing that the axis was determined by taking a sighting line from the observation point to the point on the horizon where 'the sun (or a star) is seen to rise on a chosen day' (Watkins 1974 [1925], 128). With this in mind, Watkins wrote the chapter 'Sun alignment', suggesting that the topographical sites used for such alignments and those for the ley were in some cases identical and that the alignment was often the same for both uses. He was familiar with the work of Peter L'Estrange in this connection, who, in a paper entitled 'Sun worship on the Malvern Hills', suggested that the solar observations he had conducted showed that in all probability sun-worshipping was practised by prehistoric people in Britain (Watkins 1923).

Like Duke and Lockyer before him, Watkins agreed that Stonehenge was an example of the connection between sun alignment, long-distance tracks and the use of beacons. He (1974 [1925], 102) put forward evidence of sunrise orientations at Woolhope and Holme Lacy and found a May Day sunrise line at May Hill in the Malverns, which augmented the existing theories of a prehistoric calendar. A.F. Bennett added weight to this variation on Watkins' thesis by concluding,

> All over the British Isles are to be found earthworks and mark-stones bearing names relating to the sun. Here and there similar place-names survive, but the objects to which they referred have been obliterated by time. (Bennett 1933, 120)

Additionally Watkins discovered that some of the upright stones of a dolmen called Arthur's Stone in Herefordshire were 'adjusted for a midday sun (maximum elevation) observation', a phenomenon rarely sought by the orientationists. He described the site as follows:

> although Arthur's Stone has apparently no seasonal alignments in the structure of its chamber, it, as a mound, aligns topographically for the Summer Solstice or Midsummer Day, not only to sunrise as just given, but to sunset over a pointer stone. (Watkins 1974 [1925], 151)

Watkins credited Walter Pritchard for the discovery that this dolmen was on a summer solstice ley and also relied on information sent to him by Somerville, so he was certainly aware of the work of the orientationists. He even took the alignments found by Somerville and extended them on the map to show that they extended to hill summits marked by cairns and earthworks several miles away (Watkins 1928). Watkins (1931, 66) also addressed the problem of chance alignments yet suggested that his findings could also be usefully applied to the seasonal alignments found in stone circles and dolmens by Lewis, Lockyer and Somerville, as well as to the 'profuse alignments found in prehistoric cup-markings'. F.C. Tyler (1939, 38) in similar studies also discussed fortuitous alignments, showing that this criticism of alignment studies, still current today, has a long history.

It is impossible to estimate the extent to which the long history of interest in astronomical and landscape alignments and the intellectual atmosphere it created contributed to Watkins' work. Phrases and ideas first found in antiquarian literature are often repeated by Watkins and in many respects he can be seen as a successor to Lockyer and Somerville: he certainly acknowledged their contribution even though he took alignment studies in a different direction. There are other similarities too: like Lockyer, Watkins advocated the use of other evidence such as archaeology, folklore, documentary records, anthropology and etymology. His rules were set out in 'Appendix A: ley hunting', comparable to the way Lockyer offered guidance in his *Surveying for Archaeologists* (1909). Unlike Duke, Watkins did not mention gnomons but suggested that surveying was carried out by using 'sighting staves' and that these skilled methods were kept secret to empower the surveyors. He discovered notches on the horizon which he described as sighting points to show the direction a traveller should go. This was part of his theory that the leys were aligned through the use of bonfires and surveying rods, calling the ancient surveyors 'dodmen' (Watkins 1974 [1925], 78). However, the idea that these dodmen were capable of accurate surveying was anathema to the archaeologists who had made it clear that prehistoric peoples were incapable of these sophisticated accomplishments. Furthermore Watkins believed that 'ley-man', 'astronomer-priest', 'druid', 'bard', 'wizard', 'witch', 'palmer' and 'hermit' were all more or less linked by one thread of ancient knowledge and power (Watkins 1974 [1925], 83). In this he mirrored the orientationists' view that prehistoric people possessed advanced skills, counter to the beliefs of the archaeologists. Tyler (1939, 9) agreed with Watkins, adding that, 'this idea is not, of course, at all in accordance with accepted ideas of the mental and practical capacity of our prehistoric forbears', acknowledging that the study of ancient trackways was not 'classical' archaeology.

However, there was one aspect of Watkins' work that might have been in tune with the archaeologists' beliefs. In his eyes the ancient Britons were not barbaric primitives but rational traders who created their straight pathways as the easiest way to access materials they did not have locally. In his last published book, *Archaic Tracks Round Cambridge*, he reported that 'even if sun observation became a ritual performed at stated seasons, there is strong evidence that the purport was utilitarian' (Watkins 1932, 28). His economic arguments were not inconsistent with Childe's materialist views, and this, in itself, should have made some of Watkins' ideas agreeable to the archaeologists. More recently, Johnson (2010, 5) concluded that the prehistoric inhabitants would have been quite capable of laying out these lines and thus the reasons for rejecting Watkins' thesis were completely invalid. Johnson was not making a case for leylines, indeed, he said they do not exist; he was pointing out the important epistemological difficulties of interpreting the past.

Although it is impossible to estimate the extent to which the long history of interest in astronomical and landscape alignments and the intellectual atmosphere it created, contributed to Alfred Watkins' work, phrases and ideas first found in antiquarian material are often repeated by Watkins. In terms of Romanticism, the gap between Belloc's *The Old Road* and Watkins' *The Old Straight Track* was only 14 years. However, Watkins had no academic credibility and he and his followers 'found' evidence to fit their theory. Unwittingly he diverted the path of orientation studies away from its original purpose, and, partly because of the disdain from some archaeologists, delayed its disciplinary progress. On the other hand, unfettered by the specialised language of astronomy, there was a community of ley-hunters founded by Watkins' admirers: The Straight Track Postal Portfolio Club, formed in 1926, had regular annual meetings in different parts of England and Wales (Stout 2008, 192–194). The club, to which members sent their contributions, was mainly peopled by retired military men, businessmen, scientists, surveyors and so on. Ley-hunting became a popular 'cult' for the 'ley-bitten' in the late 1920s, though, from 1930 until his death in 1935, Watkins stopped using the term 'ley' and simply used the terms 'old straight track' or 'archaic track'. It is understandable that ley-hunting had a popular following as it did not require specialist methods so was available to all walks of life. Tyler took over the presidency of the Straight Track Club following the death of Watkins and contributed his own ideas to the theory, adding that he felt that the whole subject needed lengthy study on new lines, 'novel to orthodox archaeology' (Tyler 1939, 37). Generally Watkins' ideas have been ignored by archaeoastronomers which seems to be rather short-sighted. Although he took the study of astronomical alignments in a different direction and was more a modern antiquarian than a scientific astronomer, he kept the studies alive and his influence can be clearly seen in the hybrid studies that followed.

Just a year after the publication of *The Old Straight Track* and on the other side of the world, hundreds of straight lines and geometric figures were discovered on the desert plains between Nazca and Palpa by Alfred Kroeber and Mejia Xesspe in 1926 (Pennick and Devereux 1989, 182–184). Paul Kosok, whilst visiting in 1941, happened to see the sun setting beyond the end of one of the lines which he described as 'the largest astronomy book in the world' (Pennick and Devereux 1989, 184). These lines were studied extensively by mathematician Maria Reiche, at one time Kosok's assistant, and they became the focus of her life's work. The purpose of the Nazca lines remains in question but Reiche thought that they marked certain solar and lunar positions. The only other evidence of specific interest in landscape lines comes from a paper by the French geographer André Meynier (1944) who explored the Breton countryside to find evidence of 'curieux alignements de chemin' in the trackways there.

Hybrid studies

Watkins' ley lines thesis widened the scope of orientation studies both literally and figuratively: monuments could be studied in relation to their landscape as well as in relation to one another. This gave rise to what can be called hybrid studies as they incorporated both astronomical orientations and the lines in the landscape. Hudson's work in the 1930s is clearly influenced by this idea and his examples of solar alignments are not based on findings at individual sites but instead relate to straight line connections between monuments. He seems to have been influenced by the idea of lines in the landscape which he married to solar alignments to find straight line connections between monuments in the fashion of Watkins. Hudson was also convinced that there were a great number of mark stones in the landscape that were the sighting-points of alignments to the rising and setting sun at midsummer and in May. Although he took a broader aspect by considering the landscape, his description of the scientific methodology resonates with that set out by Lockyer:

> On Midsummer Day the sun rises at its extreme North-eastern limit. They therefore placed a stone on the circumference of the circle to mark the exact point where the sun first appeared on the horizon. They placed a similar mark stone at the point where the sun set in the West (another on the meridian where it stood highest in the sky at noon), and two other stones where the sun rose and set on the shortest day of the year. In some cases we

> find that they did the same in regard to the sunrise and sunset on May 1st (Beltane). As a necessary consequence of the angle the earth's pole makes with the plane of her orbit, the sun rises in Midwinter immediately opposite the point where it sets at Midsummer. It is evident that the early astronomers made use of this alignment running N.W. and S.E. as a datum line for long measurements. They also used the alignment of the rising sun at Midsummer to give them cross bearings ... The bearing at which the sun first appears on the horizon depends upon the latitude at which the observer stands. At Stonehenge, lat. 51 degrees, it rises approximately 49 degrees E. of N.; at Edinburgh, lat. 56 degrees, it rises at a bearing of 43 degrees E. of N. (Hudson 1933, 123)

The same line of enquiry became popular in Germany and it has been suggested that Devoir's early 20th century diagrams of straight lines linking standing stones, laid the foundation for German alignment studies (Pennick and Devereux 1989, 42). Alternatively the interest might have been promoted through Tyler who was in contact with the German researcher Josef Heinsch. Whilst concentrating on landscape alignments, Heinsch (1979 [1933]) also mentioned solar alignments such as a 'solar year line', oriented 6° either north or south of east, as well as noting the pairing of solar and lunar sites. He was of the opinion that the ancient monuments were built in a certain way to harmonise the mundane on earth with the divine in the sky, an echo of antiquarian esoteric ideas.

This hybridisation can also be found in the research of Wilhelm Teudt and Otto Reuter in Germany around the same time. Teudt, who, like Somerville, was one of the first researchers to note the moon's extremes, found astronomical as well as geometrical relationships at ancient sites including meridional and equinoctial axes. Teudt, who called his methodology 'scientific' astronomy, as it was concerned with ascertaining the actual relations of the heavenly bodies and establishing a polar axis without a pole star, published his findings in a book entitled *Germanische Heiligtümer* (Germanic sanctuaries) in 1931. He added his endorsement of orientation studies by saying '*To recognize even a single phenomenon as deliberate orientation is to recognize orientation as such and all its premises, which are first and foremost based on astronomical activity*' (Teudt 1931, italics in original). In terms of assessing the results of site surveys, Teudt set out the difficulties of conducting a survey and his qualifications relating to the problematic nature of speculative enquiries indicate a degree of maturation:

> We have to deal with not only the assessment of the observational errors made by the ancient peoples in each individual case, which is left to our subjective judgement, and the inexactness of our maps, which however small it may be is inevitable because of the curvature of the earth, but also the constant difficulty that we obviously do not know the exact survey-point that the ancients used at a site. (Teudt 1931)

His research suggested that in Germany the custom had been to site 'sacred buildings' towards the northeast, finding some evidence of solstitial directions, possibly for calendrical purposes. While suggesting that the orientations were originally for recording a calendar, he thought that they became overlaid with religious significance. His proposition was that,

> *Over wide areas of Germania there was practised the custom, based on astronomical observations, of a northward and eastward siting of sacred buildings and other public places in relation to one another. Also, alignments on the direction of the solstice and other orientations can be proved.* (Teudt 1931, italics in original)

Teudt challenged ideas about the Neolithic by saying it was probably erroneous to think that the development was from burial place to cult and that more likely it was the reverse. Indeed he seemed to hold archaeologists in some contempt when he addressed the problem of dating which he felt created prejudices in the cultural history of the time. Although Teudt's *heilige linien* (holy lines) are similar in many ways to Watkins' trackways, Behrend (2013a) pointed out that Teudt (a clergyman) proposed religion as a basis for their construction whereas Watkins (a businessman) favoured trade and commerce, as noted earlier.

A few years later, Otto Sigfrid Reuter corroborated Teudt's findings by describing the predominance of north–south alignments in northern Europe in his 1934 book *Germanischer Himmelskunde* (Ancient German astronomy) (Pennick and Devereux 1989, 43). Reuter's earlier two volume work, *Das Rätsel der Edda und der arische Urglaube* (The riddle of the Edda and the Aryan original belief) (1921–23) contained charts relating to astronomical calculations, calendars and cosmology and drew on a common Indo-European heritage (Goodrick-Clarke 2011, 167). Heggie (2009, 10) suggested that some of the earliest statistical arguments for orientations were to be found in R. Müller's 1936 book *Himmelskundliche Ortung auf Nordisch-Germanischem Boden* which included an analysis of solstitial and lunar orientations at Odry in Poland. The German research spanned the inter-war years after which it declined because of its close association with National Socialist propaganda.

Indeed there is little evidence of these hybrid studies during the Second World War and its aftermath though Stout (2008, 213) recorded that Hando, who had published a couple of papers on 'Ley spotting' in the 1930s, went on to write *The Pleasant Land of Gwent* (1944) which had much to say about sunrise alignments. However, there were no such theories in his 1958 book, *Out and About in Monmouthshire*. In Britain, as interest in orientation studies and leylines had waned, the discussions went no further

Esotericism and metrology

Duke's astronomical plan of 1846 was given a new twist in 1925 by Katherine Maltwood (1878–1961), sculptor, collector and scholar, who, whilst researching the legends of King Arthur, became convinced that the adventures of his knights were recorded in a system of giant earthworks, some ten miles in diameter, around Glastonbury (Brown 1981, 11). Maltwood's map revealing Leo, Orion, the Ram, the Fishes and the Phoenix was published as a supplement to her 1929 edition of *The High History of the Holy Grail*. She claimed that the Glastonbury Zodiac, so-called after her map, was part of a ritual complex and she dated these earthworks to *c.* 2700 BC, when the sun at the spring equinox lay in the eye of the Bull in the Taurus constellation. In her books and artistic works, Brown affirmed that she was influenced both by the 19th century

Romantic Movement and Blavatsky's work, as well as acknowledging that she became a Freemason and quoted Masonic traditions in her support for the Zodiac (Brown 1981, 40–42). Unsurprisingly her work failed to win academic recognition from The Royal Astronomical Association.

Around the same time as Maltwood was publishing her Glastonbury discovery, another curiosity was added to the mix: dowsing. As a form of divination, dowsing was condemned by Martin Luther during the Reformation but as a method of deciphering the mysteries of ancient monuments it reappeared in the early 20th century (see Halliday 1937, 31). Its popularity perhaps began in the late 1920s with the foundation of the Association des Amis de la Radiesthésie (Association of Friends of Dowsing) in 1929 by Father Alexis Bouly, with the formation of The British Society of Dowsers following in 1933. The separate findings of M. Louis Merle and Reginald Smith, keeper of antiquities at the British Museum, that there was a relationship between water lines, springs and ancient monuments led to the suggestion that sites were deliberately chosen because of their connection to water (The Geo Group 2020). Charles Diot with the assistance of Merle published this theory in 1935 in his book *Les Sourciers et les monuments mégalithiques* (Michell 2007, 89). This general hankering after explanations, with no stone left unturned, was a mix of science and esotericism and included the findings of James Ritchie (1926) who mined the folklore relating to the megalithic remains in Aberdeenshire for clues (see Fig. 12).

Meanwhile, controversy over who built the prehistoric monuments continued: while Piggott (1954a, 138) felt that there was no doubt that the druids had a real existence, the druid 'legend' had become mythologised. Certainly, Lockyer (1906a, 316), although he acknowledged that in the antiquarian literature the builders were assumed to be druids, did not conform to this view, rather saying that the builders were 'astronomer-priests'. While the Hawkeses (1949, 80) had dismissed Stukeley's druids, they believed that there must have been a last phase when Stonehenge was administered by Celtic priests. Indeed, ideas about druidry, so prevalent in antiquarianism, virtually disappeared except in the esoteric literature and Hutton (2009b, 18) reported that in the 1920s the Ordnance Survey replaced 'Druidical circles' by 'stone circles' on their maps. However, in 1939, Ludovic McLellan Mann published his alternative ideas on a Druid temple in Glasgow, surmising that that 'the Neolithic philosopher and astronomer laid out the Glasgow area on a plan [which was] rigorously geometrical', as well as claiming that distant sites may have been linked in an exact geometrical relationship' (Behrend 1977a, 5).

Mann, an amateur archaeologist and President of the Glasgow Archaeological Society from 1931–1933, was also interested in collecting evidence for a prehistoric civilisation skilled in astronomy, chronology, geometry and metrology. Some of his ideas on this subject came together in an unpublished thesis which *inter alia* suggested that the measures used at Stonehenge were in an identical ratio to those at the Great Pyramid in Egypt (Behrend 1977b). Such measures had been of interest to the antiquarians, as already noted, but Mann's metrology provided completely new schemes. For example, he looked for 'long measures' in the layout of prehistoric

Figure 12. Grahame Gardner (President of the British Society of Dowsers 2008–2014) dowsing at Aboyne Stone Circle, Aberdeenshire in 2014 (Photo: Elspeth Winkler).

sites and found that a unit of 20.425 feet (c. 6.2 m) was frequently used. Linking this measurement to the celestial cycles he wrote,

> a picture of the heavens was sketched by means of earthworks over large areas suitably situated like the area whereon Glasgow is now placed ... the unit used was 20.425 feet and its multiples. (Mann 1938a, 10–11; cited in Henty 2020a, 6)

Mann also carried out a geometrical analysis of cup-and-ring marks and in *Archaic Sculpturings* (1915) commented on the geometrical relationship between prominent topographical features. While the archaeologists might have dismissed some of Mann's fanciful ideas, one aspect of his work caused a long standing controversy. Initially he had been more interested in the measurement of small portable artefacts dating from the Palaeolithic to the Iron Age and he became an avid collector of these to prove his point. He took meticulous measurements of all of them and concluded in *Craftsmen's Measures in Prehistoric Times* (1930) that there were two universal measures; 'the Alpha unit', a unit so small it measured just 0.619 inches (c. 15.25 mm), and the even smaller 'Beta' unit of 0.55 inches (*c.* 14.25 mm) (Mann 1930, 2). He even suggested that there were alpha and beta 'feet', made up of 24 of the small units which measured respectively 14.85 inches (*c.* 378 mm) and 13.28 inches (*c.* 338 mm) (Henty 2020a, 57). His controversial metrology became the subject of a three and a half year debate by a joint committee from the Glasgow Archaeological Society and the Geological Society of Glasgow (Reports 1937) of which the minority report's findings were mainly negative. Mann bounced back with a further pamphlet, *Ancient Measures: their origin and meaning* (1938b) as a reply to his critics. Nothing more was heard of Mann's measures apart from in Tyler's book (1939, 37) in which he examined Mann's 'alpha unit' which he calculated as being equal to 'the one-four-hundred-and-eightieth part of a degree of the equatorial circumference of the earth as known to the ancients'.

The first metrological theories of the 20th century had come in 1904 with the publication of measures found in Armorica in Brittany by Kerviler; a study which found an emphasis on the numbers three and seven. Also in Brittany, but this time in Finistère, Martin (1911) continued this line of questioning regarding a universal measure. Taken altogether the interest in metrology was another *leitmotif* of the early 20th century as was the persistent idea that the monument builders were geometricians. The above paper by Tyler also included an appendix by R.P. Jones who reviewed Heinsch's article, speculating that sites were connected by geometrical triangles:

> The main basis of this—in addition to basic triangulation on 30° and 60° and relations on diagonals of a square (45°) and double square (26.5° nearly)—is a number of angles based on a line joining a *moon-cult-spot* in West with a *sun-cult-spot* in East at an angle of 84° or 96° with the North–South axis. i.e. a declension of 6° from due East. (Jones 1939, 43)

Esoteric strands such as these, comparable with their antiquarian origins, were added to and embellished in the first half of the 20th century.

The implications for archaeoastronomy

Critics of landscape line interpretations or esoteric theories, despite Clay's paper (1927) on prehistoric trackways having been considered in *Antiquity*, were more united in their condemnation. Somerville noted that,

> discredit and derision have, moreover, been brought on the whole subject through the visionary ideas of some enthusiasts, who have tried to import into the subject far more than the cold facts of science can contain. (1923, 193)

Somerville mentioned how some of these notions such as, astronomer-priests, sacrifices to the sun and mystical proportions such as cubits, had provided 'an entire prehistoric arithmetic and astrology', concluding that it was unsurprising that 'the unmathematical, but otherwise scientific, archaeologist has repelled any suggestion of orientation in these ancient structures' (Somerville 1923, 193). As archaeologists could not satisfactorily explain the evidence of ancient tracks the subject was merely written off, as the supporting arguments 'did not always commend themselves to the more sceptical archaeologist' (G. M. 1935, 166). Stout (2008, 207) concluded that it was 'the *similarities*, and not the differences between 'Crawfordian' and 'Watkinsian' archaeology that made the latter so 'dangerous' to the former'. Crawford's rebuttal of Watkins was unequivocal. Yet Hauser (2009, 112) recently pointed out that the fieldwork that Crawford encouraged his readers to conduct was very much the method Watkins advocated, though the conclusions were different. Unaware of the similarities, Crawford was so incensed by Watkins' ideas that he refused a paid advertisement for one of his books to be published in *Antiquity* (Pennick and Devereux 1989, 23). Indeed, he further reviled Watkins' work in one of his editorials, which reminded readers that 'many best-sellers are written by quacks' (Crawford 1927, 2). Writing in the same edition, Clay (1927, 55) criticised Watkins of being ignorant of the fundamental principles of archaeology which led to him 'attempting to startle the world with new theories'. Nevertheless, a further investigation of 'ancient highways' was published in the *Archaeological Journal* in 1939 (Grundy 1939).

Disciplines that are relatively newly established, as archaeology was in the first few decades of the 20th century, are less secure than established ones, so any challenges to their orthodox views are dangerous and need to be firmly demolished. The continuation of esoteric archaeology in the unorthodox publications by Grafton Elliot Smith and W.J. Perry, which began to appear around the same time as Watkins' books, was completely unrelated to the ley lines theory, but their respective treatment by archaeologists was damning. Archaeology did not admit orientation studies perhaps because there may have been confusion over what its overriding message was, given the different approaches of Lockyer and Watkins; the one founded on scientific astronomy, the other based on a combination of empiricism and esotericism. Other reasons that astronomical studies were not taken up by the archaeologists may have been from an antipathy to astronomy, the difficulties of understanding the methodology or that the studies themselves declined after the first wave of Lockyer, Somerville and others because of the want of scholars capable of taking the field forward.

There may be other influences underlying the reason why archaeoastronomical enquiries did not become another angle for archaeologists to explore. During a time when archaeology was becoming increasingly professionalised, Lockyer, despite being a professional astronomer, entered the archaeological arena from the position of being an amateur hobbyist, beginning his research as a pastime in his later years, as did Somerville and Watkins. Not only that but there were different emphases: the preoccupation with culture history drew archaeologists away from the consideration of individual monuments which were generally the primary focus of the astronomical interpretations. Yet, with the exception of Crawford's attack on Watkins, the discourse did not appear to be unduly combative. However, modern commentators have taken a different view: for example, Campion (2004, xvi–xvii), referring to Lockyer, reported that 'the archaeologists' generally scathing response to his work began an academic turf war, which continues to this day, over who has the right to speak for ancient cultures'. However, the idea that astronomers and archaeologists were necessarily and acrimoniously divided, was not the contemporary position of Crawford, for example, who commissioned the *Antiquity* papers, written by 'specialists' in order to add to archaeological knowledge (Crawford 1927, 1).

Following the efforts of Somerville in particular, the field of orientation studies was on the brink of entering the mainstream, with its brief appearance in *Antiquity,* but this impetus was lost when the theory of ley lines entered the mix. Another factor which relegated astronomical studies to the margin related to the development of archaeology: with an interest in all chronological time periods, archaeology began to develop specialisms, of which prehistory was only one, whereas the main focus of orientation studies was on prehistoric structures. Despite Christopher Hawkes' acknowledgment that archaeology had no tools to study ritual and spiritual aspects, orientation studies, which could have done precisely this, were under-appreciated by archaeologists and played little role in their narrative of prehistory. Because of its ground-based methodology and focus on economic explanations, archaeology sidelined the sky from its narrative and left archaeoastronomy behind. In the contestatory battle for the past, the archaeologists were the clear winners.

On the other hand, there is little evidence of antagonism between ley-hunters and orientationists: Watkins (1931) accepted the comparison between his alignments and those of the astronomers, saying both theories faced the same criticisms. Surely an idea that could capture a large public's imagination could not simply die with the Straight Track Club's closure in 1948. Crawford (1951, 9) believed otherwise when he wrote in *Antiquity* in March 1951, 'Where today are the once famous Children of the Sun, the Old Straight Trackers or the Phoenician tin-traders? There is no room for these plausible hucksters in the crowded marketplace of modern archaeology'. Yet, after the club's closure ley-hunting fell out of fashion: for the 1950s Pennick and Devereux (1989, 207) only found evidence of further work on leys at the Essex Field Club. It was a subject that lay dormant, until it reappeared in the New Age.

Though the evidence for the 1940s and 1950s is somewhat patchy it does not deny absolutely that there was a continuing interest in astronomical alignments. Although unpublished at the time, Thom began accurate theodolite surveys from 1938 onwards (Heath 2007, 10). The two papers he published in 1954 and 1955 respectively will be examined with the main body of his work in Chapter 7. On the other hand, any decline in interest has to be placed into the context of what was happening in archaeology at the same time. The content of the *Proceedings of the Prehistoric Society* and *The Archaeology Journal* shows little to no interest in megalithic monuments over the period and this lessening interest was demonstrated in 1955 when there were no papers for the entire prehistoric period published in the *Proceedings of the Society of Antiquaries,* according to a survey by Graeme Barker (2007, 404). This picture was all to change in the 1960s.

Chapter 6

'God in the machine'

No one who lived through the 1960s and 1970s could have been unaware of the alternative worldview that the countercultural revolution brought. With increasing secularisation there was a shift from organised and often state-backed religion to a leaning towards more personal and spiritual alternatives in the New Age that followed. Writing on the cusp of this change, on 7 May, 1959, Cambridge academic C.P. Snow delivered the annual Rede lecture, entitled 'The Two Cultures and the Scientific Revolution' (Snow 1961). In making a distinction between literary intellectuals and scientists he was putting voice to a dichotomy that had existed in academic circles since the mid-19th century, one that was strengthened by the advance in science. Snow was indeed writing at a time of 'major scientific activity' and he believed that the whole of western society was being 'split into two polar groups', the scientists and the non-scientists, with such different attitudes that 'they can't find much common ground' (Snow 1961, 4–5). He was exploring how the scientific revolution, by which he meant the increasing application of scientific discoveries in the 20th century, affected academia as a whole. Science for Snow was 'more rigorous' and at a 'higher conceptual level' than literature and therefore, lacking the same 'automatic corrective', literature changed more slowly than science (Snow 1961, 9). He was at the same time critiquing the idea of scientific hegemony, that pervasive belief that the scientific narrative is true and therefore superior, as Bourdieu (1988, 28) supposed when he wrote: 'In the struggle between different representations, the representation socially recognised as scientific, that is to say as true, contains its own social force'. Although Snow was severely criticised at the time, the idea of two cultures has been used more recently as a shorthand phrase to describe the distinction between the sciences and the humanities (see, for example, Geertz 1976, 18; Polcaro 2015, 318). Retrospectively, towards the end of the 20th century, Renfrew and Bahn (1991, 10) reflected that archaeology 'is a science as well as a humanity', because the results from using scientific techniques drive cultural interpretations. Similarly Clive Ruggles (2011b, 1) thought archaeoastronomy was 'a science that asks social questions'. These views show that today both archaeology and archaeoastronomy straddle Snow's two cultures, but in the '60s and '70s they were both flexing their scientific muscles.

Although the research which examined the symbolic embedding of astronomical events in prehistoric monuments had a long history it was not consistently named. Yet within a few years these investigations metamorphosed firstly into astro-archaeology and then megalithic science, though neither came under the umbrella of orthodox archaeology. As John Eddy noted in 1974:

> It's too bad about the struggling marriage between Astronomy and Archaeology. Their child, though now well over 100, has never been recognised as legitimate by either side of the house, and as yet still has no name. Archaeologists, in whispered tones call her 'Archaeo-Astronomy'; Astronomers say 'Astro-Archaeology'. Neither side, you will note, seems willing to bestow its own surname on a being so strange and apparently inauspicious. (Eddy 1974a, 66)

While astro-archaeology and megalithic science were both relatively short-lived, the period in which they flowered was extremely fertile and innovative in providing a new paradigm for archaeoastronomy. These decades also saw the development of 'New' archaeology, otherwise called processualism, which was accompanied by the foundation of new archaeological subdisciplines.

Astro-archaeology

Gerald S. Hawkins, in a special report for the Smithsonian Astrophysical Observatory in 1966, renamed the field 'astro-archaeology'; an idea, not completely novel as Griffith (1909, 71) had referred to 'astronomical archaeology' in 1909. Hawkins' reasoning (1966, 2) was that his findings on alignments resulted from a 'direct interaction' of the two 'disciplines' of astronomy and archaeology, so therefore he merged the two to create the neologism astro-archaeology. In this subject area Hawkins (1974, 157–158) asked the same questions that he said Childe and Daniel had asked before him; namely how legitimate it is to infer non-material facts from material remains. With this consideration in mind, Hawkins' thesis claimed that alignments from megaliths or post-holes to celestial objects were 'artefacts in their own right', as durable as arrowheads, for example. In his criteria for this new field he was of the opinion that construction dates should not be derived from astronomy as he claimed that Lockyer's 'foray into egyptology' collapsed because of his dating claims. Hawkins (1973, 214) also stressed the need to follow objective criteria and criticised 'alignments based on arbitrarily chosen natural features'. In this way the stricter methodological rules for astro-archaeology were developed from those inherited from Lockyer, but without the attempt at dating. At the time, Anthony Aveni, one of the pioneers of New World archaeoastronomy, described astro-archaeology as a 'discipline capable of retrieving significant information about the scientific and religious practices' of the past (Aveni 1972, 531). Despite this, the label astro-archaeology did not achieve wide currency and it was adopted for a short while only though it appeared in the titles of two books appraising the history of prehistoric astronomy, *Megaliths, Myths and Men: An introduction to Astro-archaeology* and *A Little History of Astro-archaeology*, written respectively by Lancaster Brown (1976) and John Michell (1989) in 1970s. It has also had more recent use by Goodricke-Clarke (2011) where he used it interchangeably with archaeoastronomy, though generally its usage is delimited to the short time period which covers the researches of Hawkins, Fred Hoyle and C.A. Newham.

In the 1950s and early 1960s there had been new archaeological excavations at Stonehenge carried out by Richard Atkinson, Stuart Piggott and J.F.S Stone but although these threw new light on the construction sequences they could still not explain many puzzles such as the Aubrey holes (Parker Pearson 2013, 38–39). Stonehenge, arguably the province of archaeologists, remained a mystery until Hawkins published *Stonehenge Decoded* in 1965, nearly 60 years after Lockyer's *Stonehenge*. This controversial book was Hawkins' attempt to explain this 'puzzle-heavy' monument (Hawkins 1965a, 58). Marketed with the by-line 'An astronomer examines one of the great puzzles of the ancient world', with subsequent editions featuring the words 'a remarkable book of historical detection', it had great popular appeal. However British-born Hawkins was more than a populist writer, he was Professor of Physics and Astronomy at Boston University from 1957 to 1968 and particularly interested in studying pre-literate astronomy (Fig. 13).

Figure 13. Gerald Hawkins 1969. With permission from the Archives and Special Collections, Dickinson College, Carlisle PA.

Prior to the book's publication, Hawkins had published two papers in *Nature*, first 'Stonehenge Decoded' in 1963, a short contribution pointing out that Lockyer's summer solstice ideas were correct but that there were also many lunar alignments and other significant solar alignments. The second in 1964, 'Stonehenge: a Neolithic computer', suggested that Stonehenge might have functioned as a computer-like device. Although there had been some alignment studies published in *Nature* in the early part of the 20th century, there had been little since, so Hawkins' decision to publish there seems to be based on the fact that *Nature* was a reputable scientific journal and the counterpart of the American journal *Science*. It was not generally known for archaeological content though it did publish papers relating to the science of radiocarbon dating (see for example, Ralph and Stuckenrath 1960).

'New' Archaeology

Although Childe had introduced radiocarbon dating in his 1958 book (Childe 2009), it took some time for it to be generally implemented as a useful scientific tool for archaeology. Simply expressed, all plants, whether it be trees or grasses, convert oxygen to carbon dioxide by photosynthesis and when they die, no more carbon is produced. By measuring the radiocarbon (carbon[14]) of excavated plant remains they can be dated from the extent of their decay. Up until then archaeological dating had previously been suggested by subjective typologies, so a method which could validate dates scientifically was nothing short of revolutionary. In recognition of this, in 1960, Libby received the Noble Prize for chemistry with the citation that seldom had a discovery had 'such an impact on the thinking of so many fields of human endeavour' and archaeology was specifically mentioned as being one of them (Taylor and Bar-Yosef 2014, 15).

The impact of the radiocarbon dating revolution was that all dates had to be re-assessed. For example, the new techniques pushed back the dates of prehistoric monuments to an earlier time, relative to Near Eastern culture, which undermined the dates derived from existing typologies. Many features assumed to have arrived in Europe by diffusion were now found to be earlier than their supposed origins, so the culture-historical versions proposed by Childe and his contemporaries came under attack (Baity 1973, 399). An influential argument led by Troels-Smith was that changes occurred in indigenous cultures without outside influence and, over the course of his career, Glyn Daniel revised his position on diffusion to favour the proposition of 'independent evolution' (Daniel 1980, 88; Tilley 1996, 71). This adoption of a new and revolutionary scientific method implied that other scientific methods or technologies could also be employed in the service of archaeology as part of the move towards 'New Archaeology'. Originating in America, 'New Archaeology' led to critical developments in archaeology's praxis in the 1960s and 1970s. The term *processualism*, in preference to 'New Archaeology', was adopted by Lewis Binford in 1968, though it may have had its origin in the work of Willey and Phillips (1958) who had argued for processual interpretation. Processualism marked a period of change which transformed the existing archaeological paradigm and it was characterised by both theory change and the introduction of important scientific innovations such as radiocarbon dating, as mentioned above, faunal analysis; palaeoethnobotany and dendrochronology (Clarke 1973, 9). These scientific and technical advances in archaeology were important because the new data, emanating from science, could effectively falsify or support existing archaeological theories. Processual archaeology made these scientific breakthroughs central to its praxis so that it adopted a positivist methodology which was linked to a hypothetico-deductive model, generally used as a way of producing generalising statements from testing a specific hypothesis (Shanks and Hodder 1997, 4; Johnson 2010, 40). This resulted in a new focus on problem solving so that there were clear research questions before excavation.

The changing methodology modelled on the hard sciences not only drove but justified a shift in theory towards providing generalisations or metanarratives to explain 'socio-cultural systems and cultural processes of the past', rather than just describing them (Martin 1971). Thus, a pre-occupation with the latest technology, translated itself into a preoccupation with past technologies and it was this shift towards understanding cultures as systems, made up of various processes such as economics, technology and social relations, which led to 'New' archaeology becoming known as 'processual' archaeology. Trigger (1980, 183) described its approaches as being behaviourist and utilitarian, with archaeologists trying to extend a natural science approach into the discipline so that even cultural processes could be understood through general laws and hypothesis testing. In this way archaeology's descriptive culture history method was dropped for a systematic top-down approach to cultural processes and its most prominent advocates were Lewis Binford, David Clarke and Colin Renfrew. By the time Clarke published his seminal paper 'Archaeology: the loss of innocence' in 1973, which reviewed the then current picture of archaeology, processual archaeology was firmly established. Overall, its development led to 'new observations which could not be reconciled to past interpretations' (Clarke 1973, 12) and this observation was Clarke's loss of innocence.

Computer technology

One of the scientific innovations in archaeology was computer science, but before its adoption in archaeology Hawkins pioneered its use in astro-archaeology. Finding alignments at Stonehenge was not new but Hawkins and collaborator John B. White introduced computer analysis as a new instrument for astronomical practice. Hawkins took pains to point out the advantages of computer science by devoting an entire chapter in *Stonehenge Decoded* to 'The Machine', referring to the computer, an IBM 7090, used for their calculations (Fig. 14). Given that there were 27,060 different permutations between 165 'positions' formed by stones, stone-holes and mounds, relating to successive periods at Stonehenge, these could only be analysed by computer. Hawkins (1965a, 148) declared that for the date of 1500 BC, 'The machine has established an extraordinary sun-moon correlation' throughout the structure. Similarly, Dow (1967) used Hawkins' program for research on possible orientations of ancient cities and temples in Mexico. By contrast the acceptance of computer applications in archaeology was slow and a couple of years later Cowgill (1967) pointed out that computer analysis was largely novel in archaeology, though there had been some data processing in France in the late 1950s.

In relation to archaeology, not only could computerised algorithms facilitate a greater use of statistics, but entire archaeological datasets could be scrutinised by digital computer simulation. There was an obvious potential but this was not immediately realised because, as Doran and Hudson (1975, 334) observed, there was an 'academic gulf' between archaeologists and mathematicians. These two groups did not speak the same language, nor did their practices overlap. Nevertheless

Figure 14. IBM 7090 computer as used in 1965. Image wea01830, from the Historic NWS Collection, US Weather Bureau. Wikimedia Commons, public domain.

archaeologists generally were forced to accept the usefulness of science to provide data they could not otherwise obtain. Tasks such as producing distribution maps of geographical areas showing the incidence of different types of monuments could be more easily achieved if the programming was correct. If these could be combined with a dataset of radiocarbon dates the picture which emerged could therefore be validated scientifically. Another advantage was that information retrieval and collation time was greatly reduced (Doran and Hudson 1975, 89). The overall effect of these and other technical innovations for archaeology was described by David Clarke (1973, 8) as a 'quantitative and qualitative technical and social revolution [which] quietly transformed world archaeology', between the late 1940s and the 1970s. Another result was that, in archaeology, methodology, to a certain extent became separated from theory, so that London became important for the development of scientific techniques and Oxford's laboratory provided a home for archaeometry, a term newly coined in the early 1960s to describe these scientific methods (Schofield *et al.* 2011, 35). It was Cambridge that became home to archaeological theory from this time onwards and it was from there that Daniel, who took over Crawford's position as editor of *Antiquity* in 1958, wrote *The Idea of Prehistory* (1962).

Solving the mysteries of Stonehenge

By contrast theory and methodology were fully combined in astro-archaeology. For example in Hawkins' two *Nature* papers, he found little evidence for stars or planets at Stonehenge but, in addition to solar alignments, he discovered that the majority of the alignments were to the moon's extreme positions. Consequently he suggested that Stonehenge could have been a place for 'watching the interchange between the sun, which dominated the warmth of summer, and the moon, which dominated the cold of winter', justifying his position by saying 'If I can see any alignment, general relationship or use for the various parts of Stonehenge then these facts were also known to the builders' (Hawkins 1982, 218; see also Hawkins 1965a, vii). Another novel feature was Hawkins' consideration of eclipses whereby he claimed to have solved the 'puzzle' of the 56 Aubrey Holes by theorising that they were used as eclipse predictors for a cycle of 56 years, close to three periods of the moon's 18.6 year cycle (Hawkins 1965a, 140; see Glossary: eclipse). He speculated that the holes were used as a 'computer' by the builders, suggesting that the high priests 'could, in fact, have predicted the time of an impending lunar eclipse with an accuracy of about one hour'. Additionally he speculated that Stonehenge was important as a seasonal calendar. These snippets of theory, which would have been useful for symbolic interpretations in archaeology, were lost amidst the hype surrounding the claim that Stonehenge was designed as a computer by its builders. Writing retrospectively, Hawkins (1982, 218–219) explained that *Stonehenge Decoded* was limited to the astronomical alignments shown by the structure: the sun and moon alignments were a fact of the structure, but the counting aspects were speculative. That was the reason that he gave for separating the issues in the two *Nature* papers: the first (Hawkins 1963) dealt with the discovery of the alignments, the second (Hawkins 1964) with the possible numerological aspects.

In the years following his famous work, Hawkins published several articles on alignments and one of these was a survey of Calanais which he compared with Stonehenge, similarly believing that it was set up for calendrical and eclipse predicting purposes (1965b). This was not the solar calendar suggested by Lockyer and Lewis, but rather a soli-lunar calendar to account for the difference between the 12 and 13 lunar month years. Hawkins noted the effects of latitude and compared their differences, remarking that at Calanais the midsummer moon only skims the horizon yet at Stonehenge the sun and the moon at their extreme positions rise at a right-angle to the horizon. Although Stukeley and Lockyer had introduced the importance of latitude, Hawkins formalised it further. Additionally, at Calanais he thought that the builders were not as 'scientifically advanced' as those of Stonehenge and this was as close as he came to agreeing with the general understandings in archaeology about the lack of prehistoric skills (1965b, 130).

Hawkins' thesis was of interest to many archaeologists so Daniel invited the astronomer Fred Hoyle to examine critically Hawkins' interpretation of Stonehenge. In 'Stonehenge – an eclipse predictor', Hoyle (1966a) found precision alignments which confirmed Hawkins' results but put forward his own simpler theory for how the Aubrey Holes could have been used as a protractor for predicting eclipses, rather than being a computer-like device as suggested by Hawkins (see Glossary: precision alignments). Warning his readers that they needed to consult a text on spherical astronomy, Hoyle (1966b, 262), in examining Hawkins' thesis, attempted a mathematical solution 'thereby permitting the whole discussion to be confined to simple trigonometry'. There followed seven pages of astronomical notation and equations, in a language that would have been incomprehensible to a non-specialist, making it impossible for most archaeologists to dispute his claims except on cultural grounds. Hoyle (1966b, 270–274) explained the solar and lunar extremes where the sun and moon 'appear to stand still' and speculated that only skilled mathematicians would have been capable of working this out, but that this skill was lost by the time of the second phase of the monument. Hoyle's speculative claim about the builders' skills was overturned by Colton and Martin (1967) who thought that the Stonehenge architects could have predicted eclipses by simply using the Aubrey circle to judge when the setting sun and rising full moon were opposite one another; the condition required for an eclipse.

Before Hawkins and Hoyle sensationalised astro-archaeology with their new solutions, C.A. Newham, an amateur archaeologist and astronomer, was drawing similar conclusions about Stonehenge, based on theodolite measurements rather than through the aid of a computer. Although Lockyer had also used a theodolite to measure horizon altitude, Newham, was the first to measure a comprehensive set of horizon altitudes at Stonehenge, in order to find additional solar alignments along with alignments to the extreme northern moonrise and moonset (Atkinson 1974a, 215). Prior to Hawkins' first publications in *Nature*, Newham sent his findings to Richard Atkinson who advised him to publish in *Antiquity*. However Daniel, the then editor, replied, as cited by Newham, that 'he did not think it would be of interest to his readers and in any case he was not an astronomer and did not understand such things' (Newham 1982). Newham was not deterred and his research was written up by the *Yorkshire Post*'s science correspondent Douglas Emmott, under the headline 'The Mystery of Hole G' and published on 16 March 1963, seven months before Hawkins' first publication (Lancaster Brown 1976, 105–106). Once again 'mystery' was used as a selling point for a scientific enquiry and employed again when Newham self-published a booklet on the 'enigma' of Stonehenge in 1964. His further work on Stonehenge was finally published in *Nature* in 1966 and in a book in 1972. Emmott's article pre-dated Hawkins' first paper in *Nature* by seven months yet Newham's amateur work was completely eclipsed by that of Hawkins, a known academic, whose ideas were given the widest publicity by the press, radio and television. Similarly ignored was the work of another outsider, French architect G. Charrière, who published his own research on the Stonehenge alignments, suggesting they were regulated to reconcile the lunar and solar calendars, in 1961, again before Hawkins.

Hoyle's interpretations were more extreme and inaccessible than any that had gone before and following a severe critique by the leading archaeologists he disappeared from the scene. Nor were they interested in Alexander Marshack's discoveries, published in the same year, that Hawkins published his second paper in *Nature* (Hawkins 1964). It was Hawkins' work on the sophisticated lunar-solar lore in Britain that led Marshack to investigate whether this tradition existed earlier, elsewhere (Marshack 1964). While researching the origins of this aspect of culture, which he believed dated back some 30,000 years to the Upper Palaeolithic, Marshack chanced upon an image of a bone tool, believed to be 20,000 years old, found at Ishango at the head of the Nile. He deciphered the systematic notches scratched upon it as being evidence of a lunar calendar and sent his findings to Hawkins who found some validity in his theories (Marshack 1991). Believing these to be a record of a lunar calendar Marshack went on to find many similar examples for this period. In researching similar prehistoric bones and notations in cave paintings, he introduced the new method of using microscopic analysis and, for his work, achieved recognition in America as a researcher at the Peabody Museum of Archaeology and Ethnology at Harvard University. However, faced with the 'scientific' hypotheses of Hawkins, Hoyle and Newham, another scientific approach, from another non-archaeologist, received little British attention. Nevertheless, across the Atlantic, rock art studies had been initiated by Pohorecky (1969) in Canada and these were continued in America by Chamberlain (Baity 1973, 446) and Brandt *et al.* (1973).

Astro-archaeology, while relying primarily on Lockyer's methods, contributed a new understanding of the soli-lunar eclipse cycles, determined that at the lunar extremes the moon appeared to stand still in the same way as the sun at the solstices and added new tools, such as the use of computers and microscopes for analysis. While the archaeologists were of course adept at surveying, they lacked numeracy skills, which would have been required to understand Hawkins or Hoyle. Astro-archaeology's new methods, though operationally in tune with archaeology's scientific turn, were therefore in advance of processualism in these areas. Its research, wittingly or unwittingly, tapped into the popular desire for ancient wisdom and although novel in many respects, it was a revival of the antiquarian focus on Stonehenge, with its mysteries being the dominant theme. Although Hawkins was planning a new version of *Stonehenge Decoded* at the time of his death in 2003, astro-archaeology had long been consigned to the past (Allen 2004, 2). However it is an important episode and a historical marker in archaeoastronomy's history, less because of innovations in its practice but more because it brought astronomical interpretations to the notice of a new generation of archaeologists. However, its brief flowering was soon overtaken by radical new research which came to be known as megalithic science (see Chapter 7).

The New Age

In the background of these important academic developments towards the understanding of prehistory, was the continuation of esoteric interpretations. Never was this of more prominence than during the New Age when earth mysteries and alternative archaeoastronomy became an overt sub-culture, on the fringe of what can be called the archaeoastronomy mainstream. A prediction of a new age had already appeared in Blavatsky's 19th century claim that her thesis (1877) was a revelation of ancient wisdom and, from the spread of this knowledge, a new age would dawn. Another came in 1943 in a speech by George W. Smith, then chief of the Ancient Druid Order, which heralded 'the coming of a New Age' (Stout 2008, 150). This 'new age' was prefaced by the counterculture of the 1960s, before blossoming into the New Age spirituality of the 1970s and 1980s. Included in the overall umbrella of the New Age was an updated version of antiquarian esotericism which took into account mid-20th century developments such as the space age and computer science. Its popularity was aided by the availability of cheaply published paperback books on the subject. The Glastonbury festival was first organised in September 1970 and thereafter the date was moved to coincide with the summer solstice, with its stage for 1971 being constructed on a site 'above the Glastonbury-Stonehenge ley line' (Glastonbury Festival 2017). Attended by some 12,000 that year, it was a meeting place that brought together the 1960's 'alternative' culture; a cosmology associated with the Age of Aquarius and the 'latest archaeoastronomy' (Campion 2002, 203). Modern druidry also became a part of the pagan counterculture in the 1960s though there had been druid ceremonies at Stonehenge since 1905 (Stout 2008, 144). The publication of *Stonehenge Decoded* had helped arouse the public's imagination and this led to an appetite which was eager to solve the ancient mysteries, decipher their puzzles and enigmas and revive their customs with celebrations at the midsummer solstice rising.

Ley lines and earth mysteries

In 1961, Watkins' ley lines received a new mystical treatment from Tony Wedd who associated them with UFOs. Wedd had been influenced by two books, one by Buck Nelson, *My Trip to Mars, the Moon and Venus* (1956) and the other by Aimé Michel, *Flying Saucers and the Straight Line Mystery* (1958; Pennick and Devereux 1989, 208–209). Works such as these served to regenerate interest in ley lines and a new community, The Ley Hunter's Club, was formed in 1962 with *The Ley Hunter* magazine appearing in 1965. These complementary research areas came under the general term 'Earth Mysteries' which, according to Paul Devereux seems to have first appeared as a headline in the *Whole Earth Catalogue* in 1974. He described this new field as follows:

> Among the subjects so gathered up are aspects of: anthropology; archaeology; ancient astronomy; the study of ancient lifeways and arcane lore; divination; dowsing; ethnobotany; ethnopsychology; the experience of ancient sites and landscapes; folklore; geomantic traditions; geophysics; history; psychology; ritual and magic; sacred geometry; shamanism; unusual phenomena. (Devereux 2017)

Devereux, from his position of deep insider, assessed this esoteric trend as a fringe area, outside the academic mainstream. He reasoned that though many of the subjects were authentic research areas, it was their juxtaposition and cross-boundary treatment that presented problems for established disciplines, while Hutton (2013, 383) reported that its practitioners also referred to it as 'alternative archaeology'. From the early 1970s ley research developed along two diverging paths, research-based ley hunting and the concept of leys as energy lines. Both John Michell (1978) and Paul Screeton (1974) carried the discussion far beyond Watkins' original conceptions.

Mary Caine (1969) rediscovered Maltwood's Glastonbury Zodiac and put a New Age spin on it, wondering whether its purpose was 'a mystical path of initiation by Ancient Sumerians', or whether the 'strange lines of psychic power' had a subconscious effect on those who crossed them. In a similar vein, Guy Underwood (1969) combined traditional dowsing for water with documenting 'the Earth Force'. A further variant of the earth mysteries tradition was the Dragon Project, which was founded in 1977, becoming a trust in 1988. One of its projects was researching the Rollright Stones in Oxfordshire through a mixture of monitoring and dowsing which led to the conclusion that the stones 'pulsated with low-level magnetism', emitting high frequency ultrasound (Ancient Explorers 2016; Fig. 15). Similarly, Barnatt's *Stone Circles of the Peak: a search for natural harmony* was described by Burl (1981) as evoking a 'never-never land of ley-lines, earth magic and extra-sensory powers', whereas Graves' *Needles of Stone* 'invoked energy pillars, telepathic beams and occultism'. The combination of these different strands became an eclectic pseudoscientific area within the New Age counterculture.

Figure 15. Radiation monitoring at the King Stone, part of the Rollright Stones complex. Reproduced with kind permission of Paul Devereux.

John Michell and alternative archaeoastronomy
John Michell is regarded as one of the leading protagonists for this pseudoscience. For example, Campion (2002, 203), described Michell's *The View Over Atlantis* (1978) as a seminal text for the New Age movement and believed that Michell had 'pretty well

invented' the modern study of earth mysteries. Michell's *Atlantis* was first published in 1969 and in it Michell put his own twist on Chinese geomancy, Maltwood, Watkins and others to conclude that 'a great scientific instrument lies sprawled over the entire surface of the globe', the key of which 'lies within the contours of the landscape' (Michell 1978, 62–63). Michell (1978, 79–80) believed in a system of numerology or concealed geometry that the ancients understood, concluding that ancient monuments contained 'the whole vocabulary of the sacred language of the past'. He examined several sites including Stonehenge which he claimed (1978, 120) was laid out 'according to the geometry and the numbers of the square of the Sun'. Michell's complicated diagrams 'proved' the monuments were designed according to a magic square which was 'capable of providing a numerical formula for the symmetry of the heavens' (Michell 1978, 110). Additionally, each stone circle had an energy source, 'the flow of terrestrial magnetic current', at its centre. For the most part archaeologists ignored these New Age publications or at least kept quiet about them, though Daniel (1964, 166) denounced the appropriation of the monument 'by neo-Druids'. On the other hand Michell (1989, 66–68) concluded that 'astro-archaeology' moved into the counterculture of the 1960s on a popular level and into the counterculture of archaeology at an academic level at the same time.

The implications for archaeoastronomy

Following the dramatic proposals of Hawkins, astro-archaeology came under serious scrutiny. Before its later rejection, Hawkins' 'novel idea about Stonehenge' was introduced by Daniel in *Antiquity's* 1964 editorial on Stonehenge, where readers were reminded of *Antiquity*'s 1927 issue when Trotter wrote of Stonehenge, 'And we may prolong controversies about it until we fill a library' (Daniel 1964, 166). The difficulties caused by Hawkins' different conceptual approach caused some archaeologists to take a sceptical view. That this led to an acrimonious division is well documented in the secondary literature. For example, Lancaster Brown (1976, 111) reported that the conflict of ideas between archaeologists and astronomers, which had quietly simmered since Lockyer's day, now 'suddenly boiled over in print', with Hayman (1997, 184) saying that they clashed in 'a very public showdown'. According to Michell (1989, 7) the two sides were 'in mutual opposition', yet Colin Renfrew (1973, 222), writing at the same time, called it 'one of those agreeably fiery little controversies to which archaeology seems particularly prone'.

The root cause of the debate was two-fold: first that outsiders, like Hawkins and Hoyle, were impinging on the archaeologists' domain and, not only that, but Hawkins, rather than conducting archaeological surveys out in the field, employed a completely different method, computer analysis, which at that time was novel in archaeology. Secondly, the position of archaeology was that, following processualism, progression theory within the model of the Three Age system, altered its face to become a meta-narrative of simple to complex. In other words, it was a view of cultural evolution which showed how societies could be classified on a scale of complexity (Johnson 2010, 23). Therefore, according to the archaeologists, the monument builders would simply not have had the skill or knowledge to construct the monuments in the way the archaeoastronomers proposed. Similarly, following Christopher Hawkes' thesis that there was only a partial picture to be drawn from the material record, Daniel (1962, 127–128) thought archaeology could not speak about 'the spiritual, mental and moral culture of these societies'. Both these factors continued to limit the acceptance of archaeoastronomy by archaeologists. The origin of this latest clash is traced by most commentators to the publication of Hawkins' paper in *Nature*, but the negativity actually began in 1962 when Newham's paper was rejected for *Antiquity* by Daniel.

The initial reviews of Hawkins were derogatory as can be judged by titles such as 'Decoder Misled' (Atkinson 1966a) and 'Moonshine on Stonehenge' (Atkinson 1966b). Atkinson's 'Moonshine' review was an example of the reaction of archaeologists to interlopers. He (1966b, 213) criticised Hawkins' claims on the grounds of inaccurate site plans, poor archaeological data and misguided selection of stones as markers, suggesting Hawkins was overconfident in his use of the computer, 'the secular equivalent of divine revelation'. Not only that, but the new radiocarbon datings rendered Stonehenge older than the date used by Hawkins. This reaction could perhaps have been foreseen given the differences between Hawkins' methodology and that of the archaeologists. Yet despite these major shortcomings, Atkinson did find some positives in Hawkins' putative alignments to the sun and the lunar extremes. However, when it came to Hoyle, Atkinson (1967) added that it was Hoyles' assessment of the intellectual superiority of the monument builders that made Hoyle's thesis more difficult to accept than that of Hawkins. In the same paper, which had a number of discussants, Hawkins (1967, 92), who had believed that the Stonehenge builders were more intelligent than previously thought, nevertheless robustly demolished Hoyles' assessment of the intellectual superiority of the monument builders and said that no astronomer was equipped to act as a guide to the regions of archaeology and anthropology. Although Hoyle published a book with fuller account in 1977, by that time those archaeologists involved had lost interest in either him or Hawkins.

The incommensurability between the two fields was further reinforced by Jacquetta Hawkes' (1967) paper 'God in the machine', in which she looked at the Hawkins-Hoyle debate to question their validity and suggested their view was not only ethnocentric but suffered from selection bias. In other words, to fit their astronomical theories, they only selected measurements that would align to the extreme rising or setting positions of the sun and moon on the horizon. While she accepted the solstitial alignment at Stonehenge and conceded that the monument builders may have been interested in the lunar extremes, she was of the opinion that 'the astronomical *nouveau vague* flowing over Stonehenge' would not overturn current archaeological thinking (Hawkes 1967, 180). For her Stonehenge was a place of ritual, not evidence of intellectual and astronomical activity, concluding from their differences that 'Every age has the Stonehenge it deserves – or desires'.

Hawkins (1965a, 402) also touched on the problem of incommensurability. In this regard, he considered the problems of disciplinary distinctions and used the example of the differing beliefs of intellectual ability to remark that in archaeology the monument builders were regarded as inferior, whereas in anthropology, however far in the past, 'the species Homo sapiens was believed to be our equal'. In opposition, Atkinson (1974b, 130) pointed out the orthodox view and noted the contradiction between positive verification of prehistoric mathematics and astronomy and the negative archaeological evidence for recorded numeracy. Few outsiders had encroached on the archaeologists' territory in relation to British prehistoric monuments since Lockyer and Boyle Somerville and the central issue which caused a dispute at that time was also the intellectual capability of the prehistoric ancestors. It was difficult to find a middle ground and Newham discussed the problems of bias faced by the two opposing sides, concluding that,

> Implicit faith cannot be placed in all the interpretations given to the findings of astronomers and archaeologists alike. Perhaps the truth lies somewhere between the two extremes. (cited in Lancaster Brown 1976, 161)

He reflected the views of the early 20th century Irish archaeologist R.A.S. Macalister who had written 'Let an archaeologist become obsessed with the idea that a defaced inscription must be read in a particular way ... and he is lost, his eyes will follow the dictates of his mind' (Lancaster Brown 1976, 282). A summary of the evidence suggests that the rejection of astronomical theories may have been due to several factors of which the dispute about the mental abilities of the builders was one; the others being the inaccessible mathematical language and the antipathy towards astronomers trying to invade archaeological territory. As Eddy (1974a, 66) remarked, in the 'struggling marriage' between astronomy and archaeology', Hawkins only added to the 'clutter'.

The different standpoints of archaeology and archaeoastronomy were also heightened by the 'subjective dichotomy' between science and non-science, which Renfrew (1981) thought obscured what was an interesting development in the evolution of science. This seems to bring the argument back to Snow's two cultures; the division between the sciences and the humanities and, acknowledging that he had to some extent crossed the boundaries between the two, Hawkins dedicated *Stonehenge Decoded* to Snow. This split had always been problematic for archaeology, but Daniel (1962, 126) had earlier stressed that although prehistoric archaeology used scientific techniques, he regarded it as a humanity. It was a point reiterated by Piggott (1974b, 275) when he too likened the disciplinary differences to the 'yawning crevasse' between Snow's two cultures, though he hoped it might be a 'crack in the snow'.

Chapter 7

Megalithic science

Hawkins' *Stonehenge Decoded* (1965a) had caught the attention of archaeologists but they just as quickly dismissed it. However they simply could not brush off the contemporaneous work of Alexander Thom so easily. Thom's large body of work, which he began publishing in 1954, contained meticulous surveys of prehistoric monuments and deserved earnest attention. Initially the leading archaeologists took his whole package seriously without heeding the difficulties his new theories posed; theories which became the subject of a lengthy debate.

Alexander Thom (1894–1985) was an engineer by profession; a career which culminated in his appointment as Professor of Engineering Science at Oxford. It is certainly likely that Thom would have been aware of Lockyer's and other related astronomical works and he would have been 29 when Boyle Somerville's paper on British prehistoric monuments was published. In 1933 Thom took a trip to Calanais, was apparently reminded of Somerville's paper, and from that point onwards decided to commence a programme of accurate theodolite surveys of megalithic monuments and sites, mainly in Scotland, and interpret the alignments he found there. This he did part-time but, after his retirement in 1961, he devoted his life to making detailed studies of these monuments (see Fig. 16), often helped by his son Archibald Stevenson Thom. Though his praxis was later called megalithic science, as his work contained many examples of his usage of 'Megalithic metrology', 'Megalithic man', 'Megalithic astronomy', 'Megalithic yard', 'Megalithic fathom (2 megalithic yards)' and so on, Thom did not actually use this term. The descriptors, megalithic science or alternatively megalithic astronomy, were generally employed interchangeably by others when describing his work. Under these connected neologisms Thom's body of work included a combination of specialised astronomical terms and methods which were not easily transferrable to another discipline, further promoting the idea that the field was separate from that of archaeology. The emphasis on science in astronomical practice was already well-developed by this time, so archaeoastronomy did not have the same rupture with the past that archaeology experienced when it followed the path to processualism. Instead archaeoastronomy demonstrated some continuity with past traditions though there were certainly innovations and refinements in Thom's work

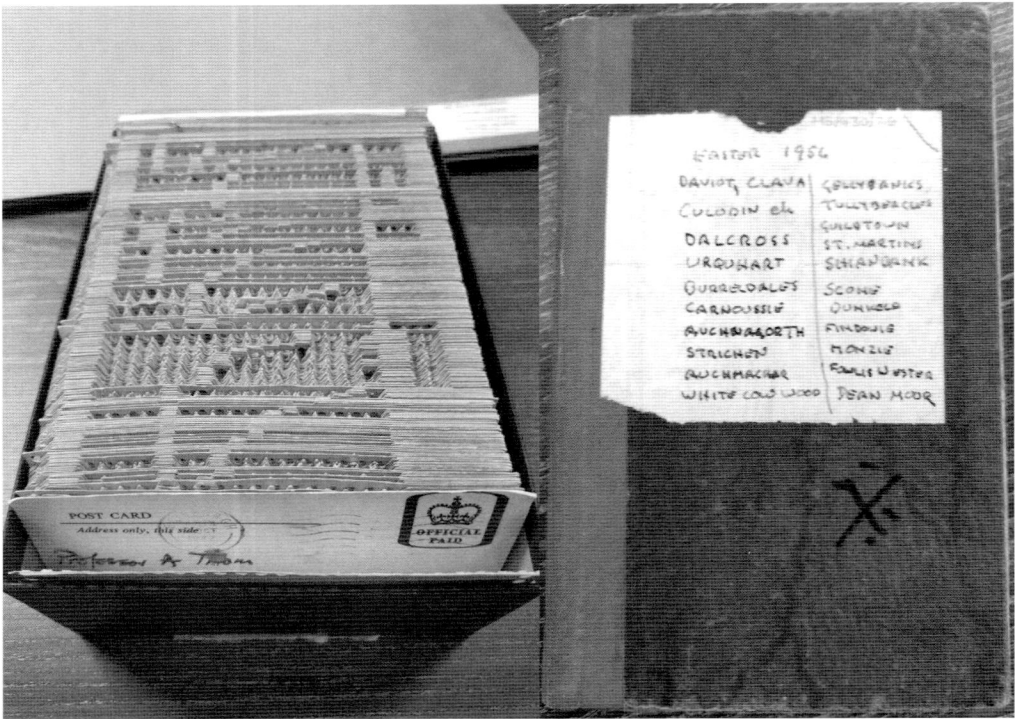

Figure 16. Alexander Thom's meticulous card index and one of the many notebooks he used in the field. Photo: Kenneth Brophy, reproduced with kind permission from Alexander Thom's great grandson Eòghann MacColl.

Without a specific platform for the subject matter of prehistoric astronomy, Thom's first nine papers, between 1954 and 1964, were scattered over several scientific and technical journals, such as the *Journal of The British Astronomical Association* (1954); *Journal of the Royal Statistical Society* (1955; 1962; 1964a); the *Empire Empirical Review* (1958); *The Mathematical Gazette* (1961a); *Archives International d'Histoire des Sciences* (1961b) and the *New Scientist* (1964b; 1964c). Some of the ideas for which he later became famous were introduced in these early papers, the content of which showed that his approach was that of a scientist, surveyor, astronomer and statistician, interested in sharing his findings with those similarly qualified rather than specifically directing them to archaeologists. It is commonly believed that because Thom published in obscure journals, his work received little attention from archaeologists. However this is not to say that some archaeologists were unaware of his work because his 1955 paper, detailing data from over 60 sites, was followed by a four-page discussion with comments from Childe and others. In 1966 Thom (1966a; 1966b) chose the more accessible journals of *Antiquity* and *Nature* to expound his ideas and followed these up in 1967 with his ground-breaking book, *Megalithic Sites in Britain*. Here he considered 450 sites, 300 of which he surveyed, but as many of the sites he surveyed showed a preference for lunar declinations, his second book in 1971 was entitled *Megalithic Lunar Observatories*, as he believed the monuments were constructed as 'scientific institutions built to study the movements of the moon' (Thom 1971, 90). With all his astronomical knowledge of the movements of the sun and the moon, the effects of parallax and refraction and lunar perturbation, Thom was unable to view the relation of the megalithic monuments to the Neolithic sky in any other way than scientific. Not that he was unaware of the archaeology of the sites because his third book (Thom and Thom 1980a) included archaeological notes by Aubrey Burl, but he did not draw on archaeological theory to examine them. His last book on standing stones, published after his death in November 1985, was a further collaboration (Thom and Burl 1990).

The Thom paradigm

The evidence shows that much of Thom's praxis was not new but an embellishment of antiquarian and early 20th century astronomical ideas and methods. For example, Lancaster Brown (1976, 194) concluded that Thom got the idea of classifying the circles from Lewis; that he found clues about lunar alignments from Somerville and derived the practices of looking for stellar alignments and of using changes in the Sun's obliquity to determine the date of megalithic monuments from Lockyer. Indeed, the only practical difference between Thom's studies and those of the early 20th century was an increase in accuracy and a greater extent of site surveys (Meadows 1975). However while there certainly was continuity, Thom introduced important innovations which taken all together have subsequently been called the 'Thom paradigm'.

Thom's paradigm, which created a metanarrative on prehistoric monumental culture, can be set in the context of archaeology's processualist metanarratives, explored in Chapter 6. Djindjian (2015, 70) concluded that processualism also led to a preference for mathematical modelling, the use of multi-dimensional data analysis methods and the implementation of statistical tests. Thom pioneered their use in his research but, while this more scientific approach in archaeology led to the formation of many archaeological subdisciplines and specialisms, it did *not* include Thom's megalithic science. The belief was that by studying isolated aspects of the archaeological record in detail it would be possible to establish a system of 'theory building', known as middle-range theory (Binford 1983). Renfrew's *Emergence of Civilisation*, published in 1973, promoted this new understanding of cultural change which blended evolutionary theory with functionalism (Shanks and Tilley 1988, 31–34). Processual archaeology has remained essentially positivist and functionalist and despite 'a wide variety of different theoretical perspectives on the past', processualism was, according to Shanks and Tilley (1988, vii–viii), an 'anti-theoretical discipline'. Similarly Hodder (2004, 1) agreed that its approaches put more emphasis on testability than theory. On the other hand, in Thom's work, both science and theory were fundamental to his megalithic science.

Elements of the Thom paradigm

Thom developed a new way of researching prehistoric monuments by borrowing methodology from other disciplines, such as astronomy, geometry and statistics. From his findings he provided an overall theory of 'megalithic man' and his megalithic remains, which could be applied universally to sites in Britain and Brittany. His paradigm was comprised of seven elemental categories: astronomy; surveying; statistics; geometry; metrology; dating and the megalithic calendar, as we will see. First, by augmenting the existing astronomical scientific method of Lockyer and Hawkins, Thom introduced new and complicated variables to make it more rigorous than anything that had gone before. He refined Lockyer's formulae for determining declination by adding mean values of parallax and lunar perturbation (see Glossary: moon) in order to minimise calculation errors to just a few minutes of arc, believing that the builders' precision suggested that they could detect these minute changes in declination. Similarly, by using temperature to obtain the correction to mean refraction, his calculations were more accurate than earlier ones (Thom and Thom 1983). The graze effect of the sun, described by the Thoms as 'the extra bend experienced by a ray when it passes over a ridge' (Thom and Thom 1980b), was also taken into account. His methodology for finding alignments was based on the trigonometrical relation between the four measurements, azimuth, declination, latitude and altitude, so that by knowing three the fourth could be found. His conclusion (Thom 1971, 90) was that the sites which were predominantly stone circles were 'scientific institutions built to study the movements of the moon' and from this he could not be swayed, reiterating it over and over again (Fig. 17).

Because solar and lunar risings or settings are so changeable only the extreme positions were generally considered, so, for example, from one new moon to the next, the moon's declination changes, while the entire lunar cycle from its widest extreme to the next takes 18.61 years to complete. Somerville had been aware of these lunar extremes but Thom (1971, 5) gave them new names; major and minor lunar standstills. He has been widely credited for this but Hoyle's phrase, 'appear to stand still', mentioned in Chapter 6, is remarkably close to the term standstill. To complicate matters further, there is the additional problem of extrapolation as the moon's maximum declination may be reached when it is not at its rising or setting point. This finding, combined with research on the ground, led to Thom's theory that the megalith builders understood these cycles and the deviations caused by the moon's perturbations (A.S. Thom 1984, 86). Although his son Archibald acknowledged that the moon's declination extremes at the minor standstill are not really unique, the importance of the minor standstill was that at that part of the cycle the perturbation cycle could be timed and that would make eclipse prediction possible. Thom himself

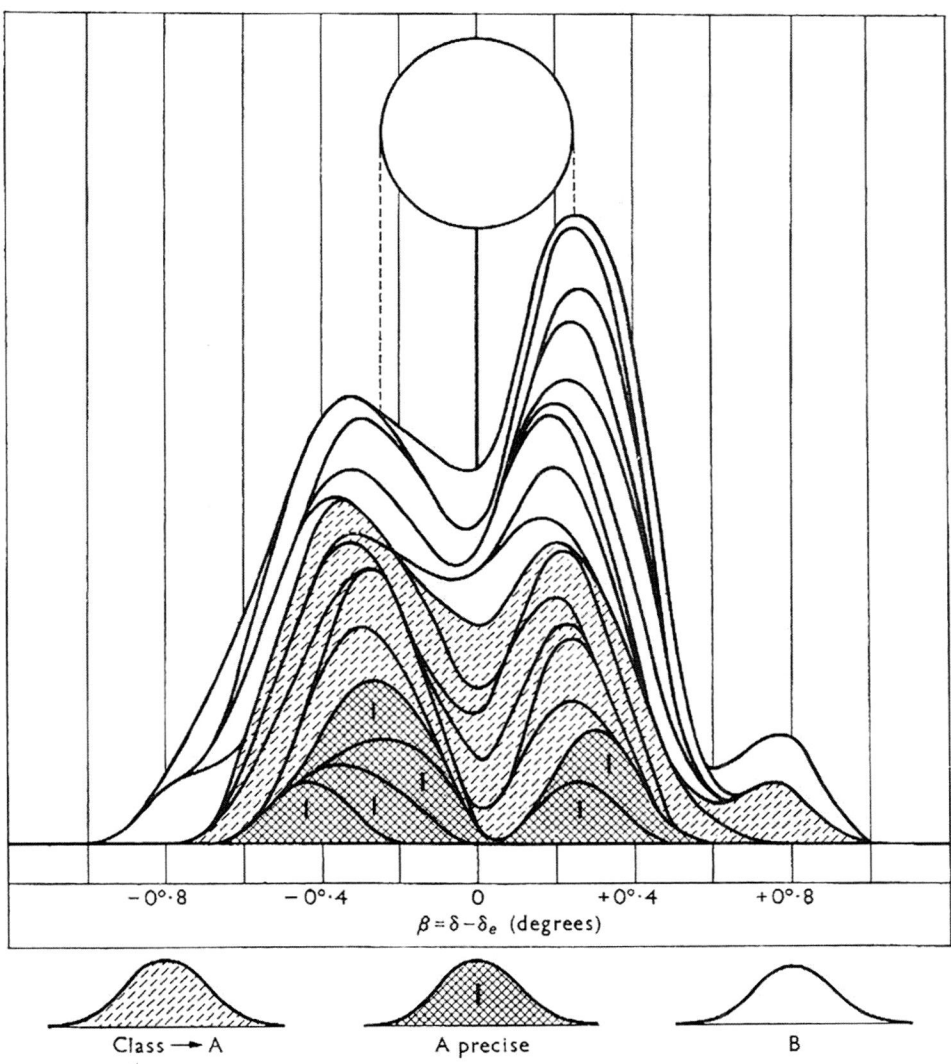

Figure 17. Alexander Thom's diagram showing the degree of precision (within 1°) he found for lunar sightlines. Taken from his Megalithic Sites in Britain (1967) and reproduced with kind permission from his great grandson Eòghann MacColl.

also suggested that 'megalithic man' was capable of working out extrapolation and proposed that the fan-shaped rows of stones at Carnac were designed to solve this problem (Thom and Thom 1971, 147). In France, Charrière similarly believed in the sophisticated ability of the builders to set out their monuments, so that what we might take to be errors in orientation were a deliberate attempt to reconcile lunar and solar calendars (Baity 1973, 395).

Like Hawkins and Hoyle before him, Thom further theorised that stone circles were used for predicting eclipses and that a period of 150 years of standstill observations was required to incorporate these lunar alignments, though Norris (1988, 269) believed the figure would have been closer to 180 years. Morrison (1980) also pointed out some of the problems of viewing the lunar standstills, the extremes of which occur only at first or last crescent, yet Thom mainly referred to full moon sightings at the standstills. Overall, Thom's astronomical methodology gave him the tools to 'see' what he thought the builders saw, within minutes of arc. Consequently his conclusion was that the builders used the same precision when placing their stones in line with certain key declinations; a conclusion that was once again at odds with most archaeologists' understanding of the rudimentary degree of prehistoric skills.

Thom's site plans were accurately drawn from his field measurements which he took by tape together with theodolite or prismatic compass readings (see for example Fig. 18). He also recorded the horizon altitudes and the azimuths of the stones, from his own measurements, Ordnance Survey maps and photographs. From these he could determine both backsights (the observing positions) and foresights or notches on the horizon (see Glossary: surveying for alignments). The utility of alignments to features on the horizon had first been mentioned by John Smith in 1771, by Lewis in 1892 and Watkins in 1925 (Watkins 1974), but Thom made them a central part of his theory by classifying nine different types of foresight (Thom and Thom 1980c). He concluded that it was the close agreement of an azimuth (taken from the backsight) with the calculated lunar declination (at the horizon foresight) 'that makes us so certain that we are dealing with genuine lunar observatories' (Thom and Thom 1980c, S94).

The third element of his paradigm related to statistical probability and Thom was at pains to back up his arguments by analysing his data statistically. It was necessary to use standard deviation to give 'an indication of the precision of a measurement' or a derived quantity (Thom 1967, 6). He classified the circles into types and set out unambiguous and strict criteria for the values used to calculate probability, finding, for example, the probability value for 19 Type A Scottish sites was 0.3%, or in other words, three chances in a thousand that those alignments could have come about by chance (Thom and Thom 1978a). The results were presented as histograms which indicated those declinations that had the highest number of incidences, as further evidence of his alignment theory. However, as most of the research was dependent on his own selection of foresights and backsights, he defended himself by saying that the problem of selection was 'a matter of personal opinion' (Thom 1967, 96), but nevertheless classified his results in terms of likelihood. This type of statistical analysis involving a large data set had not been possible before because most of the earlier work related to single sites. However, Thom's statistics came under scrutiny by P.R. Freeman (1976), a lecturer in the Department of Statistics and Computer Science at University College, who pointed out that the problem of deciding which astronomical declinations count as significant is difficult. Subsequently together with Elmore (1979) he devised a statistical procedure to test the alignment results

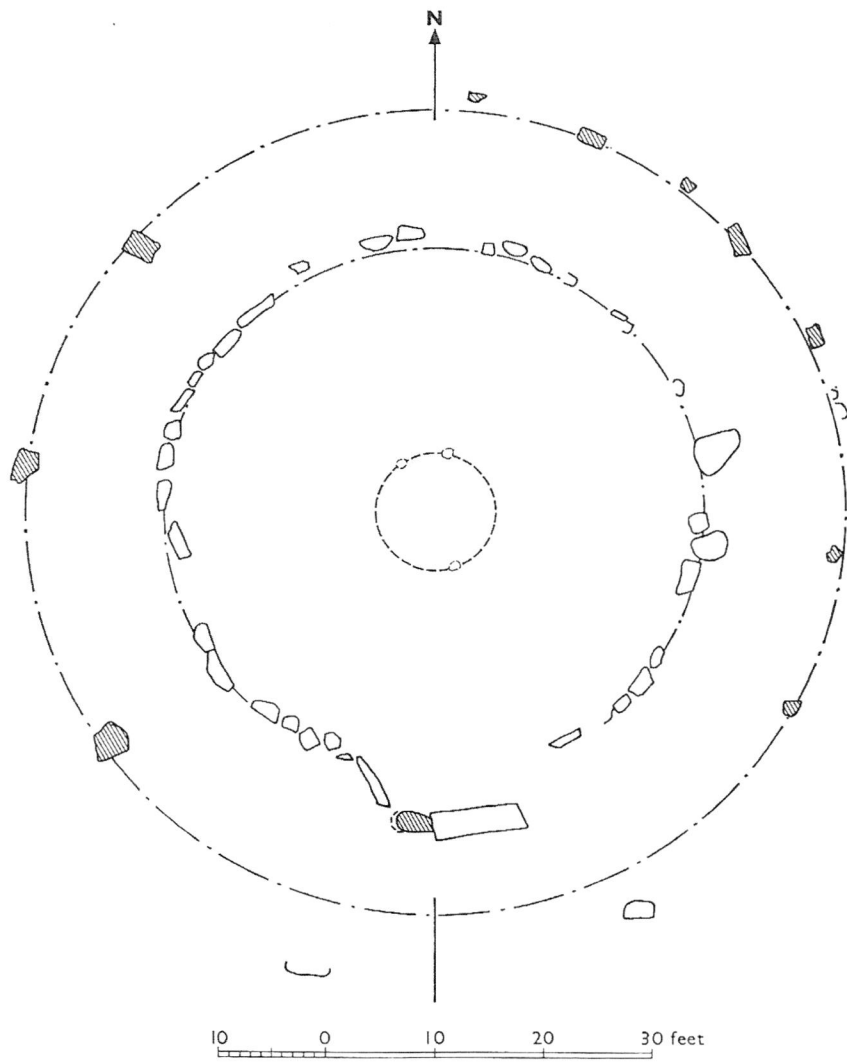

Figure 18. Alexander Thom's plan of the recumbent stone circle at Aquorthies, Kingausie in northeast Scotland. Taken from his Megalithic Sites in Britain *(1967) and reproduced with kind permission from his great grandson Eòghann MacColl.*

of three surveys, based on well-defined groups, and concluded that most did not fall into the category of precision alignments when using a degree of error of slightly over 1°, despite Thom's belief in a precision accuracy of within a few minutes of arc. Nevertheless, Thom's statistical methodology, which was innovative for astronomical studies, coincided with its adoption in processual archaeology, so the archaeologists would have at least been able to understand his arguments.

Not so with Thom's speculations about megalithic geometry. Like Stukeley, Duke and Somerville before him, Thom believed that the builders were able to set complicated geometrical designs. He thought that 'megalithic man knew the theorem of Pythagoras' or at least 'he was feeling his way toward it' (Thom 1967, 27) and used it to lay out the circles, notwithstanding the obvious fact that the circles had been laid out at least a millennium before the birth of Pythagoras. According to Thom, the circles ranged from those based on three types of Pythagorean triangles to ellipses, egg-shaped circles and flattened circles, but he noted that this geometrical knowledge was confined to the privileged few whose mathematical principles 'were sufficiently important to them to be committed to stone' (Thom 1955, 283–284). Euan MacKie, an archaeologist, attempted to rewrite the archaeological version of prehistory by concluding that in Britain 'there was some very advanced astronomical and geometrical knowledge', adding that Thom's fieldwork endorsed this view (MacKie 1977a). MacKie was fully aware of the astronomical practice and theory and explained it in simpler terms than Thom, thus making it more accessible to archaeologists. However, questioning whether Thom's approach was 'megalithic mathematics or Neolithic nonsense', Angell (1976), a statistician, pointed out a simpler method to construct circles based on triangles. Thom's Pythagorean triangles are of course evidence of his ethnocentricism and he appeared to overlook the fact, that as a matter of geometric necessity, circles contain many triangles. Ellegård (1981, 116) pointed out that there is a 'general tendency (not limited to archaeoastronomers) to project onto another culture the scientific concerns and approaches of our own'. MacKie too, worried about the assumption that mathematics could be used to infer what happened in the past on the basis of measurements of present conditions.

Allied to geometry was metrology and this proved to be another of the sticking points in Thom's paradigm. As a variant on Stukeley's notion of a druidical cubit, Thom believed that there was a universal system of megalithic metrology. He found these megalithic measures from data obtained from his surveys of stone circles and declared that there was a common unit of length, or 'Megalithic fathom' valued at 5.44 feet (*c.* 1.7 m), which when divided by two (2.72 ft) became the 'Megalithic Yard' (Thom 1955; 1961a). This megalithic yard was suggested to be the standard of measurement in use throughout Britain and Brittany. Indeed as the measure in Carnac of 2.721±0.001 feet was so close to the British measure of 2.720±0.003, Thom speculated that this standardisation emanated from 'a controlling, or at least advising centre' (Thom and Thom 1972). He divided his megalithic yard into megalithic feet and megalithic inches and so convinced was he by his own accurate empiricism that he came to regard megalithic units as 'known' rather than theoretical. Thom similarly measured cup and ring marks in megalithic inches in an attempt to tune into ancient wisdom, a theme which had permeated many antiquarian enquiries, but failed to unlock the puzzle, though thought 'doubtless they contain a message of some sort' (Thom and Thom 1978b, 45). Behrend (1977a) suggested that Thom may have been influenced by Mann's findings, detailed in Chapter 5, that a unit of 20.425 feet was frequently used: this unit equals three times Thom's megalithic rod of 2.5 megalithic yards. While it is possible, especially as Mann and Thom were contemporaries and both living in Scotland, it cannot be said for certain.

Atkinson (1979) considered the evidence for the megalithic yard at Stonehenge and acknowledged that the builders had used some agreed measure but suggested that as the values of the megalithic yard had been known before, this was an *a posteriori* test, while Freeman (1976), from performing a Bayesian analysis of Thom's evidence, concluded that it could not be a universal measure. Another critique was that Thom overlooked the obvious simpler solution which was that the positions of the stones were established by pacing the ground, so Porteous (1973) devised a statistical test to show that the average pace was 33 inches (83.8 cm), very close to Thom's 'megalithic yard'. This seemingly insignificant point about different ideas on measurement actually represented much of what was wrong with Thom's thesis in the eyes of those interested archaeologists: his picture of 'megalithic man' was at odds with the evolutionary simple to complex version of humankind envisioned by the archaeologists, as noted earlier in Chapter 4. Indeed, as we have seen, this contradiction had already stirred controversy in the early 20th century.

Working backwards from alignments to declinations and then finding the date of a site from these declinations, Thom's findings were not in line with proposed archaeological dates for these monuments. For example at Avebury he suggested a date of 1600 BC based on an alignment to Deneb's setting position, though elsewhere he found alignments to Capella *c.* 1800 BC (Thom 1967; Thom *et al.* 1976). As Thom had found similar dates at other sites, at Kintyre, where he dated a major standstill alignment to 1580 BC, he felt '*confident*' enough to say that 'the *accurate* lunar and solar lines were all set up about this time' (Thom and Thom 1979, S98). When Morrison (1980) had re-assessed Thom's findings he suggested that, because of errors in Thom's calculations, the dating of the sightlines would have been between six and four centuries earlier than Thom's dates. Morrison's evidence pushed back the date of the monuments to the Early Bronze Age, though the archaeological dates, newly revised by radiocarbon dating, suggested dates earlier than this. However, at this time, few monuments had been radiocarbon dated and many dates were inferred from the dates found for similar monuments. For example, Burl's inferential date for Avebury, was 2600 BC; a full thousand years earlier than Thom's calculation (Burl 1979, 39). Thom's dating errors came about because his precision alignments of just minutes of arc with no leeway either side could only have one date and he fell into the same trap as Lockyer when he dated monuments by stellar alignments. However, Thom later concluded (1978a, 179) that 'the large range of possible dates makes it impossible to be certain of the association of a given alignment with a definite star', but this was rather too little too late.

Though Thom's work suggested the importance of lunar rather than solar alignments, he proposed not only that the activities of 'early man' were regulated by a solar calendar which depended on the marking of solar risings and settings but also suggested a further sub-division of the year into eight parts similar to the sequence of the Scottish Quarter days. More detailed than Lockyer's May year, as statistically some declinations were more prominent than others, Thom theorised that these were the verification for the megalithic year being divided into 16 equal parts of 22 or 23 days (Thom 1967, 109). He termed these periods 'epochs' or 'months' and found they related to the equinoxes, solstices and the quarter days. For clarity, it must be noted that Thom's 'quarter days', which refer to cultural divisions are not the same as the astronomical 'cross-quarter days', calculated arithmetically (see Glossary: sun). While Thom found evidence of his megalithic calendar at Carnac, his Shetland surveys gave the most convincing proof (Thom and Merritt 1978). MacKie was so convinced by Thom's idea of a prehistoric solar calendar that he made this part of his research until as recently as 2009 (Mackie 1988; 2009).

Despite Thom and MacKie making the case for the knowledge and creation of a calendar from observations of the movements of the sun, no calendar would have been required to regulate the social existence of megalithic society. The patterns and seasons of their lives would simply have been at one with the patterns and seasons in the heavens. This understanding would have been sufficient for subsistence hunting and gathering, early domestication of animals and herding or limited cultivation and agriculture. This is because the seasons and the life/death cycle are reflected in both breeding cycles in hunted or domesticated animals and growth cycles in crops. The similarity of the cycles observed in plant and animal life to those experienced by humankind may have given rise to affinities between people, affairs of the land and patterns in the sky, an encompassing animism which governed daily life and which was reflected in the monuments.

Overall, the Thom paradigm with all its different parts combined was an all-embracing and innovative practice within which its methodologies and theories were formalised. Thom had achieved this by imposing a set of disciplinary rules relating to the seven different elements of which it was comprised: elements that had previously been scattered through the literature. Although it did not advocate computer science as Hawkins had done, Thom's paradigm was applied to a large body of evidence from numerous sites and it was therefore far in advance of astro-archaeology which had mainly focused on Stonehenge.

New Age appropriations

In some ways, Thom's entire thesis was a gift to certain New Agers. The cycle of feast days adopted by pagan religions such as Wicca in the late 1950s linked New Age paganism with Thom's megalithic calendar which depicted the same cycle of dates. At the same time, with deft yet incomprehensible logic, Michell (1978, 121–122) associated Thom's metrology with Masonic numbers, harmony and the cabalistic number of fusion which culminated in his elaborate conclusion that linked the numerical scheme of Stonehenge with that of the Great Pyramid (see also Henty

2020a, 62) Obviously this was, as Hutton concluded, 'explicitly hostile to orthodox prehistory' (2013, 382). One can imagine that Thom would have been horrified at the way his work was misappropriated.

Michell (1989) first published *A Little History of Astro-Archaeology* in 1977 at the height of New Age interest in the mysteries of ancient monuments. Subtitled *Stages in the transformation of a heresy*, it tapped into this popular market which was still active when he updated it in 1989. In his new introduction, Michell described his book as an illustration of 'the beginnings of a subject new to scholarship, concerning the relationship of ancient monuments and temples to the positions of the heavenly bodies as observed by their builders' (1989, 6). He subverted the theories of both Hawkins and Thom to fit his own ideas about geomancy and esotericism; views which were the polar opposite of archaeological orthodoxy as well as being far removed from serious archaeoastronomy. At the same time as Thom was coming under the scrutiny of some archaeologists, his megalithic science was being appropriated by the Earth Mysteries movement and had a New Age following that he could never have foreseen. It is unclear how widely Thom's books were read by the general public but television programmes such the BBC's *Cracking the Stone Age Code* (aired in 1970; BBC Archive 2020), which featured Thom's work, would have promulgated his ideas to those who were already susceptible to esoteric solutions.

The rapid appropriation and subversion of Thom's meticulous scientific research by other popular writers might also have impeded the academic acceptance of megalithic science, by association. At one extreme of the popular genre was Michell and at the other was John Edwin Wood, whose semi-academic work, found Thom's version of prehistoric science 'particularly attuned to our own time' (Wood 1978, 200). Somewhere in the middle of the spectrum lies Keith Critchlow. Drawing on cross-cultural comparisons, geomancy and numerology, Critchlow concluded that the stone circle builders laid out 'a pattern of their cosmos' to gain an understanding of their 'role in the scheme of things' (2007, 99). Several other authors stepped on this popular bandwagon: Janet and Colin Bord, authors of *Mysterious Britain* (1972) and *The Secret Country* (1976) referred to the 'cosmic energies' at 'stone observatories', while Robert Temple (1976), writing about the Dogon, a tribe living in Mali who attached special importance to Sirius, suggested that the original stimulus for these beliefs was a visit to earth by extra-terrestrial amphibians 5000 or more years ago. Also Thom's work was the inspiration behind John Ivimy's *The Sphinx and the Megaliths* (1974) (Goodricke-Clarke 2011, 178–179). Consequently, a canon of pseudoscientific publications vied with the academic literature and as Heggie (1987a) reported, 'There is no shortage of rubbish to read on "ancient mysteries", and unfortunately such pseudo-science often seems to have a wide popular appeal'. The title of one of Michell's books, *Megalithomania* (2007), could be aptly used to describe the publications of this period.

Providing a contemporary commentary, E.C. Krupp explained this obsession with fantastical explanations as being 'the dual appeal of archaeology and astronomy, both their science and their romance' that made them susceptible to authors such as

Immanuel Velikovsky, Erich von Däniken and others (Krupp 1979, 219). For example, Velikovsky's (1950) catastrophist theory suggested a new celestial order following the purported ejection of Venus from Jupiter, while von Däniken (1969) suggested that some ancient monuments could not have been constructed by ancient builders but rather by extra-terrestrials. These authors, along with Maltwood and the ley-hunters with their 'unsubstantiated challenges to modern science' had generated interest in and support of archaeoastronomy (Krupp 1979, 5–6). That Krupp included this material in a book which attempted a serious overview of archaeoastronomy in the 1970s perhaps had the unintended result of creating an association between pseudoscience and archaeoastronomy.

Writing towards the end of height of the New Age, Pennick and Devereux described how the New Age following led to the archaeologists' further suspicion of the archaeoastronomy of the time:

> Because it is outside the accepted range of mainstream research, thus having no institutionalised form of protection or augmentation, the study of ancient alignments easily becomes prey to 'New Age' cultists, would-be gurus, 'soft' or popularist theoreticians and journalistic hacks. The nonsense that is often perpetrated by these elements reinforces and justifies the suspicion and prejudices already held by archaeologists and other academics. Thus a vicious circle is created, and the study area itself becomes the victim. (Pennick and Devereux 1989, 13)

Hutton (2013, 383) suggested that Thom's ideas, whether consciously or not, sometimes drew on those of the counterculture or reinforced them and cited Thom's suggestion, that Neolithic engineers could survey straight lines between mutually invisible points, as reinforcing the idea of ley lines; a point also made by Michell (1989, 79). However, having traced how esoteric ideas were transmitted from antiquarianism and revived in the early 20th century, the record suggests that Thom's esoteric ideas on metrology and the prehistoric calendar came from these sources rather than being influenced by the counterculture which, in turn, was given a new focus through his ideas. Similarly, there is no evidence to suggest that New Age esotericism was taken seriously by other archaeoastronomers who were trying to enhance their field of study by publishing scientific research. Yet Iwaniszewski (2008, 254) maintained that archaeoastronomical narratives have continued up until the present to feed the fervour of new-ageism, occultism and hermeticism. Despite this evidence, it is difficult to judge whether this New Age association hampered archaeoastronomy's inclusion in mainstream archaeological studies or whether archaeoastronomy was rejected for other reasons which will be explored.

The never-ending language gap

For the period of astro-archaeology and megalithic science, the language gulf between archaeoastronomers and archaeologists continued. For example, the very name astro-archaeology placed astronomy as being higher on the agenda than archaeology.

Similarly the term megalithic science was a token for megalithic astronomy and statistics and, as noted earlier, not only did archaeologists lag behind in these fields, but they neither spoke the same language nor used the astronomical notation that many of the archaeoastronomical papers exhibited. Also, the commonality between the fields was limited because Jacquetta Hawkes (1967, 176) doubted that many archaeologists were capable of understanding the complicated mathematical reasoning proposed in the astronomical theories, while Childe (1955, 293–294), in his comments on Thom's 1955 paper, observed the emotional reaction of archaeologists in general when faced with 'mathematical symbols'. This has relevance because Bernard Barber (1961, 599) viewed resistance to mathematics as one of the critical factors in the non-adoption of new ideas. Only Atkinson and MacKie took the matter seriously enough to decipher the language and make a contribution to the field. That specialised language was the barrier between archaeology and megalithic science is, however, a spurious argument, because it is unlikely that the archaeologists of that time would have been able to carry out radiocarbon or faunal analysis if not for teams of specialists, so there is no reason why they could not have employed archaeoastronomers for astronomical analyses. Nevertheless at the time, many commentators pointed to language as being one of the reasons the communities did not coalesce.

There was no dedicated home for prehistoric astronomy publications until 1970. The *Journal for the History of Astronomy* (hereafter JHA) was specifically founded to fill this gap and 'to encourage future research in the history of astronomy' (Hoskin 1970, 4). The journal, which became an important venue for Thom's publications, was the brainchild of Michael Hoskin who lectured in the history of astronomy at Cambridge University from 1959 to 1988. From its inception and up until 1978, 23 megalithic science papers, relating to British sites or those at Carnac, were published in it and 17 of these were written by Thom or in co-authorship with his son and other colleagues. Only three papers by other authors volunteered new research but they were either dependent on Thom's earlier surveys or took Thom's methodology as their starting point. The remaining three papers critiqued either the methodology or the findings of megalithic science. To cope with the increasing volume of submissions the *Archaeoastronomy Supplement* of the JHA was published between 1979 and 2002. The 15 related papers published between 1979 and 1985 included five by Thom but began to show a changing picture where his research played a less dominant role. Although the emphasis remained on megalithic science, more papers, especially those by Clive Ruggles, demonstrated a more rigorous adaptation of Thom's methodology, as will be shown later in Chapter 9. The journal made up for the initial dearth of archaeoastronomy books as apart from *Stonehenge Decoded* (Hawkins 1965a) nothing similar had been published since Lockyer. Thom's two books on megalithic astronomy acted as text-books and these were complemented by his collaborative work with Burl, MacKie's *Science and Society in Prehistoric Britain* (1977a) and Heggie's (1981b) themed volume on megalithic science. After decades of little output, these developments were quite phenomenal.

Meanwhile, from its small base in the previous era, archaeology had expanded into many university departments so had a strong community to ensure self-reproduction. New departments opened, such as Sheffield in 1963 and Glasgow in 1964, and archaeology responded to the need for specialists, with some universities organising 1 year masters courses in the 1980s. Additionally, archaeologists were in touch with their peers by coming together annually at the Theoretical Archaeology Group (TAG) conferences which had been born out of conversations between Colin Renfrew and Andrew Fleming (Fleming and Johnson 1990). The first of these was held in Sheffield in 1977. By contrast, there was no community to which British archaeoastronomers could belong.

Because of the impact of Hawkins' and Thom's research, commentators, who came from both within and outside the fields of archaeology and archaeoastronomy, began an impartial appraisal of megalithic science. In 1981, two books and two papers reviewed the field, which taken together represent a historical marker for when the need for a paradigm change became apparent. In the first book, Clive Ruggles and archaeologist Alasdair Whittle drew both astronomers and archaeologists together in its pages to describe the then current situation while acknowledging that the study of astronomical practices 'is only one line of evidence' (Ruggles and Whittle 1981, 11). In a preparatory paper the mathematician and astronomer Douglas Heggie (1981a) examined the detail of megalithic science and created a number of rules about intentionality and objective criteria for the choice of data. Similarly his book (1981b), in which several authors tested Thom's theories, was described by John Carlson, a prominent American archaeoastronomer, as a turning point in the debate; 'the advent of reasoned critique and evaluation by qualified individuals of diverse professional backgrounds' (Carlson 1982a, 45).

Ellegård's (1981) article on Stone Age science was also cited by Carlson as another example of the new climate in research. Ellegård's paper, with comments from 18 experts who represented astronomy, archaeology and anthropology, did not doubt the astronomical significance of the monuments, but again queried Thom's claims for the scientific knowledge attributed to the builders. In the same paper, historians of science Owen Gingerich and Stephen McCluskey argued that it was time to 'temper the present [methodology]' (119) to include more archaeology and ethnographic and historical data from other non-literate and non-numerate cultures. Ronald Hicks, archaeologist and anthropologist, in conjunction with his own work on the Irish stone circles and henge monuments, concluded that the only correct answer was that given earlier by Heggie who felt that orientations had a symbolic rather than an observational value – they were in the right direction for important risings and settings but were never intended to be accurate enough for precise observations (Hicks 1984, 191). Hicks added that the spread of measurements in Thom's original analysis reflected local or individual variations in the standard of measurement used and that whilst all the geometric shapes pinpointed by Thom existed, 'imprecision ... is most likely the result of the megalithic builders' inability to lay them out precisely to plan' (Hicks 1984, 199). The archaeological evidence indicated a considerable amount of regional diversity and that may have dictated both culture and architecture in different areas; a picture Hicks thought was inconsistent with Thom's standardised metrology. He concluded:

> To truly understand these monuments we cannot look only at the astronomy, the geometry, the metrology, the iconography, or the archaeology and the evidence for social organisation. We must look at all of these. Those who work on any one aspect must be aware of, and make a serious attempt to understand, the work being done on all the others. (Hicks 1984, 205)

Given these perspectives, the timing of an initiative to further the debate at international conferences was not coincidental: the first international interdisciplinary 'Oxford' conference on archaeoastronomy was held in 1981. This was inaugurated by Michael Hoskin who, in addition to his duties at JHA, was President of the History of Astronomy Commission of the International Astronomical Union, in conjunction with the International Union for the History and Philosophy of Science. According to Hoskin the location was chosen because it was a convenient base from which to visit Stonehenge and Avebury. It was the first in a series of roughly 4-yearly 'Oxford' conferences, but only the first one took place in Oxford.

Megalithic science – the debate

To answer the question why the prehistoric builders would want to make a connection on earth and in stone between their landscape and the skyscape called for an assessment of culture, ideology, ritual and religion. Neither megalithic science nor archaeology could emphatically provide the answers but Thom and his followers provided a new set of evidence which had previously been inaccessible in archaeology and for which there was no precedent. As we have seen, by the end of the 1950s, archaeology's version of prehistory was the mainstream orthodox position whereas astronomical studies had virtually disappeared from view, only briefly sitting on the sidelines. With the revelations of Hawkins and Thom, astro-archaeology and megalithic science found themselves in the limelight and not only under the scrutiny of the above commentators but of the leading prehistorians of the day.

The nub of the debate was prompted by an ethnocentric fallacy created by Hawkins, Hoyle and Thom: the idea that because their research into astronomical alignments required astronomical and mathematical knowledge, the megalith builders must have possessed the same scientific interest in and understanding of the cosmos that was otherwise unattested by the archaeological record. It led to diametrically opposing narratives and it was this opposition that drove the controversy. Yet having rejected Hawkins and Hoyle, many archaeologists found that they could not dismiss Thom so summarily and without due consideration. This was because Thom's research was presented as a large and coherent body of work about prehistoric astronomy from a surveyor using a traditional archaeological method combined with astronomy. His meticulous and detailed plans of hundreds of stone circles, many of which included archaeological details by Burl, deserved some respect, especially as he was providing detail on sites that archaeologists had little knowledge of. At the time, John Barber succinctly expressed the view that:

> Thomism is severely, even paradoxically, at odds with our archaeological view of the Neolithic period. They cannot be reconciled by any adaptation of the latter but rather demand a completely new Neolithic overview. (Barber 1976, 43)

Barber's statement begs the question of what specifically in 'Thomism' was so at odds with archaeology. As noted earlier, Thom's paradigm was a complicated mixture of theory and methodology and while some aspects could be accepted, others simply did not fit in with the archaeologists' understanding of prehistory. The first element of his paradigm was astronomy and this caused two problems. First there was the language barrier noted earlier in Chapter 1, but Atkinson (1975, 51) clarified the archaeological response as being not so much a lack of numeracy on their part but simply that Thom's view of prehistory did not fit the archaeological model. This was similar to the criticism delivered to Hawkins and Hoyle before it was levelled at Thom. Indeed, without Hawkins' fame and its catalyst effect it could be questioned whether the interest in Thom's work would have been so long-lived.

MacKie (1977b, 173) also agreed that Thom's theory was too different from the general picture of a relatively simple society, barbarian and rural, possibly with a ruling hierarchy 'but with no sign of the sophisticated, semi-civilised priesthood' that Thom's work implied. Secondly, it was Thom's ethnocentric vision of prehistoric science that was at the root of many of the criticisms against him, yet Atkinson (1966b, 216) conceded that the early development of science and metrology was an aspect which was 'too often undervalued'. The criticism was similarly tempered by Cunliffe (1973, 27) who proposed that Thom's theory that the builders 'were not only highly numerate but were also carrying out complex astronomical observations, need occasion no surprise'. However these supportive statements from archaeologists were in the minority and as Thom's megalithic science came as a package with skilled 'megalithic man' at the forefront, the archaeologists' overall rejection of this aspect meant that most of them were not inclined to pursue the remainder of his paradigm. In hindsight, Atkinson (1986) noted the overall impact of these critiques when he suggested that errors in one field have no bearing on the others but that many of Thom's critics took a single error to invalidate the whole.

Concerned primarily with their own discipline which, with the advent of processualism meant asking new questions about prehistory that the new scientific techniques could help answer, the archaeologists were pre-occupied. For example, Ritchie (2009) suggested that archaeology was too beset by its own problems of classification and dating to be ready for the type of statistical testing that archaeoastronomers advocated for groups of sites. This situation, together with the idea fostered earlier by Christopher Hawkes and reaffirmed by Glyn Daniel that the mental and spiritual realms of prehistoric people could not be inferred or accessed meant that there was not an overly welcoming atmosphere for Thom's suppositions. However the hostility shown towards astro-archaeology was not replicated, as demonstrated by the way some archaeologists wrote about the problem, while trying to find a solution. Piggott (1974b, 275) advocated dialogue, adding that without care, 'we [the archaeologists] will find alinements as meaningless as the 'old straight tracks of Alfred Watkins'; while Atkinson (1975) recommended collaboration between astronomers and prehistorians.

Nevertheless the recommendation by Hammersley in Thom's 1955 paper (Hammersley 1955), that the 'existing foundations of the orthodox structure' would need to be re-examined was not taken up until 14 years later when the archaeological community began to organise symposia to examine the impact of Thom's ideas, the first being held in Glasgow in 1969 (MacKie 1988, 209). This was closely followed in December the same year by an interdisciplinary conference, sponsored by the Royal Society and the British Academy, entitled *The Impact of the Natural Sciences on Archaeology*. There were others in the same vein, such as a bi-national symposium on *Mathematics in the Archaeological and Historical sciences*, organised by the Royal Society and the Romanian Academy in 1970 and *The Place of Astronomy in the Ancient World*, jointly convened by the British Academy and the Royal Society, in 1972. Leading archaeologists such as Piggott, Atkinson and Daniel were on the latter's organising committee and, in his concluding remarks, King-Hele acknowledged that the purpose of the conference was to build bridges between scientists and historians. He added that in the past disciplines tended to become 'intellectual islands, on which were cultivated more and more specialized plants', so advances could be made by allowing a new light to shine on old problems (King-Hele 1974, 273–274). As evidenced from these conferences, it would seem that these archaeologists were not predisposed to dismiss megalithic science immediately and Daniel even invited Thom to Brittany to survey the Carnac alignments in 1970. Five years elapsed before a similar conference took place in 1975, which MacKie (1976, 136) optimistically and erroneously described as a turning point in which the field of pre-literate geometry and astronomy would be more widely accepted as another branch of archaeology.

This short period which saw the two fields coming together led Hawkins to agree that although the subject matter called on the disciplines of astronomy, mathematics, archaeology, ethnology and mythology, 'one gained the impression that one was dealing with a single, coherent area of study' (Hawkins 1973, 214). This cohesion was further demonstrated by Ruggles and Whittle's edited volume (1981), mentioned earlier, which was based on some of the papers from the 1979 conference in Newcastle-upon-Tyne. Entitled *Megalithic Astronomy and Society* it was the last conference of its kind. Apparently the stimulus behind the conference was a 2-year course on the 'Age of Stonehenge' tutored by Colin Burgess and Gordon Moir. However there were no further collaborations; neither was heed paid to MacKie's implicit suggestion that archaeoastronomy could be a subdiscipline of archaeology.

While other archaeologists had been debating Thom's paradigm, Mackie put it into practice and published his own scholarly contribution to the debate. Cautiously and critically agreeing with the majority of Thom's conclusions he tested them with his own archaeological and astronomical surveys at Kintraw (MacKie 1974). He replaced Thom's 'megalithic man' with astronomer-priests, a term possibly borrowed from Lockyer. MacKie's diffusionist view was that immigrant priests, who mixed with the Neolithic farming peoples, established 'a new sky-oriented religion with a basis in exact astronomical observation' (MacKie 1977b, 185). However, most ideas on diffusion had been overturned by the new dates discovered through radiocarbon dating, so MacKie swam against the tide of orthodoxy on both accounts. Any optimism previously generated was undermined when Gordon Moir pointed out that, although MacKie had tried to integrate archaeoastronomy into the archaeological record, his example was not taken up by other archaeologists. Although many of them accepted orientations they disputed the idea of accurate alignments because, as Moir (1980, 7) suggested, they 'see little need to overthrow existing ideas on prehistory to accommodate possible Neolithic astronomers'. He personally felt that Thom's 'hypotheses lack credibility, the methodology is suspect and the evidence poor'.

Like MacKie, Burl bridged the gap between archaeology and astronomy, being described as an archaeologist who ensured that the astronomy fitted the archaeology, not the other way round (Heggie 1982a, S69). However, despite his connection with Thom, Burl portrayed a different picture of megalithic culture in his book, *Rings of Stone* (1979), so that Gingerich (1980) gleaned the impression that Burl had conducted a solid case against prehistoric scientific society and high-precision astronomy. Nevertheless in 1983, Burl concluded that archaeoastronomy had become a respectable study and was 'no longer regarded as an activity of the lunatic fringe', and added that it 'now needs to become a respectable discipline' (Burl 1983, 42, 47). Ritchie agreed, believing that the way forward for both archaeology and archaeoastronomy was a joint programme where archaeologists took responsibility for site-interpretation, classification and chronology and archaeoastronomers supplied site-surveys and horizon-plotting: only then would statistical evaluation of groups of sites with astronomical potential be possible (Ritchie 2009, 40). Heggie (1981a) went further by suggesting that archaeoastronomy was a specialism that should be subsumed within archaeology when he wrote that the study of megalithic astronomy was part of the overall study of megalithic monuments so should be 'the business of prehistorians and archaeologists'. There is no evidence to suggest that these suggested solutions were actioned, so the opportunity was lost. However, Heggie was of the opinion that Thom's ideas stimulated archaeological research projects, statistical analyses and large-scale excavations. Ritchie concurred, stressing that Thom had spurred archaeologists to be more meticulous in recording details, but it would only be when the two worked together would statistical evaluation of groups of sites with astronomical potential be possible.

Three elements of Thom's paradigm, metrology, geometry and advanced astronomical knowledge, were subject to a combined scrutiny and rejection. By the end of this period, many archaeologists and other experts alike had, with due diligence, scrutinised the praxis of megalithic science and found it either extraneous to their own or in need of serious change. Nevertheless the literature reveals that a few archaeologists, in addition to MacKie and Burl, took astronomy into account in their reports, but these were the exceptions to the rule. For example, in 1978, Peter Topping, the archaeologist excavating the cursus at Scorton in Yorkshire, found a post-hole which he felt could represent 'the remains of some form of surveying marker' and, touching on archaeoastronomy, wrote that 'a system of uprights would lead the eye up the rising ground to a possible focal point … on the horizon' (cited by Pennick and Devereux 1989, 73). Similarly the archaeologist Michael Wysocki found a post-hole at Crickley Hill thought to house a post tall enough to cast a shadow the length of the long mound perhaps at midsummer sunrise (Pennick and Devereux 1989, 76).

Notwithstanding the initial good will on both sides which led to the joint conferences, after sustained criticism the paths of the archaeologists and archaeoastronomers diverged and they both went their separate ways either to the TAG meetings or to the 'Oxford' conferences. The position was summed up by Pedersen (2009) who noted that there was a polarisation between those who wholeheartedly adopted archaeoastronomy and those who could not take its claims seriously.

The implications for archaeoastronomy

Megalithic science was not only a challenge but was too different from the mainstream orthodox view of prehistory to be subsumed as a specialism, unlike other specialisms such as archaeobotany or landscape archaeology which came into being around the same time. In other words archaeology and megalithic science, after a full airing, were found to be incommensurable. As already noted, the focus of archaeology at that time was on social and economic processes and Thom's metanarrative of a universal culture of prehistoric astronomy and metrology simply did not fit the archaeological narrative. Additionally, although some archaeologists, such as Renfrew (1981), recognised that many prehistoric monuments contained alignments to the solstices and standstills, they were simply not interested in astronomy and to them the alignments seemed simple enough to require no special study (Hutton 2013, 378). It was the theory clash that was more important than the differing methodological approaches, because, stripped of its most extreme components, the ability to test sites for astronomical alignments could have been a useful tool. There was some irony in this as 1970's archaeoastronomy was very much focused on a methodological approach in tune with processualism, as noted in Chapter 6. The archaeological subdisciplines had been developed in order to answer archaeological questions about the material record through the use of new specialised techniques but, in general, as archaeologists were not asking questions about the sky or the symbolic aspect of sites, they had no need for archaeoastronomy and it remained outside their domain.

However, the debate was more than an argument about the incompatible approaches of science and non-science, as it had contestation at its heart. Both archaeologists and astronomers were studying the same material remains and drew on the same primary sources but they contested each other's narratives. Contestation led to what Hoskin (1976, 222) described as 'polarised attitudes' which made it difficult for Thom to receive a fair hearing. Similarly, Hawkins got to the nub of the problem when he wrote of the difficulties which arise 'when one discipline – astronomy – suddenly impinges on another – prehistory' (Hawkins 1980, S97). While arguments about incommensurability are useful, they draw attention away from the competing explanations proposed by Hawkins and Thom. While Hawkins' speculations had caused a storm, they were soon dismissed, but the reactions to Thom's thesis lasted for nearly three decades. This was partly because Thom's work, based on meticulous fieldwork, showed great knowledge of the prehistoric sites that came under the archaeologists' purview so could have usefully added to the existing facts of Scottish archaeology. At that time archaeology in Scotland, according to Barclay (2001, 11), was neglected in Piggott's book on Neolithic culture (1954b) in favour of southern England because there was inadequate evidence. From the archaeological perspective, Clarke's opinion was that if there were alternative models and rival paradigms which led to 'discordant new information' they had to be subject to 'due debate' rather than being suppressed (Clarke 1973, 6, 11). There had been much debate, but the result was that archaeological orthodoxy won the day and archaeoastronomy became subjugated knowledge, seemingly irrelevant to archaeology.

The ensuing rift, if rift it was, was based on a myth created by Hawkins and Thom: the idea that monument building was carried out by an elite class of specialised astronomer-priests who recorded their findings in stone. By propounding their theories Hawkins and Thom were trespassers on the hallowed grounds of archaeologists yet this new divide which opened up in the 1970s and the ensuing bitter debates were not new, they were a strengthening of attitudes which had been entrenched since Lockyer. In hindsight, Hutton highlighted the episode as a lesson in the politics of knowledge, expressed by the relationships between 'different kinds of professional scholar, between popular and academic culture, and between mainstream society and a counter-culture', concluding that the interaction between attitudes engendered by different 'disciplines', seems to have been more important than has generally been acknowledged (Hutton 2013, 393–394). A further example of how this played out with regard to other groups who approached the past from different perspectives, was noted by Behrend (2013b) when introducing a facsimile copy of the debate between Michell and Burl on ley lines, first aired in *Popular Archaeology*, 1983. Burl's final comment was that ley lines were 'prime examples of wishful thinking and the "evidence" for them was as insubstantial and implausible as the powers attributed to them'. The sheer weight of the popular pseudoscience at the time may have reinforced the archaeologists' retreat to the safety of their own orthodox views.

Thom's paradigm certainly flew in the face of archaeological orthodoxy and there were further reasons for it not being accepted. For example, there was a reluctance to admit the importance of the work of a non-archaeologist; a failure to distinguish Thom's work from that of the 'lunatic fringe', while at the same time, megaliths were of a minority interest even to most archaeologists (Heggie 1987b, 181). While these are all reasons that add to the complexity of the issue, the importance of orthodoxy and contestation cannot be overstated. Towards the end of the debate, Daniel from his position as editor of *Antiquity*, believing that the case for astronomical observatories had not been proven, made an attempt to put the archaeological record straight and to enforce the establishment view (Daniel 1980). While earlier he had suggested that archaeologists must give Thom's work serious consideration, he reversed his position at this time, saying it was not astronomy but advancements in radiocarbon dating that had revolutionised the picture of megalithic monuments. The opinion of Daniel, an eminent prehistorian, would have carried a great deal of weight in the archaeological community. By this time the debate had ended with most archaeologists having lost interest, but they left a legacy of some name-calling with archaeoastronomers reportedly being labelled 'archaeoastronomy buffs' and 'butterfly collectors', with Daniel (1980, 85) calling the whole field 'astronaut archaeology'.

Had their different narratives dovetailed they could have provided a much fuller picture of prehistoric culture than any that had previously been proposed. However, both fields utilised the knowledge gained through scientific methods to different ends. Archaeology explained cultural evidence in a positivist and empiricist way to rewrite their interpretation of prehistory. Megalithic science attempted to do the same but its results were predicated on an ethnocentric fallacy in which the ideas contained within archaeoastronomy were projected back onto the prehistoric builders themselves, giving the idea that they too possessed scientific and astronomical skills. This was the great flaw in the theory of megalithic astronomy: the fault did not lie with the scientific methods that both archaeology and archaeoastronomy developed.

Archaeology was simply positioned as the dominant discipline with a stronghold in universities and although megalithic science was even practised by Atkinson and MacKie, there is no evidence that it was ever really considered an essential mode of research for archaeology, even as a subdiscipline. To explain the archaeologists' reluctance some pointers can be taken from a paper by Bernard Barber. Barber (1961) theorised that if scientists are in the habit of thinking in their own conceptual models, then there is resistance to changing that model to fit new ideas. That archaeology did not change its model to admit archaeoastronomy seems to prove Barber's point. Furthermore he pointed to social reasons that come into play when discoveries are made by those of a lower standing than the qualified authorities, similar to the resistance by insiders to outsiders (Barber 1961, 599–601). This point particularly applies to the case of Newham and more generally to Hawkins and Thom. Additionally,

Barber suggested that publications have a role in furthering resistance to innovation. In this particular debate, this is illustrated first by the case where Daniel prevented the publication of Newham's work and secondly by the fact that, after 1966, no archaeoastronomy research was published in *Antiquity*. However impartial the original debate was, some of these considerations may have had an effect on the eventual sidelining of archaeoastronomy.

By contrast, in the same period every element of archaeology's praxis appeared more confident, self-assured and well-defined; a position from which it could experiment with various theories and develop associated scientific practices and sub-disciplines. It instituted learning courses to ensure continuity, had grown in numbers and become professionalised. With a growing number of textbooks, journals and the newly established TAG conferences, all of which supported a common language community, its position as a mainstream discipline and owner of the orthodox view of prehistory was seemingly unassailable. The Institute of Field Archaeologists was founded in 1982 partly as a result of the need to develop clear boundaries between amateurs and the professionals who were seeking legitimacy (Sayer 2014, 58). Unlike the professional archaeologists almost all of megalithic science's researchers were 'part-time, retired or amateur' (Ruggles, 1981a, 485). However, although Thom was an amateur he contributed sufficient scholarly work, to be regarded as an academic.

The archaeoastronomers became distanced from the archaeologists for other reasons. The joint conferences had ended; output in shared journals, such as *Antiquity* and *Nature*, ceased and while JHA and its *Archaeoastronomy Supplement* provided a home for archaeoastronomy which was a positive factor for astronomical studies, its foundation effectively removed archaeoastronomy from the archaeologists' view. Whether this was censorship or circumstance will never be known. Nevertheless, archaeoastronomy gained ground at this time. Although Thom did not call his research megalithic science, it was identified by this disciplinary name. Overall it became an autonomous, self-referential field which contained a unique paradigmatic subject with its own methods, theory, specific terminologies and language. Furthermore, Thom's first three books were deemed to be of sufficient academic quality to be published by Oxford University Press, with his last two volumes being published by British Archaeological Reports. Because Thom's *Megalithic Sites in Britain* (1967) and *Megalithic Lunar Observatories* (1971) specified everything that was needed to understand the methodology, they functioned as text-books with the field being described in hindsight as a 'legitimate new area of scholarship' and a 'respectable subject' (Carlson *et al.* 1999, 47). Certainly this period in archaeoastronomy's history was the most fertile to date so the archaeoastronomers that followed Hawkins and Thom inherited a combination of a strict fieldwork regime, computer and statistical methodology together with revised theories about the sun and the moon. The assessments of Thom's paradigm by both archaeologists and commentators left the field open for revisioning: it just needed to iron out its difficulties to evolve.

Chapter 8

New World archaeoastronomy

With ever increasing globalisation it seems almost anachronistic to talk about the Old and the New Worlds today. Yet in the 1970s and 1980s these terms were used to describe the differences between Old World (Britain and Europe) and New World (North and South America) archaeoastronomies. While British scholars were still dealing with the aftermath of megalithic science, in the Americas studies of similar relationships between events in the celestial sphere and those on the ground, gleaned from extant remains, historical texts and ethnography, were forging ahead. If evidence from Britain had demonstrated that the power of the sky had had such a strong impact on ancient civilisations, then it seemed obvious that similar evidence could be found in the Americas which had a rich and varied cultural heritage. As Ed Krupp (1984, 1–2) suggested at the time, the sky put meaning into the world and made it comprehensible so that it consequently became interwoven into traditions, temples, tombs and tales. As the lifecycle from birth, growth, maturation and death was a cycle as dependable as the cycles in the heavens, Krupp believed that the heavens provided a metaphor for life on earth. In other words symbolic thought and action are an expression of a culture's cosmology at a certain snapshot in time. Archaeoastronomy in the Americas therefore sought to unpack the particular and varied worldviews that were embedded and immortalised at different locations by particular symbolic monuments, carvings and paintings. In a similar vein, Travis Hudson (1984) used ethnographic examples from the Californian Indians to argue that understanding the origins of complex astronomies could shed light on the roots of science among ancient peoples. Hudson's work was the first detailed description of indigenous Californian astronomy and was informative in showing that as hunter-gatherers the Indians had a long-standing involvement with the sky.

This cultural and ethnographic basis for research, so lacking in British studies of alignment hunting, was characteristic of New World archaeoastronomy. The reason for this was two-fold. First, archaeology in the Americas was situated under the larger umbrella of anthropology so was therefore more concerned with why things happened, with processes and behaviour and the cultural environment in which the behaviour took place. Secondly, New World research was conducted on a much broader basis than its British counterpart as it covered the examination of the remains of a number of diverse indigenous cultures, some of which still had living descendants, as noted in Chapter 4. The area of study covered Mesoamerica which included Mayan and pre-Columbian South America. For example, much of southern Mexico, Guatemala, El Salvador and Honduras was ruled by the Aztecs until the Spaniards arrived in 1519. The ancestors of the modern Mayan people lived in southern Mexico and northern Central America while the Incas occupied Peru and western South America. Peru was also home to the Nazca culture which is famous for its ceremonial site Cahuachi and the enigmatic Nazca lines (Fig. 19). In the Mayan civilisation the discovery of the use of astronomy in sites, combined with interpretations gleaned from ancient books called codices, established the importance of the sky to these cultures. In addition there were the cultures of indigenous North American Indians and those of the American Southwest, home to the antecedents of modern Pueblo peoples (Kelley and Milone 2005). The most famous example of these is at Chaco Canyon, New Mexico, where Chimney Rock (Malville 2015a) and Fajada Butte (Zeilik 1985) are also located. More than three dozen circular stone medicine wheels were the focus of John Eddy's (1974b) research. Thought to be constructed by early Plains Indians they are found from northern Colorado to Alberta and Saskatchewan.

The time periods covered by these studies included prehistory, the early historic period and the recent past. Their very variety demanded different ways of looking at them together with new methods after the realisation that there was more to look

Figure 19. The Nazca ceremonial site Cahuachi in Peru, 2017. Photo: Alejandro López.

at in the sky than the sun and the moon; one size, for example the Thom paradigm did not fit all. Indeed, the acknowledged expert in the field of Mayan studies, Sir Eric J. Thompson (1974, 94), was sceptical about the use of intentional astronomic alignments. Because the new research combined archaeology, ethnography, history and anthropology alongside the traditional astronomical method, researchers were able to utilise the resources of these disciplines to provide a more comprehensive approach than the one in Britain which relied on astronomical alignments alone. Clearly the time was right to find a new name for this burgeoning cross-disciplinary field.

Archaeoastronomy

Astronomical studies of monuments which, in less than a decade, had changed their name from orientation studies to astro-archaeology and then to megalithic science, were subsequently renamed archaeoastronomy in 1971; a designation which has now endured for 50 years. The term archaeoastronomy was initially coined by Euan MacKie at the end of January 1971 to represent 'the study of astronomical practices in ancient times' (MacKie 1971, 120). In this review of Thom's *Megalithic Lunar Observatories*, he proposed it as a replacement for Hawkins' term 'astro-archaeology', which he felt was misleading. This renaming was taken up quite quickly in America, primarily because of Elizabeth Baity's seminal paper entitled 'Archaeoastronomy and ethnoastronomy so far', published in 1973. The separate but related field of ethnoastronomy which merged astronomy, texts, sky lore, ethnology and iconography to explain sky-related practices and phenomena was named at the same time. Nine years after Baity's paper, John B. Carlson (1982b, 2) noted that as neologisms the terms 'archaeoastronomy and ethnoastronomy' were still in the process of defining themselves; an opinion confirmed by the fact that archaeoastronomy did not appear in the *Oxford English Dictionary* until 1989.

MacKie told me that it was at his suggestion that the name archaeoastronomy was used by Baity as a description for this 'new subdiscipline', born as 'a direct interaction between astronomy, engineering, and archaeology'. In her paper, Baity summarised the work completed to date by Hawkins, Hoyle, Thom and others, concluding that 'the Stonehenge controversy and its aftermath' showed the necessity for interdisciplinary work in archaeology (Baity 1973, 394). Additionally Baity drew on worldwide research to demonstrate that studies which did not examine cultures' relationship with the sky were necessarily incomplete, suggesting that archaeoastronomy, combined with insights from ethnoastronomy, afforded the possibility of a new dimension in archaeology which would be 'the addition of astronomy to the archaeologists' conceptual tools'. Her criteria for a 'scientific subdiscipline' were 'an appropriate methodology' and text-books; both of which megalithic science had achieved, so in her view archaeoastronomy could 'move ahead on the basis of methods, criteria, [and] data' (Baity 1973, 418–419).

Baity sent copies of her synopsis to 50 scholars and included 18 of their diverse reactions which provide a picture of how archaeoastronomy was viewed at the time in North America particularly. For example, Anthony Aveni reported he saw real progress in the new 'interdiscipline' as a result of cooperation between scholars 'each schooled in his own discipline' (Aveni 1973, 431). However, Breternitz (1973, 432), an American archaeologist, suggested that the subject matter was 'somewhat esoteric', while Geoffrey Clark commented that the field suffered from 'a plethora of competing and alternative hypotheses'. As he pointed out,

> What constitutes patterning is determined ultimately by the paradigm under which the investigator is operating: change the paradigm, and you change the nature of the data and its consequent patterning ... Until the theoretical/ interpretative framework is overhauled, the potential latent in the battery of techniques for doing archaeoastronomy cannot be fully realized. (Clark 1973, 432)

Reyman (1973, 436) agreed that archaeoastronomical research was data-driven, not problem-oriented, with a dearth of hypotheses dealing with why there was interest in the sky and what it might mean in terms of 'cultural-ecological adaptations'. On the other hand, Dean Snow added that the importance of Baity's article was that it probably marked the end of the 'specimen collecting' stage in the development of the subdiscipline (Snow 1973, 438). Generally optimistic in tone, Baity's paper was an historical marker which drew a line under what had gone before and offered guidelines for how archaeoastronomy could progress in the future. This evidence suggests that in North America archaeoastronomy was viewed as a specialised field, an ancillary of archaeology, rather than it being a distinct discipline operating on its own terms. It also hints that at this time there was not complete consensus within the field.

Up until then archaeoastronomical surveys had relied on finding alignments with little heed to their relationship with local associated beliefs and practices and this was what ethnoastronomy aimed to uncover. In agreement, Anthony Aveni (1978, 593) stressed the need to establish ethnographic and ethnohistorical bases for archaeoastronomical enquiries, concluding that archaeoastronomy is 'a branch of cultural anthropology and ought to be treated that way'. It was particularly suited to uncovering material about ancient peoples in the New World, particularly South America, where there was a wealth of historical data relating to the pre-Columbian cultures through texts written at the time of the European conquests, as well as information that could be gleaned from the indigenous descendants of that time. The main ethnohistorical chronicles were held in Spain and Portugal but they were made accessible to Latin American researchers in the early 1970s, which added strength to their work. While ethnographic research in general is ideal for a historical approach, ethnoastronomy adds extra detail because it particularly examines any vestiges of astronomy, whether it be alignments, myth, iconography or social mores present within the society studied. It also requires setting aside Western preconceptions to 'see' other conceptual universes (López 2011, 41). Although Baity wrote about the categories of archaeoastronomy and ethnoastronomy, she acknowledged that there was not a sharp line between the two (Baity 1973, 402) and her subdivision was probably made to distinguish it from the greater part of her article which was spent in detailing the history of megalithic science in Europe. In the New World the division should have been a moot point and Carlson was later of the opinion that no meaningful demarcation could be made between the two (Carlson *et al.* 1999, 3). However, at that early stage, a number of researchers, such as Morley (1956), Dow (1967) and Hartung (1969), proceeded along the old lines of simply discovering alignments. Nevertheless, while New World archaeoastronomy and ethnoastronomy, as portrayed by Baity, seemed to be in their infancy with no consistent schedule of investigations nor complete agreement on the methodology to be used, the possibilities for the future were obvious.

Figure 20. Anthony Aveni surveying at Castillo de Teayo in the state of Veracruz, Mexico beside a Huastec carved relief, January 1979. Photo: E.C. Krupp.

New World archaeoastronomy was later strengthened by a large number of researchers, though Broda (1991a) credited Anthony Aveni's importance in fostering the growth of this complex field. Now Russell Colgate Distinguished Professor Emeritus of Astronomy, Anthropology and Native American Studies, Aveni has taught these subjects there from 1963. He is widely recognised as one of the founders of Mesoamerican archaeoastronomy and his numerous insights on the field have helped further New World archaeoastronomy generally (Fig. 20).

From its very inception there was the recognition that interdisciplinary collaboration could have a beneficial effect and consequently American archaeoastronomy had a further reach than that in Britain. Baity had already tapped into this interdisciplinary potential and Carlson endorsed this view, concluding:

> It [archaeoastronomy] yields results at the interfaces between many traditional disciplines and makes contributions in unexpected....ways. These new results enrich not only the individual disciplines but also contribute to the general understanding of the origins of science and the roots of human culture. (Carlson 1979a, 9)

Carlson also thought it was beneficial for archaeoastronomers to have a working knowledge of the language and scholarship of other related fields. In this respect, American archaeoastronomy was in advance of its Old World cousin, because it included ethnoastronomy and recognised the need for interdisciplinary cooperation from the start. For example, the papers from the 1983 Northridge Conference on archaeoastronomy published later as *Earth and Sky* (Benson and Hopkinson 1985) highlighted the 'crucial role of ethnography', which received a strong emphasis in the papers (Williamson 1987).

Ethnoastronomy

In Latin America the picture was somewhat different as there had already been a long tradition of research into its large range of different monuments and cultures, as part of archaeological, ethnographic and myth study in general. Though traditionally there was a split between highland and lowland areas in these studies, after it was realised that there was an important interaction between the two the studies became more heterogeneous. Despite this, the earliest studies of the Andean region tended to use archaeoastronomical methods whereas in the rest of South America they tended to employ ethnoastronomy. This separation can be evidenced by where the studies appeared in the published literature, with archaeoastronomy being associated with archaeological literature while ethnoastronomy research was found in ethnography publications (López, pers. comm.) While of course each nation has a slightly different timeline, research began early in the 20th century with Martin Gusinde, an Austrian anthropologist, who worked in Tierra del Fuego between the 1910s and 1930s, becoming the leading expert on its indigenous culture (see for example Gusinde 1922). Other early researchers included Nordenskiöld, a Swedish scholar who worked mainly in Argentina, Peru and Bolivia in the 1910s and 1920s and León Cadogan, a Paraguayan ethnologist whose foundational research on the cosmovision of the Guaraní was conducted over 50 years between the 1920s and 1970s (see also references to early work in Chapter 4). Cadogan's book *Ayvu Rapyta* (1959), written in the Mbyá Guarani language, recorded the myths and religious tradition of these Paraguayan peoples. Then there was Alfred Métraux (1946) who made an enormous contribution relating to the worldview of Chaco groups; research which was later followed by Tomasini's (1997) exploration of shamanism in the Nivaklé Chacoan culture. Contemporaneously, Grebe Vicuña's (1998) ethnographic study of the Chilean indigenous cultures, explained the Mapuche worldview. While astronomical knowledge was considered in general in these works, it was at the forefront in Robert Lehmann-Nitsche's monographs of the early 20th century (López, pers. comm.).

Archaeoastronomical studies in Mexico were expanded by Franz Tichy from the 1960s onwards (see for example Tichy 1993) and by Hortz Hartung in his 1971 book, *The Diœ Zeremonialzentren der Maya* (*Mayan Ceremonial Centres*), where he proposed that the buildings were oriented astronomically to ensure balance and harmony. The Austrian archaeologist Johanna Broda made Mexico her home in the late 1960s and has produced a large volume of work relating to Aztec archaeoastronomy (see for example, Broda 1969; 1991b). Stanislaw Iwaniszewski, Ivan Sprajc, Jesús Galindo Trejo and others have expanded this work and put their own stamp on it. In Peru, Reiner Tom Zuidema published his doctoral thesis on the Ceque System of Cuzco in 1964 and continued publishing his research on the Inca civilisation up until his death in 2016 (see for example Zuidema 1964; 1990). Aveni, so influential for archaeoastronomy in North America, also published a series of papers on Inca astronomy in the early 1980s (see for example Aveni 1981a) but, according to López (pers. comm.), they were largely ignored by the local researchers in favour of work written in Spanish, published around the same time. Slightly earlier the theses of the anthropologists Stephen and Christine Hugh-Jones appeared; both with a strong astronomical and cosmological content relating to the cultures in Columbia and Brazil in the northwest regions of the Amazon (S. Hugh Jones, 1979; C. Hugh-Jones 1979). New areas, such as the Caribbean were also being explored by Edmundo Magaña (1984) and Fabiola Jara (1987). In 1992, the North American anthropologist Stephen Fabian published *Space-time of the Bororo of Brazil*, an important ethnoastronomical study of the Eastern Bororo Indians of Mato Grosso, Brazil. In the same year, Brian Bauer (1992) revisited the Inca ceque system, continuing this research in collaboration with David Dearborn (Bauer and Dearborn 1995).

According to López (pers. comm.), the contemporary period of Latin American ethnoastronomical research began at the end of the 1990s, but this was surely prompted by the long history of seminal research, briefly summarised above, which came before it. Recent archaeoastronomical investigations have been those carried out in Chile, by, for example, Bustamente, sometimes working in collaboration with Boccas or Moyano (Boccas *et al.* 2000; Moyano 2002; Bustamente 2013). For Bolivia and Ecuador, recent research has been boosted by Pereira (2004) and Christóbal Cobo (2008) respectively. Importantly, for the discipline as a whole, there was a new methodological manual, *Patterns in the Sky: an introduction to ethnoastronomy*, by Fabian (2001). Up until this time, most of the research effort had been towards collecting data anthropologically from cultures that were fast becoming affected by the intrusions of modern day living, but now there was a revisioning which put more focus on theory (see for example Iwaniszewski 2011; López 2011). New anthropological theory, related to ontology and the ontological turn (see for example Alberti *et al.* 2011; Holbraad and Pedersen 2017) may provide insights and a new way of working in Latin American anthropology and ethnoastronomy, though this may be difficult to accomplish.

The above-named authors singled out here, only provide a tiny snapshot of the work that was being carried out in different areas of South America throughout the

20th century and in the first two decades of the 21st century. There are too many pioneers of Latin American anthropology, archaeoastronomy and ethnoastronomy to acknowledge all of them by name but they have all played their part in providing a strong foundation for the methods used and the questions asked today. While Americans in the USA, such as Aveni and Carlson highlighted the importance of ethnography in archaeoastronomical studies, they seemed to be unaware that anthropology and ethnography had been at the heart of Latin American studies right from their very beginning: accordingly ethnoastronomy seemed a more fitting name than archaeoastronomy.

Communities

For an emerging field to have authority, legitimacy and recognition it needs to be institutionalised. Not only that but it has to demonstrate its autonomy from other disciplines through forming field-specific associations, hosting conferences, having dedicated journals and publishing books. By the early 1980s, North American archaeoastronomy had achieved all these milestones and achieved what Aveni (1981b, 57) called 'the appropriate cultural underpinning'.

The Center for Archaeoastronomy

Almost from the very start, American archaeoastronomy benefitted from institutional backing with the establishment of The Center for Archaeoastronomy at the University of Maryland in 1978. Aiming 'to advance research, education, and public awareness of archaeoastronomy', the Center was within and supported by three of the university's academic divisions; Mathematical and Physical Sciences and Engineering; Arts and Humanities; and Behavioural and Social Sciences (Carlson 1979b). The Center's primary mission was to,

> foster the interdisciplinary approach in research and education towards the understanding and appreciation of the astronomies, sky lore, and world-views not only of ancient peoples but also of the rapidly-vanishing indigenous cultures of our world. (Carlson 1978, 1)

The idea to found the Center was primarily the brainchild of John B. Carlson and Ray Williamson who were also the editors of the *Archaeoastronomy Bulletin*, which was first published in 1977. As the Center's primary function was to promote interdisciplinary understanding of the astronomies of a variety of cultures through diverse methods, at Maryland, Snow's two cultures came together and American archaeoastronomy benefitted as a result. American archaeoastronomers also promoted the discipline through their publications and courses. For example, Aveni's *Skywatchers of Ancient Mexico* (1983) was described as serving a 'serious pedagogical purpose' in presenting the fundamental principles of positional astronomy necessary for archaeoastronomy, which could be useful 'as a supplementary text in college-level courses which were seriously concerned with archaeoastronomy' (Hively 1981, 205).

There is some evidence that archaeoastronomy also appeared on other university curricula at that time: at the Center of Archaeoastronomy when Carlson was Adjunct Professor at the University of Maryland, he taught several interdisciplinary courses related to astronomy in culture (Fig. 21). Another two courses came under the respective tuition of Derral Mulholland at the University of Texas and David Kelley and Eugene Milone at the University of Calgary, while there was also there was a BS degree in archaeoastronomy at the University of Washington, Seattle. Through this development, Hicks (2006) was of the opinion that New World studies had 'moved into the mainstream' of archaeological and anthropological study and added that by 1996 there were other courses available such as the Internet Resource Center established by Bryan Penprase. Currently there is a postgraduate certificate in archaeoastronomy at the University of Oklahoma, taught by Steven Gullberg, Director for Archaeoastronomy and Astronomy in Culture, which came online in 2019.

Figure 21. John B. Carlson at the Second International Conference on Archaeoastronomy held in Merida, Yucatan, Mexico in January 1986. Photo: E.C. Krupp.

Latin American developments

In all subject areas, groups of like-minded researchers tend to get together to discuss their work and related problems but institutionalisation was not realised in Latin America until the 1990s. In 1994 the group, Intijalsu, was formed to further studies of astronomical knowledge amongst the peoples of the Andes and Chile. Another such research community was founded by Armando José Quijano Vodniza, who was attached to the Architecture Programme of the CESMAG University Institution, San Juan de Pasto, Columbia. Doubtless there were many other small groups such as this, including a study group at the Faculty of Astronomical and Geophysical Sciences of the National University of La Plata, Argentina, formed in 1998, which brought together Alejandro López, Sixto Giménez Benítez and latterly Cecilia Gómez and others.

However, what was needed was an organisation that took in all aspects of South American archaeoastronomical and anthropological ethnoastronomy under its umbrella; one which discounted national borders. As a preliminary, some Latin American researchers began to establish systematic forms of collaboration and think about a space for the circulation of their material in Spanish to enable a more global reach within their area. The first step for this was taken at the *Ethno and Archaeoastronomy Symposium in the Americas* in Santiago, Chile in 2003; the third such meeting was associated with the International Congress of Americanists. During it, it was decided to found The Sociedad Interamericana de Astronomía en la Cultura (SIAC). By this time in Latin America, following the work of Iwaniszewski who first coined the term *astronomía cultural* (cultural astronomy) in his PhD thesis (1988; see Chapter 10 for more detail), the term cultural astronomy had become an umbrella term to describe what had previously been designated ethnoastronomy and archaeoastronomy. Its subsequent followers were not just South American researchers but also an important group of Mexican researchers including Broda, Šprajc and others, who, because of their close ties with their South American counterparts were also instrumental in founding SIAC. They were joined by William Breen Murray from the south of the USA and Juan Antonio Belmonte from Spain. According to López, financing was obtained through a 3-year subsidy from CYTED (Programa Iberoamericano de Ciencia y Tecnología para el Desarrollo). In 2013 SIAC was officially formalised and its members today include some 79 researchers from 14 different countries.

As research expanded in Latin America, education followed suit. In Colombia in 2008, the topographer Julio Hernán Bonilla Romero founded the 'Archaeoastronomy Research Seedbed' at the Francisco José de Caldas District University in Bogotá, which has generated several related student research projects (Romero *et al.* 2019). Between 2004 and 2008, López and Gómez worked together at the Planetarium of Buenos Aires, teaching a cultural astronomy programme and filming the first Argentinean planetarium show on indigenous astronomy. Around the same time, in Mexico City, at The National Autonomous University of Mexico, there were seminars on archaeoastronomy which trained new researchers. To foster this effort throughout South America, from 2012, SIAC has organised a series of Inter-American Schools of Cultural Astronomy which have taken place in a different Latin American country each year (Fig. 22). These were as follows: FCAGLP, National University of La Plata, Argentina in 2012; Centro QUITSATO, Ecuador, in 2013; IIH–UNAM and INAH, Mexico, in 2014; MAST, Rio de Janeiro, in 2015; Astronomical Center of San Cosme and San Damián, Paraguay, in 2016; MNAAH, Orval University, Planetarium María Reiche and IPA, Lima-Nazca, Peru, 2017; Samaipata, Bolivia, 2018; and at the University of La Serena, Chile, 2019. These courses are designed to train researchers, particularly advanced undergraduate and postgraduate students from related disciplines such as astronomy, anthropology, mathematics, sociology, archeology, history, engineering, architecture and so on. There certainly seems to be an appetite for this, as Corrado and Benítez (2020, 274) reported that although there were only 100 places at La Plata in 2012, 170 students enrolled.

Figure 22. First Inter-American School of Astronomy in Culture, in the Facultad de Ciencias Astronómicas y Geofísicas, Universidad Nacional de La Plata, Argentina, 2012. © SIAC.

Since 2013, the schools have been associated with the SIAC conferences in order to promote theoretical and methodological debate and exchanges between established researchers and students. Additionally, SIAC has supported important outreach and relationship ventures with local communities and in primary and secondary schools in various countries such as Argentina, Brazil, Colombia, Mexico, Paraguay and Spain. During this time some Latin American research reached a wider audience with the publication of the *Handbook of Archaeoastronomy and Ethnoastronomy* (Ruggles 2015a; see Chapter 11 for more details): of the 243 chapters, 37 were written by SIAC members and of the six section editors, half of these also belonged to SIAC (López, pers. comm.). Despite all these positives, Corrado and Benítez (2020, 273), who teach archaeoastronomy at the University of La Plata, feel that archaeologists tend not to consider the sky in their work, despite their appreciation of the cultural landscape on the ground. Accordingly they thought that cultural astronomy should be included in anthropology university courses, while associated disciplines should also be made aware of it. Indeed, at La Plata, cultural astronomy is offered as an option in both astronomy and anthropology courses, with an average of 20 students per year since 2016.

Publications

In Britain, as we have seen in Chapter 7, the *Journal for the History of Astronomy* (JHA), in which Thom published so many of his papers, was a stand-alone initiative by Michael Hoskin, but its American counterpart *Archaeoastronomy* was closely tied to the University of Maryland. Initially titled the *Archaeoastronomy Bulletin*, it was then a short pamphlet published quarterly which included notices of conferences, research notes and work in progress. By 1979, the same year as the *Archaeoastronomy Supplement* to the JHA was first published in Britain, the bulletin had become a regular quarterly journal called *Archaeoastronomy: Bulletin of the Center for Archaeoastronomy*. The new journal, which changed to annual publication in 1983, claimed to be the only publication devoted exclusively to world archaeoastronomy and ethnoastronomy and from the outset it was bolder than the JHA because it offered space for the controversial debates that perhaps had a profound influence on the development of the discipline. Certainly it is to the credit of the *Archaeoastronomy Bulletin*'s editors, John Carlson and Ray Williamson, that the journal closely followed the progress of the discipline throughout the following years by creating forums for discussion, giving detailed conference reviews, publishing new research and sourcing new books.

Many of the papers were heavily reliant on ethnographic detail that gave them an authority that European studies could not hope to achieve. In practice the journal articles tended to cover a mixture of the American Southwest, home to the antecedents of modern Pueblo peoples, indigenous American cultures and Mesoamerica which included the Maya and pre-Columbian South America. In terms of reach, Carlson claimed that the mailing list in 1978 was comprised of 600 persons and institutions, so it certainly had a wide readership. As a further measure of the popularity of archaeoastronomy in the Americas, in the same year, Collier and Aveni published a bibliography of 1480 articles and books relating to New World archaeoastronomy. One of these books was by Jonathan Reyman, an American archaeologist, who set out his ideas for the discipline in a volume entitled *The Nature and Nurture of Archaeoastronomical Studies*, published in 1975 (Reymann 1975a). A short version of this appeared in Aveni's *Archaeoastronomy in Pre-Columbian America*, published the same year (Reymann 1975b). By comparison there was only a handful of authors who published work on British sites that were included in Collier and Aveni's list.

In Britain, as editor of the *Archaeoastronomy Supplement* to the JHA, Clive Ruggles had set the level high for archaeoastronomy publications, but it was the lack of such professional standards that continued to be a problem in America because there was such a range of competence in the work published that archaeoastronomy as a whole laid itself open to criticism by other disciplines. To address this issue, archaeoastronomy publications needed to be more robust than the online *Archaeoastronomy & Ethnoastronomy News* (A&E News) (1991–1999), edited by Carlson, David Dearborn and LeRoy Doggett, which was mainly a platform for announcements and short opinion pieces. In 1998 the *Bulletin* changed its name to *Archaeoastronomy: The Journal of Astronomy in Culture* and the University of Texas Press took over its publication. Under the editorship of Carlson, Dearborn, Ruggles and McCluskey, it only published peer-reviewed academic papers from 1999 onwards. Recognising that archaeoastronomy had a close association with archaeology the editors chose a style that was 'consistent with one of the premier archaeological journals' in the USA and invited archaeologists such as Richard Bradley, Johanna Broda and Stanislaw Iwaniszewski onto their advisory board (Carlson *et al.* 1999). The editors, had a preference that the broader cultural contexts should be addressed in the American journal, leaving the 'more data-oriented focus' to JHA's *Archaeoastronomy Supplement*, therefore very few British or European papers focusing on alignments were published. The first issue of the new look journal contained papers from invited contributors in order to create a framework within which to develop theoretical archaeoastronomy.

In 2005, its issues 12 and 13 were published as a book entitled *Songs from the Sky: Indigenous Astronomical and Cosmological Traditions of the World* (Chamberlain *et al.* 2005). Remarkably this book had taken 22 years to come to fruition as it was the proceedings of the *First International Conference on Ethnoastronomy* which was held at the Smithsonian Institution in Washington DC in 1983. It was a novel multidisciplinary offering bringing together the disciplines of anthropology, archaeology, astronomy, engineering and art history as well as the history of science, history of religion, folklore, and mythology. Twenty of the 32 papers concerned the Americas while the remaining 12 detailed research in the Arab world, sub-Saharan Africa, southern India, Java, Melanesia, Australia and Polynesia.

However, despite the disciplinary offerings gradually being refined in this way, it was perhaps in the 1970s and 1980s that American archaeoastronomy was at its heyday in the coverage it received from outside its domain. *The Technology Review* published by the Massachusetts Institute of Technology devoted its December 1977 issue to archaeoastronomy with contributions by John Eddy and Owen Gingerich amongst others, under the headline 'The origins of science; the astronomy of the ancients' (Dobyns 1980). This was good progress but the promotion of scholarly archaeoastronomy was hampered by popular works including Immanuel Velikovsky's *Worlds in Collision* (1950) and Erich von Däniken's *Chariots of the Gods?* (1969). It was a similar situation to that already referred to in Britain (see Chapter 7). As noted, Krupp (1979) referred to this material but, by describing archaeoastronomy as 'reliable and scientific', he tried to distance the discipline from the wealth of popular 'pseudoscientific' material published in these decades.

Other examples of fringe output included *Astronomy of the Ancients* (Brecher and Feirtag 1979) and the article 'America's prehistoric astronomers' (Alexander 1978) which did little to enhance archaeoastronomy's professional standing (Aveni 1981b, 2). Because archaeoastronomy looked for evidence for the sacred as expressed in ritual monuments, art and symbolism, this may have encouraged a resurgence of interest in ancient sites by some people in their quest for New Age spirituality. José Argüelles' *The Mayan Factor* (1987) brought the New Age to Chichén Itzá, by suggesting devotees repair there to hold various rituals which included crystals, humming and power points (Carlson 1999a, 147). Of course the event that inspired the greatest number of fantasists, New Agers, esotericists and pseudoscientists was the 2012 phenomenon. That year coincided with the 5125 year cycle in the Maya Long Count calendar, the period of 13 'Baktuns' or 13 ×144,000 days (Carlson 2011, 2) and the speculations about the approach of 2012 fostered a multitude of non-scholarly publications.

In Latin America, much archaeoastronomical research was carried out by English-speaking scholars and their work received more global attention than similar works published in Spanish. For example Zuidema (1964), who made a study of Cusco in Peru, once the centre of the Inca Empire, came from the Netherlands and of course Aveni and his colleagues had their bases in the United States of America. Similarly the journal *Andean Past* has been published in English by Cornell University since 1987. By contrast, in the early days there were few locally produced journals: one was *Latin America Research Review*, established in 1965 as the official scholarly journal of the Latin American Studies Association, though archaeoastronomical content was extremely rare. Also, given the number of countries within Latin America that experienced political difficulties which hampered their economic and social growth, their journal *Research Review* was taken up with commentary on these issues to the exclusion of the humanities and social sciences that were part of its original remit. In the 1990s more local journals were founded and *Latin American Antiquity*, which was established in 1990, appears to have filled this gap with 42 papers either on or mentioning archaeoastronomy up to 2020.

Other related journals include *Ancient Mesoamerica* from 1990 onwards; *Arqueología Mexicana* from 1993 and *Estudios de Cultura Maya*, *Estudios de Cultura Náhuatl*, from 1999. Yet because the majority of the papers published within them are in Spanish they tend not to be cited by English speaking authors and vice versa; a situation which has created a language-based cultural divide in Latin American archaeoastronomical research. That this continues can be evidenced by the recent volume *Cosmology, Calendars, and Horizon-Based Astronomy in Ancient Mesoamerica* (Dowd and Milbrath 2015) which is clearly geared up for an English-speaking audience. On the Latin American side of this divide, which López, has expressed as 'a good example of colonial relations in academia' (pers. comm.), SIAC branched out by publishing its own journal *Cosmovisiones* (*Cosmovisões*) in Spanish in 2020. Its original aim was to publish articles presented at the SIAC conferences and its two volumes to date have featured articles by Trejo, López, Gómez and Iwaniszewski amongst others.

Organisations and conferences

The importance of conferences to a discipline is difficult to evaluate but they can bring life to the discipline and keep it up to date by disseminating new theories and methods. The meeting together of like-minded academics creates a flow of information both into the conference theatre and outwards from it as delegates return to their own spheres of influence and spread the word. As Aveni (1993) said of archaeoastronomical conferences, 'we all evidently share a collective goal, lest why would we reassemble again and again?'. It was the recognition of the usefulness of archaeoastronomy in collaborative and interdisciplinary work which led to a different pattern of conferences in the Americas from the early 1970s onwards and these were more specifically focused on New World interests. There was no repeat of the British conferences which had primarily examined megalithic science; rather an emphasis on attempting to admit American archaeoastronomy into the mainstream. Over the years they were organised by various academic bodies and organisations, some in a series like the *Archaeoastronomy in the Americas* conferences and some as one-off events.

In June 1973 there was a joint meeting in Mexico City convened by Anthony Aveni and Horst Hartung, arranged by the American Association for the Advancement of Science (AAAS) and CONACYT, the Mexican Council for Science and Technology. It was entitled *Science and Man in the Americas* and 18 papers from this conference were published under the title *Archaeoastronomy in Pre-Columbian America* (Aveni 1975). In his conference review, Gerald Hawkins (1973, 214) suggested that although the subject matter called on the disciplines of astronomy, mathematics, archaeology, ethnology and mythology, 'one gained the impression that one was dealing with a single, coherent area of study'. The content covered alignments, including those to Venus and Capella in pre-Columbian structures; the rock art of the North American Indians; the Great Basin petroglyphs; the ethnohistorical materials and the astronomical orientation of buildings and structures in Mesoamerica, as well as Maya stelae and codices. The overall collection underlines how differently archaeoastronomy developed in the New World because it incorporated so many different cultural sources and evidence. Carlson (1976, 206) pointed to the significance of this volume as establishing archaeoastronomy as a legitimate interdisciplinary field, 'the whole of which has the potential to contain much more than the sum of its parts'. Mexico City seemed like a more appropriate choice of venue than the Mesoamerican symposium organised at Cambridge University in England a year earlier where Marshack and Baity amongst others discussed recent archaeoastronomical research. Sandwiched between these two conferences there was an archaeoastronomy seminar at the University of North Carolina in March 1973.

The AAAS, which was comprised of several divisions to cover the broad spectrum of science and its societal implications, also organised archaeoastronomy symposia on its own behalf. For example, at their annual meeting in San Francisco in 1980 there was a symposium on archaeoastronomy, organised by Ed Krupp and sponsored by AAAS sections D (Astronomy) and H (Anthropology) because, according to Carey (1984), 'astronomy appears to be a fundamental component of culture, making the scope of archaeoastronomy worldwide'. The resulting conference proceedings, *Archaeoastronomy and the Roots of Science* (Krupp 1984), are notable because they juxtaposed New World archaeoastronomy with Old World megalithic science, which was one of the last occasions the latter was taken into account in America.

The International Astronomical Union (IAU), originally founded in 1919, is a body aimed at promoting astronomical research through various organised Commissions.

The History of Astronomy Commission 41 was one such research group which began organising similar meetings. Owen Gingerich, president in 1973, was of the opinion that the Commission provided an unprecedented opportunity to recognise the history of astronomy as a serious discipline (Bracher 1999). In 2015, Commission 41 was replaced by Commission C3, which hosts a group, currently chaired by Steven Gullberg, called the Working Group for Archaeoastronomy and Astronomy in Culture (WGAAC). In 2021 its 89 members variously represented North, South and Central America; Britain and Europe; India, Australia, Indonesia, Nigeria and Japan. Set up to promote discussion and collaboration, one of its aims is to promote education, providing links to other international archaeoastronomy organisations.

In the 1970s when Commission 41 was particularly active, the American Astronomy Society (AAS) also hosted conferences which were a response by archaeoastronomy-minded astronomers who had found, according to Bracher (1999), that 'mainstream astronomers, by and large, regarded such topics as marginal to their concerns'. Their meeting in January 1979 included an archaeoastronomy session which was attended by around 200 people (Bracher 1999). As a result of conversations between Kenneth Brecher, the organiser of this AAS meeting, John Eddy and Gingerich, the Historical Astronomy Division (HAD) was founded. Set up as a separate division, the HAD organised a series of interdisciplinary conferences which have continued into the 21st century. The description 'historical astronomy' was used so that the work covered could include archaeoastronomy, in addition to the beginnings of modern astronomy.

Interdisciplinary research was clearly an ideological aim in American archaeoastronomy and from the conference programmes it seemed as if this was an aim which was being realised. The affiliates of the HAD, for example, included historians of science, anthropologists and archaeologists. The *American Indian Quarterly* (1984) was of the opinion that American archaeoastronomy started defining itself in the context of these interdisciplinary symposia and it is clear from the range of papers given at these conferences that archaeoastronomy embraced many disciplines from the start: for example, the contributors included astronomers, archaeologists, anthropologists, historians, architects and geographers. Williamson (1987) later concurred that the key to progress was the maintenance of archaeoastronomy's cross-disciplinary character with ethnography playing a crucial role. However in reality, most papers were individual research efforts so, despite the acknowledgement of the cross-disciplinary nature of the subject matter, it did not lead to many collaborations. It would seem therefore that the notion of American archaeoastronomy being an interdiscipline stemmed from the different resources it had at its disposal, rather than its contributors joining together and actually conducting research with academics from these separate disciplines.

In 1979, Ray Williamson organised the *Archaeoastronomy in the Americas* conference held in Santa Fe, New Mexico and the resulting collection of 28 papers was later published by the Center for Archaeoastronomy under the same title. Aveni (1980,

294) reported that 19 papers or 43% of the total addressed North American Indian astronomy; a measure of how quickly ethnoastronomical studies were progressing. In a review of the subsequent publication *Archaeoastronomy in the Americas*, which was edited by Williamson (1981), Mulholland (1983) suggested that 'not to have read it is to be uninformed of the mainstream'. The 'jurisdictional jealousies and cross-disciplinary incomprehensions', described by Mulholland, belonged to the past as far as American archaeoastronomy was concerned. He cited the anthropologist Thomas Zuidema as saying, 'We should not look at these systems from the point of view of the prehistory of western science and astronomy, but from the standpoint of analysing the human propensity to classify the social and physical universe'.

Similar conferences were held in the early 1980s; for example, Urton and Aveni organised a conference entitled *Conference in Ethnoastronomy and Archaeoastronomy in the American Tropics* at the New York Academy of Sciences, which introduced Latin American studies into the mix. Two years later, *The First International Conference on Ethnoastronomy: Indigenous Astronomical and Cosmological Traditions of the World* was organised jointly by the Center of Archaeoastronomy, the Smithsonian Institute and the HAD. Others included *Archaeoastronomy and Ethnoastronomy in Mesoamerica* in Mexico City in September 1984 and the *International Conference on Rock Art and Archaeoastronomy* at Little Rock, Arkansas in October of the same year. Additionally there were symposia on *Anthropology and Astronomy: A Marriage made in Heaven*' in August 1983 as part of the 11th International Congress of Anthropological and Ethnological Sciences in Quebec and *Astronomy and Ceremony in the Prehistoric Southwest* in October 1983 at the Maxwell Museum of Anthropology at the University of New Mexico, Albuquerque. The aptly titled *Symposium on Ethnoastronomy and American Archaeoastronomy* was the theme of the 45th conference of The International Congress of Americanists held in Bogotá, Colombia, in 1985. Their next conference was held in Amsterdam in 1988 where Edmundo Magaña and Aveni organised a similar outing. According to López, the proceedings were published in two volumes, the North American papers edited by Aveni with the South American ones edited by Magaña.

Not all the organisations were centred in the United States of America; CONACYT, the Mexican Council for Science and Technology being one example of a South American organisation. At this time there was also the Instituto Nacional Antropologia de Mexico and similar organisations in Guatemala and Honduras. The Institute for Andean Research had been founded in New York in 1937. Originally primarily interested in the Andean region of South America, its charter was amended in 1948 to extend its sphere of activities to all of South America, Central America, Mexico and the United States of America. However, though it aimed to cover ethnographic and anthropological studies, its main publications centred on archaeological excavations, with no interest in archaeoastronomy. Yet, overall, the number and frequency of these conferences suggests that the community of ethnoastronomers and archaeoastronomers was growing in size, that ethnoastronomy had received full recognition and that research in South America was keeping pace with that in the North.

The result of these American initiatives, which included archaeoastronomy's institutional presence at the University of Maryland and university courses elsewhere; its recognition by important organisations such as the HAD and AAAS; together with its textbooks, numerous publications and journals and interdisciplinary conferences, was that in the USA particularly, archaeoastronomy achieved legitimacy as a discipline in the 1970s and 1980s. Not only that but it had a community of many practitioners and followers which should have been enough to sustain its continual presence. Yet, as in Britain, this momentum which started so promisingly began to slow down by the early 1990s. Although Crowe and Dowd (1999, 25–26) pointed out that some historians continued to show interest in archaeoastronomy as evidenced by its inclusion in, for example, North's *The Norton History of Astronomy and Cosmology* (1994) and Hoskin's *Cambridge Illustrated History of Astronomy* (1996), they reported that there was a decline in archaeoastronomical papers presented at the HAD from 35% (1981–1986) to 10% (1993–1997). This falling off was also reflected in the publications of the American *Archaeoastronomy* journal which changed from annual publication to biannual for the 1987–1988 Volume 10 with the subsequent volume (11) covering five years from 1989–1993. Its 2011 issue on the Mayan phenomenon was its last.

Five years elapsed before *The Journal of Astronomy in Culture*, which should have been a continuation of the *Archaeoastronomy* journal, was founded in 2016. It is the official journal for the International Society of Archaeoastronomy and Astronomy in Culture (ISAAC) but since the 2016 opening issue, there has been no further publication. On the other hand, there was perhaps a regeneration with the founding of new societies such as the Society for Cultural Astronomy in the American Southwest (SCAAS) which began organising conferences in 2009. Although still concerned with the American Southwest, it has now shifted its focus to include the indigenous cultures of northern Mexico and Mesoamerica. The purpose behind the change was to be more inclusive of the cultures, past and present, which influenced the development of those in the Southwest together with the desire to treat the Native American and Indigenous perspective more sensitively (Greg Munson, pers. comm. 2021). Also there continues to be a venue for New World research at the ongoing 'Oxford' conferences: the 1986 and 2011 conferences were held in Merida, Mexico and Lima, Peru respectively. Unfortunately the meeting at La Plata, Argentina, scheduled for 2020, had to be postponed because of the Covid-19 pandemic. This was to have been a joint conference with the Sociedad Interamericana de Astronomía en la Cultura (SIAC) which, as we have seen, is important for fostering new Latin American research.

Debates and divides

Through all these activities, New World archaeoastronomy therefore obtained a legitimacy that was never realised in Britain before or since, but this is not to say that it did not come under the same kind of scrutiny as British megalithic science experienced in the 1960s and 1970s. Again the relationship between archaeology and archaeoastronomy was called into account because, as Reyman (1979, 11) concluded, archaeoastronomers and archaeologists have 'blind spots' with regard to the other's work. This evidently was still a problem in the 1990s when Dearborn (1991), in an article entitled 'Bridging disciplines & falling in cracks', felt that the 'artificial partitioning of Knowledge into disciplines affects our perceptions and limits our actions'. Throughout, archaeoastronomers had to overcome derogatory descriptions, such as 'transit jockeys', similar to those levelled at them in Britain, so to overcome this they had to display a lot more knowledge of the related disciplines. American archaeologist Keith Kintigh (1992) weighed into the debate by explaining his thoughts, which he said were shared by other archaeologists, on what he called the chasm or void between the disciplines. In an argument which could also have been directed at the similar circumstances in Britain, he suggested that archaeologists simply ignored archaeoastronomers because their claims added nothing to the current interpretive questions, so they were therefore 'pretty marginal to mainstream archaeology'. He claimed that archaeological collaborations with, for example, geology, botany and zoology, worked because the relevant disciplines had shared goals. Though Kintigh regarded most of archaeoastronomy as 'celestial butterfly collecting' he did see its potential for adding another layer to understanding cultures, given the fact that astronomical alignments were artefacts. Kintigh's comments as an outsider to archaeoastronomy were completely at variance with how American archaeoastronomers perceived themselves as part of the mainstream. For example, Aveni (1992) promptly replied to Kintigh and while he agreed that the research agendas of physical and social scientists were not the same, nevertheless he felt that the discipline of archaeoastronomy was making progress away from the simple documenting of alignments. Certainly emotions ran high as evidenced by Farrer's cutting response:

> Perhaps it is research that archaeologists cannot understand, since they are limited to the detritus of the long-gone rather than being privy to the arcane of the still-here. It is their loss if they are so bound to their own cultural models that they do not understand what they have before their eyes as they unearth a building oriented to light and shadow patterns, or as they contemplate a pot or textile encoded with important cultural knowledge. That some of this knowledge is astronomical cannot be doubted. Archaeologists may, if they wish, reinvent the wheel, or they can open their eyes and join hands with those of us who are archaeo- and ethnoastronomers. (Farrer 1993)

These emotive exchanges were reminiscent of the earlier debates in Britain but on balance, in many parts of the New World, the archaeoastronomers were winning the war against their critics. For example, Aveni (1992) gave examples of joint investigations in Mexico and, from researching sessions at the Society for American Archaeology and the American Anthropological Association and so on, he concluded that rather than divergence he saw 'a slow convergence of research agendas over the years'. The Kintigh/Aveni debate, first aired in 1992, was revisited by Aveni in 2016 who continued to view archaeoastronomy's methods, techniques and skills as useful to social scientists when needed and thought that it would better succeed when it was '*fully* integrated' into the culture-based disciplines (Aveni 2016, 248). The argument over the usefulness of archaeoastronomy to archaeology trundles on however. Michael Smith (2003, 221), an American archaeologist who specialises in Mayan studies, while accepting the argument for the role of cosmology in planning Mesoamerican cities, found generally that some of the arguments for it were 'vague, weak, and unconvincing' and that the research area required 'rigorous and explicit methods' to be accepted by archaeologists. In response, Ivan Šprajc (2005), an archaeoastronomer working in the same area, called for more collaboration to close the communication gap and pointed to the many excellent research papers that had been conducted with the rigour and exactness Smith called for. As noted earlier, Corrado and Benítez (2020) have confirmed that these territorial problems continue.

The green/brown dichotomy
If the accounts of the above conferences and those in Britain, detailed in Chapter 7, give a picture of two archaeoastronomies, those of the New and the Old Worlds, with their different approaches, methodologies and positions within academia, then this divide was made even more apparent with the publication of the proceedings of the first 'Oxford' International Archaeoastronomy symposium held in 1981. They were contained in two volumes, respectively *Archaeoastronomy in the New World: American Primitive Astronomy*, edited by Anthony Aveni (1982) and *Archaeoastronomy in the Old World*, edited by Douglas Heggie (1982b). The New World approach by such authorities as Aveni, McCluskey, Zuidema, Murray and Williamson, was both anthropological and ethnoastronomical and covered some of the most important sites and cultures of the New World through their respective analyses of astronomically related structures, rituals and symbolisms. The Old World view was mainly from a British and Irish perspective though there was one paper on Polish stone rings and one on the orientation of Neolithic sites in central Europe. The contributors in the Old World volume were 'those whose professional background is in the pure and applied sciences' who had raised 'technical issues which have aroused the interest of statisticians and astronomers' (Heggie 1982b, vii). Indeed, the papers which make up the Old World volume are full of diagrams, tables, data records, histograms and orientation pie charts and are not easy reading for those outside Heggie's suggested disciplines. Nevertheless at this 'Oxford' conference both New World and Old World research proceeded under the disciplinary title of archaeoastronomy. In the majority of cases, the difference between the two reflected not only the different questions that researchers were asking but also the researchers' intellectual background which in the Old World was predominantly astronomy. On the other hand, in the New World, 'research paths opened by astronomers, archaeologists, historians, anthropologists and ethnologists' were

coming together, according to Aveni (1982, viii); a situation which helped increase the validity of the various case studies.

The books themselves have achieved a fame in the history of archaeoastronomy, not so much for their contents but for the colour of their covers, brown for the New World and green for the Old World; a distinction that led to Aveni (1989a, 3), in his introduction to the proceedings of the second 'Oxford' conference, calling it the 'green-brown dichotomy'. This differential which he explained afterwards had arisen from his analysis of the contents of the volumes where he found that in the Old World green volume all sixteen papers dealt with the possible astronomical alignments at prehistoric sites in the British Isles and central Europe (Aveni 2008, 8). By contrast, in the New World brown volume only three of the nine papers dealt with alignments and two of those used ethnohistorical evidence for corroboration. Aveni also noted that the majority of the New World material either made no reference to alignments or only indirectly, yet he pointed out that both volumes carried the word archaeoastronomy in their titles. He stressed that the 'brown' approach was better in answering the question of *why* people oriented buildings accurately rather than the 'green' approach which argued about *whether* they could align them accurately; adding that there was a danger of drawing firm conclusions on the basis of employing statistical methods alone. He regarded this as a dilemma, saying,

> We find ourselves in the archaeoastronomy of the mid-1980s in a curious quandary. The questions asked by those in the quantitative sciences do not seem to elicit all that much interest in anthropological circles, and those astronomical matters that impress people engaged in the study of culture are given too little attention by the astronomers. (Aveni 1989a, 10)

More to the point, he reported that in the 1981 *Old World* volume there was not 'a single discussion of water, mountains, or, for that matter, any environmental parameters or phenomena other than celestial that might have influenced the placement of the standing stones' (Aveni 1989a, 6). Consequently he believed that there was an 'isolation of culturally based evidence from astronomical argumentation' and cited McCluskey as saying that the ultimate goal of archaeoastronomy should be the 'deepening of our understanding of culture'. In the same volume Iwaniszewski (1989), who had conducted research in both the Old and the New Worlds, examined archaeoastronomy via the discipline of anthropology. He agreed that the intellectual core of anthropology is the study of culture and cited Keesing who observed two distinct concepts of culture: behavioural-ecological (relation to environment) and ideational-symbolic. He emphasised that cultural systems are information systems and that 'through the careful examination and observation of the assemblages of cultural products, anthropologists can make inferences about culturally patterned behaviour' (Iwaniszewski 1989, 25). Therefore he thought that astronomy should be studied as a cultural subsystem and that 'archaeoastronomy is a perfect field in which the ideational-symbolic and behavioural-ecological approaches can be used in conjunction with one another'. Recognising that the importance of observable astronomical phenomena would be determined by cultural preference, for Iwaniszewski, the main question was what different functions did astronomy play in particular sociocultural systems. Far from being at odds with archaeology, Iwaniszewski suggested that archaeoastronomy with its new tools was crucial for archaeology, since no adequate strategy to study the cognitive part of the ancient cultures had so far been developed. Rather than experiencing the friction between British archaeoastronomers and archaeologists, Aveni (1989a, 9) also believed that archaeology 'offers us the clay out of which to mould ideas and suppositions that can be tested empirically', though he later suggested that there was a 'natural methodological mismatch between disciplines based in science versus social science' (Aveni 2008, 7).

The contrast between the two archaeoastronomies had been already discussed at the 1979 Santa Fe conference where Ronald Hicks (1981) had presented a paper entitled, 'Archaeoastronomy and related problems: Old World approaches vs. New'. The methodological differences that Hicks and Aveni drew attention to were later called a 'divide' by Ruggles and Saunders (1993a), who not only felt it hindered a cohesive identity for archaeoastronomy, but that it continued to promote statistical methodology which was often inappropriate for New World sites or cultures. However, because there was so little cultural evidence for Old World prehistory, the green methodology was one of the only ways the monuments could be examined at that time. Reflecting the decline of 'green' studies in Britain and elsewhere and the growth of studies in the Americas, by the time of the second Oxford conference in 1986, New World archaeoastronomy was dominant and British archaeoastronomy was only represented by Ruggles, with Hoskin and Iwaniszewski making an appearance for Europe. The proceedings, edited by Aveni (1989b), were misnamed *World Archaeoastronomy* because it was obvious from the list of contributors that the conference was really a showcase for New World archaeoastronomy whose proponents were asking different questions from those of the Old World.

Given these distinctions it is not surprising that Aveni (1989a) asked 'whither archaeoastronomy' and accordingly he questioned how and why archaeoastronomy was conducted and what it hoped to achieve. He wanted to know for example, 'what did the Maya observe, how did they observe and exactly what ends did their empiricism serve?'. He felt that these were the central questions that a growing number of New World archaeoastronomers were asking. Surely these questions were not that different from those being asked in the Old World. Heggie's introductory enquiry in the Old World volume, 'was astronomy practised here in the late Neolithic and Bronze Ages, and if so, what was its purpose?', is basically the same as Aveni's question. What might have constituted the divide was that in the Americas, whilst, as already mentioned, research paths were converging, by implication, in the Old World, their respective paths were divisive and unconstructive. But this notion is not correct either, yes there had been a debate about megalithic science but the green volume did contain papers by archaeologists such as Ritchie, Atkinson, Burl and MacKie. The nub of the problem was that anthropological evidence, on which much of New World archaeoastronomy relied, was simply not available in the Old World.

The implications for archaeoastronomy

Of course it is simplistic to combine the histories of archaeoastronomy in North and South America together and call them New World archaeoastronomy, because they clearly have their differences. Yet they both draw on evidence from other disciplines, especially anthropology and ethnography in a way that completely separates them from Old Word archaeoastronomy. Much of the early research in Central and Latin America was carried out by researchers from North America and Europe, who brought their methods with them but fitted them to a very different set of monuments or symbolism. Yet little of this was done from an archaeoastronomy perspective, but rather from using methods already employed by local anthropologists, where anthropology became combined with ethnography and ethnoastronomy. While it appears from English language publications that there were fewer projects than in North America, this is simply misleading and can be put down to the language barrier which hid much Latin American research from English-speaking eyes. As can be seen from the authors cited above, there is evidence of their research being published in every decade.

In North America, in the early 20th century, there was less evidence of this type of work, partly because there was very little ethnohistorical literature and the researchers only had the indigenous Indian cultures to study anthropologically. It was not until the naming of archaeoastronomy and its subsequent acceptance by Baity and others in the early 1970s, that archaeoastronomy studies flourished. The naming itself was hugely important in creating a sense of identity for studies which referenced the sky in their investigations. The foundation of the The Center for Archaeoastronomy and its subsequent journals further underlined this move to give archaeoastronomy an institutional presence and validate it. This acceptance was responsible for a large flowering in terms of reseach and publications which were enthusiastically received at conferences and symposia, arranged by other interested organisations. These organisations were led by astronomers who thought archaeoastronomy should come under their wing. Again this progress was not the same as in Central and Latin America where research into astronomy in culture simply fed into and expanded the current programme of anthropology, far removed from the natural sciences. Snow's two cultures were very much divided between North and South American research agendas, or at the very least, blurred.

Conferences have played a very important part in the forging of communities and the dissemination of research in the New World, but at a time when North American conferences seem to be in decline, the opposite is true in Central and South America. For North America it may be that the early pioneers who were so enthuisastic in the '70s and '80s, have reached or come close to retirement age. Active particpants today have also had other venues to air their work such as the 'Oxford' conferences or the European archaeoastronomy conferences which commenced in the early 1990s. Although new names have entered the field, with the lack of educational courses their research seems to have been influenced by the previous literature and methods, giving this new work a rather old-fashioned feel. Added to this, with the demise of the archaeoastronomy journal, there are few publishing outlets for their work. Since 2015, some archaeoastronomers based in North America, such as Gullberg, Krupp, Malville, Milbrath and Vadala, Richman, Von del Chamberlain and Pachak for example, have published their work in the *Journal of Skyscape Archaeology*. Yet, this British journal may have very few readers in the Americas. Unfortunately, with a dearth of scholarly literature, the fringe publications and television shows have become more prominent and, according to Gullberg (2020, 101), this has increased the scepticism towards archaeoastronomy by archaeologists and anthropologists.

In contrast, Latin American research has been re-invigorated by the foundation of SIAC, its archaeoastronomy courses, conferences and journals. Because they were associated with anthropology from the start and ethnoastronomy from the 1970s, researchers have been less associated with the disputes that have always surrounded archaeoastronomy. This has allowed them to adapt and create new anthropological theories and in the near future they may lead the field by combining ontological insights with their archaeoasatronomical work.

Chapter 9

A turning point for British archaeoastronomy

The new term archaeoastronomy was not taken up immediately in Britain because, at the time it was suggested by MacKie in 1971, megalithic science was at the height of its popularity. However, it came into fashion after 1979 when the *Journal for the History of Astronomy* published the first volume of its *Archaeoastronomy Supplement*. At that time, advocates of alignment studies in Britain were at a crossroads because they were concerned with both the consequences of Alexander Thom's corpus and how the field could reinvent itself by framing a new methodology which would be rigorous enough to convince their archaeology peers. It seemed as if the first 'Oxford' conference had prompted a universal desire to review critically the claims of the past and place the discipline of archaeoastronomy in a broader context from which it could move forward. This of course was easier to do in the Americas, as shown in Chapter 8, because researchers had such a wide variety of cultural sources to draw from.

In Britain, where sources were limited to the monumental remains in the landscape, the renewed scrutiny resulted in changes which inevitably took place over a number of years particularly from the late 1970s to the early 1980s; changes which were more fully implemented following a turning point in 1985. It was a revisioning which continued, in fits and starts mainly because of the lack of interested researchers, to the end of the 20th century. Archaeology also had its own turning point but this was not related to its methodology as such, rather a re-appraisal of the theories which drove it. This saw the introduction of postprocessual theory which drew insights from philosophy to provide more nuanced interpretations than those based on processual scientific techniques alone.

1985: a milestone year

It is difficult to pinpoint disciplinary changes or even to suggest whether such change is a revolutionary event or the result of a gradual shift in attitude. Similarly it is not easy to assess what constitutes a paradigm change when there are only subtle modifications. In many cases acceptance of the proposed modifications takes time so, for example, following the name change to archaeoastronomy, seven years elapsed between Baity's paper and John Eddy recognising 1980 as the start of the second wave of archaeoastronomy, following the earlier wave of Hawkins and Thom. Eddy (1980) was referring to the development of American archaeoastronomy but it was 1985 that marked a turning point for archaeoastronomy in Britain. The last of Thom's articles, in which he suggested, 'Not many more lunar sites are being reported – at least one writer we know is being put off by adverse criticism, and so statistical analysis can go no further at present' (Thom and Thom 1984, S146), had been published the year before. In 1985, the year that Alexander Thom died, Richard Atkinson (1985) who doubted whether, without Thom's contribution, archaeoastronomy would have existed at all, made his last contribution to the *Archaeoastronomy Supplement*. 1985 also signalled a change in the content of the *Supplement* because this was the year that Michael Hoskin (1985), who proved to be influential in the field, made the first of many surveys of prehistoric European monuments, in this instance the Talayotic culture of Menorca. Before then the *Supplement* had not published any European archaeoastronomy (see Chapter 10).

Drawing the period to a close, Clive Ruggles assessed the last five years of megalithic astronomy acknowledging that Thom had led the way in making archaeoastronomy a vigorous field of enquiry. However, Ruggles (1984a, 232) pointed out that the picture painted by archaeologists told a different story because it drew on data, not just from megalithic sites, but also on that from settlement sites, artefacts and the environment. To bridge the gap he suggested that:

> Only if the data can be seen to have been selected fairly (that is without regard for the astronomical possibilities), and the presence of significantly more astronomical alignments than would have been expected by chance can be demonstrated statistically, can the archaeoastronomers present the archaeologist with reliable evidence that astronomical considerations did affect site design. (Ruggles 1984b, 15)

Ruggles' retrospective in 1984 prefaced a new era of British archaeoastronomy because, following megalithic science, archaeoastronomers were left with the choice of retreating from the debate with archaeologists, discussed in Chapter 7, or proceeding in isolation. From that position they could change their practice from within without recourse to other disciplinary approval and this was the choice that Ruggles made by creating a new definition of archaeoastronomy. From his position as newly appointed editor of the *Archaeoastronomy Supplement*, and drawing on developments in the Americas, Ruggles gave British and European archaeoastronomy a broader avenue of enquiry than just the study of prehistoric megalithic monuments: 'Archaeoastronomy and ethnoastronomy seek to investigate astronomical practice and celestial lore in human societies past and present' (Ruggles 1988). He underlined this shift by emphasising that papers concerned with cultural context would be encouraged.

Archaeoastronomy certainly appeared to be thriving as in 1985 the *Archaeoastronomy Supplement* filled two volumes, the only time that happened in its history. 1985 might also be considered to be the year of the divorce between British archaeoastronomy and archaeology, after years of the latter weighing up the claims of the former. For example, the archaeologist Evan Hadingham published his book on ancient worldwide cosmology in 1985, deliberately omitting the words 'archaeoastronomy' and 'astroarchaeology'. This was because he thought 'these words may suggest that we can examine astronomical lore separately from the total pattern of beliefs and values of a vanished people' (Hadingham 1985, front matter author's note). After this time Ewan MacKie (1988) appeared to be the only archaeologist who looked for an archaeoastronomical interpretation of megalithic sites.

Archaeoastronomy: new name, new practices

To distance British archaeoastronomy from megalithic science its entire practice needed to be re-envisioned because, for it to progress, it was not enough to simply give it a new name and definition. First of all, in a move to discipline the field, a new methodology was proposed by J.A. Cooke, R.W. Few, J.G. Morgan and C.L.N. Ruggles, astronomy students who had been working together surveying megalithic sites for four years, in their 1977 paper on the Calanais sites found on the Isle of Lewis in the Outer Hebrides. All members of the Cambridge Astronomical Society, they, together with M.E. Bailey, had earlier published a short survey of three megalithic sites in Argyllshire in 1975 (Bailey *et al.* 1975), when the influence of Thom's megalithic science was still strong. By contrast, the Calanais paper was a detailed recommendation for a new code of practice to be applied to statistical data. While not addressing Thom's other claims for megalithic science the authors made it clear that they were only assessing his claims for astronomical alignments at the sites. Although Thom had already considered a procedure for deciding on indicated horizons, he had only made preliminary observations at Calanais, so Cooke *et al.* (1977) chose these sites as a first test for their new approach. Of the 46 lines surveyed by Thom, the authors found only six which might have been astronomical and that the only line which had an accurate astronomical indication could have occurred by chance. Therefore they argued that if the criteria used for selecting the lines were well-defined, objective and not biased by theories already proposed, then a valid statistical analysis assessing probability could be performed in order to judge whether or not the alignments were intentional. The Calanais paper represented an advance because it set out clear rules and took the importance of statistical analysis much further than previously by arguing that only statistical verification could settle the questions of megalithic astronomy. At that time the authors did not use statistics but earlier MacKie (1974) had already proposed similar tests to those in the 1977 Calanais paper, which he had applied in his surveys of Ballochroy and Kintraw.

Indeed the Calanais study must be regarded as a landmark event in the history of British archaeoastronomy, not least because it showed the early promise of Clive Ruggles' distinguished career as an archaeoastronomer, but also because it turned the tables on megalithic science, removing Thom's ethnocentric vision and placing science where it belonged, as a tool for 20th century archaeoastronomers. In several related papers, Ruggles went on to re-assess Thom's claims at a number of different locations, particularly those relating to lunar sightlines, and in this way honed his

Figure 23. Clive Ruggles at the European Society for Astronomy in Culture (SEAC) conference in 2010. © Michael Rappenglück.

new praxis on what he criticised in Thom (see for example Ruggles 1981b; 1982; 1983). To assess whether the sightlines were deliberate or chance occurrences, Ruggles classified the status of the observing position in great detail: given that in some cases he was re-analysing multiple lines, the permutations of the different criteria were almost endless and, in one paper (Ruggles 1983), ran into some 30 pages of discussion and tables which would be incomprehensible to anyone other than a skilled statistician.

It has to be made clear that Ruggles (Fig. 23) did not introduce a *new* method of measurement for archaeoastronomy: he used the methodology inherited from Thom but refined it with regard to data selection, statistical analysis of the results and the inclusion of archaeological and cultural evidence. In this way archaeoastronomy methodology was prioritised over interpretation because Ruggles (1989, 23) was of the opinion that 'statistical rigour must precede interpretative reasoning'. Optimally, his early work fulfilled two objectives: the provision of clear guidelines for archaeoastronomy practitioners and the assurance to archaeologists that the subject was methodologically sound. Yet Ruggles' ultimate aim for British archaeoastronomy argued for research 'in its fuller archaeological context through an integrated programme of excavation, locational analysis, horizon survey, and statistical investigation' (Ruggles and Martlew 1989, S137). There is some irony in this as the majority of Ruggles' research was published in the *Archaeoastronomy Supplement* which probably most archaeologists did not read. This lack of dissemination further concretised the Thomist mythology of megalithic science in the eyes of archaeologists.

Following on from his belief that statistics were key for archaeoastronomical research, Ruggles also recommended a further change when conducting surveys because he believed that more attention should be focused on sites that were archaeologically similar and where marked orientation trends were evident, rather than on archaeologically diverse sites (Ruggles 1982b, 99). This focus on groups of similar monuments became a feature of his subsequent research, for example, his survey of the group of Recumbent Stone Circles (RSCs) in northeast Scotland (Ruggles 1984c). Thom's rules for precision had been questioned by both Reyman and Heggie, with the latter suggesting 2° was acceptable for judging whether or not the alignments were intentional. In partial response, Ruggles relaxed Thom's standard measure of arc minutes by using a measure of 1° instead. Subsequently Ruggles (1985a) surveyed 300 linear settings in Argyll and Mull where there was only marginal preference for the moon's southerly limits at the most precise level. Although he had hoped that the eventual aim of archaeoastronomy should be to consider the astronomical data in the light of their archaeological and cultural context, this later paper did not go beyond conclusions about the orientations. Indeed with the best will in the world archaeoastronomers could do little more than this as there was so little archaeological evidence for the sites they chose to survey.

Ruggles' body of work, which Ellegård (1985) thought 'the indispensable starting-point for any further work on British "megalithic" astronomy', moved the debate away from precision alignments to less precise orientations while attempting to incorporate what little archaeological evidence there was into the interpretation. Despite this, Ruggles only occasionally collaborated with archaeologists because few of the sites he examined had been excavated or radiocarbon dated. However, part of his research on RSCs was conducted with Aubrey Burl, who had earlier published his own findings (Burl 1970; Ruggles and Burl 1985). Burl was another advocate of large-scale studies of close-related groups, as opposed to single-site investigations, though less for the purpose of finding common alignments but rather to indicate symbolism in prehistoric culture, believing that 'orientation was a fundamental of funerary ritual' (Burl 1980, 1982, 142). Neither was Burl a fan of the obsession 'with risings and settings', rather believing that the moon low in the sky, skimming over the erected stones, would have been a more likely symbolic target to represent an association between the moon and death (Burl 1980, 194, 198). In tune with his New World colleagues, Burl (1982, 164) felt that archaeoastronomy and archaeology might provide the answers to 'how' and 'what' happened, but only anthropology could tell us 'why it happened'. What was missing from Ruggles' methodology were tools to uncover symbolism, rites or rituals as it only included methods for finding astronomical alignments.

Ruggles' strict criteria and statistical method brought much needed rigour to the field but while there was no lack of prehistoric monuments in Britain to study many of them were unique individual sites which excluded them from the type of data set that Ruggles advocated. Much was missed because of this one-dimensional view as each site has a unique location and visual landscape horizon but the individuality of the sites does not rest there. Some circles, for example, have different dimensions and numbers of stones, some being rough-hewn boulders while others are carefully dressed and shaped, as well as there being differences in colour and geological makeup. That there were only five such individual studies on British and Irish sites published in the *Archaeoastronomy Supplement* for the entire period of Ruggles' editorship, underlines this finding. Aveni (1984) was similarly cautious of the statistical approach saying that, by tending to isolate and examine one facet of a phenomenon at a time, it could be counter-productive, while others raised doubts as to 'whether the mathematical modelling required for the statistical analyses can ever truly reflect the situation "on the ground"' (Pennick and Devereux 1989, 236).

However, alignment studies remained as important as they had been in Thom's day yet, perhaps because Thom's ideas about megalithic man had been so controversial, there was, as noted above, little willingness to interpret the results. For example, in Ruggles'

Figure 24. Looking from the centre of Stonehenge towards the west. To the left are stones 57 and 78 with their lintel. The stones in front of them are bluestone pillars and in the background are some of the remaining uprights and a lintel of the outer sarsen circle. Photo: Susan Greaney, July 2020.

series of papers examining the stone rows of Mull, while he suggested that there were more complicated hypotheses relating to natural horizon features and their astronomical significance, he failed to spell out these hypotheses. Similarly, both his north Mull and the southwest Irish stone rows surveys hinted that the data-driven methodology was undermined by local conditions, a problem for which Ruggles had not worked out a solution. These challenges would have to be met 'as part of the shift towards more contextual studies of the possible patterns of thought and symbolism that helped to define the location and orientation' of the monuments (Ruggles 1996a, S69). Yet Burl's earlier arguments for interpretations which took symbolic expressions into account should have been a reminder to alignment-seeking archaeoastronomers that the real reason for the investigations was to shed light on prehistoric culture and had archaeoastronomy done so it would have been more in tune with archaeology. This overall lack of theory expansion left archaeoastronomy as being simply a scientific methodology, redolent of archaeology's processual methods. It was a tool which could have been employed by any established discipline, particularly archaeology, but its overall flaw was that it overlooked the importance of individual sites, some of which, like Stonehenge were iconic (Fig. 24).

A turning point for archaeology

Around this time in the 1980s, when archaeoastronomers were honing their scientific methods, some archaeologists were beginning to question their own hypothetico-deductive model by responding to the shift in the wider intellectual climate that followed Jean François Lyotard's seminal text, *The Postmodern Condition* (2001), first published in 1979. In it he argued that scientific knowledge does not represent the totality of knowledge but that it exists alongside narrative. He called into question the legitimacy of universal truths, particularly the hegemony of science and, although he made no mention of Snow's two cultures, he took up his air of dissatisfaction with the way science dominated academic discourse. As argued earlier in Chapter 6, the turn to science in archaeology had led to a trend towards generalising metanarratives and Lyotard (2001, xxiv–xxv), from the broader perspective of science in general, decried these by preferring a postmodern 'incredulity towards metanarratives'. This, he argued, would allow 'sensitivity to differences' and reinforce 'our ability to tolerate the incommensurable'. In this way Lyotard made the distinction between scientific knowledge and the other, that critical, reflexive or hermeneutic kind, which he argued was about values or aims. The new epistemology meant that postmodernism expressed what Charles Jencks (1986), an architect with influential views on postmodernism, called a 'condition of doubt' which gave rise to 'anarchic and creative departures from orthodoxy'.

Archaeology's response to postmodernism, though it was not recognised as such in the archaeology theory books of the time, was a theoretical shift from processual explanations to more multivocal postprocessualist enquiries which encouraged more interpretive perspectives. Early indications of this shift to postprocessualism came with the publication of Ian Hodder's edited volume, *Symbolic and Structural Archaeology* in 1982. Hodder had started off as a processualist but found there was no satisfactory way to differentiate between different forms of process where they left the same archaeological trace. He still recognised process but emphasised situatedness, context and change beyond the simple dichotomies of processualism (Hodder 2004, 75). Andrew Sherratt (1995) pointed out that as each generation observes reality from a different angle, the processual metanarratives were not wrong but simply out of temper with the times. Indeed postprocessualism did not mean the obsolescence of processual archaeology, but rather indicated a new way of approaching data in a complementary way; a reformulation in which culture took centre stage rather than the processual attempts to achieve what Hodder (1982, viii) described as 'an apparent rigour and the veneer of a natural science'. This appeared to be the motivation for postprocessualism which included looking at science, the building block of processualism, with new eyes, especially with the realisation that scientific knowledge was not purely objective but socially constructed (Johnson 2010, 44–46). Hodder explained it as a political struggle between a closed view of science and an open view which sought out qualities and values. Therefore, postprocessualism broadened the range of questions asked to include elements of sociology, anthropology and behavioural psychology and it was augmented by a number of philosophical strands such as phenomenology and reflexivity.

An argument proposed by Julian Thomas (2006, 54) was that it was Christopher Tilley, one of the architects of postprocessualism alongside Hodder and Michael Shanks, who was the 'principal inspiration' behind the phenomenological approach. In his groundbreaking work *A Phenomenology of Landscape* Tilley (1994) proposed that you could only learn about a particular landscape by visiting it in person and experiencing it through all one's senses. However, to accept Thomas's conclusion would be to ignore Timothy Ingold's (1993) work on taskscapes and Richard Bradley's (1993) perceptions of monumental culture; both of which pre-dated Tilley's book. For example, Ingold drew on Merleau-Ponty's ideas of participation, as opposed to observation, to find a more meaningful narrative, while Bradley (1998) examined the built-in experiential nature of monuments. The premise was that landscapes are not places devoid of meaning but part of a cultural lifeworld for the people who inhabit them and phenomenology helps recover this. For Thomas (2006, 57), the keystone of the phenomenological approach was that 'the subjective aspects of experience are not superficial elements … but are the means through which the material world reveals itself to us'.

It was Hodder (2008, 196) who introduced reflexive methods with the aim of 'doing archaeology differently … at all levels', from the initial research design to the final writing up. As he explained, 'By reflexivity here, I mean initially the recognition and incorporation of multiple stakeholder groups, and the self-critical awareness of one's archaeological truth claims as historical and contingent' (Hodder 2003, 56). Political changes brought about by globalisation which required that more voices be heard, demanded this new ethical and reflexive approach. Tilley suggested (1998, 69) that, from that point onwards, archaeology became increasingly self-reflexive, critically interrogating its intellectual presuppositions, procedures and practices. That might have been Tilley's aim, rather than what actually happened, because in practice theoretical propositions may take a long time to implement at the trowel's edge. It would be many years later before archaeoastronomy tried to catch up with the turn to phenomenology and reflexivity.

Shanks and Tilley advocated pluralism as a way of encouraging healthy debate within archaeology. Without mentioning postprocessualism they set out its manifesto by saying:

> Rather than attempting to formulate positions which would once and for all explain the past in an absolute sense, we should be emphasizing that there are no absolutes, no fundamentals to dig down to in order to ground our analyses. (Shanks and Tilley 1988, 56)

As archaeology moved away from its traditional metanarrative it allowed the possibility of many archaeologies, those disconnected 'subtheories' noted by David Clarke (1973, 18) who wanted them to come under 'a common theoretical hat-rack'. While Clarke envisioned a general unifying theory, Parker Pearson (1998, 681), in a retrospective of Clarke's seminal paper, felt there was a 'battleground of contested approaches'. Postprocessualism offered the possibility that allowed them to step along in tandem.

However, theory implementation, like new methodology, takes time and often requires new approaches. According to Gathercole (1994, 3), the more interpretive options available, the greater the likelihood there is of correcting bias and eliminating error. Postprocessualism admitted to and accepted the limitations of subjectivity and partiality and some archaeologists attempted to transcend these problems by becoming phenomenological and reflexive, as mentioned earlier. While there was clearly a repositioning of archaeology's praxis, the inertia of tradition within the discipline weighed heavily. The adoption of postprocessualism in archaeology was not a complete paradigm change because it retained all the best of processual methodology which in turn provided the data for the postprocessualists to interpret; rather it was a complementary transition which favoured pluralism over monism. As Hodder argued (1995, 76), the emphasis of processual archaeology was a critical approach to method and theory which postprocessualism took a lot further, but he did not regard the resulting diversity as a need to 'set up a new dominating paradigm'. In other words, postprocessualism combined scientific rigour, maintained by the technology introduced by processualism, with multivocality, while admitting to and accepting the limitations of subjectivity and bias. By the middle 1990s, postprocessualism was firmly established and had become 'an unceasing reworking of the past' (Shanks and Tilley 1992, 28). This reworking can be seen in the new holistic interpretations of Neolithic and Bronze Age monumental culture from the perspective of their landscapes which, in some cases, included a brief examination of religion, ritual and cosmology (see for example, Darvill 1997; Bradley 1998; Thomas 1999). Many of these issues were thrashed out in the archaeological communities, such as the ongoing TAG meetings (see Chapter 7), yet while archaeologists were joining the dots of ritual, sacred space and 'culturally specific cosmological concepts', there was a gap where the dot for astronomical orientations might have been found.

Archaeoastronomy: advancing but lagging behind

On the other hand, while postprocessualist theory was being explored and adopted in theoretical archaeology, archaeoastronomy, despite its new rigour and accountability, lacked the accoutrements of cultural theory, which was still the province of mainstream archaeology. Having abandoned Thom's extreme interpretive speculations about prehistoric culture, in many ways archaeoastronomy in this period was merely a more streamlined but complex tool to be utilised in wider research. For example, Ruggles' quantitative methodology, by having no room for qualitative explanations, was reliant on the alignment metanarrative. At its inception archaeoastronomy was in tune with scientific processual methods, but it failed to adapt to the postprocessual approach. Yet, as already stated above, Ruggles did not introduce a *new* method for archaeoastronomy because the statistical evaluation of a large number of sites, combined with rigorous surveying methods, had already been practised by Thom, though he made it more robust. What changed was that those extreme interpretive elements of Thom's praxis, which dealt with geometry, metrology, dating and the prehistoric calendar, were stripped away while ambitious interpretations which contested the contemporary archaeological view ceased. This was not a revolutionary paradigm change but a minor shift towards a clarified praxis for the future. Martin's opinion, relating to paradigm shifts in archaeology, is relevant here. He thought that to claim that some archaeologists have adopted a new paradigm 'is equivalent to asserting that when they look at their world they see something new and different' (Martin 1971, 4). Ruggles' practice was certainly a major improvement but it was not something *that* new or something *that* different. The critical change was the field's renaming from megalithic science to archaeoastronomy, which potentially allowed it to have a new relationship with archaeology.

Yet no matter how refined methodology becomes, its practice may require qualification. Certainly Ruggles' view became modified over time and in 1994 he concluded that the paradigm which concentrated on solar and lunar extremes was outdated. Instead archaeoastronomers needed 'to admit the possibility not only of symbolism associated with the solstices, equinoxes and standstills but also broader, lower-precision alternatives' (Ruggles 1994a, S2). Similarly Hicks (1993) stressed that it was important to move beyond astronomy towards understanding possible religious symbolism, as this symbolism undoubtedly involved the whole site not just the alignments. It had taken thirteen years to accept Burl's 1980 argument in favour of symbolism. However, despite Ruggles (1989, 19–20) having already called for 'more interpretative discussions of more subjective evidence', archaeoastronomy failed to accomplish this. Therefore in practice, the tightening of archaeoastronomy's methodological rules meant that other lines of enquiry were generally overlooked: quantitative methodology was set above qualitative explanations and archaeoastronomy with its singular narrative on alignments, in tune with archaeology's processualist metanarratives, lagged behind the more interpretive postprocessualist perspective of contemporary archaeology. For example, in the case of Stonehenge, Ray (1987, 246) felt that it was not the solstitial alignment that was the most important question but 'the overall design and purpose of the site in relation to others in the Wessex area'. However, archaeoastronomers failed to branch out to examine complexes of sites which the archaeologists were beginning to do. Perhaps the real dichotomy was the difference between Snow's two cultures (1961) which led to this quantitative and qualitative mismatch between archaeoastronomy and archaeology.

Other advances
Ruggles' method, focused on horizon astronomy, was specific but not all encompassing. There were a few exceptions to the rule such as the recognition of the sunlight effects at Maeshowe in Orkney and also at Newgrange, following the discovery of the roof-box there by Michael O'Kelly in 1967 (O'Kelly and O'Kelly 1982). Generally, however, one of the failings of the archaeoastronomy of this period was this focus on horizon astronomy to the exclusion of other events or sequences of events in the sky which occurred along and above a particular stretch of the horizon. In this, once again archaeoastronomy lagged behind developments in archaeology where landscape archaeology had come into its own in the 1970s following the publication of *Landscape Archaeology* by Aston and Rowley in 1974. It was not until the end of the

1980s that ideas about landscape began to filter into archaeoastronomy. Additionally, there was an excessive interest in the luminaries of which Ruggles was aware when he indicated that the focus on the sun and the moon was perhaps a limitation (Ruggles et al. 1991, S72). Neither was there room for Schaefer's (1993) reminder that comets, meteor showers, eclipses, multiple conjunctions of planets and supernovas were not taken into account in archaeoastronomy, despite those events possibly being awesome omens for skywatchers. While American ethnographic archaeoastronomy was better equipped for this, British archaeoastronomy shared many of the same problems as archaeology in that both had only partial evidence to go on, coupled with an incomplete understanding of how the development of sites and their later use might distort the original alignments. Nevertheless British archaeoastronomy advanced during this period and caused none of the controversy that beset megalithic science.

It was apparent that to be an archaeoastronomer required various skills, the most important of which were surveying, astronomy, computing and statistics and in this period there were several advances in these areas. There was a change to surveying techniques as a result of technical innovation; a change which came from outside the field. First of all, the American Department of Defence launched its first Navigation System based on satellite readings in 1978, though the 24 satellite system only became fully operational in 1993 (NASA 2017). Secondly, Magellan launched its first hand-held device (the Magellan NAV 1000) earlier in 1989 (Sullivan 2012). These developments potentially improved the accuracy of archaeoastronomical surveys and American archaeoastronomer Kim Malville told me that he 'started using GPS seriously beginning in 1990 in various places around the world', occasionally 'with two stations, one mobile and one stationary'.

Whatever paths archaeoastronomers followed, they still had to master the astronomy and use it accurately. The known problem of finding stellar alignments because of the slow movement of the fixed stars caused by precession was further complicated by the difficulty in evaluating the extinction angle of stars (see Glossary: the stars' motions). This can render a star invisible on the horizon because of atmospheric haze, so Schaefer (1986) devised a new formula which he claimed was more accurate than Neugebauer's which Thom had used. In addition, Schaefer conducted a detailed examination of the lengths of the lunar month and explained the principles of heliacal rising (Schaefer 1987; 1992). Because many cultures used the dates of these risings for calendrical or alignment purposes, it was important that archaeoastronomers became familiar with the phenomenon. Schaefer and Liller (1990) added to the growing literature on refraction with Weiss (1990) observing that their new findings would help resolve a long-standing controversy in archaeoastronomy, as they threw doubt on the precision of alignments.

Hawkins had been innovative in using computer technology and in the 1980s and 1990s the growth of computer software programs had a facilitating effect for archaeoastronomy. Dearborn and Bell (1984) reported on early software applications for analysing archaeoastronomical data and Ruggles listed additional aids in his

1999 textbook. He also offered, for free downloading, his own DECPAK programmes, adapted from those written by himself, Cooke, Few and Morgan between 1975 and 1984 and these are still available online on Ruggles' website (Ruggles 2021). This access was important because although Michael Hoskin (1989) used planetarium software provided by the National Air and Space Museum in Washington in 1989 for his research in Europe, this would not have been freely available. Ruggles (1999a, 159, 256) also foresaw the use of virtual reality modelling, drawing on recently published archaeological experiments by Glyn Goodrick (1998). In this vein, Prendergast (1991) added AutoCAD modelling and digital photogrammetry to explore shadow casting phenomena (Fig. 25) while Higginbottom *et al.* (2000) used Andrew Smith's 'Horizon' profiling software for a reassessment of Ruggles' findings for Western Scotland sites.

Ruggles' methodological refinements had pushed statistics to the fore so probability assessment became another skill to master. This subject introduced a completely new vocabulary which would have been difficult for non-specialists to comprehend. For example Gates (1986) talked about 'maximum likelihood', 'angular tolerance', 'the eigenvalues of ZZ"' and a 'collinearity measure', to name a few terms used. Ruggles (1984b) employed the Nearest Neighbour Test when testing the statistical probability of alignments at 300 western Scottish sites but Higginbottom and Clay (1999) criticised

Figure 25. At the Newgrange passage tomb the standing stone GC-1 casts a moving shadow over the highly decorated central kerbstone. These shadow casting phenomena are thought to have led to a seasonally-related ceremonial role for the prehistoric users of the tomb. Photo: Frank Prendergast.

this approach suggesting that an alternative method Z_m^2 was preferable. This was because their method could eliminate background 'noise', in other words 'random error, or statistical uncertainty'. In a related study, mentioned above, Higginbottom *et al.* (2000) used the Kolmogrov-Smirnoff test to ascertain the significance of horizons in relation to monuments in western Scotland. Generally, before this time, Ruggles was alone in using what most archaeoastronomers perceived as sophisticated statistical methods. However, there were some parallels between archaeoastronomy and archaeology as at least one practice in both fields was incorporated at roughly the same time. For example, while Ruggles was advocating the use of Bayesian statistics into archaeoastronomy's methods (see for example, Ruggles 1986; Ruggles and Saunders 1993a), Caitlin Buck and colleagues (1991) were exploring the use of Bayesian techniques to bring more accuracy to radiocarbon dating in archaeology.

Yet, overall, archaeoastronomy failed to catch up with the advances archaeology had made in expanding and improving interpretations of the cultural record: Ruggles (1989, 23) seemed unable to overcome the problem of marrying together what he termed, 'the 'statistical' approach of the numerate scientist and the 'interpretative' approach of the archaeologist or ethnographer'. All its methodological advances, helped by techniques drawn from other disciplines, added a new layer of sophistication to archaeoastronomy's praxis and potentially made the results more accurate, but if British archaeoastronomy could have adopted the ethnographic elements of the New World practice, an entirely different picture might have emerged. It was as if the researchers, having accepted the pre-literacy of the builders, drew a line under the possibility of understanding their culture, which blinded them to survivals in the culture of later centuries. Consequently, while postprocessual archaeology forged ahead, British archaeoastronomy, remained a scientific methodology, redolent of archaeological processualism, so was out of temper with the times. However, although it was under-theorised, it was not necessarily incommensurate with archaeology's processual methods: as a methodological tool it could not only have provided useful data for archaeologists in the overall examination of sites but might also have prompted different questions.

Esotericism

As we have already seen, popular esoteric literature, pertaining to both archaeology and archaeoastronomy, existed outside the academy. In 1986 this genre was named pseudoarchaeology following a meeting of the Society for American Archaeology, organised by Ken Feder, Luanne Hudson and Francis Harrold. The resulting volume was *Cult Archaeology & Creationism: understanding pseudoarchaeological beliefs about the past*, edited by Harrold and Eve (1987). The term pseudoarchaeology was not new and its hyphenated form can be found in an article entitled 'Archaeological frauds' by E. Foreman in 1877, just over two decades after archaeology had been established as a discipline. However, following Harrold and Eve's book, it came to be used as an umbrella term to describe a particular genre of esoteric and alternative histories, in order to set them apart from academic output.

From the late 1980s this genre was led by Robert Bauval whose interest in ancient mysteries was piqued by reading Temple's *The Sirius Mystery* (1976), referred to in Chapter 7. Bauval, an engineer, was a self-styled Egyptologist who, after publishing his ideas in the academic journal *Discussions in Egyptology* (Bauval 1989), collaborated with Adrian Gilbert to elaborate the theory that the placing of the pyramids mirrored the stars in the Orion constellation (Bauval and Gilbert 1995). While megalithic science was no longer considered in academia, Campion (2004, xxi) believed Bauval's suppositions were an appropriation of Thom's megalithic science. Additionally Bauval's work, which he actually described as 'Alternative history', mimicked that of an academic publication, with chapter notes, bibliography and index. Together with Graham Hancock, who published similar alternative histories such as *The Sign and the Seal* in 1992 and *Fingerprints of the Gods* in 1995, they published *Keeper of Genesis* (1996) which by Bauval's own account was the pursuit of 'the quest for the science of immortality' (Bauval 2017). Bauval's *Secret Chamber* (2000), which was timed for the millennium, 'as our civilisation stands poised at the end of a great cycle', picked up on the link between ancient wisdom and hermeticism; a link which, as suggested earlier, had been in evidence since antiquarianism. Other volumes in this category included books such as *A Key to Stonehenge* by Robin Heath (1999) who also co-authored *Measure of Albion: the lost science of prehistoric Britain* (1999) with John Michell, whose New Age publications have already been discussed in Chapter 6. This public appetite for secret codes, conspiracy theories, heroic quests and mysteries had been already whetted by other books, particularly Michael Baigent's *The Holy Blood and the Holy Grail* (Baigent et al. 1982) which purported that Mary Magdalene had a child fathered by Jesus Christ, thereby giving birth to a sacred royal bloodline.

William Stiebing (1984, 170) suggested that it was the reliance on subjectivity over scientific methodology and the usage of 'compact answers' to complex questions that characterised pseudoarchaeology. Alternatively Paul Jordan (2001, 292) regarded it as an act of amateur archaeological practice which resembled scholarly literature without actually being scholarly, thereby blurring the distinction between scholarship and alternative output. Similarly, Fagan and Feder (2006, 270) concurred that many alternative histories are 'farragoes of misdirection, fallacious logic, [and] manufactured evidence'. As a footnote to this controversy, they disassociated archaeoastronomy from the 'pseudoarchaeological abuse of the technique', but that was not the view at the time. Given that archaeoastronomy had been derided by some archaeologists in the past, the danger to archaeoastronomy was that esoteric books such as those described above, particularly those which used speculative astronomy as a basis for their conjectures, would come to be bracketed with scientific archaeoastronomy. Identity, as an essential disciplinary requirement, must be guarded jealously. It was not just archaeoastronomers who were concerned with delimiting their boundaries; archaeologists, such as Feder (1984), similarly decried pseudoarchaeology's invasion into their own territory.

Learning resources

From 1977 onwards Ruggles was a prolific author, publishing not only his archaeoastronomical site-based research and theories but also other papers (see for example Ruggles 1997a; 2000), which served as mission statements for archaeoastronomy practitioners as they overviewed the entire field. Up until 1999 only Thom's books served as learning resources until Ruggles (1999a) published his own text-book, *Astronomy in Prehistoric Britain and Ireland*, replete with astronomy, archaeology and statistics text boxes, with practical explanations from his own case studies. In the same year he became Professor of Archaeoastronomy within the School of Archaeology and Ancient History at Leicester, which was apparently the first such post in the world.

Unlike mainstream archaeology which was sustained by university teaching, degree programmes and qualifications, in Britain there was no formal route into archaeoastronomy. Most archaeoastronomers who gained their experience through fieldwork and the application of astronomy to their results were autodidacts in the true sense of the word. Yet, for Ruggles, the key to archaeoastronomy's future success was dissemination through academic bodies, peer-reviewed research, teaching and training and the possibility of interdisciplinary postgraduate training programmes. In 1989, Ruggles joined the School of Archaeological Studies at the University of Leicester, splitting his time between that and other departments before finally moving fully into the School in 1997. There, drawing on his newly disciplined archaeoastronomy methodology, he initiated a course entitled 'Archaeoastronomy: theory and practice', which ran from the academic years 1989–1990 to 2002–2003 as a 20-credit third-year option in the BA and BSc single-honours archaeology degrees. A former student, Alun Salt who took the module in 1999, returning to it in 2003 as a revision course for his PhD, told me that on both occasions the class was at capacity with 30 students (pers. comm.). In the last couple of years a longer version, 'Archaeoastronomy: theory, method and practice', which was supplemented by material on practical field techniques, ran as a 30-credit module, in the one-year MA degree in Landscape Studies, yet compared with the popular undergraduate course, Salt found there were only a few MA students.

The aims of Ruggles' 12-week course were to look at the scope of problems addressed by archaeoastronomy; to teach its methodological principles and to understand the role of archaeoastronomy within archaeology. While the course was centred on the Neolithic and Bronze Ages in Britain and Ireland, the students were introduced to world archaeoastronomy and ethnoastronomy. Archaeoastronomy's position relative to mainstream archaeology was discussed but Thom's work was not considered 'partly because many of the issues are no longer of current archaeological interest' (Ruggles 2003). Therefore the syllabus deliberately moved away from megalithic science towards the practice that Ruggles had put in its place. For example, simple probability arguments were discussed in relation to balancing 'statistical evidence from trends at local groups of monuments against broader contextual evidence from single sites' (Ruggles 2003). However, Ruggles (1993a) had earlier found that the disadvantage of teaching archaeoastronomy was the amount of time taken in teaching basic astronomy. Despite being located within the School of Archaeology, the main reading list only featured books on archaeoastronomy, not texts on archaeology. Nevertheless, Ruggles acknowledged that archaeoastronomical research required a critical appraisal of evidence from archaeology, history, anthropology, astronomy and statistics, thereby leaning towards archaeoastronomy being an interdiscipline, rather than an autonomous discipline. Yet, although he was increasingly aware that interdisciplinary work was essential to the development of interpretation, he regretted that 'the constraints of the discipline-based system act against interdisciplinary developments at every level' (Ruggles 1993a, 8–9). Overall, the course material suggests that, despite these interdisciplinary aims, Ruggles' course naturally leaned more towards a scientific, methodological approach rather than towards the humanitarian, societal analysis that archaeology favoured.

When Ruggles' course at Leicester ended, Salt told me that development started on the BSc Interdisciplinary Science Course, which was to have a one 20-credit module covering 'Archaeoastronomy, archaeology, physics and geology'. Salt himself took on the lead role of creating a module based on the idea of creating an authentic Stonehenge replica, including asking if astronomical features could be replicated. This, he reported, ran a couple of years until the course was redesigned 'to work around pyramids using the expertise of Sarah Symons', one of Ruggles' former students. Graham Shipley, Professor of Ancient History at Leicester since 2002, reported that since Ruggles took early retirement in 2003, archaeoastronomy on its own has never re-appeared on the curriculum (Shipley, pers. comm.). The existing course has changed completely and Salt confirmed Shipley's report that the archaeoastronomy element has been removed.

Nevertheless, Ruggles' teaching had a long-lasting influence as it enabled some of his students to further the field through their own publications, some of which were not completed until some years after his course had ended. For example, at least three related PhD theses were awarded to Ruggles' students; respectively, Sarah Symons (1999); Efrosyni Boutsikas (2007) and Alun Salt (2009). Similarly, another of Ruggles' students Erin Nell went on to publish *Astronomical Orientations and Dimensions of Archaic and Classical Greek Temples* in 2003 and later collaborated with Ruggles in a paper on the orientations of the Giza pyramids (Nell and Ruggles 2014).

In 1993, four years after Ruggles put archaeoastronomy on the university curriculum, Lionel Sims, Head of Anthropology at the University of East London (UEL), offered a course entitled 'Decoding Stonehenge' which ran until 2011 as an optional choice on a BSc (Hons) anthropology degree programme. The course was, as its title suggested, a new examination of Britain's iconic monument, though it included Avebury and monuments at Bru na Boinne and Loughcrew in Ireland. Unlike Hawkins' work from which the course title derived, Sims' course did not focus solely on astronomical alignments but attempted to examine how archaeoastronomy could deal with cultural complexity. It was more focused on understanding the needs which drove a culture to enshrine alignments in their monuments rather than on the methods of finding alignments. Like Ruggles, Sims (Fig. 26) approached the material from an interdisciplinary perspective, combining a number of methodologies and approaches, though his choice differed. If Ruggles represented processualism in archaeoastronomy, then Sims spoke for postprocessualism. His praxis revolved around an anthropological critique of five disciplines; archaeoastronomy; archaeology; behavioural ecology (socio-biology); Indo-European poetics; and cultural anthropology, and key texts from these were part of the reading material. He drew on theories from those disciplines 'to model the likely scenarios for late Neolithic monument building cultures' (pers. comm.) and to argue for a new approach to prehistoric monuments which could shed light on similar sites of the period. In Sims' words, his praxis 'included archaeoastronomy as part of the American definition of anthropology which integrates biological, social, cultural anthropology with archaeology, linguistics, myth and folk lore' (pers. comm.).

Sims has described his methodology as 'emergence – the product of integrating all of the extant methodologies' which came about as a result of his being 'struck by the lack of integration between anthropology and archaeology into the origins of social complexity' (pers. comm.) He believed that one 'sub-discipline' in particular 'stood at the centre of this intersection yet itself was in disarray – archaeoastronomy' (Sims 2013, 8). According to Sims, the integrated methodology approach required

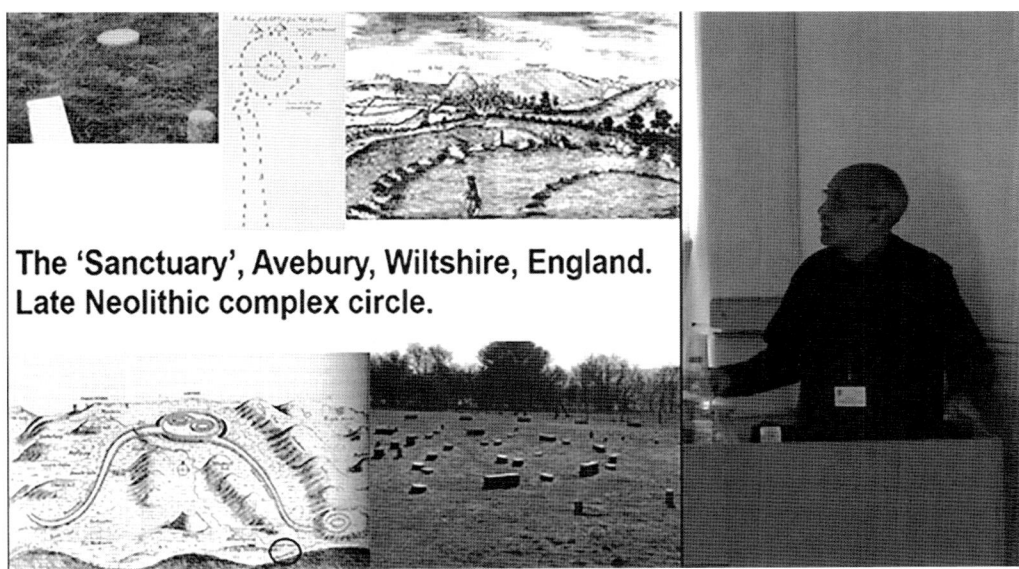

Figure 26. Lionel Sims presenting at the Theoretical Archaeology Group Conference, December 2017. © Open Past CC BY.

not just a new way of conducting field work, but also a new interpretive method. A further rationale for his point of view was that other disciplines which specialise in prehistory only have access to 'fragments' which reveal some aspects of the culture so that no one discipline 'possesses a rich enough set of data to independently interpret a prehistoric culture as a whole' (Sims 2013, 22). In contrast to Ruggles, Sims believed that by exploring single sites such as Stonehenge, which was the main focus of the course, new insights could be found. Additionally, his approach was informed by landscape phenomenology and the module essay title, 'Evaluate Neolithic Revolution theory using the theory of lunar-solar conflation', encapsulates the anthropological nature of this module. Overall, the content of Sims' course, being an innovative combination of theories and methodologies founded in other disciplines, enabled the humanitarian, societal analysis missing from Ruggles' course. Yet while Sims' course and his publications followed the postprocessual trend by valuing the use of other disciplinary approaches, it is unlikely that archaeologists would have been aware of his complementary work. As a turning point towards a more comprehensive approach, it could not have been more different from the turning point identified earlier in 1985.

The implications for archaeoastronomy

During this period British archaeoastronomy became isolated from the view of all but a few archaeologists so there was little repeat of the debates which followed megalithic astronomy. There were over 80 participants from 20 countries at 'Oxford' III in Scotland in 1990, yet the archaeologists who made such a useful contribution to the 'green volume' of 'Oxford' I were missing from the pages of the proceedings. Atkinson was 70 in that year; Burl aged 64 was approaching the end of his active archaeological career and MacKie (2000) and Ritchie (1998) had turned their attention to Iron Age brochs. For the archaeologists who replaced them, faced with so little British archaeoastronomical research, there was little to comment on or contest, despite Ruggles' stringent methodology being aimed to appeal to the archaeologists. The net effect for archaeoastronomy in terms of its relationship with archaeology was small.

There was still doubt about how archaeoastronomy could add to the narrative about prehistory. To overcome contestation or sidelining, archaeoastronomers had to begin thinking like archaeologists, or as Zeilik (1989) expressed it, 'We should work with an archaeological awareness for every site and culture and even generate hypotheses that the archaeologists can test for us!'. This was a thought echoed by Hoskin and Zedda (1997, S4) who felt that rather than trespassing on the domain of archaeology, archaeoastronomers should 'regard themselves and be regarded, as members of the archaeological team'. These were however pipe-dreams for the future because archaeoastronomy and archaeology failed to come together in this period, though they had some common ground with recognised astronomically-oriented sites. For example, archaeologists acknowledged the existence of the solstitial alignment at Stonehenge and the sunlight effects at Maeshowe and Newgrange, already mentioned. There was also the recognition of the sacred aspects of landscape which the archaeologists were beginning to address. Generally however, the sky was ignored by most archaeologists. An exception to this rule was Bradley (1998, 109) who referenced its importance, noting that 'circular constructions reflect a perception of space that extends outwards from the individual and upwards into the sky'. Despite feeling that archaeoastronomical questions were legitimate, they were too limited, as in Bradley's eyes 'the operation of such complexes was first and foremost an experience' (Bradley 1993, 47). Similarly Thomas (1999, 53) believed that astronomical phenomena did not 'indicate any scientific observation of the heavens, so much as a perceived unity of earth and sky, life and death, past and present'. In the same vein, Tilley (1994, 26) continued this trend by acknowledging 'the physical and biological experience of landscape – earth, water, wood, stone, high places and low places, the wind, rain, sun, stars and sky'. In a complementary manner, Timothy Darvill (1997) recognised the sacred geography in the Stonehenge landscape.

The influence of this material was not lost on Ruggles (1999b) who showed how the debate about astronomical alignments had moved on by quoting Bradley (1991, 58) as saying, in regard to the Dorset cursus, 'by incorporating into its structure an important astronomical alignment, those who built it made those developments appear to be part of the functioning of nature'. Further confirmation came from Carlson (2000) who pointed to the 'new' development of interdisciplinary studies involving landscape archaeology and the analysis of archaeoastronomical sites within a 'ritual landscape', suggesting that it was this interdisciplinary nature that was driving archaeoastronomy into a 'third epoch'. In practice, however, the complementary narratives of some archaeologists who were moving closer to recognising the sky and its cycles and those of archaeoastronomers such as Sims veering in the direction towards encompassing symbolism, proceeded along separate paths and were isolated from one another. To be successful archaeoastronomy's paradigm of data-driven studies of large groups of monuments would have to be relinquished in favour of a more interpretative narrative. This dilemma was voiced by *Archaeoastronomy*'s editors as 'squaring post-processual modes of explanation with scientific methods of data analysis' (Carlson *et al.* 1999, 9). In the words of Murray (1998, S1) 'if paradigmatic contradictions make this [interdisciplinary] consensus impossible, collaboration of the kind contemplated in archaeoastronomical research is foreclosed'. With postprocessual archaeology moving forwards in a new interpretative direction, the archaeoastronomy of data-driven studies of large groups of monuments seemed outdated. Certainly in Britain, at the close of the 20th century, because archaeoastronomers failed to engage with the complementary narratives of archaeologists, the opportunity for fruitful collaboration was lost.

When archaeoastronomy no longer rivalled archaeology's narratives on prehistory archaeologists stopped their commentary against it. Some leading archaeologists, as noted above, were beginning to have their own ideas about the relative importance of the sky to past cultures so they did not need to learn the archaeoastronomers' language. This left archaeoastronomy on the sidelines though it received some support from an unlikely source, that of philosophy. Whitlock (1994) argued that in philosophy, archaeoastronomy has a special bearing on the history of philosophy, cosmology, philosophy of science, philosophy of religion and culture and so on. He added that, 'while archaeoastronomy does not solve philosophical questions, it sheds light on how cultures attempt to do so'. Cosmology, Whitlock argued, was the common ground between philosophy, astronomy and archaeology. Nevertheless archaeoastronomers were still concerned with the gulf between themselves and the archaeologists so they tried to devise strategies accordingly. For example, to improve the relationship between archaeoastronomy and related mainstream disciplines the decision was made to publish two volumes of the third 'Oxford' conference proceedings. Accordingly *Astronomies and Cultures* (Ruggles and Saunders 1993b) was aimed at a wider interdisciplinary audience while *Archaeoastronomy in the 1990s* (Ruggles 1993b) was intended primarily for an 'internal' readership of archaeoastronomers. This action reveals a lack of self-confidence in the face of mainstream criticisms and despite a willingness by some to enter the wider academic framework, archaeoastronomers made few attempts to integrate with other disciplines.

Writing in hindsight, Hutton (2013, 376) suggested that in 1980 'it really seemed as if archaeoastronomy was going to become a full-blown international academic discipline, with its own departments and a clutch of mainstream journals'. Certainly Ruggles (1985b, S64) thought that if it could be shown that astronomical practice was universal and that the practice could be correlated with social activity, it could be a discipline in its own right, though at that stage he did not believe it 'satisfactorily justified its separate existence' because he felt that the study of astronomical practices was only one line of evidence. In 1996, reiterating these earlier remarks, Ruggles continued to shed doubts on whether archaeoastronomy could be recognised as a stand-alone discipline and noted that it was still striving to find its identity and to define its precise scope and goals (Ruggles 1996b, 9). The alternative was that it could become a subdiscipline of archaeology because it asked questions about the sky, not otherwise considered, and was increasingly reliant on data provided by archaeologists. At best it could become interdisciplinary if it adopted Carlson's stricture that an interdisciplinary attitude involves 'being aware of the non-superiority of one's own disciplinary view, seeing one's own deficiencies when stepping into a new field, and listening to what those already there have to tell us' (Carlson 1999b).

Archaeoastronomy's standing in Britain was not helped by the decline in its output in the 1990s, somewhat mirroring the same situation as in the Americas. Ruggles had moved away from new British research so the number of researchers publishing their investigations of British and Irish prehistoric sites in archaeoastronomical publications had fallen to eight. They included Myatt (1988), Scott (1990) plus Higginbottom and Clay (1999) for Scotland, Farrah (1993) for Lundy and Powell (1995) for Wales, and for Ireland, Stooke (1994) and Prendergast (2000). Of these only three appear to be still working in the field today. This decline was one of the reasons which led to the cessation of the *Archaeoastronomy Supplement* of the JHA in 2002. Apart from the optional courses at Leicester and East London, archaeoastronomy was not taught at British universities and any research was carried out on a part-time or amateur basis. Though it had a textbook and a professor, for it to be wholeheartedly included on the academic curriculum it would have needed specialist tutors and only Sims and Ruggles were expert enough at this time to fulfill this role to ensure archaeoastronomy's continuance in the university arena.

The renaming of the field to archaeoastronomy was an important feature of its development in this period but Baity's optimistic view that archaeologists would take up the tools of archaeoastronomy was not realised in British archaeology. Ruggles' methodology, developed from research at British and Irish sites, was more stringent and reliable than any that had gone before and should have drawn the line under the controversy over megalithic science. However, although this gave archaeoastronomy a more respectable voice, his results existed in a vacuum, divorced from mainstream archaeological enquiry into British prehistory. Nevertheless, Ruggles' impact on the development of archaeoastronomy cannot be overstated and though his retirement signalled the end of his course at Leicester, he has continued to make a valuable contribution to the field. Additionally, he is one of the few archaeoastronomers that archaeologists turn to, for example Parker Pearson, having invited him to assess alignments at Stonehenge, devoted two pages to Ruggles' archaeoastronomical survey in his subsequent book (Parker Pearson 2013, 48–49, 246) and agreed with his results. Hutton (2013, 389) has described Ruggles as the 'voice of reason' in connection with the archaeoastronomy of Stonehenge, believing that the default position of archaeologists generally was to repeat the views of Ruggles as they regard him as representing the consensual view of archaeoastronomers. Despite this, although there was the intention to incorporate more archaeology and more landscape studies into archaeoastronomical hypotheses, this was rarely achieved and British archaeoastronomy remained redolent of 'green' archaeoastronomy. While either side could have provided a fuller picture by taking the other's data into account, historic scepticism on the part of archaeologists and ignorance of archaeology on the part of the archaeoastronomers left the two fields in vacuums of their own making, without lines of communication between them. In part the lack of dialogue between the two could be attributed to the lag in theory development; archaeoastronomy following scientific processualism at a time when archaeology was adopting postprocessualism.

Chapter 10

Archaeoastronomy and cultural astronomy in Europe

Europe is a vast land mass made up of many different countries whose national boundaries today bear no relation to their occupation by many diverse prehistoric cultures that were once in existence: cultures which have left their evidence in the form of a variety of material remains in the landscape, ranging from megalithic monuments to earthworks and beyond. As there are too many different academic traditions of archaeology in Europe, it will not be possible to cover archaeoastronomy's relationship with archaeology in the same way as it can be studied in Britain, despite many parallels in their interests. In Europe archaeological research covers all the different prehistoric ages from the Palaeolithic to the Bronze Age. Evidence from Alexander Marshack (1972) highlighted a suggested lunar calendar from markings on a Palaeolithic bone tool (see Chapter 6) but during the Mesolithic to Neolithic transition, lunar time reckoning was replaced with solar year computation (Iwaniszewski 1999, 92). The first developments of European Neolithic and Eneolithic (that period between the Neolithic and the Bronze Age) were in the Balkans, which led to the expansion of farming communities associated with longhouse settlements of the Linear Pottery Culture. However it was generally only the archaeoastronomy of megalithic monuments in Western Europe that had been researched since antiquarianism and beyond, but these were few and far between until from 1985 onwards Michael Hoskin reinvigorated these studies. On the other hand Central and Eastern Europe had a different monumental legacy which led to the development of two archaeoastronomies, that of Western Europe and that of the East.

This chapter will explore their different trajectories and the influential work that was produced by the end of the 1990s, which ultimately led to the suggestion to broaden the scope of archaeoastronomy by calling it cultural astronomy. This effectively moved archaeoastronomy closer to the 'brown' version employed in the Americas. From the late 1980s a series of conferences was organised in different European countries which culminated in the inauguration of the Société Européenne pour L'Astronomie dans la Culture (SEAC) (European Society for Astronomy in Culture) in 1993. Shortly afterwards, in 1996, the International Society for Archaeoastronomy and Astronomy in Culture (ISAAC) was founded.

Michael Hoskin

Michael Hoskin (1930–2021) was a renowned astronomer who lectured in the history of astronomy at Cambridge University from 1959 until his retirement in 1988. He was a Fellow of Churchill College Cambridge; emeritus Fellow of St Edmund's College Cambridge; Honorary Fellow of the Royal Astronomical Society and holds medals of the American Astronomical Society and the European Society for Astronomy in Culture. The International Astronomical Union has named an asteroid Minor Planet after him while the authorities at the archaeological site at Antequera, Spain, have named one of their buildings the 'Centro Solar Michael Hoskin' in recognition of his achievements. His importance to the field of archaeoastronomy began in 1970 when he founded the *Journal for the History of Astronomy* (JHA), as already mentioned in Chapter 7, and which he edited for 44 years until 2014. In addition to these accomplishments, after Hoskin retired he spent many years conducting archaeoastronomical fieldwork relating to megalithic monuments in Atlantic and Mediterranean Europe. Hoskin had learned archaeoastronomy from Alexander Thom and archaeology from the American archaeologist William Waldren; his aim being to present a body of work to the prehistorians so that they could take orientations into consideration, as he never believed that archaeoastronomy could 'go it alone' or provide all the answers (Hoskin 2001, 1–3).

He published his first paper on the prehistoric buildings of the Talayotic culture in Menorca in the *Archaeoastronomy Supplement* of the JHA in 1985. This in itself was something of a landmark development because he used planetarium software provided by the National Air and Space Museum in Washington DC. It would be at least a decade before such software, of invaluable importance to archaeoastronomy, was made commercially available as detailed in Chapter 9. Hoskin's surveys were conducted over a wide area of megalithic Europe and after his work in Menorca he moved on to Pantelleria in Italy where he investigated some 50 communal passage tombs or *sesi* which belonged to the Bronze Age Rodi-Tindari-Vallelunga culture (Tusa *et al.* 1992). In Crete he measured the orientations of 209 tombs at the Late-Minoan Cemetery at Armenoi (Papathanassiou *et al.* 1992) before going on to survey orientations at the Maltese temples (Serio *et al.* 1992) and the megalithic tombs and temples in Sardinia (Hoskin *et al.* 1993). He also studied the Portuguese and Spanish dolmens along the Atlantic Façade in Iberia and continued to publish the results of his fieldwork in the JHA and its *Supplement* until 2008, but thereafter confined his content to papers and books on the history of astronomy. During this long period he had surveyed over 2500 monuments with help from his colleagues and written 26 papers detailing his findings.

Archaeoastronomy based on the 'green' methodology generally lacked interpretation while its theory remained static but Hoskin tried to broaden its scope in his work by combining it with archaeology to find cultural explanations. Consequently, in all his research, Hoskin tried to liaise with archaeologists to make sure that his results fitted the known archaeology though he admitted the archaeological context in his work was 'sketchy and inadequate' (Hoskin 2001, 3). Nevertheless, where he was unable to collaborate with archaeologists, he reviewed the archaeological literature to assess the types of structures for which an archaeoastronomical explanation might answer some of the questions posed by archaeologists. His view of archaeoastronomy as a sub-discipline of archaeology can be inferred from his suggestion that an archaeological team should include an archaeoastronomer, capable of providing astronomical data and interpretation. Hoskin's work was foundational in demonstrating how archaeoastronomy could add weight to archaeological results and how archaeology in turn could enhance the astronomical hypothesis. Conscious of the critiques against archaeoastronomy he thought that, 'in a climate where archaeologists and astronomers alike are sceptical of the claims of archaeoastronomy, it surely behoves archaeoastronomers to proceed with greater caution' (Hoskin 1994, S89). He was also influenced by the work of Edoardo Proverbio, who had already surveyed some of the Sardinian tombs and found that there were many factors which could have influenced tomb orientations such as the avoidance of farming land or orientation to sacred mountains (Proverbio *et al.* 1987). As such Proverbio's research was an advance towards viewing alignments in the context of culture and this focus on culture can be seen in many of Hoskin's individual papers published in the *Archaeoastronomy Supplement* to the JHA; the results of which were condensed in his major study, *Tombs, Temples and Their Orientations* published in 2001. This was described by Juan Antonio Belmonte (2001b, S86) as a 'Corpus Mensurarum, probably the largest corpus of orientation data in scientific history'.

Though Hoskin used a stringent methodology, he preferred to talk of orientations rather than alignments. Additionally, in contrast to earlier approaches, Hoskin advocated a softening in the horizon-based methodology by suggesting orientations to the sun that did not rely on rising and setting positions on the horizon. For example, for the vast majority of the sites he surveyed, he posited orientations towards the positions of the sun either climbing or descending in the sky or even overhead at the sun culminating positions when the orientations were closer to the south (see for example Hoskin *et al.* 1995). Belmonte's only criticism was that Hoskin rarely looked for a lunar explanation (Belmonte 2001b, S86). Certainly Hoskin (2001, 100, 216), although he did consider the moon, found no compelling evidence that it could account for the narrow range of orientations he discovered and preferred to call himself a 'solarist'. Earlier, following on from Thom, Ruggles had measured alignments from a defined viewing point, but, by contrast, from 1990 onwards, at many sites in Menorca, northern Iberia and Malta, Hoskin, when measuring tombs, was concerned with the field of view through the precinct entrance (see for example Hoskin *et al.* 1990). This measurement, the width of the tomb entrance, gave him a range of orientations which he termed the builders' 'signature of azimuth' while later on he devised an axis of symmetry which narrowed the possibilities (Hoskin and Nùñez 1991; Fig. 27). Hoskin preferred to present his data in easily understood circular polar charts, though he also utilised histograms for selected regions or agglomerates of regions in the last chapter of his book. These easily read charts

Figure 27. The Naveta d'Es Tudons, a megalithic chamber tomb in Menorca (see Hoskin and Nùñez 1991). Photo: Juan Antonio Belmonte.

showed the frequency of declination values for his large data sets. He generally avoided the statistical language that Ruggles employed which made his work more accessible to readers untrained in astronomy and statistics.

Some of the monuments he surveyed faced too far south for them to be directed to the sun, moon or planets, so Hoskin (1989) suggested that the Menorcan *taulas* (Fig. 28) might have been oriented to the four stars in the Southern Cross, which because of precession are no longer visible today at that location. He matched the declination of one taula oriented just south of east to Sirius, Rigel and the Orion constellation and this hypothesis meshed with the archaeological data concerning the timings of ritual animal slaughter. Although Ruggles' methodology had not proscribed stellar alignments, he made no claim for them, whereas at some sites Hoskin considered them, finding further verification in Malta that the Southern Cross was a target, together with some evidence of observation of the heliacal risings of the Pleiades (Ventura *et al.* 1993).

Another innovative feature of Hoskin's body of work was his interest in the cultural significance of orientations and how certain patterns were common to certain societies but less strong in others; where for example migration had diffused cultural patterning in Sardinia or where the cultures of eastern Catalonia were relatively isolated from other Iberian cultures (see for example, Hoskin and Pérez 1998). Although Thom had compared metrology in Britain with that in Brittany,

Figure 28. The precinct of Torralba d'en Salort in Menorca with its distinctive stone taula (see Hoskin 1989). Photo: Juan Antonio Belmonte.

this type of cross-cultural comparative research was new to archaeoastronomy and Hoskin's work included non-astronomical findings where there was no evidence of the incorporation of astronomical directions. Noting that archaeology was impoverished by its hostility to astronomical orientations, Hoskin suggested that instead of pursuing archaeoastronomy, researchers should utilise the term 'archaeotopography' rather than being limited to the measurement of tombs and the altitudes of the horizons. He felt that 'archaeotopography' was a neutral description which covered all orientations not just astronomic ones, so could include the significance of the landscape in influencing how the monuments were oriented (Hoskin 1997). For example, the entrances of 209 Cretan Late Bronze Age tombs faced the easterly horizon which was dominated by Mt Vrysinas, home to an earlier lunar sanctuary. Despite the fact that the average target was closest to the equinoxes, because the tombs faced this sacred mountain, Hoskin suggested that, in this case, a lunar explanation was the most likely (Papathanassiou and Hoskin 1996). Hoskin's archaeotopography, because it included looking for significance in the landscape and cross-cultural comparisons, was more encompassing than the alignment studies so routinely offered. Archaeotopography was a fashion briefly taken up by Belmonte (1997) who referenced the orientations of 34 Palestinian Early Bronze Age dolmens in the Jordan Valley to the sacred mountain, Mt Nebo. It has been used more recently by Giulio Magli (2010), but, like astro-archaeology, although its principles were embedded in archaeoastronomy, the terminology was short-lived. Nevertheless it was from Hoskin's archaeotopography that ideas about the landscape began to filter into archaeoastronomy.

Hoskin's extensive surveys in Europe incorporated several changes to the existing archaeoastronomical methodology, moving it away from the emphasis on the horizon. At the time archaeoastronomy had little theory so Hoskin's insights into cultural analysis and the importance of the landscape not only moved the field forward but inspired a new generation of European archaeoastronomers. Not only that but he was of the opinion that by calling the field archaeoastronomy, it claimed in advance that the prehistoric builders selected the orientations on the basis of astronomy (Hoskin 1997). His research was a marked change from some of the ethnocentric views unwittingly portrayed by other archaeoastronomers at the time, despite his being a self-confessed solarist. Had the model proposed by Hoskin in Europe, which envisaged archaeoastronomy as a data-gathering tool to enhance the known archaeology in order to aid explanations of the cultural processes underlying monumentalism, found more traction within British archaeology then the history of British archaeoastronomy could have had a different outcome.

European studies

Hoskin's research led to a renewed interest in Western European archaeoastronomy but it is difficult to trace his impact on research completed in the rest of Europe where the methods used have not been universal. In this respect, this has led to an apparent split between Western and Eastern Europe, as evidenced by their different histories.

Western Europe

Hoskin brought the archaeoastronomical study of Atlantic and Mediterranean megalithic monuments to British and American eyes through his numerous publications in the *Archaeoastronomy Supplement*. Many of these focused on the Iberian monuments in Portugal and mainland Spain as well as the Balearic Islands. The latter prompted Spanish archaeoastronomers to take up the study from the early 1990s onwards (Cerdeño *et al.* 2006, 21). Their research methodology was similar to that advocated by Ruggles so it focused on finding alignments with the aim of verifying their probability, first through the use of curvigrams and latterly by statistical analyses, though Belmonte (2009) claimed, that following Hoskin, the Spanish discipline was pioneered by an approach which combined archaeology, astronomy and history in a cultural context. The main proponents of this 'Spanish school' were Juan Antonio Belmonte and César Esteban before they were joined by A. César González-García and other like-minded astrophysicists or astronomers, who have continued to make an important contribution to the field. Indeed, according to Cerdeño *et al.* (2006, 25) they are responsible for 80% of the archaeoastronomical studies in Spain. Further details of how archaeoastronomy developed in Spain can be found in *Arqueoastronomía Hispánica*, edited by Belmonte (2000), which was first published in 1994, before being revised and reprinted in 2000. In his review for the JHA, Iwaniszewski (1996, S81–S82) wrote that it was difficult to keep up with the expansion in European cultural astronomy, suggesting that the book's contents represented the traditional view of astronomical knowledge being possessed by priests; that its study was located in the history of astronomy and that to date it did not recognise the full implications of the cultural context. However he conceded that the use of ethnohistorical evidence by Esteban, Belmonte and Aparicio (1994) in the last chapter of the book was a step towards a more mature approach to archaeoastronomical research in Spain (Iwaniszewski 1996, S84). Most of the material in the book was upgraded and updated and published as *Reflejo del Cosmos* (Belmonte and Hoskin 2002). Following this shift towards interdisciplinarity, the Spanish community has expanded (Esteban 2014, 9). This is advantageous because 'raw archaeoastronomical data are themselves not the important thing', according to Esteban (2014, 10), rather they only acquire meaning when used to interpret the culture that created them. He pointed to interdisciplinary groups, led by Cerdeño, Criado-Boado and González-García respectively, as taking cultural astronomy forward in this respect.

There have been a few archaeoastronomy courses in Spain such as the one given by Belmonte in 1998 at the International University Menendez Pelayo of Tenerife or the University of La Laguna's 'Classic astronomy' course which included a section on archaeoastronomy (Cerdeña *et al.* 2006, 25). At La Laguna, from 1994 onwards, Belmonte coordinated the PhD course on the history of astronomy which in 1999 was converted into a course on the history of astronomy and archaeoastronomy for MA students who wished to start a PhD, before it was delisted in the mid-2000s. Belmonte told me that Michael Hoskin, Clive Ruggles, Eulalia Pérez Sedeño, Julio Samsó, Stan Iwanizewski, Rolf Krauss and Ivan Šprajc were among the tutors. Other universities such as Alicante, Seville and Salamanca have offered related courses though the distancing between specialisms persists (Cerdeña *et al.* 2006, 27). There were also a few journals, such as *Complutum*, *Trabajos de Prehistoria* and *Revista de Arqueologia* that published archaeoastronomical papers (Cerdeña *et al.* 2006, 21), but not in any great number. This may have been because archaeologists in Spain were sceptical of archaeoastronomy, as they were in Britain. There were exceptions: the Spanish archaeologists Almagro-Gorbea and Gran-Aymerich directed the first archaeological project that included a wide archaeoastronomical study in Bibracte, France (Almagro-Gorbea and Gran-Aymerich 1991; Cerdeña *et al.* 2006, 23). Residual antipathy has lessened in recent years with some archaeologists beginning to believe the study of orientations should be part of landscape archaeology (Esteban 2014, 14–15; see also Criado and Quintela 2007).

The picture in Portugal is somewhat different, though researchers were similarly influenced by Hoskin. His collaborations with Portuguese archaeologists and amateur astronomers were extensive and responsible for training a generation of scholars interested in the field. Unfortunately, their impact on Portuguese academia has been rather limited, despite the constant and innovative research stemming from Portuguese archaeoastronomers. For example the paper by Marciano da Silva (2004, 475) theorised that the crossover of the spring full moon and the sun at the equinox might have had significance for prehistoric people, as an indicator of the arrival of Spring (see Glossary: crossovers). Thom's earlier contention of a megalithic equinox was never fully investigated, but here da Silva conflated it with the moon, later designated the equinoctial full moon (EFM) by Fabio Silva (da Silva 2004, 107; Silva 2016). By computing the azimuth and time of the moonrise for a period of 110 years, more than five lunar node cycles, da Silva found that the azimuth interval was between 85° and 110°, which effectively meant that all prior alignments to the equinox sun would need to be re-examined. Some new research took these findings into account (see for example González-García and Belmonte 2010).

As crossovers occur twice a month, not just at the equinoxes, Fabio Silva and Fernando Pimenta (2012) looked at the autumn full moon which da Silva had dismissed, as well as the crossover of the crescent moon for both first and last crescents in summer and winter near the solstices. They created a model of declination distributions for the crescent moons which they used for existing data sets, two in Portugal and one in Ireland. Their results for the crossovers showed broad peaks in the distribution range. This range was large enough to include the solstices and the minor standstill, therefore suggesting an alternative interpretation for lunar standstill alignments. Also in Portugal, Pimenta and Luís Tirapicos, who had both worked with Hoskin, joined with archaeoastronomical software developer Andrew Smith to produce the only application of Bayesian statistics within the field to date (Pimenta *et al.* 2009). At the central Alentejo megalithic enclosures they found some evidence that the autumn full moon might have been an orientation target (Pimenta *et al.* 2009, 11). What these papers had in common was a theoretical engagement with cultural context. In other words, rather than just producing alignment data the authors looked at how monuments captured celestial events in a symbolic way and what this might mean for the societies that built them, rather than being preoccupied with the alignments themselves, in contrast with much of the work that came from Spain. The Portuguese papers were published in English, two in the JHA and the latter in the American journal *Archaeoastronomy*, as there were and are no home-grown journals for archaeoastronomical content in Portugal. Although at least one major international conference was organised and hosted in the city of Évora (SEAC 2011), archaeoastronomy has no official presence in Portuguese universities: there are no courses, chairs, positions or official bodies that focus explicitly on archaeoastronomy or cultural astronomy. What exists is a small group of enthusiasts that routinely engage with an equally small group of open-minded archaeologists and historians to work collaboratively on research projects.

As we have seen in Chapter 4, the study of archaeoastronomy in France began during the antiquarian period with Gaillard's research at Carnac. Baudouin, Devoir and others took up the mantle in the early decades of the 20th century while Charrière painted a picture of lunar observation in the 1960s. He made a systematic study of French megaliths and published a typology of alignments (Charrière 1964). The picture after that is not clear: other than what can be gleaned from Thom (1971),

Burl (1993) and Hoskin (2001), little research seems to have been carried out locally, with the exception of that by French archaeologist Yves Chevalier. In 1997, he was intending to publish his work on the orientations of 935 dolmens located in southern France and although his doctoral thesis had been published in 1984, he died before this latest work could be published. In Hoskin's introduction to Chevalier's research, published posthumously in 1999, he wrote that, as the original paper did not include the orientation data, he managed to include them by retrieving them from Chevalier's family (Chevalier 1999, S47). Hoskin also included a translation of Chevalier's thesis summary and his article on Basque tombs, and these both adapted by Hoskin, form the basis of the 1999 paper. More recently French archaeologists have been more concerned with the significance of the landscape setting of the megalithic remains than with the sun, moon and stars (Le Roux 2002, 550–551).

During the Second World War (1942), Georg Innerebner, an Austrian, published *Sonnenlauf und Zeitbestimmung im Leben der Urzeitvölker* (Sun path and time reckoning in the life of primeval man) in the German journal *Germanien*, suggesting that as the sun was viewed as a god, each settlement would have its own system of time-reckoning because of their different landscapes and locations (Dow 2018, 52–53). It was part of his work for the Cultural Commissions organised by Himmler and as such has become politicised and fallen out of view. Similar but more serious problems faced archaeoastronomy in Germany. There, following the output of Nissen in the 19th century and that of Heinsch, Teudt and Reuter in the 1930s, archaeoastronomy took a sinister turn when it became linked with Nazi ideology, prior to and during the Second World War. For example Rolf Müller, perhaps unwittingly claimed the stone circles at Odry were built by the Aryans (Iwaniszewski 2008, 256). This tarnished image persisted for decades though more recently archaeoastronomical or cultural astronomical studies have been included in the context of the history of science, particularly natural science, through the work of anthropologist Hertha von Dechend. During the 1980s and 1990s she gave various lectures on the subject at the University of Frankfurt which resulted in a chair for the history of natural sciences and ethnology. By contrast, earlier in her career she had co-written *Hamlet's Mill* with Giorgio de Santillana; an esoteric volume, written in a popular style with scant referencing, which even they described by as 'highly unconventional' (Santillana and Dechund 1977, 57), and which Iwaniszewski more recently (2008, 255) defined it as a continuation of astralism. First published in 1969, *Hamlet's Mill* is reminiscent of the antiquarian search for ancient wisdom encoded in sky-related myths and drew some inspiration from Dupuis' *L'Origine de tous les cultes* (2005 [1798]; Santillana and Dechund 1977, ix), referred to earlier in Chapter 3. The English translation of *Hamlet's Mill* appeared in 1977 at the height of the New Age and fitted well with its esoteric culture. The book's main thesis was that Neolithic peoples gained knowledge about celestial mechanics, particularly the precession of the equinoxes, through observing the sky, which led them to adopt religions based on the changing constellations. Evidence for this could be found in myths or artefacts from around the world: stories and myths which were either transmitted from culture to culture or arrived at independently by societies who studied the heavens. Although the authors argued (Santillana and Dechund 1977, 329) that myth requires to be studied with open eyes, having set out the terms of the initial quest, they were unable to interpret their evidence in any other way.

Further interest in German archaeoastronomy was promulgated by Rolf Müller who regained his reputation by publishing *Der Himmel über dem Menschen der Steinzeit (The Sky above Stone Age Man)* in 1970. Müller carried out many surveys and was one of the first to suggest that conclusions about orientations could only be made if a statistical analysis was made of a large number of sites (Schmeidler 1988). At the Ruhr University at Bochum a research group headed by Wolfhard Schlosser (and including Gerhard Mildenberger, Michael Reinhardt and Jan Cierny) made systematic researches of prehistoric grave orientations spanning the period from the Upper Palaeolithic to the Early Bronze Age. Schlosser and Cierny published their own work entitled *Sterne und Steine* (Stars and Stones) about prehistoric astronomy and methods for recovering it in 1997.

Around this time, two discoveries prompted a resurgence of interest in sky-related subjects. A fourth Bronze Age golden hat, thought to have originated in Germany was located in a private collection in Switzerland in 1996. Two others had been found in the 19th century while the third was excavated in 1953. The hats were believed to be associated with astronomical/calendrical knowledge (Amendola 2021). The second major find was the discovery in 1999 of the Nebra sky disc; a circular Bronze Age artefact inlaid with symbols believed to represent the sun, moon and the stars, with a wealth of articles both academic and popular being written about it. However it was not until more recently that German archaeoastronomy became respectable with the founding of the society, Gesellschaft für Archäoastronomie (Society for Archaeoastronomy) in 2008, as its founder Michael Rappenglück told me. The society holds annual conferences and has organised several published volumes, such as *Prähistorische Astronomie und Ethnoastronomie (Prehistoric Astronomy and Ethnoastronomy)*, edited by Gudrun Wolfschmidt and published in 2008. Another aim of the society is to bring archaeoastronomy to the attention of the German-speaking countries (Germany, Austria and Switzerland).

Currently there is a lack of academic research or teaching of archaeoastronomy in Germany (Sticker-Jantscheff 2015, 21). This is in contrast to the situation in Switzerland where Rita Gautschy (2020) teaches two archaeoastronomy courses within the Institute for Integrative Prehistory and Archaeological Science at the University of Basel. A contributory factor for this absence in Germany might be the archaeologists' disdain for the subject, referring to it as fiction or esoteric (Sticker-Jantscheff 2015, 31–32), though in 2014 there was a symposium, entitled *Archaeoastronomy and Archaeology – Pros and Cons*, to discuss these problems. The issue that essentially prompted this conference was the controversial paper by Allard Mees (2007) about the archaeoastronomy of what was dubbed the early Celtic 'Stonehenge' discovered at Magdalenenberg in the Black Forest (Sticker-Jantscheff 2015, 33; Fig. 29). While the meeting concluded that archaeologists had no objection to archaeoastronomical interpretations, the methodology posed several issues for them and there the matter was left hanging.

Figure 29. The reconstructed wooden poles at Magdalenenberg, October, 2014. Photo: M. Sticker-Jantscheff.

In 1980s' Italy, Anthony Aveni collaborated with Giuliano Romano (1986) to look at alignments in Veneto-Friuli in the northeast of Italy. They approached their research from the American ethnographic viewpoint, considering alignments to stars named in early Latin literature. Their paper is interesting evidence of how differently the two archaeoastronomies, the green and the brown, had developed because at that time there was a complete dearth of ethnographic material in Western European archaeoastronomy. Aveni's influence continued because in the following year Proverbio and Romano also teamed up with him (Proverbio *et al.* 1987) to consider the astronomical orientations of five *tombes dei giganti* (megalithic tombs) in Sardinia. The alignment of burial sites to astronomical directions was already well-documented so this paper was more far-reaching because the authors pointed out that there were many factors which could have influenced tomb orientations, such as the avoidance of farming land, orientation to sacred mountains or the need to locate conspicuous sites. However, they felt that if they could demonstrate the non-randomness of alignments by finding a significant number of astronomically oriented points then *additionally* an astronomical hypothesis could be considered.

At this time in Italy, both archaeoastronomers and archaeologists were interested in prehistoric architecture which led to a conference in 1989, the proceedings of which were published as *Colloquio Internazionale: Archaeologia e Astronomia*, edited by Romano and Traversari in 1991 (Ruggles 1995). The first part focused on Italian contributions while the second part contained a diverse range of evidence from other cultures throughout the world. Archaeoastronomy was also the subject of three conferences held at the Accademia Nazionale dei Lincei, respectively in 1994, 1997 and 2000. These conferences paved the way for the foundation of the Italian Society for Archaeoastronomy (La Società Italiana di Archeoastronomia (SIA)) which has been organising conferences since 2000 under the presidency of Edoardo Proverbio: their proceedings have been published since 2002. The society also publishes a journal *Rivista Italiana di Archaeoastronomia*, and judging from the number of contributors, archaeoastronomy seems to be very popular in Italy. However, there seems to be no cross-fertilisation between this group and Giulio Magli, who is one of the most well-known archaeoastronomers in Italy. Magli is a professor at the Politecnico di Milano, where he is Faculty head for a MOOC course (Massive Open Online Course) on archaeoastronomy, the only one in Italy. His lecture notes for students were published in book form in 2016 and he has written other books on the subject, including the 2009 volume, *Mysteries and Discoveries of Archaeoastronomy*. Originally it appears that Italian archaeologists were sceptical of archaeoastronomy but that situation has gradually improved (Antonello 2013). Elio Antonello believes that this may be because the archaeoastronomers are now helping anthropologists and archaeologists to understand the archaeoastronomical data.

Central and Eastern Europe
By contrast, from Western eyes, little was understood about Central and Eastern European sites. This was not because of a lack of similar research but rather that any papers published were in a variety of national languages such as Bulgarian, Romanian, Czech, Polish, German or Russian. As these were to be found generally in local journals, they were therefore inaccessible to most British/American scholars (Iwaniszewski 1998, 177; 1999, 87). The differences between east and west did not end there because the central and eastern areas of Europe are not home to the megalithic monuments that were the focus of British and Western European research. Instead the monuments in this part of Europe were predominantly made of earth or timber, though there were circular enclosures, earthen and stone barrows with many more still to be discovered. Before the entire range of material remains came into consideration, the early archaeoastronomical research focused on the study of calendrics and ancient astronomy. For example, in Bulgaria there were finds of four different types of calendars together with clay models showing representations of the sun and the moon, while cult pillars possibly served as calendrically scheduling devices (Iwaniszewski 1998, 179). The starting point for the research was the Palaeolithic and bone engravings from that era which shed light on early lunar calendars (see for instance Marshack 1972); their importance confirmed by the ethnographic studies of Orlova (1966) and Konakov (1994), for example. In addition Iwaniszewski (1998, 180) found that the 'social and ritual space of central European Neolithic societies was

carefully ordered and often incorporated astronomical alignments', particularly for the Lineabandkeramik (Linear Pottery) Culture. Later societies such as the Funnel Beaker Culture oriented their long barrows towards the sunrise and sunset throughout the year, while the way burials faced also gave evidence of deliberate alignments. Much information was gathered about these Neolithic astronomical alignments and calendrical divisions of the year (for example, see Schlosser 1989; Iwaniszewski 1995a; 1997), though the preference for orientations depended on the communities, whether they be the Corded Ware Culture, Beaker peoples and so on (Iwaniszewski 1999, 97). A similar pattern of orientations was found for Bronze Age sites but at this time the emphasis on alignments to the sun prevailed as well as a preference for solar imagery on portable artefacts (Pásztor 1995a). This solar symbolism was pervasive and Pásztor found it in models of sun chariots or depictions of spiked circles and swastikas on funerary urns. Further areas of research included rock sanctuaries, dolmens and fortresses in the Thracian region (modern day Bulgaria, Greece and Turkey) (Iwaniszewski 1998, 184).

Nevertheless, as Iwaniszewski (1999, 87) pointed out, there was such a wealth of different cultural styles as expressed in architecture, cave paintings, rock art and other symbolic features, that it was difficult to find a common thread. Similarly, he found (1994a; 1999, 87) that this type of research was generally conducted by a small and diverse group of scholars, with different approaches and beliefs, rather than them employing a single set of theories and methods. They tended to work in relative isolation while carrying out their investigations outside their professional careers. The exception to this was that in Poland (and possibly elsewhere) some students travelled to Latin America to carry out research there. For example, Iwaniszewski (1992a, 57–62) analysed the output of Polish scholars and found that between 1970 and 1989 there were 106 papers published at home or abroad, with over three-quarters of these being Latin American research. While he felt that this hampered the growth of home-grown studies of archaeoastronomy and ethnoastronomy, he found that, unlike in Britain, much of the work was by or in collaboration with archaeologists who used the results 'to corroborate other archaeological and historical data' (Iwaniszewski 1994a).

As demonstrated here, in general it can be said that Central and Eastern European archaeoastronomy developed differently from that in Britain and Western Europe. Here the publication problem had a different angle because although, as shown, their research was not published in English, the reverse was true as only a few archaeoastronomical texts in English were translated into national languages; Hawkins' *Stonehenge Decoded* being one of the few accessible texts there (Iwaniszewski 1998, 178). Because those publications came from the 1960s and 1970s, they were both outdated and irrelevant for investigating the variety of remains found in past European cultures. Generally Central–Eastern European archaeoastronomy was carried out in the shadow of the megalithic studies in Atlantic Europe yet Iwaniszewski thought (1998, 190) that it was 'more "brown" than "green"' because its methods used textual evidence rather than statistics and there was more emphasis on theory.

Following a series of changes in the political, social and economical climates that took place in central and eastern Europe at the latter end of the 20th century, Iwaniszewski (1999, 112) found that there was a greater opportunity for stable and closer contacts between leading archaeoastronomers. This atmosphere may have prompted them to get together to discuss their work, which resulted in several edited volumes, such as *Readings in Archaeoastronomy* (Iwaniszewski 1992b) or *Archaeoastronomy from Scandinavia to Sardinia* (Pásztor 1995b), as well as several conferences. These consisted of a series of bi-annual conferences organised by Carlos Jaschek and Pierre Erny from 1986 onwards, which included the 1988 meeting at Tolbukhin (present day Dobrikh), Bulgaria and the following year's outing in Venice (Iwaniszewski 1994b). These meetings continued in a slightly different format under the name of *Current Problems and Future of Archaeoastronomy*, first in Warsaw, Poland in 1990, followed by ones in Székesfehérvár, Hungary in 1991 and Strasbourg, France in 1992.

This sense that the wider European community was coming together was underlined by the establishment of a new journal, *Astronomie et Sciences Humaines*, in 1988. This publication, which was largely the brainchild of Jaschek and Erny, emanated from the Strasbourg Astronomical Observatory in collaboration with the Institute of Ethnology in Strasbourg University's Faculty of Social Sciences. At the time it ceased publication in 1996, it had published 13 issues of papers, largely based on the presentations delivered at the biannual meetings which Jaschek and Erny had organised. An additional issue in 1992, entitled *European Meeting on Archaeo and Ethnoastronomy*, detailed the international meeting, mentioned above, which took place in Strasbourg in November 1992. At that meeting a new society, the Société Européenne pour l'Astronomie dans la Culture (SEAC: European Society for Astronomy in Culture), was created with its statutes being adopted the following year at its inaugural meeting in Smolyan Bulgaria, organised in conjunction with the National Astronomical Observatory Rozhen, the Institute of Astronomy and the Bulgarian Academy of Sciences. Writing about the various symposia detailed here, Ziolkowski and Lebeuf pointed out (1991, 21) that one should not get the impression that there was a consensus over theory or methodology and there were many other factors still to be taken into account.

This summary of European archaeoastronomy research is not meant to imply that it was only researchers from the above countries that were conducting related research. On the contrary, the first SEAC Newsletter (Iwaniszewski, pers. comm.), prepared for their inaugural meeting, listed research conducted in Albania, Bulgaria, the Czech Republic, Georgia, Greece, Hungary, Lithuania, Romania and Russia. Clearly SEAC is the most important organisation for European research but recently the Romanian Society for Cultural Astronomy (SRPIC) was founded in 2017. It holds annual conferences and publishes proceedings (SRPIC 2021) and members Marc and Simina Frincu (2019) recently published a monograph entitled *Astronomia străbunilor* (*Astronomy of the Ancients*). Other local groups, in addition to those mentioned, may follow. While there is evidence that most European countries have a legacy of some form or other of archaeoastronomical research dating back to antiquarianism and the early years of the 20th century, there have also been periods, such as the time between the 1940s and 1950s already described for Britain, when progress seems to have stalled. However, because of the taught courses in the last couple of decades, which have brought a new generation into the field, and the various symposia which have encouraged attendees to share research, discuss current problems and raise awareness of the prehistoric cultures of the different countries concerned, the Europe-wide interest seems to have found a sustainable form. That is not to say that all countries are equal in the quality of their academic output: too often results reflect preconceived ideas, anachronistic premises and a lack of engagement with cultural context or other disciplines while alignment hunting continues to result in overinterpretation. These vie with truly inspirational work, but it is a mixed bag overall.

Cultural astronomy

While in the Americas, archaeoastronomy and ethnoastronomy became subsumed under the general term archaeoastronomy, it was somewhat of a misnomer for these combined studies. Originally referring to the study of the presence of astronomical alignments relating to buildings and their orientation, archaeoastronomy's usage became increasingly problematic. Stanislaw Iwaniszewski was the first to recognise this and consequently coined the term *astronomía cultural* (cultural astronomy) in his PhD thesis (1988) (see Chapter 8). Subsequently he used it in his archaeoastronomy seminars at the University of Mexico from 1986 onwards. In 1991, his paper that followed his presentation at the Tolbukhin conference in 1988, not only considered a 'new paradigm', which married archaeoastronomy with ethnoastronomy, sociology astronomy and the history of astronomy, but that this paradigm should be a working framework to underpin the creation of a new discipline, that of cultural astronomy. This was the first use of the term in English (Iwaniszewski 1991, 286–287). The editorial in a Russian journal described his 1991 paper as 'a serious step towards theoretical consideration of archaeoastronomy's seat among other closely related scientific studies of a historical nature' (Gurshtein 1990, 15). Iwaniszewski told me that cultural astronomy as a term achieved gradual use in Mexico at least and was possibly picked up by the anthropologist Nicholas Saunders who was conducting research there at the time.

Iwaniszewski has defined cultural astronomy as a study of human-astronomical relations carried out in a cultural context because 'the central subject of cultural astronomy focuses on the ways people use the sky' (Iwaniszewski 1995b, 20–21). Yet he pointed out that as each society has its own lifeworld, it must be understood within the context in which it functions (Iwaniszewski 2008, 253). He had already hinted at this in a footnote (Iwaniszewski 1995b, 25) where he suggested that perhaps there was no single theory for cultural astronomy; rather it was best approached by a number of different models. The term subsequently became disseminated in European studies because of its use as part of SEAC's title (Iwaniszewski 1995b, 17).

More recently, Iwaniszewski's view was that in order to confirm an astronomical alignment hypothesis, it is necessary to examine how past and non-Western societies conceived, used and manipulated time and space categories (Iwaniszewski 2001, 5). Only if the alignment corresponded to that culture's time/space ordering and agreed with that culture's symbolic logic could it be considered astronomical: referents had to be placed in context and could only be established where there were repetitive practices. For him the main question was to do with the examination of the different functions that astronomy plays in particular sociocultural systems. As he believed that the importance of observable astronomical phenomena would be determined by cultural preference, Iwaniszewski's view of cultural astronomy therefore placed the discipline within the humanities rather than the sciences (Iwaniszewski 1989). In this respect Burl was ahead of his time when he suggested in 1982 (p. 164) that while archaeoastronomy and archaeology may provide the answers to 'how' and 'what' happened only anthropology can tell us 'why it happened' as already cited in Chapter 9. In other words Burl was advocating cultural astronomy long before the term had been coined.

Following Iwaniszewski's thesis, Clive Ruggles together with Nicholas Saunders (1993a) made an impassioned plea for the renaming of the discipline to 'cultural astronomy' as a solution to the problem of having two different archaeoastronomies, the Old World and the New. Viewing the sky as a cultural resource and because different cultures' usage of astronomy is an integral part of their behaviour, they proposed that researchers should attempt to understand it by promoting the study of the way cultures 'perceive celestial objects and integrate them into their view of the world' (Ruggles and Saunders 1993a, 1). The authors reasoned that, by combining 'complementary' evidence from related disciplines, collaboration could provide a hitherto missing link as well as providing cross-cultural comparisons. As an adjunct to this, given the limitations of the material record, analogical inference might suggest correlations that could be applied to explain cultural change. Yet this paper was not an abandonment of Ruggles' preference for statistical verification, on the contrary they promoted Bayesian statistics as a method whereby data of many different kinds can be used to corroborate a theory.

Seemingly unaware of Iwaniszewski's earlier ideas, Aveni (2008, 722), thought the importance of Ruggles and Saunders' approach was because it proposed 'nothing less than a reorientation, replete with renaming, of the interdiscipline of archaeoastronomy'. In terms of changing fashions he noted that cultural astronomy was the 'catch label' of the 1990s (Aveni 1995, S74). Despite Aveni's view of its popularity, the term cultural astronomy was not adopted wholeheartedly until Aveni used it in the title of his book, *Foundations of New World Cultural Astronomy* in 2008. Kelley and Milone's encyclopedia initially preferred archaeoastronomy in the title though this was changed to cultural astronomy in the 2011 edition. However, in Britain the term was adopted into the academy in 1997 with the first publication of *Culture and Cosmos: a journal of the history of astrology and cultural astronomy*.

Theoretically, the name change from archaeoastronomy to cultural astronomy, made alignment seeking archaeoastronomy research just part of cultural astronomy's wider ambitions. The title cultural astronomer indicates a researcher looking for any evidence of astronomy within culture; so is broader than the title archaeoastronomer, which implies a narrower focus. While this difference may be subtle, cultural astronomy had the advantage of removing itself from past perceptions of archaeoastronomy and megalithic science which had caused so much controversy, though Iwaniszewski (1989, 34) believed it had no adequate strategy to study the cognitive part of the ancient cultures. Despite this, it began to ask the sorts of questions that interpretive postprocessual archaeologists were raising. There had already been a move in archaeology towards the study of past thought processes gleaned from material remains through cognitive archaeology, following Renfrew's published lecture *Towards an Archaeology of Mind* in 1982. There he reflected that symbols were the 'clearest indicators of the functioning of mind' and that they could be understood through the use of 'cognitive archaeology' (Renfrew 1982, 13). Following these leads, Muglova and Stoev (1996) debated the limits of cognition in archaeoastronomical interpretation.

Around the same time, archaeologists were beginning to examine the symbolism embedded in monuments and sites. In Tilley's view, expressed in 1996, the separating out of utilitarian and functional aspects of behaviour from the symbolic and stylistic aspects of material culture was a misconception, ignoring Burl's earlier attempts to unite the two (Tilley 1996, 5). Many postprocessualist archaeologists, as well as believing that thoughts and ideas were as important as the material world, favoured experimentation with multiple interpretations over a final conclusion which explained everything (Johnson 2010, 93, 110). However, having set the material record straight through processual archaeology, the postprocessual discipline of archaeology could theoretically turn to the most difficult rung on Hawkes' ladder around the same time as cultural astronomy was attempting to do so.

Communities

SEAC
The adoption of cultural astronomy in Europe is reflected in the name of its most important association SEAC, as mentioned above. According to Iwaniszewski (1995b, 20–21) the usefulness of this organisation was that it stimulated research, dissemination, created contacts and common databases as well as helping develop common research projects. At least, these were the lofty aims at its inception, which it did not altogether achieve in the intervening years between then and now. Importantly it aimed to bring together researchers from both the east and west of Europe and it continues to do so partly through offering reduced prices for the poorer eastern European nations. SEAC's formal inauguration took place in Smolyan, Bulgaria in 1993, under the presidency of Ruggles, with Jaschek among the vice-presidents and Iwaniszewski as secretary. SEAC's formal aims included the interdisciplinary promotion of cultural astronomy and the encouragement of research (Koleva and

Kolev 1996, xiii). Ruggles suggested (1994b) that as the scope of these activities was wider than earlier debates about megalithic astronomy, he felt that Europe could be said to have taken up its place alongside the Americas 'as a centre for up-to-date research in archaeoastronomy and cultural astronomy'.

The primary aims of SEAC were set out in the following statutes, published in SEAC's first proceedings (Koleva and Kolev 1996, xiii):

- to promote the interdisciplinary study of astronomical practice in its cultural context as a topic of considerable importance within the general study of human societies and their relationship to their environment;
- to promote research seeking to develop our understanding of the cultural significance of astronomical knowledge through the integration of techniques and methods within the humanities and social sciences, astronomy, and methodological disciplines.

Since then, the wording has been changed slightly in favour of a more neutral and inclusive description: 'the humanities, natural sciences, social sciences and other disciplines', notably ensuring that astronomy was not singled out, but rather included as part of the natural sciences (SEAC 2020).

SEAC conferences (see Fig. 30), which attract around 85 invited talks, presentations and posters each year, have been held annually in different European cities since 1993, though the 2020 conference was cancelled because of the coronavirus pandemic. They mainly provide an off-campus institutional base primarily for British and European archaeoastronomers, though it has welcomed some participants from the Americas and around the world. Yet while SEAC is in an ideal position to be an educator, Sims reported that its 'educational initiatives have so far been stillborn, since no consensus exists on method or models' (pers. comm. 2014). Although its popularity has waned over the years, dropping from 140 members in 2017 to 87 in 2021, largely as a result of a re-organisation of membership criteria. SEAC's original statutes included the unrealised ideal of establishing a journal, but in 2014 it was announced that their

Figure 30. The 18th meeting of the European Society for Astronomy in Culture (SEAC) at Gilching, Germany, September 2010. © vhs Gilching, 2010.

conference proceedings 'may in fact be considered as a substitute for an annual journal'. A set of proceedings is published after each annual conference but their content and quality varies, though the volumes for 2004, 2010 and 2011 (Pásztor 2007; Pimenta *et al.* 2015; Rappenglück *et al.* 2016) were published by British Archaeological Reports (BAR) after a much higher level of peer review than in the past. The influence of their proceedings is debatable as they are difficult to access, often delayed and mainly available to conference attendees only, so it is unlikely that their content is accessible for mainstream archaeological review, apart from those published by BAR.

While alignment studies continue to proliferate, the switch from archaeoastronomy to cultural astronomy has encouraged many ethnographic papers as a result of the widening of the field. Between archaeology and archaeoastronomy the sacred, cultural link was missing and European archaeoastronomy has looked increasingly towards ethnography to bridge the gap; research such as that of Roslyn Frank (1996), Emilia Pásztor (1993) and Arnold Lebeuf (1996) amongst others, for example. Ruggles (1993c, 121) welcomed this initiative as he believed that ethnographic fieldwork, where available, was a far more promising resource than any form of archaeoastronomical data. Accordingly, the previously narrow scope of prehistoric research has widened to include time periods from the Palaeolithic through to the 19th century and its geographic footprint extended beyond Europe with its cross-cultural parallels. Also the entire sky became open for consideration, not just the sun and the moon but comets, planets, constellations and the Milky Way.

The theme of each SEAC conference is determined by the local Organising Committee of the country concerned, and the venues have alternated between western and eastern European cities since its inception. For the 1998 conference in Dublin, organised by Ruggles, Prendergast and Ray, the theme was 'Astronomy, cosmology and landscape', chosen because:

> the theme of landscape perception has provided one of the most important links between archaeoastronomy and recent developments in theoretical archaeology, through their strong common interest in questions of cosmology and cognition. (Ruggles *et al.* 2001, vii)

Consequently archaeologists Aubrey Burl and Professors George Eogan and Gabriel Cooney were invited speakers. It was a positive step forward in reconciling the fields and showed evidence of a slow shift by archaeoastronomers towards acceptance of concepts already explored within archaeology and anthropology, such as landscape and culture. Only the Malta conference in 2014 has since tried to bridge the gap between archaeoastronomy and archaeology.

ISAAC

To further cultural astronomy beyond Europe, the International Society for Archaeoastronomy and Astronomy in Culture (ISAAC) was founded in 1996. The idea for this new international community came from Ruggles and Steven McCluskey, a historian of astronomy who has a special interest in archaeoastronomy. Referring back to the Kintigh debate, they felt that archaeoastronomers still sensed a lack of respect from other disciplines (Ruggles and McCluskey 1996). One of the reasons for this was that they believed archaeoastronomy had no single set of professional standards to answer the social questions that archaeologists were asking. Although there were regional groups such as SEAC in Europe or the Historical Astronomy Division in America, there was no representative international body to advocate the significance of archaeoastronomy. Also, while there was 'an internal sense of scholarly community' they recognised that the 'largely personal efforts, building on the efforts of a few dedicated individuals ... have limited influence outside of our interdisciplinary community (Ruggles and McCluskey 1996). Although the closest thing to a worldwide international group was the International Steering Committee for the 'Oxford' Conferences under the leadership of Aveni and Hoskin, it was not a membership organisation. It was these factors which led Ruggles and McCluskey to establish ISAAC while the names of both SEAC and ISAAC recognised the transition from archaeoastronomy to cultural astronomy.

Under the presidency of Ruggles, ISAAC only admitted to full membership those applicants who were active in the field, as evidenced by published research, though this has recently changed so that full members have to be 'professional PhD-qualified cultural astronomers' (ISAAC 2021). In addition, the professional status of cultural astronomy could be further advanced by forming ties with existing international, regional and national academic bodies, and with this in mind ISAAC took over the 'Oxford' conferences in 2004. There had been no new journal to replace *Archaeoastronomy, the Journal of Astronomy in Culture* since its demise in 2011 so ISAAC decided to found its own journal, the *Journal of Astronomy in Culture* in 2016, as mentioned in Chapter 8. Aimed to cater for interdisciplinary facets of cultural astronomy, it has only ever published one issue and in that there was no British or European content.

INSAAP

On the margins of SEAC and ISAAC is INSAP (The Inspiration of Astronomical Phenomena), a small community founded in 1994, which holds conferences every three years. INSAP boasts an interdisciplinary home for sky-related issues stemming from various fields, though it deliberately excludes ethno- and archaeoastronomy as these subjects are 'better handled by other, more specialized meetings' (INSAP 2021). In 2017 all three organisations combined to host a joint meeting at Santiago del Compostela, which boasted an audience of 300 participants (Boutsikas 2018, 134).

EAA

In Europe, if archaeoastronomers wish to promote archaeoastronomy and engage with archaeologists the European Association of Archaeologists (EAA) conferences are the place to do it. The EAA had its inaugural meeting in 1994, just one year later than SEAC. Its first annual meeting took place in Santiago de Compostela in 1995 with subsequent conferences taking place in a different European country each year. Primarily an association for European archaeologists it welcomes 'other related or interested individuals or bodies in Europe and beyond' (EAA 2021). Currently it has over 15,000 members, some of whom are prehistorians interested in the same material legacy that archaeoastronomers survey. One of its primary aims is to promote the development of archaeological research and it achieves this by organising annual conferences which host multiple sessions.

Yet archaeoastronomers did not realise the potential of taking part in the EAA conferences until 1999, when in Bournemouth, England, Emília Pásztor organised a specific archaeoastronomy session precisely to discuss the relationship between archaeoastronomers and archaeologists and to evaluate 'archaeoastronomy's potential for adding new knowledge to our understanding of prehistoric cultures' (Pásztor 1999). Stanislaw Iwaniszewski attended her session and went on to host *Astronomy, Materiality and Changing Landscape* at Esslingen, Germany in 2001, while there was a third session, *Ad Astra per Aspera et per Ludum* in 2002 at Thessaloniki, Greece, organised by Amande Alice Maravelia. Unfortunately these sessions were not as promising as they sounded because Iwaniszewski has told me that since they were mostly attended by archaeoastronomers, not archaeologists, SEAC decided not to participate any further, especially as the dates of SEAC and EAA conferences often overlapped.

However, this hard-line mood changed eventually so that at SEAC 2017, Felipe Criado-Boado, president of the EAA from 2014 to 2021, in line with his association's policy of promoting 'cooperation with other organisations with similar aims', hinted that the EAA might host an archaeoastronomy session in the future. Subsequently a formal invitation was offered and, at the EAA conference in Bern in August 2019, the 27th annual SEAC conference took place within the larger conference. This comprised three SEAC archaeoastronomy sessions: 'Frontiers in theory, methodology and education within cultural astronomy'; 'Cultural astronomy, skyscape and ontology: how celestial objects and events have featured in the belief systems, cosmologies and worldviews of different societies' and 'The archaeology of astronomy: concepts of space and time materialised in cultures'. This latter session illustrated the potential of archaeoastronomy and its relevance to archaeology (Zotti 2019, 217). In addition there was a Round Table discussion, 'Archaeology and cultural astronomy, bridging the gap between trench and sky' which had two archaeologists and two cultural astronomers on the panel for a public discussion. Unfortunately Zotti (2019, 219) reported that there were only 20 participants who were mainly SEAC members and this and the lack of well-planned promotion meant that SEAC had really missed its chance. SEAC has not planned future collaborations and SEAC did not offer a virtual event for its cancelled 2020 conference. By contrast the EAA hosted a massive online conference with two archaeoastronomy sessions, one hosted by Emilia Pásztor and the other by Stanislaw Iwaniszewski, both of which were well attended.

The implications for archaeoastronomy

Through the JHA and its *Supplement*, Hoskin brought his surveys of monuments in Europe to a wide English-speaking audience which was largely unaware of how archaeoastronomy had been developing locally in Europe. Yet, in almost every European country there was a history of and continuance of the practice of archaeoastronomy, as shown above. Nevertheless, because most of the publications were in local languages they were not widely distributed and this was detrimental for archaeoastronomy's development because their input of new ideas and methods, tailored particularly for the many different types of monuments under consideration, were not widely disseminated. It was not until some Spanish research papers appeared in the JHA in English in the early 1990s or when the publication of SEAC proceedings became more accessible because of a change in publishers, could the British and American communities begin to keep up with this research from outside their areas.

Cultural astronomy, as an umbrella term for both green and brown archaeoastronomy, was the suggested name change, but despite Aveni's assessment of its popularity and its inclusion in the names of the SEAC and ISAAC's communities, archaeoastronomy still appears to be the preferred short-hand term for both types. This seems to be because the name of a field conveys identity and autonomy from other disciplines and becomes so rooted in tradition that changes are often misleading, internally and externally. What was practised in the New World from the 1970s onwards could easily have been called cultural astronomy but it had not been thought of at the time when archaeoastronomy seemed a brave new term. This was especially true in Britain as the name change there indicated the demise of the unpalatable megalithic science. For Ruggles (1993a, 6), because cultural astronomy combined the varying aspects of astronomy, whether archaeo- or ethno- into a single mode of enquiry, it would be strong enough to foster cross-disciplinary exchanges with mainstream disciplines. Following Dogan's suggestion (1996, 297) with regard to hybridisation, the hybrid field, in this case cultural astronomy, could be independent or claim an allegiance with another speciality, that of archaeoastronomy. Cultural astronomy is an example of a bottom-up approach where complementary specialisms merge to form a larger field.

It was the European organised conferences and symposia from the late 1980s onwards that led to the formation of SEAC which, from the very start, adopted cultural astronomy fully. Together with the ISAAC and 'Oxford' conferences the effect was two-fold. First, they helped consolidate the archaeoastronomical community which Schaefer (1999, 93) thought was still, in 1999, living with 'the fallout of those days when a large fraction of the results were merely bad science'. As cultural theorist Mary Douglas expressed it (1970, 166), 'When the community is attacked from outside at least the external danger fosters solidarity within'. Secondly, they widened archaeoastronomy's reach, so for example, the fifth 'Oxford' conference was publicised on the internet as well as being widely advertised to archaeologists and anthropologists, which accounted for a larger and more varied audience (Fountain and Sinclair 2005, x). Similarly, in 1999, Oxford VI combined with SEAC for a joint conference in Tenerife where it was noted that the interdisciplinary character of cultural astronomy was reflected by the attendance of astronomers, historians, anthropologists, archaeologists and historians of science (Esteban and Belmonte

2000a). It was Esteban and Belmonte's opinion that 'not many scientific disciplines can be enriched with so [many] diverse points of view'. So, once these communities had been established, which in some small way made up for the lack of institutional presence at universities, the only problem for archaeoastronomy and cultural astronomy was that there seemed to be no cross-fertilisation within the relevant disciplines of the attendees that they boasted. Nevertheless, these organisations and the conferences they spawned brought some coherent sense of unity to the field, not just in Europe but internationally. Yet there was one crucial difference between British and European archaeoastronomy in that much archaeoastronomical fieldwork in Europe was carried out with, or commissioned by, professional archaeologists and used to corroborate other archaeological and historical data. Therefore, in the whole continent of Europe, Britain remained an isolated instance where archaeoastronomy was seemingly divorced from archaeology.

To overcome contestation or sidelining, archaeoastronomers had to begin thinking like archaeologists, or as Zeilik (1989), expressed it, 'We should work with an archaeological awareness for every site and culture and even generate hypotheses that the archaeologists can test for us!'. Yet, despite the invitations to members of other related disciplines to their conferences, there was not that much chance of a new dialogue because the founding SEAC and ISAAC, though providing internal validation, added to archaeoastronomy's isolation. In this respect the archaeoastronomers were certainly concerned with self-image. This can be evidenced by their questions, constantly posed during this period, as to whether archaeoastronomy was a discipline in its own right, whether or not it should be regarded as a subdiscipline of either anthropology or archaeology, or whether it was an interdiscipline. How influential and important these debates were is unquantifiable but clearly they are of value in assessing the practice and progress of the discipline. Additionally, the conferences serve as arenas for peer approval in an otherwise generally sceptical academic climate. On balance though, the two cultural astronomy societies, one European and one international, together with the smaller regional associations in Europe and the Americas, have helped enhance self-reproduction, continuity and longevity. When archaeoastronomy only rarely appeared on the academic curriculum, these conferences and their published output constituted the discipline itself. Yet while there were some positives, the opportunity to take archaeoastronomy and cultural astronomy out of the safe havens of the dedicated communities and engage with archaeologists at the EAA conferences has largely been lost. This is detrimental to both archaeoastronomy and cultural astronomy and ultimately to archaeology.

Chapter 11

Archaeoastronomy in the 21st century

Despite the twists and turns in its history, archaeoastronomy has survived and is still a relevant field of enquiry today: indeed Clive Ruggles thought in 2011 that archaeoastronomy and ethnoastronomy were 'burgeoning' in terms of published research (Ruggles 2011b, 2). However he questioned whether archaeoastronomers had been 'running round the same circles' for the last 30 years, or 'pushing back the frontiers' (Ruggles 2011b, 3). This implied that, unless there was a fresh impetus, archaeoastronomy would be locked into the existing framework of using horizon astronomy to measure alignments to the sun, moon and occasionally stars and, when the data permitted, subjecting the results to statistical evaluation. Research based on this practice continues to dominate conference presentations and proceedings: for example in the proceedings of the 2014 SEAC conference, there were nine papers in Part 3, 'Astronomical orientations' plus five others ordered by their geographical location; a total of 14 in all (Silva *et al.* 2016). The remaining 13 were equally divided between cosmology, the history of astronomy and cultural astronomy. There is of course room for alignment studies but the issue Ruggles was more concerned with was whether archaeoastronomy had broadened its scope from being primarily a methods-based tool towards a more interpretive approach to mirror developments in theoretical postprocessual archaeology (Ruggles 2011b, 3; 2015b, 360; see also Henty 2020b). Ruggles' question rather hinted at the idea that archaeoastronomy was stagnating, so now a decade on from that paper it is time to reassess whether there has been any progress in the intervening years.

This chapter will bring archaeoastronomy's history up to date and show that far from stagnating, archaeoastronomy has been re-invigorated by improvements in methodology, the addition of new astronomical concepts and several theoretical shifts. Not only that, but it has strengthened its core by engaging with the various turns to ontology, reflexivity and phenomenology. More than at any time in its history, archaeoastronomy has proved to be adaptable to what is occurring in other related disciplinary areas and that has had a positive impact on its relationship with archaeology, especially after the introduction of skyscape archaeology from 2014 onwards.

Re-invigorating archaeoastronomy

The new impetus that Ruggles was looking for in 2011 had already started some years earlier, yet while there was no *fundamental* theoretical shift many creative ideas contributed to a fresh way of looking at things. Unlike earlier periods in archaeoastronomy's history where key personalities such as Stukeley, Lockyer, Hawkins, Thom and Ruggles had prefaced significant paradigm changes, in the early years of the 21st century many archaeoastronomers played their part in revitalising archaeoastronomy. Some of them began to look at the sun, the moon and the stars in a different way and here certain ideas which had never really gained traction were re-explored. The first related to shadows cast by the sun, originally considered by Chapple in 1778 (see Chapter 3). Although it was briefly taken up again in 1912 (see Chapter 4), the notion then lay dormant until Prendergast's 1991 research (see Chapter 9). In the current period it was revived in terms of solar hierophanies respectively by Belmonte *et al.* (2013) and McCluskey (2015). Additionally, new findings with respect to shadow phenomena were proposed by Daniel Brown (2016a) and Olwyn Pritchard (2016). Secondly, because Thom's megalithic calendar, based on solar positions throughout the year, had generally been dismissed, only solstitial or equinoctial alignments were sought in the following decades. However, new research from Douglas Scott (2016) and Bernadette Brady (2017) showed that the cross-quarter days, particularly those in November and February, might have been a focus for alignments.

While the overall influence of the sun was being re-evaluated in this way, research which discovered new aspects of the moon's cycle threatened the dominance of Thom's lunar metanarrative with its focus on standstills, an emphasis which was rarely questioned. The initial impetus came from Marciano da Silva (2004), as described earlier in Chapter 10. Generally lunar standstill alignments were simply treated as data but da Silva's research was innovative in that he drew on anthropology to try and picture prehistoric cosmology in order to underpin the significance of his findings on crossovers. Similarly Silva and Pimenta's work (Silva and Pimenta 2012; Silva 2016) on crossovers was an overt challenge to the paradigm of minor standstill alignments. By noting distributions, these three research papers went beyond the traditional focus of archaeoastronomy which relates single values of declination to major events. Around the same time Lionel Sims (2007a) used the anthropological template of Chris Knight (1991), whose thesis was influenced by Claude Levi-Strauss and Alexander Marshack, to propose a theory of the symbolic importance of dark moon as hunter-gather societies transitioned to Neolithisation.

Stellar alignments were also revisited and examples can be found in Morgan Saletta's (2011) research on the megalithic monuments at Arles-Fontvieille which suggested that the heliacal rising of the Pleiades and Orion may have been observed and represented in the rock art there, and Belmonte and González-García's (2015) findings at Carthago Nova, relating to Canopus. Other research has also found alignments to the Pleiades and Orion at Augusta Raurica in Switzerland (Sticker-Jantscheff 2018); Orion at Tomnaverie Recumbent Stone Circle (Henty 2014) and Aldebaran at the Carregal Do Sal dolmens in Portugal (Silva 2014a), while evidence of precession was found in the alignment of the Sardinian Nuraghic *tombes di giganti* to the Southern Cross (Zedda and Belmonte 2004). Bernadette Brady's specialised studies of star phases, which regulate their periods of visibility and invisibility, and star paths as possible identifiers of critical sunrises and sunsets, have brought much clarity to this previously under-researched field (Brady 2015a; 2015b).

The predominant archaeoastronomical method was to look at either individual sites or groups of similar sites constructed in the same period. However, following on from Ruggles and Saunders' idea of using archaeoastronomy to explain cultural change, as noted in Chapter 10, González-García and Costa-Ferrer (2011) experimented with a new approach, that of looking at one geographical area diachronically, taking into account 'a long archaeological sequence' to see whether evidence of evolution or radical change in the customary patterns of orientation matched the cultural changes inferred from the material evidence. Their study spanned from the Neolithic to the Roman era, while another examination of continuity and change, in monuments found in a small area in northeast Scotland, looked at the time span from the Mesolithic to the Bronze Age (Henty 2015). This type of archaeoastronomical study could potentially aid explanations of cultural and material transitions or change that many archaeologists are concerned with.

While it was recognised that archaeoastronomical investigations had to mesh with the known archaeology, some archaeoastronomers began looking to other disciplines for insights, as well as mixing techniques and methods to come up with something new. Frank Ventura (2017) proposed that substantive questions cannot be answered by looking for alignments alone but require conceptual schemes to consider motivation and meaning before interpretation is possible. Similarly Sims, as discussed in Chapter 9, drew on other disciplines to create a more effective model for research (Sims 2013). However, in general archaeoastronomers were simply out of tune with developments outside their own specialised interests, despite the nudge given by Ruggles in 2011. While it was generally accepted in archaeoastronomy that bias could affect interpretation, there seems to be no evidence at this time that archaeoastronomers adopted reflexivity in the way that Hodder had suggested for archaeology (see Chapter 9).

In conjunction with the theory changes detailed above, methodology was also scrutinised. On the practical side, large data sets still needed to be statistically examined for evidence of intentionality. In this context, Silva (2017a) compared the curvigram method with the maximum likelihood method, finding the latter to be more precise. He followed this up with a plea that uncertainty in measurements needs to be accurately recorded along with the other statistical evidence (Silva 2020a). There were also useful technical advances in surveying and 'geo-spatial measurement technologies', which, because they demand a 'high level of technical expertise', have developed into specialisms within archaeoastronomy (Prendergast 2015; see also Schiavottiello 2009). Similarly computer graphics and digital terrain models may also need to be created by experts (see Zotti 2015). For example, John MacDonald's (2006) paper introduced an advance in methodology by using a 3D simulation model of Stonehenge and a 3D visualisation model projected onto the sky created with the planetarium software 'SkyMap Pro'.

Planetarium software was in its infancy at the start of the 21st century and there are now many options available. One of these is 'Stellarium' which is an invaluable freeware planetarium program. It provides a realistic 3D sky which shows celestial bodies in the sky for any date or time in history or prehistory (+/–200,000 years) and for any longitude and latitude on earth: fully searchable it has a catalogue of over 600,000 stars and a realistic Milky Way depiction. First launched in 2001, it was not at first wholly reliable, but its version 0.21.0, released in March 2021, has many useful features for archaeoastronomers, such as a plug-in for 'archaeolines', which show the paths of the sun and moon or, if required, user defined declinations for the cross-quarter sun for example (Stellarium 2021). Andrew Smith's 'Horizon' (2018) is a landscape visualisation tool using Digital Terrain Model/Digital Elevation Model mapping data which enables a site panorama to be uploaded into Stellarium. Landscapes can also be generated by horizon profiling software 'HeyWhatsThat' (2021). Another variant is Silva's 'skyscapeR', an open-source R package for data reduction, visualisation and analysis in cultural astronomy (Silva 2021). Archaeoastronomy, because of its technical methodology, has generally been a closed field to those who cannot practice it but the development of these computer applications has meant that it has become more accessible for those with a background in other fields.

The overall result of these new approaches has meant that some archaeoastronomers have been shying away from the singular methodology of finding alignments towards a more plural approach in line with postprocessual archaeology; a move which has produced a more modulated and complex picture than that created by using astronomy alone. New questions have been asked and these have been underlined by a willingness to question the existing and restrictive practices of the 1980s and 1990s, when their narrower focus on finding the usual alignments by examining large data-sets generally deterred experimentation.

The ontological turn

While archaeoastronomers were looking at their practices with new eyes, radical and far-reaching theory developments within sociological, philosophical and anthropological literature were making the case for the turn to ontology. Innovations included the Actor-Network Theory developed by the sociologist Bruno Latour (2005) and the Material Engagement Theory developed by Lambros Malafouris (2013), which combined archaeology, philosophy and anthropology with cultural neuroscience. These theories can be linked together as they propose a similar understanding of the world. For example, Latour (2005, 193) suggested that all systems in reality are driven by networks of relationships and that these relationships extend to both human and non-human actors, while Malafouris (2013, 213) questioned the division between organic and inorganic, arguing that human cognition is in constant interaction with the material world. By removing these dichotomies then many different 'things' can be combined together to make what can be considered as 'a single whole' (Harris and Cipolla 2017, 139; see also DeLanda 2016, 8). In this respect there is a close connection between ideas of assemblages put forward by the French philosopher Gilles Deleuze and those of Ingold's meshworks. Additionally, Deleuze's theory of assemblages signifies an approach that looks at the 'whole as an inextricable combination of interrelated parts' (Little 2019). Similarly, Ingold looked at the material world as the 'fluxes and flows of *materials*' in a 'meshwork of interwoven lines of growth and movement' (Ingold 2010, 3).

In archaeology, these tacit assumptions that existing concepts, such as the dualisms inherent in nature/culture, human/non-human or animate/inanimate, are inadequate to explain the world in its entirety have prefaced what has come to be known as 'the ontological turn' which investigates 'the fundamental character of worldly entities' (Thomas 2015, 1290). These new ideas have certainly given archaeologists pause for thought and they began to be thrashed out at TAG conferences from 2005 onwards, some years before they were published in mainstream archaeological texts (see for example Downes 2005, 3–4; Pollard 2005, 4). The discussion appeared to culminate with a session entitled 'Archaeological ontologies' at TAG 2008, where the following proposition was presented: that the difference between the epistemological divide between human culture and non-human things could be solved through ontological thinking (Jones and Hicks 2008, 45). Only by escaping the subject/object dichotomy is there the potential of really understanding the past (Cobb *et al.* 2008). Pluciennik's warning (2012, 34) in general was that the academy 'tends to valorise the new' over the repetition of existing models, yet overall uptake has been slow.

This new way of trying to comprehend essential issues in archaeology follows other developments in anthropology which began with a critique of the very notion that we can understand other worldviews by visiting them from a worldview that is culturally our own, where our concepts are simply inadequate to 'translate *different* ones' (Henare *et al.* 2007, 12). The underlying ideology of the ontological turn is that there are many different worlds (ontologies) and that they can only be uncovered by 'thinking through things' in order to conceive of a world in the way that the inhabitants of that world do (Henare *et al.* 2007, 15). Expressed in this way, 'things' such as stones or pots are not inanimate objects but may have agency and relationships, thereby placing animism and alterity (otherness) at the heart of ontological thinking.

Holbraad and Pedersen, proposed the ontological turn as a new methodology in which 'reflexivity, conceptualization and experimentation' are key, so that it is not so much a matter of 'seeing differently' but of 'seeing *different* things (Holbraad and Pedersen 2017, 6, 9). An example of this would be how a consecrated powder, which may just be powder to us, is power to Afro-Cuban diviners (Holbraad and Pedersen 2017, 220–227). In other words, they argued that anthropological concepts have to be rethought or transformed to understand cultures that are different from that of the analyst. In *Thinking Through Things*, the point was made that '"different worlds" reside in things' (Henare *et al.* 2007, 14). Similarly Alberti agreed that ontology could be a tool for 'unsettling our uncertainties', or an invitation to 'think difference' (Alberti *et al.* 2011, 901; Alberti 2016, 141).

If implemented in the way Holbraad and Pedersen envisaged, then the ontological turn would be a change which could disrupt the continuity of the astronomical methodology and it is evident that some archaeoastronomers were influenced by the new anthropological thinking, especially as Ruggles had already noted the gap between western and non-western views of the sky (Ruggles 2011b, 2). While acknowledging that we need to break out of the dichotomies such as the nature/culture split, Malville (2010) favoured an emic (insider) ethnographic approach to obtain the 'thick descriptions' favoured by Geertz (1973). In an effort to avoid ethnocentricism, Malville tried to envisage the ontology of the Incas and theorised that the Andean *huacas* (shrines) 'possessed supernatural power and an animating essence for people, crops, and animals'. In this instance Malville was attempting to recapture the essence of the Incas ontologically as opposed to recreating their worldview epistemologically. Similarly, Iwaniszewski (2010) was also attempting to extricate pre-modern worldviews from 'socially and culturally disembedded cosmologies relying on specific epistemological frameworks'. However, his description of ontologies as worldviews or cosmologies was more redolent of an epistemological approach. Nevertheless, more recently, while describing cultures that do not recognise the nature/culture split of the inanimate/animate world, by contending that many instances from the ethnographic record attest to celestial bodies being seen as animate entities whose motions in the sky are recognised as social relations, he allowed that these could be studied 'in ontological terms', rather than through epistemology (Iwaniszewski 2011). By moving away from traditional archaeoastronomy, Iwaniszewski, informed by Bourdieu's notions of habitus and field, advocated an approach which he called 'the sky-as-a-social-field', which was 'capable of highlighting the multiplicity of celestial interpretations observed within the same society'(Iwaniszewski 2011, 35–36). The underlying theory was that the implicit act of agency involved in the design of monuments changed the very nature of the sky from an immutable entity outside the capability of human interference into something mutable; in other words the sky belongs to nature, the skyscape belongs to society. Importantly Iwaniszewski (2011, 36) suggested that this methodology mirrored recent developments in theoretical archaeology, for which he cited Latour's actor-network theory (2005) and Ingold's 'dwelling ontology' (2000), which had drawn on anthropological perspectives to offer new solutions to treating celestial bodies as animate entities.

In this vein, Vadala and Milbrath (2016), by looking at the components of the assemblage as being the sky and the natural and built environment, followed Delanda's approach to ontology where he argued that all objects of study should be viewed as heterogeneous parts rather than *a priori* or pre-defined objects of study. By employing a 3D virtual reality model Vadala and Milbrath argued (2016, 26) that this gave them a phenomenological and subjective 'first-person view of how things might have looked to the ancient Maya'. While these authors represent some engagement with the turn to ontology, the uptake of these ideas in archaeoastronomy is slow. It may also be problematic for those archaeoastronomers reliant on archaeoastronomy's scientific methodology because as López (2011, 42) pointed out, when considering measurement precision, in many cultures 'the "fuzziness" of measurements is in fact both necessary and desirable': his view is a palimpsest of the problem. As Iwaniszewski (2015a, 4) argued, 'despite the growing interest in ancient epistemologies and indigenous ontological views, archaeoastronomers rarely deal with spatial and temporal representations of cultures and peoples'. Nevertheless, there is a move to keep developments in archaeoastronomy contemporaneous with those in the humanities, particularly those in anthropology, and the turn to ontology was the motivation for a round table discussion at SEAC in 2018. Overall, the turn to ontology may be a marginal phenomenon for most archaeoastronomers who focus primarily on finding alignments rather than considering theory and in this respect they have not yet mirrored this shift in interest, despite the above attempts to reconstruct the ontologies of cultures, particularly in the New World.

Skyscapes and skyscape archaeology

The emergence of the concepts of *skyscapes* and *skyscape archaeology* was prefaced by a new way of looking at the archaeological record phenomenologically. Archaeoastronomers have of course always been concerned with the sky but by focusing on rising and setting events at the horizon, the dynamism, movement and sheer spectacle of the sky got lost (Henty 2020b, 25). If there was less focus on horizon events, the entire skyscape could come under consideration. This had been made clear by the archaeologist Jan Harding and his colleagues in their ground-breaking research in 2006 relating to Neolithic beliefs and practices at the Thornborough monument complex in Yorkshire, where they described the sky as '[the] people's skyscape' and suggested that 'the skyscape was an integral part of beliefs and practices' (Harding *et al.* 2006, 26, 48). In their seminal paper, they described how they placed themselves 'in an environment whereby the phenomenology of experience could be considered' (Harding *et al.* 2006, 28). Rather than looking for the traditional solar and lunar horizon events, they wanted to collate as much information about the sky as possible, including the movement of stars. Their research suggested that the henges at Thornborough might have deliberately referenced the midwinter sunrise, Orion's Belt and other celestial phenomena; therefore suggesting that there was a close relationship between the 'people's skyscape and life cycles' (Harding *et al.* 2006, 26).

While archaeology had already embraced phenomenology, it was this paper by Harding *et al.* that laid the foundation for phenomenological archaeoastronomy. The first archaeoastronomer to use the phenomenological method explicitly was Sims in 2009 when he combined 'the phenomenology of a particular monument with another robust method, in this case archaeoastronomy', to 'address different properties of the same monument [Silbury Hill]' (Sims 2009, 389). Other phenomenological approaches followed, such as Silva's (2014a) examination of Portuguese dolmens, the results of which were also corroborated by folklore, or Ilaria Cristofaro's (2017) exploration of the reflection of the sky in water which was an auto-ethnographic project using reflexive phenomenology. As researchers attempted to re-conceptualise the dynamic element of the sky through the eyes of the monument builders, new insights were gained. For example, Sims rejuvenated North's 1996 theory to propose that the builders of Stonehenge deliberately constructed 'windows' to the sky to watch the trajectory of the solstice sun and the standstill moon (Sims 2007a). The idea of monuments containing deliberately constructed windows to the sky gained traction with Silva's research on the 'window of visibility' formed by the entrances of Portuguese dolmens (Silva 2013, 103; 2014a). Around the same time, I published research on the window framed by the recumbent arrangement at Tomnaverie stone circle in Aberdeenshire, the view from which allowed the possibility that many celestial events were of importance (Henty 2014).

According to the *Oxford English Dictionary*, the term skyscape first appeared in print in a poem by S.T. Coleridge in 1811 and was popularly used to describe paintings where the sky figured prominently, but its subsequent use in archaeoastronomy appears to be a 21st century appropriation. Skyscape(s), both as a term and a concept, was introduced to explore the cultural engagement that societies had/have with the sky and why skyscapes are important (Silva 2015a). Silva also suggested that its use would distance it from old archaeoastronomical assumptions so that 'new connections can be crafted' (Silva 2015a, 3). When defining skyscape, his caveat was that ideas about skyscapes (or landscapes), are not necessarily universal and that cultures, though accessing the same sky, may see completely different skyscapes (Silva 2015a; 2017b). Harding and his colleagues did not explicitly explain their use of skyscape but it can be inferred from a close reading of their paper (2006). This shows how they made a distinction between the sky as being part of the natural world, which could be reproduced with the use of planetarium software, and the people's skyscape which is imbued with meaning. Drawing on Cumming's use of landscape, Silva (2015a, 2) confirmed

Figure 31. Fabio Silva and Liz Henty opening the Visualising Skyscapes session at the Theoretical Archaeology Group conference in Southampton, 2016. Photo: Georg Zotti.

this idea by saying 'the sky is a natural phenomenon that is turned into a cultural skyscape through human agency'. Its current usage varies; for example, Sims (2009, 389) spoke of 'a less restricted definition of landscape which includes skyscape' while Brown (2015, 95) recognised skyscape as the sky 'set in scene by people, landscape and monument'.

If, as noted in Chapter 10, cultural astronomy became the 'catch-label' of the 1990s, then from 2012 onwards, skyscapes became the new catch-word for British archaeoastronomy through its dissemination. For example, what would have been called 'archaeoastronomy sessions', were described as 'skyscape sessions', following initiatives at the TAG conferences. In December 2012 Fabio Silva and Nicholas Campion organised a session entitled, 'The role and importance of the sky in archaeology', with the aim of showing how the concept of skyscapes demonstrates how integrated approaches can add to our understanding of past cultures, in order to bring new archaeoastronomical ideas to the attention of archaeologists (Silva and Campion 2012, 17; Fig. 31). Similar sessions followed in 2013, 2014 and 2016, while at around the same time Daniel Brown organised several gatherings at the National Astronomy Meetings (NAM) with the aim of giving young astronomers the opportunity to learn more about archaeoastronomy and skyscapes (Fig. 32). These outings at TAG and NAM, together with their subsequent publications (see Silva and Campion 2015; Brown 2016b; Henty and Brown 2020), were aimed to circulate and popularise the idea of skyscapes within archaeoastronomy, archaeology and astronomy.

Published by Oxbow in 2015 and edited by Silva and Campion, *Skyscapes: the role and importance of the sky in archaeology* is a volume based on the first TAG skyscapes meeting. In its preface Malville (2015b, xv) referred to 'skyscape archaeology', as utilised in the papers on windows referred to earlier, where both Silva and I had trialled the term 'skyscape archaeology', alongside an idea of its methodology:

> Archaeoastronomers should become more phenomenological and grounded on the archaeological record and context of the prehistoric structures they study. In a sense, archaeoastronomy should become more of a 'skyscape archaeology'. (Silva 2014a, 25)

> The use of detailed excavation data, the awareness of location and landscape and the integration of the sky with all its associated events, creates a multivalent approach to prehistoric archaeoastronomy which has no written history or ethnography to support cultural interpretation. This new approach which moves archaeoastronomy away from orthodoxy and outdated paradigms could be better named as 'skyscape archaeology'; similar in scope to taskscape and landscape archaeology, but in relation to the sky. (Henty 2014, 57)

In Timothy Darvill's afterword to the *Skyscapes* volume, he acknowledged the naming and associated methodology of skyscape archaeology by saying 'Continuity and change will be a major theme of skyscape archaeology in future and no doubt come to play a key part in understanding shifting cultural and religious attitudes' (Darvill 2015, 146). As archaeoastronomical neologisms *skyscape* and *skyscape archaeology* are still in the process of being defined but skyscapes can be researched in a similar way to landscapes and as such may be more relevant for archaeologists (see Darvill 2016, 264). Significantly, skyscape archaeology was the first attempt to rename the field since cultural astronomy was proposed as an alternative name for archaeoastronomy in 1991, as detailed in Chapter 10.

The very premise of skyscape archaeology was underlined by Ruggles' remark that 'archaeoastronomical interpretation can never proceed in isolation from archaeological endeavour as a whole' (Ruggles 2015b, 354). However, from its inception, Silva and I felt that skyscape archaeology represented more

Figure 32. Table-top planetarium demonstration with Daniel Brown (left) and Frank Prendergast (right) at the National Astronomy Meeting in Llandudno, July 2015. Photo: Pamela Armstrong.

than a name change: it aimed to be a new theoretical approach to uncover human relationships with the sky, as a departure from earlier archaeoastronomy paradigms. Although it still applies archaeoastronomy methodology to the archaeological record, it includes the usage of other data, both quantitative and qualitative, ethnography, history, texts, art, phenomenology, reflexivity and so on, in close proximity to archaeology's postprocessualist theory and methods (see Silva and Henty 2015, 1–3; 2018, 3). By reconceptualising the sky as multitudinous encultured skyscapes, the methodology of skyscape archaeology has become more akin to that of archaeology and anthropology, where traditional archaeoastronomical methods are only one part. If, as Aldana suggested (2009, 109), cultural astronomy was the 'companion of the move from Processual to Post-processual archaeology', then in many ways skyscape archaeology follows this progression. However, skyscape archaeology attempts to go much further than this because, by studying the skyscape in the same holistic way as landscape archaeology approaches the land and integrating the two, 'previously unseen patterns can be identified' (Armstrong 2016, 270). As such it represents more than a paradigm shift because its aim is to create an interdisciplinary model, unfettered by traditional distinctions. Silva and I have expressed this aim as being the possibility of answering questions relating to 'religion, belief, ritual, theology, ecology, social memory, cosmology and ontology'; questions that are unanswerable by the archaeoastronomical method alone (Silva and Henty 2018, 2–3).

While these were bold aims it has to be questioned whether skyscape archaeology was substantively different from what had gone before. Sims (2008, 220–221) had already suggested that 'Weaknesses in both archaeoastronomy and landscape archaeology can be overcome by their combination', citing Tilley's 1994 phenomenological approach as a guide. However, Sims' suggestion referred to phenomenology as being key, whereas Silva and I (2018, 3) had argued for reflexivity, which is one of the key pillars of Holbraad and Pedersen's (2017) ontological turn. In the reviews of the *Skyscapes* volume, some archaeoastronomers were critical of this new approach, for example Belmonte (2016a) thought that by separating the skyscape from the landscape created a problematic dichotomy between the two sister disciplines, which rather missed the point that skyscape archaeology would bring them together. However, González García (2016, 3–4) thought it was a 'commendable effort to break new ground in cultural astronomy', thereby placing it under the umbrella of cultural astronomy, and added that 'skyscape archaeology' would be 'a useful field for archaeologists'. We anticipated that archaeoastronomers might be cautious but we were really reaching out to archaeologists so were pleased that there was approval from Darvill (2015, 141) who noted that skyscapes are 'enculturated', a comment which aligns with Iwaniszewski's (2011) assessment of 'sky-as-a-social-field'. Similarly Timothy Insoll (2016, 120) indicated that 'skyscapes matter' and that 'skyscapes should not be ignored'. Even if most archaeologists do not engage with or adopt skyscape archaeology, this renewed interest in the sky is developing in tandem with new concepts in archaeological theory, for the first time since antiquarianism.

Esotericism

The many alternative variants appearing outside academic archaeological and archaeoastronomical narratives continued: examples in this contemporary period included Robin Heath's *Powerpoints* which put a modern twist on Watkins' ley line thesis (see Chapter 5), to suggest that power points such as Didcot power station and 'modern power grids' are arranged on 'ancient linear alignments' (Heath 2005, 11, 42). A similar volume *Island of the Setting Sun*, by Anthony Murphy and Richard Moore (2008), in the context of Irish monuments in the Boyne valley, also speculated on landscape lines, referring to them as the 'cosmic grid' while postulating that the Plain of Muirthemne in Co. Louth contained a giant replica of the Orion constellation. These works, and others such as Peter Marshall's (2004) foray into 'Europe's lost civilisations', tend to continue the Earth Mysteries tradition (see Chapter 6), though in the case of Murphy and Moore their theory can be related back to Duke's 1846 planetarium or Maltwood's 1925 Glastonbury Zodiac. These titles are unleashed on an unsuspecting public who may not appreciate the distinction between academic and speculative archaeoastronomy.

What continues to be of concern to many archaeologists is the proliferation of pseudo-academic content; pseudo-academic because by adding footnotes and references the authors mimic the academic style (Schadla-Hall 1999, 154). Alternative archaeologies are distinctly outside the consensual mainstream of archaeology, though the distinction of fringe material only comes about if there is a 'mainstream' where one side has access to the supposed truth while the other is 'wrong' (Stout 2012, 249). However, Holtorf (2005, 550) argued that alternative archaeology should be considered, because in a pluralist world not to do so would be absolutism. In a stinging rejoinder, Fagan and Feder (2005, 720) described alternative archaeology projects as 'farragoes of misdirection, fallacious logic, [and] manufactured evidence'. Schadla-Hall's view (2004) was that the development of archaeology depended on the ability to distinguish rational enquiry from speculation but, as objectivity was less certain as a goal, archaeologists have come to realise that there is no such thing as a black and white distinction between 'them' and 'us'. Similarly, Moshenka (2017) was also of the opinion that the boundaries between the two are not that clear. A reason for this could be that what seems fallacious to archaeologists and archaeoastronomers alike, may achieve an authority in popular culture. For example, take the case of 'ancient observatories', a speculative term, the wholesale use of which Belmonte (2015) has taken issue with, and compare his academic argument with a sensationalist headline in the *New Scientist* by Clare Wilson (2017) about 'star-gazing observatories'. The latter narrative was actually based on serious archaeoastronomical research but was manicured in this way for popular consumption.

Findings such as these draw archaeoastronomy into the debate about what constitutes the difference between mainstream and more speculative accounts, many of which have been mentioned in earlier chapters. In a hierarchy of alternative archaeology, Andersson (2012) placed archaeoastronomy at the top and Atlantis at the bottom, with earth mysteries, ley lines and so on in between, though despite admitting that archaeoastronomy was now an established field within academia, she thought it was closely associated with alternative ideas. Holtorf (2005, 547) agreed that some elements of archaeoastronomical research were so similar to those of archaeology, that a separation between alternative and professional archaeology was very difficult. With seemingly little awareness of recent archaeoastronomy, Fagan and Feder brought up the old arguments that it was 'a stand-alone interpretative (let alone dating) tool, where it is routinely presumed, rather than argued, that star alignments perceived by modern minds were intentionally established by ancient builders' (Fagan and Feder 2005, 722–723). This rather misses the point that archaeoastronomers decry 'the sensationalism' of pseudoarchaoastronomy as much as archaeologists rail against 'the gross errors and wild guesses' of pseudoarchaeology (see for example Henty and Silva 2018; Witcher 2018, 3). A conclusion drawn from Alfredo González-Ruibal is that 'we may not know whether stories come from specialists or amateurs' (González-Ruibal *et al.* 2018, 527). It is this blurring of the lines which may be the real reason behind the professionals' disdain. What academics generally fail to realise is that the general failure to write accessible archaeology books for the general public, aids the proliferation of alternative accounts (Pratt 2015). An exception and a model might be Parker Pearson's *Stonehenge* (2013), described on its cover as 'A detailed account ... expressed in a genial style'.

Disseminating archaeoastronomy

Of course, all the innovations in archaeoastronomy and skyscape archaeology were important for the archaeoastronomy community but they tended to be in-house developments and without dissemination they exist in a vacuum. Nevertheless, in the 21st century the number of archaeoastronomy books and specialised journal issues published approximately equalled the output (Lockyer (2), Watkins (1), Thom (5), Hoskin (1), Ruggles (1)) for the entire 20th century. This publishing phenomenon had begun in 2005 with Ruggles', *Ancient Astronomy: an encyclopedia of cosmologies and myth* (Ruggles 2005a). In over 500 pages it explored the key themes and issues relating to ancient astronomy, presented case studies from a variety of societies and covered the basic concepts of horizon astronomy. Contemporaneously Kelley and Milone (2005) published *Exploring Ancient Skies*, a 600 page volume that they described as an encyclopaedic survey of archaeoastronomy, intended primarily as a textbook. These books were necessarily long because nothing like them had ever been written before except as brief chapters in proceedings and journals. Kelley and Milone's book came into being because, as a result of teaching archaeoastronomy over a number of years, they realised that there needed to be a cogent body of scholarly materials and methodology for undergraduates (Kelley and Milone 2005, vii). To this end there are helpful appendices together with sample exercises for students. Similarly, Giulio Magli's *Archaeoastronomy* (2016) was designed as a textbook for undergraduates while

Bryan Penprase's *The Power of the Stars* (2017), represents a beginner's guide to cultural astronomy.

With all the developments mentioned earlier, archaeoastronomy appeared to be at a turning point and two books published in 2015 highlighted the difference between the old and the new: one appeared to concentrate on processual archaeoastronomy, while the other, the *Skyscapes* volume (Silva and Campion 2015), explored above, seemed to usher in postprocessual skyscape archaeology. The first, Ruggles' edited *Handbook of Archaeoastronomy and Ethnoastronomy* (2015a), is encyclopaedic in form as it combines archaeoastronomy, cultural astronomy and ethnoastronomy research from around the world. Published in three volumes, it features many prominent archaeoastronomers, while placing 'green' and 'brown' methodologies (see Chapter 8), side by side. Of course there were countless references to the sky, yet, despite its use in prior literature, only six of the 217 chapters referred to skyscapes. Fabiola Jara's chapter fully engaged with the idea while describing the cosmology of the Amazonian Arawak people 'where notions of landscape are extended to include the skyscape' and where oral traditions 'stress continuity between the earth and the sky(land) scapes' (Jara 2015, 934, 942). With the exception of Jan Harding (2015), mentioned above, and David Pankenier (2015), who explored Chinese architecture in the context of the circumpolar skyscape, skyscape was only mentioned in passing in the three others. Though the *Handbook* painted an absorbing picture of archaeoastronomy and ethnoastronomy worldwide, by contrast the second volume *Skyscapes* was attempting to show that skyscapes could be studied in the same way as archaeologists thought about landscapes.

In the same vein as *Skyscapes*, the papers from the second TAG session were also issued in 2015, as a special issue on *Landscape – Seascape – Skyscape* in *Culture and Cosmos* (Silva 2015b). The 2014 meeting at NAM gave rise to a dedicated issue of the *Journal of Physics: Conference Series*, in which the majority of papers featured an interdisciplinary approach towards examining monuments in relation to their skyscapes (Brown 2016b). The NAM sessions received wide media coverage in newspapers and periodicals, including the online *Archaeology* magazine (2016; see also *Science Daily* 2014; *Heritage Daily* 2014; *The Guardian* 2016). A further edited volume, *Visualising Skyscapes: material forms of cultural engagement with the heavens* (Henty and Brown 2020), was published by Routledge in 2020, to add to the corpus of skyscape studies by drawing together researchers who see skyscapes as an integral part of their work. As Oxbow and Routledge are leading publishers of archaeology books, potentially the inclusion of these volumes in their catalogues may capture the attention of archaeologists who would not normally read archaeoastronomical literature and make them aware of its recent developments. From this evidence, it would appear that Sims' view that 'the [publishing] issue revolves around the academic boundary disputes triggered by the work of Hawkins and Thom', is no longer a problem (Sims, pers. comm.).

While these new publications were enlarging the corpus of archaeoastronomy and skyscape archaeology, the traditional dedicated archaeoastronomy journals were in decline. From 2000 onwards the archaeoastronomy content of JHA, decreased to an average of one paper per year. Its American counterpart, *Archaeoastronomy: The Journal of Astronomy in Culture*, ceased publication in 2011, being briefly replaced by one issue of the new version, *Journal of Astronomy in Culture*, in 2016, as detailed in Chapter 8. The failure of these journals spawned a one-off initiative in 2010 by Kim Malville and Jarita Holbrook, editors of Volume 9 of the online *Journal of Cosmology*. Entitled 'Archaeoastronomy: cosmology of ancient cultures', it contained archaeoastronomy research papers, some of which were beginning to question the old green/brown research strategies (see for example Sims 2010 in Malville and Holbrook 2010). However it must be remembered that these journals are insider publications, and, as such, they may attract little interest from other disciplines.

Frustrated with this lack of venues for our own publications, Fabio Silva and I talked about the relationship between archaeoastronomy and archaeology and the likelihood that most archaeologists did not read archaeoastronomy journals. After several hours' discussion at TAG 2013, we became committed to improving archaeoastronomy's profile by putting our ideas into action through founding the *Journal of Skyscape Archaeology* (JSA) in 2015 (*Journal of Skyscape Archaeology* 2021). In order to explore a multidisciplinary approach to archaeoastronomy, the journal's aim is to provide a venue for 'cross-fertilization' between archaeoastronomy, archaeology, cultural astronomy, anthropology and history (Silva and Henty 2015). Additionally JSA acknowledges and attempts to bridge Snow's (1961) two cultures by saying,

> thus skyscape archaeology sits comfortably in the hybrid chair of archaeology, halfway between the sciences (of which archaeology already involves many) and the humanities (which traditionally is the domain of archaeology). (Silva and Henty 2015, 3)

While considering a name for the journal we wanted to avoid using archaeoastronomy because of its connotations with megalithic science in the past, so looked for a more palatable way of presenting it. As archaeology had adopted *landscape archaeology* in the 1970s, we thought *skyscape archaeology* would have some appeal for archaeologists, because we wanted not only to present a new version of archaeoastronomy but also locate it in archaeology. Consequently we trialled the term in our own papers, both published in archaeological journals, before the journal's launch (Henty 2014; Silva 2014a), as noted above. Our decision was also fuelled by other reasons which included irritation at the singular archaeoastronomical method which was out of tune with contemporary postprocessualism and frustration with archaeoastronomy's isolation. The inaugural issue of JSA was published in July 2015, the first of its programme of two issues per year, and in 2021 it entered its seventh year. Its content reflects our new version of archaeoastronomy and there is also evidence that skyscape archaeology appeals to some archaeologists, such as Kenneth Brophy, David Connolly, Vince Gaffney, Timothy Darvill, Brian Hayden, Timothy Insoll and Timothy Pauketat who have all contributed short articles since JSA was first published.

Learning resources

While books and journals may be mined for insights into how archaeoastronomy is practised, nothing is more valuable than a taught course for a would-be archaeoastronomer. Earlier Ruggles (1993a, 9) had suggested that 'we need to persuade at least one University somewhere to support cultural astronomy as a mainstream activity in itself, with a concentration of research and perhaps a specialist taught Masters course'. This wish was realised in October 2002 with the establishment of the 'interdisciplinary' MA in Cultural Astronomy and Astrology at Bath Spa University, with Nicholas Campion as its director (Campion 2004). The MA, situated in the Sophia Centre for the Study of Cosmology in Culture, transferred to the University of Wales Trinity Saint David (UWTSD) as a distance learning course in 2008, with its aim being 'to explore the ways in which human beings attribute meaning to the planets, stars and sky, and construct cosmologies which provide the basis for culture and society' (UWTSD 2021).

Lionel Sims' course had ended with his retirement from the University of East London in 2011, but the optional 'Archaeoastronomy module', part of the UW TSD MA, came on-stream one year earlier in January 2010, as an attempt 'to create an academic programme in archaeoastronomy' (Campion and Malville 2011, 358). It is not as popular as some of the other modules but remains on the curriculum where other modules have been dropped. Fabio Silva, one of the original students, became one of the teaching assistants on the course in 2011, before taking over as main tutor in 2013 in conjunction with Campion and Kim Malville, from the University of Colorado. The UWTSD course has evolved and developed from its original launch when it focused on the 'astronomical component' with webinars on celestial mechanics and naked-eye astronomy which covered the basics. These were supplemented by a demonstration of simple surveying techniques, an explanation of declination, along with the horizon coordinates of azimuth and altitude (see Glossary: azimuth; altitude), and so on (Fig. 33).

As Campion and Malville (2011, 357–358) pointed out, the module was an 'introduction to practical archaeoastronomy' and seen as 'a training course'. What was missing from the module was archaeology but this gap was filled when it was renamed 'Skyscapes, cosmology and archaeology' in the academic year 2014–2015. Silva explained that the label change was to mirror the 'evolution of the module's content into a more far-reaching exploration of what people see in the sky and how they make sense of and engage with it, via the study of their structures and other material remains' (Silva 2014b). In the 2020–2021 academic year, after Silva had left to go to Bournemouth University, the module was renamed again to 'Sacred skies' which has a broader remit than the earlier modules. It covers such topics as 'The sky in myth', 'Sky and spirit' and so on, alongside skyscape archaeology tutorials on surveying and basic astronomy taught by Bernadette Brady.

Figure 33. Learning how to use a theodolite for the UWTSD archaeoastronomy module with Bernadette Brady (left) Fabio Silva (centre) and Nicholas Campion (right) (Photo: author).

While the UWTSD module was uniquely important for teaching archaeoastronomy, its wider impact has been in its role in bringing archaeoastronomy to the archaeologists at the TAG skyscapes sessions. These fostered a small informal community which has resulted in a renewed, if small, interest in the archaeoastronomy of British monuments. For example, five out of ten presentations at the TAG 2016 session, concentrated on British sites while elsewhere in 2016, two papers, which looked at sites in Scotland (Scott 2016) and Wales (Pritchard 2016) respectively, were published in JSA. However, the overall number of archaeoastronomers researching British monuments is still very small being made up of a tiny core group and a few independent amateur researchers, many of whom are retired and have had no formal archaeoastronomy education.

This situation may improve as, since the academic year 2020–2021, skyscapes are now part of the Bournemouth University archaeology curriculum, in Fabio Silva's unit 'Gathering time' (Silva, pers. comm.).

Towards convergence

The relationship between archaeologists and archaeoastronomers has never been easy, yet in the Americas of the 1990s Aveni thought that despite them operating under different paradigms, he had witnessed 'a slow convergence' (Aveni 1992). However, in Britain it is only in more recent years that there has been an improvement. The new field of skyscape archaeology was and remains an attempt to heal past differences between archaeoastronomy and archaeology by replacing them with 'a more engaged and equal relationship', to borrow words from Rowlands (1997, 129) and, as noted earlier, some British archaeologists have shown their support of this new venture. This might suggest that some archaeoastronomy sits within mainstream archaeology, but here the results are mixed. Harding *et al.*'s 2006 paper was published in the American *Archaeoastronomy* journal but in the follow up archaeological volume, *Cult, Religion and Pilgrimage* (Harding 2013), only a relatively brief summary of the archaeoastronomy was present. Indeed Harding had earlier acknowledged that archaeoastronomy was mostly marginalised and that its 'all-too-often absence from mainstream studies' severely limited the scope and depth of interpretations of the Neolithic period (Harding *et al.* 2006, 26–27).

This sidelining of archaeoastronomy is still in evidence: for example in a recent book on the Neolithic by Keith Ray and Julian Thomas (2018), other than a brief reference to solstitial alignments at Newgrange and Maeshowe, archaeoastronomy is ignored (see also O'Donnell 2019, 230). Another instance of the omission of archaeoastronomy comes from a book by Barbara Bender and colleagues. It attempted to be a new reflexive approach in order to get away from the 'rhetoric of authority' assumed in archaeological reports which render them closed to other possibilities or multiple interpretations (Bender *et al.* 2007, 27–28). *Stone Worlds*, an account of an archaeological project undertaken at Leskernick on Bodmin Moor, is an interesting experiment involving both archaeologists and anthropologists which tried 'to question and work across disciplinary boundaries' (Bender *et al.* 2007, 16). This prehistoric landscape contains various structures such as stone circles and stone rows, which cry out for astronomical surveys, if you were an archaeoastronomer. On the cover of the book is a photograph of the Propped Stone, an intentionally created window between a long linear rock and a triangular slab propped against it, through which the summer solstice sun can be seen setting on the horizon. Only a couple of sentences referred to this alignment and no archaeoastronomy was mentioned in the report at all, thereby failing in its brief of working across disciplinary boundaries.

These examples have to be set against other projects which do involve collaboration with archaeoastronomers, such as Hilary Murray's 2009 archaeological report on

Mesolithic pit alignments at Warren Field in Aberdeenshire (Murray *et al.* 2009). The authors commissioned an archaeoastronomical survey by Smith and Higginbottom (2009) but only a small sample of this appeared in the book and the main 19 page report now languishes in the archives of Historic Environment Scotland, formally RCAHMS (H. Murray, pers. comm.; Henty 2020b, 19). While the archaeoastronomical data was drastically curtailed for the 2009 volume, in Vince Gaffney's later reassessment of Warren Field it took centre stage (Gaffney *et al.* 2013). With an appendix by Ruggles on how sequences of moonrises can be observed along the horizon, the main thesis of the new research was that the pits were deliberately set up for use as a Mesolithic calendar. Notably, in the Ray and Thomas volume archaeoastronomy does not feature in their examination of either Warren Field or Thornborough.

Yet, a few other archaeological surveys have followed this practice of using an archaeoastronomer to corroborate archaeological findings (see for example Bradley 2011; Bradley and Nimura 2016; Bennett and Gale 2017). Further evidence of archaeoastronomy can be found in the relatively new work on Stonehenge, which continues to be the main site of interest in Britain (Parker Pearson 2013): because of its famous solstice alignment it invites collaboration between archaeologists and archaeoastronomers. Other recent examples of cooperation include a chapter by Ruggles in Cunliffe and Renfrew's (1997) edited volume on *Science and Stonehenge* and Sims' National Geographic film, *Stonehenge Rediscovered* (2003), which contained a commentary by the archaeologist Barry Cunliffe. Interest in the sky has not been restricted to Neolithic monuments or Mesolithic pits, for example Josh Pollard (2017) drew on cultural astronomy to propose that the Uffington White Horse was a geoglyph of a sun-horse. Additionally, in the online *Oxford Handbook of Light in Archaeology*, most of the chapters have been either authored by archaeoastronomers or relate to archaeoastronomy (Papadopoulos and Moyes 2017). Similarly the *Journal of Lithic Studies* devoted an entire issue to mainly archaeoastronomical content (for example, Meaden 2017).

In the last few years there is evidence that some archaeologists now have a more favourable attitude to archaeoastronomy and in some instances archaeoastronomy is becoming part of the archaeological mainstream, though generally only when it is on the initiative of archaeologists. For example, in Scotland, archaeologists Brian Wilkinson and Murray Cook contributed to a new learning resource for primary school teachers, with the following rationale: 'the study of stone circles will allow discussion of the movement of the planets, the changing of the seasons and why in the past this might have been of great importance to our ancestors' (Forestry Commission Scotland 2015). Similarly at the skyscapes session at TAG 2014, a group of young archaeologists concluded from their examination of Yadlee Stone Circle that solar movements were a socially significant phenomenon (Gardner *et al.* 2017). While these individual instances may seem insignificant details, when taken together they demonstrate not only that there is a broader acceptance of archaeoastronomy by archaeologists, but also that they are willing to engage with the material. Encouragingly, Darvill (2015,

147) concluded recently that the potential of bringing skyscapes into archaeological thinking was considerable.

The improved relationship between archaeologists and archaeoastronomers has been a long time coming. A few years earlier, Sims (2007b) had introduced his version of cultural astronomy in a session entitled 'Reconstructing the underworld: the anthropology and archaeology of other-worlds' at the TAG 2007 conference in York; views which led to an attack by a leading archaeologist present (Sims, pers. comm.). By contrast, at the end of the TAG 2014 skyscape session there was a robust discussion between archaeoastronomers and archaeologists which demonstrated how their relationship had mellowed. In his review David Connolly found that,

> what began as rather combative challenges soon became a search for a common language, and here the key issue was understood as the need to communicate the concerns of all parties in such a way that methodologies and interpretation are cross-disciplinary. (Connolly 2015, 148)

Indeed he suggested that, on the basis of one paper at least, archaeoastronomical techniques can be combined with traditional archaeological methods 'to provide a more nuanced and complex picture of societal change than before' (Connolly 2015, 143).

From these examples it seems that archaeoastronomical science, when employed as a specialism under the umbrella of archaeology, can coexist with archaeological science. Generally, however, archaeoastronomy is not part of archaeology's normal practice and work such as that listed above is rare. It is less easy for archaeoastronomers to bridge the gap: for example, an early version of Sims' (2006) publication on the solarisation of the moon at Stonehenge was rejected by the then *Cambridge Archaeology Journal* editor but, after the National Geographic film was broadcast worldwide, it was subsequently accepted (Sims, pers. comm.). Nevertheless, more recently other archaeoastronomers are intentionally bridging the gap between the mainstream and the marginalised, by publishing archaeoastronomy papers in archaeology journals, such as *Papers from the Institute of Archaeology* (see Silva 2013; Henty 2014).

Importantly, it does not appear that all British archaeologists are simply uninterested in archaeoastronomy, which seemed to be the case in the 1980s and 1990s. For example, in 2016 a new look was taken at the controversy Kintigh provoked in 1992 (see Chapter 8), when he suggested archaeoastronomy was of only marginal interest to archaeologists (Kintigh 1992). Darvill wrote that the debate 'could perhaps unkindly, be seen as an attempt to privilege particular contributions to understanding of the ancient past' (Darvill 2016, 261). Significantly, he added that postprocessual archaeology has an interest in archaeoastronomy, but for disciplines to work together effectively there has to be 'a shared epistemology: common methods of constructing arguments and of creating and validating knowledge' (Darvill 2016, 262). Indeed, that there is an active interest by some archaeologists was demonstrated by two conferences, held towards the end of 2018. The first at Dublin in September saw eminent archaeology professors Richard Bradley, Chris Scarre and Gabriel Cooney share the bill with leading archaeoastronomers, Clive Ruggles, Frank Prendergast and Fabio Silva. The organisers advertised that the conference was a response to the interest in astronomical heritage and its aim was to explore the meaning of the sky to the builders of megalithic monuments in Ireland and Atlantic Europe (Archaeology Ireland 2018; Doyle 2020). Prendergast, one of the co-organisers told me that the discovery of the intentional winter solstice illumination of the Neolithic passage tomb at Newgrange, mentioned in Chapter 9, 'began an enduring positive relationship between Irish archaeologists and scientifically-grounded archaeoastronomy which has continued to the present' (pers. comm. 2017). Evidence for this is a paper published in *Archaeology Ireland*, entitled 'Facing the sun', in the winter of 2017 (Prendergast et al. 2017).

A similar collaborative symposium, entitled 'Cosmology in archaeology' was held in Malta two months later in November 2018. Here Maltese archaeologists, together with Mike Parker Pearson, shared the stage with archaeoastronomers including Kim Malville and Fabio Silva. The results of taking archaeoastronomy to the heart of archaeology conferences at TAG may be behind the ethos of these two recent conferences. It would appear that Bloland's prescient view (1995, 537), that in the advent of plurality, academic disciplines might find their borders dissolving, has some substance in the improvement of the relationship between archaeologists and archaeoastronomers. Can this be described as convergence? Probably not, but some inclusion of archaeoastronomy in archaeological literature is a good step forward towards endorsement.

The implications for archaeoastronomy

As examined in earlier chapters, throughout its history, archaeoastronomy has mainly developed in isolation and despite progress it still found itself on the fringe of academia at the beginning of the 21st century. On the other hand, Aveni (2008, 2) suggested that because archaeoastronomy had integrated the attitudes and methodologies of other disciplines and was increasingly involved with symbolism and belief systems, it had adopted the 'hallmarks' of postprocessual archaeology. He was, of course, speaking from a New World perspective and the same could not be said of British archaeoastronomy until the move towards skyscape archaeology. Ruggles' (2015) *Handbook* seems to mark the end of purely processual archaeoastronomy though it is likely that archaeoastronomy will always rely on scientific techniques in the same way postprocessual archaeology does. Up until that time interpretative archaeoastronomy was something that the archaeoastronomers had not been engaging with, nor were they trained to do so (Ruggles 2005b, 11) but skyscape archaeology ushered in a different theoretical perspective and the 2015 *Skyscapes* volume appears to consolidate the start of postprocessual archaeoastronomy. Also, while most archaeoastronomers continued as before, some researchers were branching out by opting for a 'broader approach' such as taking topography, foundation myths, intervisibility, iconography and so on into account (Rappenglück 2015, 139). Indeed, in this period archaeoastronomy borrowed names and concepts from other disciplines. These included phenomenology, computer graphics, digital modelling, augmented reality visualisation and ontology. With regard to the latter, as both archaeology and archaeoastronomy are now considering the turn to ontology they are more in tune with one another than they ever have been. At the same time common terms such as windows were used alongside more specialist terms like equinoctial full moons, crossovers, first and last quarter crescents, all adding to archaeoastronomy's distinguishing vocabulary which now also includes skyscapes.

Evidence of the acceptance of archaeoastronomy by archaeologists, as gleaned above, shows a mixed picture but turning points such as the TAG sessions and the foundation of the *Journal of Skyscape Archaeology* have helped to shine a light on the improvements in both practical and theoretical archaeoastronomy. These have largely come about because a small community of archaeoastronomers left the safe havens of their specialised conferences to take their work to the archaeologists' door in order to try to form a closer bond. In this respect I must point out that I am both participant and deep insider, but while writing about how skyscapes and skyscape archaeology are a development in archaeoastronomy's history, it has not been my intention to over-exaggerate my own importance or that of skyscape archaeology. On the contrary my status has allowed me to provide details about the emergence of skyscape archaeology that might otherwise have remained unknown. For example, the bookending of the preface and afterword in the *Skyscapes* volume, the first written by archaeoastronomer Kim Malville and the latter by the archaeologist Timothy Darvill, in tune with the 'sky' and 'archaeology' of the title, was of course deliberate on the part of the editors, but it does show a coming-together of the fields, rather than the contestatory encounters in other decades of archaeoastronomy's history. A similar strategy was followed for *Visualising Skyscapes* (Henty and Brown 2020) where the foreword was by archaeologist Gabriel Cooney and the afterword by the astronomer Andrew Newsam. Other archaeoastronomy authors have deliberately sought out archaeology journals for their own work. For example Sims' paper in the *Cambridge Archaeology Journal* has already been mentioned and shortly before his death in 2021, he published in the *Proceedings of the Prehistoric Society* (Sims 2021). A paper on the orientations of Portuguese dolmens also found its home there (Figueirdo *et al.* 2018). Additionally, Silva has published two papers (2014a; 2020b) in archaeology journals, the first in *Advances in Archaeological Practice,* and the second in the *Journal of Archaeological Science*. The two entries in *Papers from the Institute of Archaeology* were mentioned earlier. Similarly the editorial board of the JSA is peopled by prominent academics from relevant disciplines, such as archaeology, archaeoastronomy, ethnoastronomy, astronomy and anthropology, who have given their support to this new venture.

Overall the atmosphere suggests more collaboration, which would have been unheard of in earlier periods of archaeoastronomy's history in Britain and the policy of taking archaeoastronomy to the archaeologists seems to be working. For example, at the skyscapes session at TAG 2014 an initiative was suggested in order to make archaeologists aware that their methods of collecting data fall short of providing archaeoastronomers with enough detail about measurements essential for their work (Connolly 2015, 148). After discussion with David Connelly of the British Archaeological Jobs and Resources portal (BAJR), Connolly agreed to produce a short BAJR Guide, *Archaeoastronomy for Archaeologists* (Connolly 2016). He claimed that 'this could outline the methodologies required, give guidance on the use of the data and the issues associated with the interpretation as well as a description of the benefits that could be gained' (Connolly 2015, 148). Published in 2016, by 2018 it was the 9th most popular of the 53 published guides. While it is difficult to judge the impact of this guide, it may well have an influence on how archaeoastronomy is received or even practised by archaeologists, and in the general absence of archaeoastronomy education it may have a pedagogical purpose.

Unfortunately, most archaeoastronomers have been slow to reach out to archaeologists, preferring to debate the issue within their own communities or publications. However others, as described above, have been examining its possible usefulness to archaeology. According to Iwaniszewski (2007, 15), mainstream archaeoastronomy, and here he cited Ruggles, was still blindly open to a quantitative, scientific and statistical approach, which Aveni had earlier called 'scientific imperialism'. As Prendergast pointed out, this is not necessarily detrimental, because when an archaeoastronomical investigation is commissioned for analysing an archaeological site it can complement existing specialisms within archaeology, such as radiocarbon dating and so on (as reported by Armstrong 2015, 282). Also, Iwaniszewski, eight years on from his original comments, suggested that archaeoastronomy could be categorised as 'a type of a thematic archaeology or as a part of symbolic and cognitive archaeologies' (Iwaniszewski 2015b, 318). On the other hand Polcaro theorised that cultural astronomy was 'an interdisciplinary science' which can inform related disciplines variously, and as such can be of 'benefit in bridging' Snow's (1961) two cultures (Polcaro 2015, 318). Earlier Ruggles (2011b, 3) was even more optimistic when he assessed that that archaeoastronomy's increased emphasis on cognitive factors had allowed it to enter the archaeological mainstream. Here he was referring to the inclusion of his relatively short description of archaeoastronomy that appeared in Renfrew and Bahn's (2005) *Archaeology: the Key Concepts* (Ruggles 2005b). Certainly this was an important breakthrough given that in Renfrew and Bahn's earlier textbook on archaeology the only mention of archaeoastronomy came in connection with measuring time: Thom's 'preoccupation with such calendrical events' and the Mayan calendar were referred to in this context (Renfrew and Bahn 1991, 350). However, this is only part of the picture: Victor Fisher (2015) conducted a survey of introductory archaeology textbooks to find out whether archaeoastronomy featured in them and was met by a 'chorus of silence'.

Archaeoastronomical research in the first decades of the 21st century has shown that its security of tradition and historical continuity has allowed for internal experimentation, transformative ideas and the beginnings of a more holistic focus with the introduction of skyscape archaeology. Unlike earlier periods in archaeoastronomy's history where key personalities led the significant paradigm changes, innovations in this period have come from many different voices. The understanding that archaeology, landscape, skyscape and culture must be considered alongside specific astronomical targets has broadened the scope of archaeoastronomical studies. These later and important advances have mainly originated in Britain but from the international research featured in JSA, it appears that the influence of skyscape archaeology seems to be spreading. During this period there were improvements in relationship between archaeoastronomy and archaeology and some, but not all of these, can be attributed to this new way of looking at the skyscape.

Chapter 12

Final thoughts

The idea that, as research fields develop over time and contain elements of their past in their present their histories can contain crucial clues to their present form and relationships, has been the underlying rationale of this history. I was grateful for Severin Fowles' remark that disciplines 'have intellectual histories that must be worked through' (in Alberti *et al.* 2011, 899), because having it in the back of my mind inspired my efforts to understand today's archaeoastronomy and its relationships with archaeology and esotericism. Having brought archaeoastronomy's chequered history up to the date of writing in 2021, my final thoughts relate to some questions that hovered at the back of my mind during my research. At times there seemed to be an intellectual divide which left archaeoastronomy on the sidelines but unfortunately, for a long time, many archaeoastronomers ducked the problem and seemed content to pursue their studies out of the limelight without fully comprehending the reasons. The result was that, yes, archaeoastronomers did run round Ruggles' circles for decades and did neglect to make sufficient changes for them to move from the outside to the inside.

Ideally, in a perfect world, archaeoastronomical research would mesh with the known archaeology to provide insights into the cosmologies of the cultures the archaeologists are interested in. That this has not happened may be the result of contestation which I touched on in the introductory chapter, so its historical context needs to be re-assessed. In the early period of antiquarianism, archaeology and archaeoastronomy were combined but archaeoastronomy was understandably sidelined after the 19th century esoteric musings which, at the time, Higgins (1827) called 'aerial castle-building', because this was the period when archaeologists were developing their science. However, at the beginning of the 20th century F.C. Penrose and Sir Norman Lockyer worked together and Boyle Somerville contributed papers to *Antiquity*, so the relationship was restored for the time being. Later, there was some precedent for archaeologists to consider the sky because although Gordon Childe, writing in the 1930s, did not consider alignments he was aware of the influence of the sun and the seasons while, in the 1940s, Christopher and Jacquetta Hawkes acknowledged sun-oriented prehistoric stone circles. Yet, although the alignment at Stonehenge was well-known, it was perceived as an interesting case rather than a reason for other sites to be investigated as a general norm. The real contestation occurred during the time of Gerald Hawkins and Alexander Thom and that related to the cognitive skills of the monument builders. The archaeologists were in agreement that the abilities of prehistoric peoples were only rudimentary but Thom, in particular, challenged the archaeological narrative by claiming that the builders had sophisticated knowledge of the movements of the sun and the moon which they encoded in their monuments. This was contestation, red in tooth and claw, which led to the many conferences and articles which debated Thom's megalithic science. After a full airing, the archaeologists dismissed the archaeoastronomers' claims and the two fields went their separate ways.

Contestation may not play a part today because most archaeoastronomers recognise that the collection of archaeoastronomical data should always be assessed in the context of cultural record: the only thing left for archaeoastronomers to contest is the scope of archaeological enquiry which generally excludes looking for a connection between the monumental landscape and the skyscape. So, today the differences between archaeologists and archaeoastronomers are more nuanced, particularly because, as evidenced, some archaeologists do indeed consider the role of the sky. Of course, you will never find ley lines, dismissed in Alfred Watkins' day and further reviled after their New Age appropriation, in an archaeological text but research which takes the wider landscape into account may find evidence of processional routes or other such markers.

If contestation is no longer an issue, can the problem be related to sidelining? Here again there are subtleties to the problem because it is difficult to decide whether the non-appearance of archaeoastronomy is intentional or unconscious on the part of the archaeologists in question. The corollary to this question is to what extent have archaeoastronomers contributed to their own sidelining or did archaeoastronomy's relationship with esotericism and pseudoscience have a part to play? To answer these questions it is helpful to look at both sides; the archaeologists and the archaeoastronomers.

The archaeologists

Archaeological research includes a wide spectrum of specialist knowledge. A typical (prehistoric) site report might include soil and pollen analysis, lithics, worked stone and pottery details, radiocarbon dating, isotope analysis of human and animal bones and so on. This post-excavation work is conducted by experts and/or dedicated archaeology laboratories, working together with their colleagues newly in from the field. While broader accounts may consider the landscape surrounding site excavations, only rarely is archaeoastronomy considered because it is not relevant to most of the archaeologists' work; it depends on the research question. For example, research which studies the development of tools, the domestication of animals, the available foodstuffs and so on does not need to explore sky-related themes. There are other reasons why archaeologists do not consider the sky and one of these may be the lack of expert archaeoastronomers to carry out the work for archaeologists who are unlikely to have the necessary astronomical knowledge to do it for themselves. As archaeoastronomers have little university presence, archaeologists are unlikely to bump into them at their coffee breaks: that archaeoastronomical terms have not become part of archaeology's vocabulary could be attributed to the archaeologists' lack of exposure to it. This lack of exposure is the result of several factors not just archaeoastronomy's absence in universities: it is related to the fact that archaeoastronomers' work is generally only published in specialist journals or proceedings that archaeologists are unlikely to read and that archaeoastronomers do not attend archaeology conferences and vice versa. The problem is exacerbated by the different tools they use: trowels and sieves versus clinometers and compasses. Because of the combination of these factors many archaeologists seem ill-informed about archaeoastronomy's practice and feel that it is a difficult subject to learn.

However, while these practical problems could be overcome relatively easily, there may be a historical precedent as to why archaeologists fail to recognise the importance of the celestial realm. In 1954 Christopher Hawkes published his famous ladder of inference paper which, in a similar way to the non-negotiable Three Age system, delineated archaeological research in the following decades: questions relating to the first three rungs on Hawkes' ladder *techniques*, the economics of *subsistence-economies* and *social/political institutions* were routinely asked but those relating to the *religious institutions and spiritual life* were left hanging for a very long time because those questions seemed to be too difficult. Hawkes' thesis put the emphasis on the details while the over-arching picture was neglected. This coincided with the time archaeoastronomers focused solely on alignments, rather than interpreting what they might have said about the cosmologies of the cultures concerned. But fashions change and today the particularities singled out in the research objectives of both archaeologists and archaeoastronomers in the field mainly show a lack of engagement with newer theories and methods prompted by the ontological turn where anthropology has largely rejected the western epistemology of the nature/culture divide. For example, if archaeologists looked at the material record anthropologically or used anthropological analogies to recognise that in the ontology of a society all things may be inter-related, then the separation of categories that Hawkes proposed as a hierarchy loses its validity.

Sidelining may also be the result of the pervading scepticism engendered by work which the archaeologists thought was of questionable quality. Certainly, the longevity of this scepticism can be traced throughout archaeoastronomy's history. It was evident in late 19th century antiquarianism and later noted by Lockyer; a suspicion which continued with Crawford's angry rebuttal of Watkins' ley lines thesis, Daniel's sidelining of Newham and the eventual rejection of Thom's megalithic science. It seemed to stop after that because archaeologists simply stepped out of the arena. Yet recently a JSA Forum sounded out a few archaeologists (Silva and Henty 2020b). Vince Gaffney (2020) reported that debates about archaeoastronomy were discouraged from the point of view that Thom's work should be seen as a cautionary tale to warn off archaeologists who might be interested in it. This combined with some naivety as to the potential use of GIS for investigating the 'sky/land interface', the 'lack of a comprehensive structure' to study the sky and 'intellectual selfishness' has led to this failing on the part of archaeologists. Kenneth Brophy (2020, 272) agreed that there had been a fixation on the flaws of the past while Amanda Chadburn (2020, 276), from a heritage perspective, described archaeologists' continued resistance to archaeoastronomy. These archaeologists seem to be aware that old attitudes (and the reasons for them) die hard and I have long sensed that the embarrassment felt by archaeologists concerning Thom's contributions and their reaction to it, first embracing it and lastly denouncing it, has left a significant feeling of 'once shy, twice bitten'; a presentiment which has so far been detrimental for the inclusion of archaeoastronomy in British prehistoric archaeology. These insights are encouraging because they point out, not only that scepticism towards archaeoastronomy began in the past, but that in these archaeologists' opinions it should be consigned to the pages of history.

The archaeologists may also have been influenced by the sheer volume of esoteric literature that was inspired by archaeoastronomy and became linked to it. It is quite chilling to read that from Brophy's experience, 'it is just as likely that archaeoastronomy crops up in a lecture on pseudo-archaeology as it is in a session looking at Neolithic and Bronze Age stone circles' (Brophy 2020, 268). Esotericism reached its height in the New Age and affected both archaeology and archaeoastronomy: it has never really gone away as there remains a voracious appetite for ancient mysteries, lost knowledge and secrets. Today it is satisfied somewhat differently via extravagant social media claims, television programmes about ancient aliens and dubious newspaper articles and it is an ongoing battle to keep it out of academia especially because archaeoastronomy and its alternative appropriation have mistakenly been linked together. For example, Dragana Mladenović (2021, 39–40) pointed to archaeoastronomy papers, which were of 'dubious quality' or sensationalist, as deterring Roman archaeologists, adding that many of them lacked suitable archaeological, cultural and historical context and unfortunately the same critique could be applied to many published archaeoastronomy papers. Steven Gullberg (2020, 101), writing from an American perspective has also laid the blame on fringe publications and television shows as continuing to fuel the fire of the scepticism voiced by archaeologists. At least the archaeologists and archaeoastronomers are united in their disapproval of pseudoscience.

While these considerations may help to shed light on the relationship between archaeoastronomy and archaeology today, there seems no doubt that archaeologists have colonised the past and have dominion over it. Indeed there is anecdotal evidence, drawn from my own experience of trying to research archaeoastronomy at PhD level, as detailed in Chapter 1, together with my surveys of archaeology students (see Henty 2020b), to suggest that in many cases the omission of archaeoastronomy from the archaeological discourse was, or is, deliberate. Encouragingly there seems to be a mismatch between this neglect of archaeoastronomy and how archaeology students regard its usefulness. In my survey I found that 83.5% of the archaeology students questioned thought archaeoastronomy was relevant to archaeology while 79.3% thought archaeoastronomy has a role in the study of British prehistory, though some commented that they had been discouraged from conducting archaeoastronomical research by their tutors. Although 46.8% of archaeology students did not believe that it should be taught as a degree in its own right, 51.6% of them agreed that archaeoastronomy should be taught as part of an archaeology degree programme. This rather indicates that the two fields are not incommensurable, as they were judged to be in the past.

So, it is possible that attitudes are changing, though Gaffney (2020, 267) pointed out that a 'generational shift may still be required to fully relinquish some of these historical shackles'. There are some positive endorsements from archaeologists; for example, Brophy (2020, 268) reasoned that it is impossible to understand the history of monuments without exploring how they might have related to the sky. However, he pointed out that while the sky is only one part of the story, then skyscapes are only one part of the archaeologists' toolkit (Brophy 2020, 272), as recognised above. I have mentioned some exceptions in the work of Richard Bradley, Mike Parker Pearson, Hilary Murray and others who have used the service of archaeoastronomers, but these are a rarity, perhaps because of the lack of experienced archaeoastronomers to call on. The most that can be hoped for is that, where relevant, archaeologists not only include the sky in their list of research questions, but also read the pertinent archaeoastronomical literature and reference it in their reports. Logically archaeoastronomy should at least be considered by archaeologists as its findings add elements to their studies that otherwise would not be considered in their research: surely no over-riding interpretations of the Neolithic and Bronze Ages can be complete without a consideration of the role the sky and the heavens played in their cultures.

The archaeoastronomers

Other than the suggested reasons above for archaeoastronomy's marginalisation, some of which are legitimate, sidelining is a complex issue which is compounded by the actions of archaeoastronomers themselves. They generally have little awareness of what lies beneath the problem and what they can do to tackle it. Again, the history of archaeoastronomy can provide some clues about how the archaeoastronomers see themselves. Despite both archaeology and archaeoastronomy beginning with amateur activities, only archaeology emerged as a recognised discipline in the mid-19th century. Archaeoastronomy and other antiquarian pursuits were left behind, being consigned 'to the fringes of historical expertise where their efforts posed no threat' to the newly established disciplines (Levine 2003, 173). More recently, a similar type of fringe development outside the academy has been described as *modern amateurism* (Stebbins 1977, 582). Stebbins suggested it occurs alongside the professional life of the participant and is best described as a vocation rather than an avocation. For example, Mortimer Wheeler (1955, 74) wrote that Flinders Petrie once set himself the holiday task of visiting stone circles and cairns. The archaeoastronomer, equipped with a theodolite, compass and clinometer, is free to pursue his or her 'modern amateur' studies anywhere and most of them practise it in their spare time. And this is what the majority do because only a handful conduct archaeoastronomical research professionally, full time.

Additionally, timing factors may have played a contributory part in their isolation because archaeoastronomers, submerged in their own efforts, have always been out of temper with changes in archaeological theory. For example, Lockyer advanced the scientific method first devised in antiquarianism while archaeology was developing a culture-history approach. Similarly, Ruggles honed archaeoastronomy's praxis to a rigorous level, in tune with archaeology's processual innovations, at a time when leading prehistorians in archaeology were immersed in postprocessual theory. In the paradigm shifts between processualism and postprocessualism which occurred in both archaeology and archaeoastronomy, though in different decades, it was not so much *doing* things differently as *seeing* things differently. There was one period when the fields were more in tune and the first was when Thom's scientific processualism matched the uptake of processual scientific and analytic methods in archaeology. This led to the interdisciplinary conferences, mentioned earlier, where both sides conferred before going their separate ways.

For a long period afterwards, archaeoastronomers became obsessed with their disciplinary status, rather than interacting with other disciplines Certainly most archaeoastronomers describe their field as a discipline and have faith in its importance, so in another survey, when asked if archaeoastronomy was a discipline in its own right, 63.5% agreed that it was. However, while Ruggles began by considering it a discipline, he more recently asked whether archaeoastronomy was 'theoretically sustainable in its own right' (Ruggles 2011b, 6). He suggested that a viable alternative could be that it regard itself as a 'mini-discipline' or 'service discipline', that used its methods, techniques and skills to aid archaeologists, anthropologists and historians when they confronted issues relating to the sky. As Ruggles properly recognised that there was no sense in studying astronomical practices and beliefs in isolation, archaeoastronomy's services could be applied either where needed, as and when, or as part of an interdisciplinary collaborative effort. There is little difference between Ruggles' recent proposal and that of Lockyer who made his suggestion that astronomical studies should be taken into account in archaeological interpretations in 1894! Archaeoastronomy's struggle for recognition by archaeologists has a very long history indeed.

Of course, archaeoastronomers remain concerned with archaeoastronomy's place in the academy and over the years Clive Ruggles has made several mission statements, the highlight of which was his oft-cited 'thirty years on' paper (Ruggles 2011b) where he underlined the lack of progress away from data driven analyses without theoretical interpretation. Lionel Sims also had his reservations about whether archaeoastronomy is sustainable on its own, and his work, by setting archaeoastronomy within a 'four-field anthropology (archaeology, social anthropology, biological anthropology and linguistics)', advocated multidisciplinarity (Sims 2010). Having assessed archaeoastronomy's development against 'the weight of archaeological disfavour', he felt that if archaeoastronomy stands still waiting for others to accept it, then it is 'a discipline in danger' (Sims 2013, 185). These concerns are valid but few archaeoastronomers seem able to address them.

Recently, in response to the problem, some archaeoastronomers shared their opinions in the first part of the JSA Forum mentioned above (Silva and Henty 2020a, 86). Daniel Brown (2020, 92) thought at this time neither archaeoastronomy nor skyscape archaeology could be a discipline in its own right. Yet it seems to be effectively taught as a subdiscipline of archaeology in Rita Gautschy's courses in Switzerland. In her view 'skyscapes, cultural astronomy or archaeoastronomy – whatever one prefers to call it – clearly belongs to archaeology in academia (Gautschy 2020, 99). She thought it would be pointless to set archaeoastronomy apart as a separate discipline, rather that archaeoastronomers should be reaching out to collaborate with archaeologists. Javier Mejuto (2020, 105, 107) seemingly summed up the situation by saying that what hampers archaeoastronomy is the lack of theoretical work which impedes its entry into the academic arena and without sufficient opportunities to learn it, he concluded 'cultural astronomy is doomed to remain stagnant'. Fabio Silva (2020c, 112), echoing Gautschy, added that he saw skyscape archaeology as a subdiscipline of archaeology and in that way it would no longer live in isolation. His best option (2020, 110), as yet unfulfilled, is for it to be included as part of an archaeology degree with landscape and skyscape archaeology being taught in tandem. This position unknowingly reflects the very beginnings of archaeoastronomy in antiquarianism before disciplinary divisions, where the first musings about the sky and the landscape treated them in unison. Archaeoastronomy's lack of acceptance spills over into academic benchmarks which describe what gives a discipline its coherence and identity as well as setting out expectations about standards, but in Britain archaeoastronomy is not a benchmarked subject under the Quality Assurance Agency categories. Neither is it included under the archaeology benchmark and Darvill (2020, 262) said that this is because 'no representations were made to the benchmark panel'. Though he suggested that this does not proscribe it, he noted that its presence there would give it recognition. Without such benchmarking archaeoastronomy has to claim allegiance to other disciplines and at the University of Wales Trinity Saint David it comes under the benchmarks of history and anthropology (Campion, pers. comm.). Given that archaeoastronomy, in some form or other, has been on the curriculum as an optional course at a British university since 1989, this omission, mainly because those involved failed to take the appropriate steps, is detrimental. Because of this inward-looking struggle about their status, the archaeoastronomers have not knocked on university doors asking to be let in and indeed they have added further obstacles by isolating themselves and contributing to their own marginalisation, which suggests a certain amount of hubris on their part. Instead of arguing their case with the archaeologists, archaeoastronomers have mainly withdrawn to their own communities such as SEAC and ISAAC, outside the reach of their mainstream rivals and, as mentioned, publish their work in insider journals and proceedings. Not only that but only rarely do the majority of archaeoastronomers place their research within the archaeological context, and indeed, until skyscape archaeology there was little precedent for them to do so.

Archaeoastronomy still struggles with its identity as demonstrated by its various name changes and, historically, previous failures occurred because their names were indelibly linked to flawed practices and theory which, respectively, after due scrutiny, were rejected by archaeoastronomers and archaeologists alike. Additionally, there are minor confusions over its classification which also relate to identity. For example, at Aberdeen University library, Thom's key texts are classified in the 'History and geography' section under the sub-heading 'History of the Ancient World', while Ruggles' (1999) text-book, together with such works as Krupp's (1984) *Archaeoastronomy and the Roots of Science* are classified under the general heading 'Astronomy and other allied sciences'. This problem with identity is found elsewhere; for example in the library of Leicester University, where archaeoastronomy was taught, the Thoms' (1980a) *Megalithic Rings* is shelved in the history and archaeology section whereas *Megalithic Lunar Observatories* (1971) is found in the astronomy and astrophysics section. Neither is there consensus today amongst archaeoastronomers about its practice, whether this relates to theory and methodology or positioning: in Europe and North America archaeoastronomy comes under cultural astronomy, in South America it falls under the remit of anthropology, while in Britain some archaeoastronomers refer to it as skyscape archaeology. These developments reflect theory modification rather than an essential change to identity as generally the same method is used to measure and pinpoint alignments; and because the name archaeoastronomy has been used worldwide since 1971 it is likely that this practice will continue, especially from the outside looking in.

Because of the conflict of interests around archaeoastronomy, Belmonte (2016b, 259) described archaeoastronomy as being in 'no-man's land', adding that its future 'depends on the *desirable* convergence between archaeoastronomy and archaeology' (my emphasis). From 2012 onwards there have been initiatives from a new generation of archaeoastronomers who have been actively knocking on archaeology's door with the conscious objective of bringing archaeoastronomy to the attention of archaeologists, particularly at the TAG and EAA conferences and this was also the rationale behind founding the *Journal of Skyscape Archaeology*. We are much further down the line now and archaeoastronomy has much more recognition: the TAG, EAA, Dublin and Malta conferences suggest that the relationship between the two fields is becoming closer. While archaeoastronomy remains an autonomous field, the boundaries seem to be becoming blurred. Of course, overall, archaeoastronomy occupies a very minor place in the academy but so do most specialist subjects: its potential use in archaeology is being recognised more and more.

Current attitudes and steps towards the future

At the beginning of this volume, I introduced archaeoastronomy as the study which seeks to discover the impact of astronomy on culture. The theory that in some way cultures observed the cycles of the sun, the moon, the planets and the stars and incorporated them into their monuments in an intentional way, has not fundamentally changed since the connection was first remarked by Diodorus in the 1st century BC: it is a theory which underlies all archaeoastronomical research past and present and will likely do so in the future. However, this does not mean that there is a 'one size fits all' scenario and, as we have seen, different regions in the Americas and Europe have refashioned it in the image of the work of its motivated pioneers who took it forward for the next generation. We do indeed stand on the shoulders of giants on a platform of existing methods, data and theory, honed over time from antiquarianism onwards and it is this realisation which motivates archaeoastronomers to improve things for the future.

However, it will not be all plain sailing and many long-lasting problems still need to be addressed. Internationally, among archaeoastronomers, there is a lack of consensus over methods and theory and there are many variants of its practice vying for inclusion. Also, archaeoastronomy as a stand-alone field is undermined by its general absence in university departments and programmes. Untrained archaeoastronomers, those unlucky enough not to have received formal training, have to become autodidacts, picking up their skills and methods from the literature and/or by attending conferences. This, of course, makes it even more difficult for the field to operate consensually, as there are no set standards or expectations. In general, archaeoastronomers have been too complacent by ignoring criticisms not only between themselves but also from other disciplines, archaeology particularly. Another part of the problem is that so many different aspects come under archaeoastronomy's remit. Its methods require understandings of positional astronomy, the material record itself, which is the prime source material of archaeology, the history of astronomy, the history of culture, anthropology and ethnography, together with philosophical methods such as reflexivity and phenomenology. These different facets do not mesh easily and without these insights from other disciplines, archaeoastronomy would not have been able to progress from alignment seeking.

Currently there is only a small group of archaeoastronomers, mainly in Britain, who are actively engaged in skyscape archaeology in its fullest sense. Yet, from the historical perspective there is no reason to believe that skyscape archaeology may not suffer the fate of its previous incarnations. It could just be a passing fashion of which archaeoastronomy has seen several and a latter-day Jacquetta Hawkes might still describe it as an 'astronomical *nouveau vague*' (see J. Hawkes 1967, 180). This will happen unless we can learn the lessons of the past and improve things in the future.

There are three aspects to the question of whether or not archaeoastronomy has a future; first does it have a future as a stand-alone field largely reliant on its dedicated conferences and conference proceedings? The answer to this is yes it surely will, in some guise or another. In North America, largely through the efforts of Aveni, Carlson and others, archaeoastronomy achieved the status of a discipline early on in its history and though it has embraced ethnoastronomy and the ethnographic methods of anthropology, it retains its independence. In Latin America, the situation is more fluid because the cultural astronomy practised there proceeded from and is in tune with anthropology rather than the traditional focus on finding alignments. In Europe there is a mixture of archaeoastronomy and cultural astronomy and researchers have to fight for acceptance according to which country they live in. Yet, despite the lack of unity, international organisations like SEAC and ISAAC provide a very broad church where 'green' archaeoastronomy and 'brown' cultural astronomy can happily sit side by side. In their arenas, questions about archaeoastronomy's place in the academy or its relationship with archaeology are rarely aired. This is unlikely to change.

The second aspect relating to archaeoastronomy's future is whether or not more archaeologists will admit archaeoastronomy. Positive evidence in the form of those archaeology publications that have included archaeoastronomy findings; the opinions gleaned from the contributors to the JSA Forum and archaeoastronomy's welcome at the TAG and EAA conferences, shows that skyscapes may well be considered by archaeologists in the future. Indeed, Chadburn (2020, 277) cited González-García and Criado-Boado, the one an archaeoastronomer and the other an archaeologist, as saying 'we need each other'. Mladenović (2021, 40) agreed and concluded that 'Culturally contextualized archaeoastronomy requires expertise of two very different and complex fields'. Today, while a minority of archaeologists are using archaeoastronomy in their research or actively collaborating with archaeoastronomers, at the same time, some archaeoastronomers are making an effort to contextualise archaeoastronomy research within the larger archaeological picture and incorporate theories that archaeologists routinely use. This has impacted the relationship between archaeologists and archaeoastronomers so it is no longer as contestatory as it was in the past. This is not to say that all differences have been healed, but these differences may not play out in the generations to come.

12. Final thoughts

The third aspect also relates to the relationship between archaeoastronomers and archaeologists. By recognising the advantage of creating bridges between intellectual islands, it would be helpful for the future if more interdisciplinary collaborations could be encouraged. An exciting example of this is a recent paper where the lead authors were respectively an archaeologist and an astronomer who teamed up to conduct new research into The Hurlers stone circle complex in Cornwall (Nowakowski *et al.* 2020). This is perhaps the ideal way forward and one which skyscape archaeologists encourage. Overall, the problem which faces both archaeoastronomers and archaeologists alike is that of attributing meaning to the sites: layers of meaning could include astronomical, magical, ritual, symbolic, calendrical, sociological, economic or political factors, which when combined could provide a comprehensive picture. Whatever narrative you read, whether it be archaeology or archaeoastronomy, the account will always be quantitatively and qualitatively selective: in other words, interpretations are 'creative and empowering acts that actively produce, rather than simply transmit, what we call the past (Bender *et al.* 2007, 27). Interdisciplinarity helps prevent one-sided views on the past and listening to or adopting theories and methods from archaeoastronomy could provide archaeologists with a more balanced and holistic view of our material remains and that is all we archaeoastronomers can ask for. Now we have to persuade our archaeology colleagues to collaborate with us.

Although, in the study of British monumental culture, archaeoastronomy has always sat in the shadow of archaeology, some positive steps have been taken, so it touches on inclusion today, not least through its own efforts. This is because in the last twenty years archaeoastronomy has incorporated many multidisciplinary innovations in methodology and theory and since the introduction of skyscape archaeology some archaeoastronomers are beginning to approach the material record like archaeologists. This bodes well for its future relationship with archaeology if this impetus can be maintained. So far, these developments have been evidenced by a large volume of publications in this period, which show a renewed sense of purpose, but to avoid reaching an impasse archaeoastronomy must build on these recent achievements to develop and grow the field. But in what direction will it go given the many different strands of archaeoastronomy that are being practised, not just in different countries but often within the same country? Skyscape archaeology offers a line of communication with archaeologists far more so than traditional archaeoastronomy and perhaps, given that historical prejudices are difficult to change, this might be the way forward to break the deadlock both internally and externally. There is some support for this from some leading archaeologists as shown, but obviously I am biased, given the effort put into promoting skyscape archaeology. In Britain at least, this version is most likely to secure 'the suffrages of the archaeologist', which it has failed to do any time since Sayce penned these words about Lockyer's methods in 1914.

Entry into the university arena is another way forward and the importance of university courses, mainly from the perspective of the three courses taught in Britain, has been pointed out as an aid to enabling dissemination and reproduction. Currently there are some positives because there are at least six PhD students who have chosen to conduct archaeoastronomical research or incorporate archaeoastronomy in some way in their doctoral research: they are all placed in archaeology departments at different British universities. The impact of this cannot be quantified as yet but it does show that some archaeology supervisors regard archaeoastronomy as a worthwhile subject to base research on. As these studies will help spread the word there may well be a knock-on reproductive effect, so there are reasons to be optimistic.

For Britain, my conclusions, from the position of deep insider, are that in the future, archaeoastronomy, in the guise of skyscape archaeology, needs to be taken up as a subdiscipline under the umbrella of archaeology, in order to continue its existence. This would allow it to grow and enable important new insights into prehistoric culture and design. Without recognition from archaeologists it could remain in its current position, largely sidelined and isolated. To prevent this from happening, there are things that can and need to be done in addition to the steps already achieved: these include continuing to promote it at archaeology conferences, not just within the UK but also at the EAA annual meetings. Having participated in all the TAG skyscape sessions and attended the Dublin conference, I am only too aware of how productive it is when archaeoastronomers and archaeologists come together in conversation. The aim should be to organise more interdisciplinary conferences to enhance collaboration; to advertise archaeoastronomy extensively through social media and to form wider interdisciplinary networks which have broader aims than the ones we currently have. These meetings may well prove to be a tipping point but there is a lot more to be done such as persuading archaeoastronomers to publish their research in archaeology journals and to write more books relating to archaeoastronomy practice and theory for archaeology publishing houses. Finally we need to persuade archaeologists to introduce elements of skyscape archaeology to their courses, possibly in conjunction with landscape archaeology which is already accepted. As there is only one archaeoastronomy course left in Britain, it is important to consider how the next generation can be trained. Archaeoastronomy must come out of the shadows to ensure its academic future so that other disciplines can use its methods and expertise, in line with its aim to be interdisciplinary. We need to learn the lessons of history and these recommendations are all essential steps which need to be taken to ensure that archaeoastronomy's future is secure. We must continue with new research, grapple with new problems and come up with innovative solutions, not in isolation but in an interdisciplinary way: as Alan Salt (2015, 213) aptly stated, 'archaeoastronomy is an ongoing conversation'.

Bibliography

Achim, M. 2014. Skulls and idols: anthropometrics, antiquity collections, and the origin of American Man, 1810–1850. In P.L. Kohl, I. Podgorny and S. Gänger (eds), *Nature and Antiquities: the Making of Archaeology in the Americas.* Tuscon AZ, University of Arizona Press, 23–46.

Alberti, B. 2016. Archaeologies of risk and wonder. *Archaeological Dialogues* 23 (2), 138–145.

Alberti, B., Fowles, S., Holbraad, M., Marshall, Y. and Witmore C. 2011. 'Worlds otherwise', archaeology, anthropology, and ontological difference. *Current Anthropology* 52 (6), 896–912.

Aldana, G. 2009. Aveni honoured. *Journal for the History of Astronomy* 40 (1), 109–120.

Alexander, G. 1978. America's prehistoric astronomers. In *Nature Science Annual.* Alexandria VA, Time-Life Books, 132–153.

Allen, H. 2004. Hawkins way: remembering astronomer Gerald S. Hawkins. *Culture and Cosmos* 8, 1–6.

Almagro-Gorbea, M. and Gran-Aymerich, J.M.J. 1991. *El Estanque Monumental de Bibracte. Complutum.* Extra 1.

Amendola, L. 2021. The Golden Hat of Schifferstadt: an astronomically significant deposit location? *Journal of Skyscape Archaeology* 7 (1), 113–142.

American Indian Quarterly. 1984. Review of R. A Williamson (ed.), *Archaeoastronomy in the Americas. American Indian Quarterly*, 127.

Ancient Explorers. 2016. The Legend of the Rollright Stones. [online] Accessed May 2016, ancientexplorers.com/blog/the-legend-of-the-rollright-stones/ [link no longer active]

Anderson, J.M. 1734. *The Constitution, The History, Laws, Charges, Orders, Regulations, and Usages, of the Right Worshipful Fraternity of Accepted Free-Masons.* Philadelphia PA. [online] Accessed September 2014, https://digitalcommons.unl.edu/cgi/viewcontent.cgi?article=1028&context=libraryscience

Andersson, P. 2012. Alternative archaeology, many pasts in our present. *Numen* 59 (2/3), 125–137.

Andrews, E.W. 1959. Dzibilchaltun: lost city of the Maya. *National Geographic* 115, 90–130.

Angell, I.O. 1976. Stone circles: megalithic mathematics or Neolithic nonsense? *The Mathematical Gazette* 60, 189–193.

Anon. 1900. Societies and academies. *Nature* 61, 529–532.

Anon. 1908. University and educational intelligence. *Nature* 77, 572–574.

Anon. 1912. Prehistoric time measurement. *Nature* 89, 619–620.

Antonello, E. 2013. Cultural astronomy and archaeoastronomy: an Italian experience. In I. Šprajc and P. Pehani (eds), *Ancient Cosmologies and Modern Prophets: proceedings of the 20th conference of the European Society for Astronomy in Culture.* Ljubljana,, Slovene Anthropological Society, 507–513.

Archaeology. 2016. Did megalithic tombs double as telescopes? 30 June. [online] Accessed December, 2017, www.archaeology.org/news/4611-160630-megalithic- tomb-astronomy

Archaeology Ireland. 2018. Pathways to the Cosmos, the alignment of megalithic tombs in Ireland and Atlantic Europe Dublin conference, 15.09.18. [online] Accessed September, 2018, archaeologyireland.ie/2018/06/19/pathways-to-the-cosmos-the- alignment-of-megalithic-tombs-in-ireland-and-atlantic-europe/

Armstrong, P. 2015. Review of National Astronomy Meeting, Portsmouth (United Kingdom), 23–25 June, 2014 *Journal of Skyscape Archaeology* 1 (1), 281–284.

Armstrong, P. 2016. Review of 'The Land, the Sea and the Sky', Prehistoric Society Conference, Society of Antiquaries, London, 5 March 2016. *Journal of Skyscape Archaeology* 2 (2), 265–271.

Argüelles, J. 1987. *The Mayan Factor, Path Beyond Technology.* Sante Fe NM, Bear and Co.

Aston, M. and Rowley T. 1974. *Landscape Archaeology: an introduction to fieldwork techniques on post-Roman landscapes.* Newton Abbot, David and Charles.

Atkinson, R.J.C. 1966a. Decoder misled, *Nature* 210, 1302.

Atkinson, R.J.C. 1966b. Moonshine on Stonehenge. *Antiquity* 40, 212–216.

Atkinson, R.J.C. 1967. Hoyle on Stonehenge: some comments. *Antiquity* 41, 92–95.

Atkinson, R.J.C. 1974a. C A Newham and Stonehenge *Antiquity* 48, 215–216.

Atkinson, R.J.C. 1974b. Neolithic science and technology. In Hodson (ed.) 1974, 123–131.

Atkinson, R.J.C. 1975. Megalithic astronomy – a prehistorian's comments. *Journal for the History of Astronomy* 6, 42–52.

Atkinson, R.J.C. 1979. Review of A. Thom and A.S. Thom, *Megalithic Remains in Britain & Brittany. Archaeoastronomy Supplement to the Journal for the History of Astronomy* 1, S99–S102.

Atkinson, R.J.C. 1985. William Stukeley and the Stonehenge sunrise. *Archaeoastronomy Supplement to the Journal for the History of Astronomy* 8, S61–S62.

Atkinson, R.J.C. 1986. Obituary of Alexander Thom. *Journal for the History of Astronomy* 17, 73–75.

Aveni, A.F. 1972. Astronomical tables intended for use in astro-archaeological studies. *American Antiquity* 37 (4), 531–540.

Aveni, A.F. 1973. Comments. In Baity 1973, 431.

Aveni, A.F. (ed.). 1975. *Archaeoastronomy in Pre-Columbian America.* Austin TX, University of Texas Press.

Aveni, A.F. 1978. Comments, 593–594, in D. Turton *et al.*, Agreeing to disagree, the measurement of duration in a Southwestern Ethiopian community [and comments and reply], *Current Anthropology* 19 (3), 585–600.

Aveni, A.F. 1980. *Skywatchers of Ancient Mexico.* Austin TX, University of Texas Press.

Aveni, A.F. 1981a. Horizon astronomy in Incaic Cuzco. In Williamson (ed.) 1981, 305–318.

Aveni, A.F. 1981b. Archaeoastronomy. *Advances in Archaeological Method and Theory* 4, 1–77.

Aveni A.F. (ed.). 1982. *Archaeoastronomy in the New World, American Primitive Astronomy.* Cambridge and New York, Cambridge University Press.

Aveni, A. F. 1983. *Skywatchers of Ancient Mexico.* Austin TX, University of Texas Press.

Aveni, A.F. 1984. Comment following C.L.N. Ruggles and N.J. Saunders, The interpretation of the pecked cross symbols at Teotihuacan: a methodological note. *Archaeoastronomy Supplement to the Journal for the History of Astronomy* 7, S101– S110.

Aveni, A.F. 1989a. Introduction, whither archaeoastronomy. In Aveni (ed.) 1989b, 3–12.

Aveni, A.F. (ed). 1989b. *World Archaeoastronomy, Selected papers from the 2nd Oxford International Conference on Archaeoastronomy, held at Merida, Yucatan, Mexico, 13–17 January, 1986.* Cambridge and New York, Cambridge University Press.

Aveni, A.F. 1992. Nobody asked but I couldn't resist. A response to Keith Kintigh on archaeoastronomy and archaeology. *Archaeoastronomy and Ethnoastronomy News* 6 (1), 4. [online] Accessed June 2021, http,//terpconnect.umd.edu/~tlaloc/archastro/ae6.html

Aveni, A.F. 1993. Archaeoastronomy in the Americas since Oxford 2. In Ruggles (ed.) 1993b, 15–32.

Aveni, A.F. 1995. Review of Iwaniszewski *et al.* (eds), *Time and Astronomy at the Meeting of Two Worlds ... Archaeoastronomy Supplement to the Journal for the History of Astronomy* 20, S74–S78.

Aveni, A. (ed.). 2008. *Foundations of New World Cultural Astronomy: a reader with commentary.* Boulder CO, University Press of Colorado.

Aveni, A. 2016. Reidentifying archaeoastronomy. *Journal of Skyscape Archaeology* 2 (2), 245–249.

Aveni, A.F. and Romano, G. 1986. Archaeoastronomical research in Veneto-Friuli, Italy. *Archaeoastronomy Supplement to the Journal for the History of Astronomy* 10, S23– S31.

Baigent, M., Leigh R. and Lincoln, H. 1982. *The Holy Blood and the Holy Grail.* London, Jonathan Cape.

Bailey, M.E., Cooke, J.A., Few, R.W., Morgan, J.G. and Ruggles, C.L.N. 1975. Survey of three megalithic sites in Argyllshire. *Nature* 253, 431–433.
Baity, E. 1973. Archaeoastronomy and ethnoastronomy so far [and comments and reply]. *Current Anthropology* 14 (4), 389–449.
Bann, S. 1987. Clio in part: on antiquarianism and the historical fragment. *Perspecta* 23, 24–37.
Barber, B. 1961. Resistance by scientists to scientific discovery. *Science* 134, 596–602.
Barber, J. 1976. Comments. In Freeman 1976, 43–44.
Barclay, G. J. 2001. 'Metropolitan and parochial'/'core and periphery': a historiography of the Neolithic. *Proceedings of the Prehistoric Society* 67, 1–18.
Barker, G. 2007. Changing roles and agendas: the Society of Antiquaries and the professionalisation of archaeology, 1950–2000. In S. Pearce (ed.), *Visions of Antiquity: the Society of Antiquaries of London 1707-2007*. London, Society of Antiquities of London, 341–366.
Barnatt, J. 1978. *Stone Circles of the Peak: a search for natural harmony*. London, Turnstone Books.
Baschmakoff, A. 1930. Les alignements de Carnac (Morbihan). *L'Anthropologie* 40, 40–75.
Baudouin, M. 1912. Procédés et techniques pour l'étude de l'orientation des gravures sur rochers et de l'axe d'érection des megaliths par rapport a l'astre solaire. *Société Préhistorique Française* 9, 711–716.
Baudouin, M. 1913. Technique de la determination de l'orientation des dolmens. *L'Homme Préhistorique* 2 (1), 369–377.
Baudouin, M. 1917. La préhistoire des étoiles. *Société Préhistorique Française* 14, 290.
Bauer, B.S. 1992. Ritual pathways of the Inca, an analysis of the Collasuyu Ceques in Cuzco. *Latin American Antiquity* 3 (3), 183–205.
Bauer, B.S. and Dearborn, D.S.P. 1995. *Astronomy and Empire in the Ancient Andes, The Cultural Origins of Inca Sky Watching*. Austin TX, University of Texas Press.
Bauval, R.G. 1989. A master plan for the three pyramids of Giza based on the configuration of the three stars of the Belt of Orion. *Discussions in Egyptology* 13, 7–18.
Bauval R. 2017. Home page. [online] Accessed November 2017, www.robertbauval.co.uk/index.html.
Bauval, R. 2000. *Secret Chamber: the quest for the Hall of Records*. New York, Arrow Books.
Bauval, R. and Gilbert A. 1995. *The Orion Mystery: unlocking the secrets of the pyramids*. London, Mandarin.
Bauval, R. and Hancock, G. 1996. *Keeper of Genesis: a quest for the hidden legacy of mankind*. New York, Random House.
BBC Archive 2020. *Chronicle, Cracking the Stone Age Code* [online] Accessed June, 2020, https://www.bbc.co.uk/archive/chronicle--cracking-the-stone-age-code/zdkrhbk
Behrend, M. 1977a. A forgotten researcher: Ludovic McLennan Man citing L.McL. Mann, *Archaic Sculpturings* (Glasgow 1914). [online] Accessed June, 2013, www.cantab.net/users/michael.behrend/repubs/mann_afr/pages/intro.html
Behrend, M. 1977b. Ludovic McLellan Mann, Salisbury Plain – an astronomical blackboard, no date, transcribed by Michael Behrend. [online] Accessed, April, 2019, www.cantab.net/users/michael.behrend/repubs/mann_afr/pages/sal_plain.html
Behrend, M. 2013a. Wilhelm Teudt. [online] Accessed June, 2013. www.cantab.net/users/michael.behrend/repubs/teudt_hl/pages/intro.html
Behrend, M. 2013b. Living leys or laying the lies? Introduction to a reprint of a debate between Aubrey Burl and John Michell. *Popular Archaeology* 1983, 13–18. [online] Accessed April, 2015, www.cantab.net/users/michael.behrend/repubs/burl_michell/pages/main.html
Belloc, H. 1911. *The Old Road*. London, Constable & Co.
Belloc, H. 1913. *The Stane Street*. London, Constable & Co.

Belmonte, J.A. 1997. Mediterranean archaeotopography and archaeoastronomy: two examples of dolmenic necropolises in the Jordan Valley. *Archaeoastronomy Supplement to the Journal for the History of Astronomy* 22, S37–S43.

Belmonte, J.A. (ed.). 2000. *Arqueoastronomía Hispánica: prácticas astronómicas en la prehistoria de la Península Ibérica y los archipiélagos balear y canario* (revised edition). Madrid, Equipo Sirius.

Belmonte, J.A. 2001a. On the orientation of Old Kingdom Egyptian pyramids. *Archaeoastronomy Supplement to the Journal for the History of Astronomy* 26, S1–S20.

Belmonte, J.A. 2001b. Review of Michael Hoskin, *Tombs, Temples and Their Orientations: a new perspective on mediterranean prehistory*. *Archaeoastronomy Supplement to the Journal for the History of Astronomy* 26, S84–S89.

Belmonte, J.A. 2009. Prologos to 2nd edition. In J.A. Belmonte (ed.), *Arqueoastronomía Hispánica*, Spain, Equipo Sirius.

Belmonte, J.A. 2015. Ancient observatories' – a relevant concept? In Ruggles (ed.) 2015a, 133–145.

Belmonte, J.A. 2016a. Landscapes, skyscapes, archaeoastronomy. *Journal for the History of Astronomy* 47 (4), 445–446.

Belmonte, J.A. 2016b. Is there a conflict between archaeology and archaeoastronomy? An astronomer's view. *Journal of Skyscape Archaeology* 2 (2), 255–260.

Belmonte, J.A. and González García, A.C. 2015. The pillars of the earth and the sky. *Journal of Skyscape Archaeology* 1 (1), 9–38.

Belmonte, J.A., González García, A.C. and Polcaro, A. 2013. Light and shadows over Petra, astronomy and landscape in Nabataean lands. *Nexus Network Journal* 15 (3), 487–501.

Belmonte, J.A. and Hoskin M. 2002. *Reflejo del cosmos: atlas de arqueoastronomía en el Mediterráneo Antiguo*. Madrid, Equipo Sirius.

Bender, B. 1992. Theorising landscapes, and the prehistoric landscapes of Stonehenge. *Man* NS 27 (4), 735–755.

Bender, B. 1998. *Stonehenge: Making Space*. Oxford & New York, Berg.

Bender, B., Hamilton, S. and Tilley, C. 2007. *Stone Worlds, Narrative and Reflexivity in Landscape Archaeology*. Walnut Creek CA, Left Coast Press.

Benedict, R. 1935. *Zuni Mythology*. New York, Columbia University Press.

Bennett, A.F. 1933. Preface to Herbert Hudson 'Ancient sun alignments: the meaning of artificial mounds and mark stones'. *Proceedings of the Suffolk Institute of Archaeology and Natural History* 2, 120–138.

Bennett, F.J. 1904. On the meridional position of megaliths in Kent compared with those of Wilts, and also with those of earth-works and churches. *South Eastern Naturalist* 9, 29–36.

Bennett, G.A. and Gale, J. 2017. Lines of enquiry, linear organisation of the High Lea Farm Bronze Age barrow cemetery. *Proceedings of the Dorset Natural History & Archaeological Society* 138, 127–136.

Benson, A. and Hopkinson, T. (eds) 1985. *Earth and Sky, Papers from the Northridge Conference on Archaeoastronomy*. Thousand Oaks CA, Slo'w Press.

Binford, L.R. 1968. Some comments on historical versus processual archaeology. *Southwestern Journal of Anthropology* 24, 267–275.

Binford, L.R. 1983. *Working at Archaeology*. New York, Academic Press.

Black, W.H. 1871. Boundaries and landmarks. *Journal of the British Archaeological Association* 27, 268–274.

Blair, A. 2008. Disciplinary distinctions before the 'two cultures'. *The European Legacy* 13 (5), 577–588.

Blavatsky, H.P. 1877. *Isis Unveiled*. New York, J.W. Bouton/London, Bernard Quaritch.

Bloland, H.G. 1995. Postmodernism and Higher Education. *The Journal of Higher Education* 66 (5), 521–559.

Boccas M., Bustamante, P., González, C. and Monsalve, C. 2000. Promising archaeoastronomy investigations in Chile. In Esteban and Belmonte (eds) 2000, 115–124.

Boesce, H. 1527. *Historia Gentis Scotorum.* Paris

Boece, H. 1575. *Scotorum Historia.* Paris. [online] Accessed August 2015, http://www.philological.bham.ac.uk/boece/

Bond, G.C. and Gilliam, A. (eds). 1997. *Social Construction of the Past: representation as power.* Oxford Routledge.

Bord, J. and Bord, C. 1972. *Mysterious Britain.* London: Garnstone Press.

Bord, J. and Bord C. 1976. *The Secret Country.* London, Walker.

Boule, M. 1930. Peut-on calculer, á l'aide de l'astronomie, la date approximative de certain monuments mégalithiques. *L'Athropologie* 40, 202–203.

Bourdieu, P. 1988. *Homo Academicus* (trans. P. Collier). Cambridge, Polity.

Boutsikas, E. 2007. Astronomy and ancient Greek cult: an application of archaeoastronomy to Greek religious architecture, cosmologies and landscapes. Unpublished PhD thesis, University of Leicester.

Boutsikas, E. 2018. Review of Road to the Stars. Oxford XI; European Society for Astronomy in Culture (SEAC) 25. *Journal of Skyscape Archaeology* 4 (1), 134–137.

Bracher, K. 1999. *History of the Historical Astronomy Division.* [online] Accessed July 2012, https://had.aas.org/resources/hadhistory.

Bradley, R. 1991. The evidence of earthwork monuments. In J. Barrett, R.J. Bradley and M.T. Green (eds), *Landscape, Monuments and Society: the prehistory of Cranborne Chase*, Cambridge, Cambridge University Press, 35–58.

Bradley, R. 1993. *Altering the Earth. The Rhind Lectures 1991-92.* Edinburgh: Society of Antiquaries of Scotland Monograph 8.

Bradley, R. 1998. *The Significance of Monuments: on the shaping of human experience in Neolithic and Bronze Age Europe.* London, Routledge.

Bradley, R. 2011. *Stages and Screens: an investigation of four henge monuments in northern and north-eastern Scotland.* Edinburgh, Society of Antiquaries of Scotland.

Bradley, R. and Nimura, C. 2016. *The Use and Reuse of Stone Circles.* Oxford, Oxbow Books.

Brady, B. 2015a. Star-paths, stones and horizon astronomy. In Pimenta *et al.* (eds) 2015, 58–63.

Brady, B. 2015b. Star phases, the naked-eye astronomy of the Old Kingdom Pyramid Texts. In Silva and Campion (eds) 2015, 76–86.

Brady, B. 2017. The dual alignments of the solstitial churches in North Wales. *Journal of Skyscape Archaeology* 3 (1), 5–28.

Brandt, J.C., Maran S.P., Williamson, R.A., Harrington, R.S., Cochran C., Kennedy M., Kennedy, W.J. and Chamberlain V.D. 1975. Possible rock art records of the Crab Nebula supernova in the western United States. In Aveni 1975, 45–58.

Braudel, F. 1958. Histoire et Sciences sociales. La longue durée'. *Annales, Histoire, Sciences socials*, 13 (4), 725–753.

Braudel, F. 1995. *The Mediterranean and the Mediterranean World in the Age of Philip II, Volume 1.* Berkeley CA, University of California Press.

Brecher, K and Feirtag M. (eds). 1979. *Astronomy of the Ancients.* Cambridge MA, MIT Press.

Breternitz, D.A. 1973. Comments. In Baity 1973, 432.

Broda, J. 1969. *The Mexican Calendar as Compared to Other Mesoamerican Systems.* Vienna, Acta Ethnologica et Lingüística.

Broda, J. 1991a. Review of A.F. Aveni (ed.) *New Directions in American Archaeoastronomy. Archaeoastronomy Supplement to the Journal for the History of Astronomy* 16, S76

Broda, J. 1991b. *Arqueoastronomía y etnoastronomía en Mesoamérica.* Mexico City, UNAM.

Brophy, K. 2020. Teaching skyscapes: keeping our feet on the ground *Journal of Skyscape Archaeology* 6 (2), 268–272.

Brown, D. 2015. Exploring skyscape in Stellarium. *Journal of Skyscape Archaeology* 1 (1), 93–112.

Brown, D. 2016a. Phenomenology of shadow. *Mediterranean Archaeology and Archaeometry* 16 (4), 25–32.
Brown, D. (ed.). 2016b. *Modern Archaeoastronomy, From Material Culture to Cosmology*. *Journal of Physics Conference Series* 685.
Brown, D. 2020. Archaeoastronomy within astronomy at UK universities. *Journal of Skyscape Archaeology* 6 (1), 88–93.
Brown, R.A. 1981. *Katherine Emma Maltwood: artist 1878-1961. Monograph from an exhibition at The Maltwood Art Museum and Gallery. University of Victoria, Australia*. Victoria, Sono Nis Press.
Browne, H. 1823. *An Illustration of Stonehenge and Abury in the County of Wilts: pointing out their origin and character*. Salisbury, Brodie and Dowding.
Buck, C.E., Kenworthy, J.B., Litton, C.D. and Smith A.F.M. 1991. Combining archaeological and radiocarbon information: a Bayesian approach to calibration *Antiquity* 65, 808–821.
Bunzel, R. 1932. Introduction to Zuni ceremonialism. *Bureau of American Ethnology Annual Report* 47, 467–544.
Burkitt, M.C. and Barnes, A.S. 1921. Congress at Lieges. *Proceedings of the Prehistoric Society* 3 (3), 453–460.
Burl, H.A.W. 1970. The recumbent stone circles of north-east Scotland. *Proceedings of the Society of Antiquaries of Scotland* 102, 56–81.
Burl, A. 1979. *Rings of Stone: the prehistoric stone circles of Britain and Ireland*. London, Frances Lincoln.
Burl, A. 1980. Science or symbolism: problems of archaeo-astronomy. *Antiquity* 54, 191–200.
Burl, A. 1981. Review of J. Barnatt, *Stone Circles of the Peak: a search for natural harmony* and T. Graves, *Needles of Stone*. *Archaeoastronomy, The Journal of Astronomy in Culture* 4 (2), 35–36.
Burl, H.AW. 1982. Pi in the sky. In Heggie (ed.) 1982b, 141–169.
Burl, A. 1983. *Prehistoric Astronomy and Ritual*. Princes Risborough, Shire.
Burl, A. 1993. *From Carnac to Callanish: the prehistoric stone rows and avenues of Britain, Ireland and Brittany*. New Haven CO, Yale University Press.
Burnham, A. 2013 Rare paintings of prehistoric life revealed. [online] Accessed November, 2015, https://www.megalithic.co.uk/article.php?sid=2146414141
Bustamante P. 2013. Santiago de Chile, una ciudad con pasado mapuche-incaico. Orientaciones orográficas, orientaciones astronómicas y posible sistema de ceques Simposio, TAWANTINSUYU 2013, XVII Congreso Nacional de Arqueología Argentina, La Rioja, 22–26 April 2013. *Xama* 24–29, 177–190.
Butler, G.F. 1998. Review of G. Parry, *The Trophies of Time: English antiquarians of the seventeenth century*. *Renaissance Quarterly* 51 (2), 717–718.
Caesar, J. *The Gallic Wars*, trans. W.A. McDevitte and W.S. Bohn. [online] Accessed September 2016, http://classics.mit.edu/Caesar/gallic.6.6.html
Cadogan, L. 1959. *Ayvu Rapyta*. São Paulo, University of São Paulo.
Caine, M. 1969. The Glastonbury Giants. *Gandalf's Garden* 4. [online] Accessed June, 2013, www.users.globalnet.co.uk/~pardos/GGZodiac2.html
Callender, H. 1856. Notice of the stone circle at Callernish, in the Island of Lewis. *Proceedings of the Society of Antiquaries of Scotland* 2 (2), 380–384.
Camden, W. 1722. *Britannia: a chorographical description great of Britain and Ireland together with the adjacent lands* (2nd edition, revised E. Gibson). London, Awnson Churchill.
Campion, N. 2002. From Stonehenge to Seattle: eco-protest, archaeoastronomy and New Age cosmology In S. Salvatore (ed.), *Proceedings of the INSAP III Conference*. *Journal of the Italian Astronomical Society* Special 1, 202–205.
Campion, N. 2004. Introduction: cultural astronomy. In N. Campion, P. Curry and M. York (eds), *Astrology and the Academy: papers from the inaugural conference of the Sophia Centre, Bath Spa University College, 13-14 June 2003*. Bristol, Cinnabar Books, xv–xxx.
Campion, N. 2008. *The Dawn of Astrology*. London and New York, Continuum Books.

Campion, N. 2009. *A History of Western Astrology*, vol. 2. London and New York, Continuum Books.
Campion, N. and Malville, J.M. 2011. Masters-level education in archaeoastronomy at the University of Wales Trinity Saint David. In Ruggles (ed.) 2011a, 357–363.
Carey, W.D. 1984. Frontispiece. In Krupp (ed.) 1984, unnumbered
Carlson, J.B. 1976. Review of Aveni 1975. *Journal for the History of Astronomy* 7 (20), 205–206.
Carlson, J.B. 1978. Editorial. *Archaeoastronomy Bulletin* I (4).
Carlson, J.B. 1979a. In search of archaeoastronomy, discussions at the American Astronomical Society meeting in Mexico City, January 1979, archaeoastronomy – the scope and implications in interaction with other disciplines. *Archaeoastronomy Bulletin* 2 (2), 9.
Carlson, J.B. 1979b. Editorial. *Archaeoastronomy Bulletin* 2 (2).
Carlson, J.B. 1982a. In the current literature. *Archaeoastronomy Bulletin* 5 (1), 44–49.
Carlson, J.B. 1982b. Editorial. *Archaeoastronomy Bulletin* 5 (4).
Carlson, J.B. 1999a. Pilgrimage and the equinox 'Serpent of Light and Shadow' phenomenon at the Castillo, Chichén Itzá, Yukatán. *Archaeoastronomy, The Journal of Astronomy in Culture* 14 (1), 136–152.
Carlson, J. 1999b. Editorial: a professor of our own. *Archaeoastronomy and Ethnoastronomy News* 33. [online] Accessed March 2015, http://terpconnect.umd.edu/~tlaloc/archastro/ae33.html
Carlson, J.B. 2000. Conference report: Oxford 6. *Archaeoastronomy Supplement to the Journal for the History of Astronomy* 25, S89–S90.
Carlson, J.B. 2011. The Maya Calendar and 2012 Phenomenon. *Archaeoastronomy, The Journal of Astronomy in Culture* 24, 1–7.
Carlson, J.B., Dearborn, D.S.P., McCluskey, S.C. and Ruggles, C.L.N. 1999. Introduction: astronomy in culture *Archaeoastronomy, The Journal of Astronomy in Culture* 14 (1), 3–21, back matter, 47
Carr, E.H. 1973. *What is History*. Harmondsworth, Penguin.
Caso, A. 1932. Monte Albán: richest archaeological find in America. *National Geographic* 62, 487–512.
Cerdeño, M.L., Rodríguez-Caderot, G., Moya, P.R., Ibarra, A. and Herrero, S. 2006. Los studios de Arqueoastronomía en España: estado de la cuestión. *Trabajos de Prehistoria* 63 (2), 13–34.
Chadburn, A. 2020. Where next for archaeoastronomy? A personal view from a cultural heritage adviser. *Journal of Skyscape Archaeology* 6 (2), 276–282.
Chamberlain, V.D. 1994. Reflections on rock art and astronomy. *Archaeoastronomy and Ethnoastronomy News* 14. [http://www.wam.umd.edu/~tlaloc/archastro/ae14.html]
Chamberlain, V.D., Carlson, J.B. and Young, M.J. (eds). 2005. *Songs from the Sky, indigenous astronomical and cosmological traditions of the world*. Bognor Regis, Ocarina Books.
Charleton, W. 1663. *Chorea Gigantum*. London.
Charrière, G. 1961. Stonehenge: rythmes architecturaux et orientation. *Bulletin de la Société Préhistorique Française* 58, 276–279.
Charrière, G. 1964. Typologies des orientations mégalithiques et protohistoriques. *Bulletin de la Société Préhistoriques Française* 60 (1), 160–168.
Chevalier, Y. 1984. *L'architecture des dolmens entre Languedoc et centre-ouest de France*. Bonn, Dr. Rudolf Habelt GmbH.
Chevalier, Y. 1999. Orientations of 935 dolmens of southern France. *Supplement to the Journal for the History of Astronomy* 24, S47–S82
Childe, V. G. 1935. Changing methods and aims in prehistory: Presidential address for 1935. *Proceedings of the Prehistoric Society* 1, 1–15.
Childe, V.G. 1955. Discussion on Professor Thom's paper, 293-294 in A. Thom, A statistical examination of the megalithic sites in Britain. *Journal of the Royal Statistical Society* Series A (General), 118 (3), 275–295.
Childe, V.G. 1960 [1942]. *What Happened in History*. London, Max Parrish.
Childe, V.G. 1973 [1925]. *The Dawn of European Civilisation*. St Albans, Granada.

Childe, V.G. 1981 [1936]. *Man Makes Himself*. Bradford-on-Avon, Moonraker Press & Pitman Publishing.
Childe, V.G. 2009 [1958]. *The Prehistory of European Society*. Nottingham, Spokesman.
Clark, G. 1958. Review of ARCHAEOMETRY. *Proceedings of the Prehistoric Society* 24, 233–234.
Clark, G.A. 1973. Comments. In Baity 1973, 432.
Clarke, D. 1973. Archaeology: the loss of innocence. *Antiquity* 47, 6–18.
Clay, R. 1927. Some prehistoric ways. *Antiquity* 1, 54–65.
Cobb, H., Harris, O., Jones, C. and Richardson P. 2008. Different perspectives on subjects and objects, confronting tensions in fieldwork and theory TAG Session and Paper Abstracts, University of Southampton. [online] https://antiquity.ac.uk/sites/default/files/downloads/tag/TAG_2008_abstracts.pdf.
Cobo, C. 2008. *Astronomía Quito-Caranqui, catequilla y los discos líticos, evidencias de la astronomía antigua en los Andes ecuatoriales*. Quito, Quimera Dreams Editores.
Coles, F.R. 1900. Report on stone circles in Kincardineshire (North) and part of Aberdeenshire, with measured plans and drawings obtained under the Gunning Fellowship. *Proceeding of the Society of Antiquaries of Scotland* 34, 1899–1900, 139–198.
Collier, B.A. and Aveni, A.F. 1978. *A Selected Bibliography on Native American Astronomy*. Hamilton NY, Department of Physics and Astronomy, Colgate University.
Collis, J. 2013. The development of archaeological thought as evidenced in the *Yorkshire Archaeological Journal*. *Yorkshire Archaeological Journal* 85, 5–26.
Colt Hoare, R. 1812. *The History of Ancient Wiltshire*. London, William Miller.
Colton, R. and Martin, R.L. 1967. Eclipse cycles and eclipses at Stonehenge. *Nature* 213, 476–478.
Connolly, D. 2015. Review of 'Cosmologies in transition, continuity and transformation in the material record'. Session at the 36th TAG conference 2014, Manchester. *Journal of Skyscape Archaeology* 1 (1), 142–149.
Connolly, D. 2016. *Archaeoastronomy for Archaeologists* Guide 43. [online] Accessed June 2021, www.bajr.org/BAJRGuides/43_Archaeo-Astronomy/43_ArchaeAstronomy.pdf
Cooke, J.A., Few, R.W., Morgan, J.G. and Ruggles, C.L.N. 1977. Indicated declinations at the Callenish megalithic sites. *Journal for the History of Astronomy* 8(2), 113–133.
Copernicus, N. 1543. *De revolutionibus orbium coelestium.* Nuremburg
Corrado, G. and Benítez, S.G. 2020. Archaeoastronomy in South America, is there a future? *Journal of Skyscape Archaeology* 6 (2), 273–275.
Cowgill, G.L. 1967. Computer applications in archaeology', In *AFIPS 67, Proceedings of the November 14-16, 1967, Fall Joint Computer Conference* 1967. New York, Association for Computing Machinery, 330–337.
Cox, T. 1738. *Magna Britannia Antiqua & Nova.* London.
Crawford, O.G.C. 1927. Editorial notes. *Antiquity* 1, 1–4.
Crawford, O.G.C. 1951. Archaeological History: a review. *Antiquity* 25, 9–12.
Crawford, O.G.C. 1953. *Archaeology in the Field*. London, Phoenix House.
Criado, F. and Quintela, G. 2007. Landscape, archaeology and ethno-astronomy: a union foretold. In Zedda and Belmonte (eds) 2007, 87–99.
Cristofaro, I. 2017. Reflecting the sky in water, a phenomenological exploration of water-skyscapes. *Journal of Skyscape Archaeology* 3 (1), 112–126.
Critchlow, K. 2007. *Time Stands Still, New Light on Megalithic Science* (2nd edition). Edinburgh, Floris Books.
Crowe, M.J. and Dowd, M.F. 1999. Archaeoastronomy and the history of science. *Archaeoastronomy, The Journal of Astronomy in Culture* 14 (1), 22–38.
Cunliffe, B. 1973. Introduction. In Childe 1973, 15–28.
Cunliffe, B. and Renfrew, C. (eds). 1997. *Science and Stonehenge*. Oxford, Oxford University Press/ *Proceedings of the British Academy* 92.

Daniel, G. 1962. *The Idea of Prehistory*. London, C. A. Watts.
Daniel, G. 1964. Editorial. *Antiquity* 38, 165–170.
Daniel, G. 1978 [1950]. *150 Years of Archaeology*. London, Duckworth.
Daniel, G. 1980. Megalithic monuments. *Scientific American* 243 (1), 78–90.
Däniken, E. von. 1969. *Chariots of the Gods?: unsolved mysteries of the past*. New York, Bantam Books.
Darvill, T. 1997. Ever increasing circles: the sacred geographies of Stonehenge and its landscape. In Cunliffe and Renfrew (eds) 1997, 167–202.
Darvill, T. 2015. Afterword, dances beneath a diamond sky. In Silva and Campion (eds) 2015, 140–148.
Darvill, T. 2016. Spirits in the sky. *Journal of Skyscape Archaeology* 2 (2), 261–264.
Darvill, T. 2020. When worlds collide. *Journal of Skyscape Archaeology* 6 (2), 261–264.
Darwin, C. 1909 [1859]. *On the Origin of Species By Means of Natural Selection, or the Preservation of Favoured Races in the Struggles for Life*. New York, P.F. Collier and Son.
da Silva, C.M. 2004. The Spring full moon. *Journal for the History of Astronomy* 35 (4), 475–478.
Dawkins, W. B. 1874. *Cave Hunting*. London, Macmillan.
Dearborn, D. 1991. Bridging disciplines & falling in cracks. *Archaeoastronomy and Ethnoastronomy News* 2. [online] Accessed March 2015, https://terpconnect.umd.edu/~tlaloc/archastro/ae2.html
Dearborn, D.S.P. and Bell, B. 1984. New tools for ancient skies. *Archaeoastronomy, The Journal of Astronomy in Culture* 7, 96–104.
DeLanda, M. 2016. *Assemblage Theory*. Edinburgh, Edinburgh University Press.
Del Rio, A. 1822. *Description of the Ruins of an Ancient City*. London, H. Berthoud, Sutterby, Evans and Fox.
Devereux, P. 2017. Earth Mysteries. [online] Accessed February, 2017, www.pauldevereux.co.uk/body_earth_mysteries.html [link no longer active]
Devoir, A. 1909. Urzeitliche Astronomie in Westeuropa. *Mannus* 1, 71–82.
Devoir, A. 1911. Orientations mégalithiques de la presqu'île de Crozon. *Société Archéologique du Finistère Bulletin* 38, 338.
Devoir, A. 1915–1916. Contribution à l'étude de l'ère monumentale préhistorique: L'architecture mégalithique Bretonne et les observations solaire. *Société Préhistorique Françaises* 12, 369–37, 403–416, 458–463; 13, 70–80, 115–128.
Dicuiri, L. 2010. Reviving Puritan history: evangelicalism, antiquarianism, and Mather's *Magnalia* in Antebellum America. *Early American Literature* 45 (3), 565–592.
Dinsmoor, W.B. 1939. Archaeology and astronomy. *Proceedings of the American Philosophical Society* 80, 95–173.
Diodorus of Sicily. *Biblioteca Historica*. [online] Accessed July, 2015, maryjones.us/ctexts/classical_diodorus.html#B36.
Dixon, S.E. 1916. Some earthworks and standing stones in East Anglia: in relation to a prehistoric solar cultus. *Proceedings of the Prehistoric Society of East Anglia* 2 (2), 171–173.
Djindjian, F. 2015. A short history of the beginnings of mathematics in archaeology. In J.A. Barcelo and I. Bogdanovic (eds), *Mathematics and Archaeology*. Boca Raton FL, CRC Press, 65–85
Dobyns, Z. 1980. Archaeoastronomy, a new frontier in science. *Geocosmic News* 6 (4).
Dogan, M. 1996. The hybridization of social science knowledge. *Library Trends* 45 (2), 296–314.
Doran, J.E. and Hodson, F.R. 1975. *Mathematics and Computers in Archaeology*. Cambridge MA, Harvard University Press.
Douglas, J. 1785. *A Dissertation on the Antiquity of the Earth*. London, George Nicholl.
Douglas, J. 1793. *Nenia Britannica: or, a sepulchral history of Great Britain; from the earliest period to its general conversion to Christianity*. London, John Nicholls.
Douglas, M. 1970. *Purity and Danger*. London, Penguin Books.

Dow, J.W. 1967. Astronomical orientations at Teotihuacán, a case study in astro-archaeology. *American Antiquity* 32, 326–334.

Dow, J. 2018. *Heinrich Himmler's Cultural Commissions: programmed plunder in Italy and Yugoslavia*. Madison WI, University of Wisconsin Press.

Dowd, A.S. and Milbrath, S. (eds). 2015. *Cosmology, Calendars, and Horizon-Based Astronomy in Ancient Mesoamerica*. Boulder CO, University Press of Colorado.

Downes, J. 2005. Perceptions of ontology in a Bronze Age world, materials, artefacts and order in the Northern Isles of Scotland TAG Session and Paper Abstracts, Sheffield. [online] https://antiquity.ac.uk/sites/default/files/downloads/tag/TAG_2005_abstracts.pdf

Doyle, P. 2020. *Pathways to the Cosmos: the alignment of megalithic tombs in Ireland, Britain and Atlantic Europe*. Dublin, Wordwell and National Monuments Service.

Dryden, J. 1672. *The Conquest of Granada.* No publication details.

Duke, E. 1846. *The Druidical Temples of the County of Wilts*. London, John Russell Smith.

Dupuis, C.F. 2005 [1798]. *L'Origine de tous les cultes* (facsimile edition). Ann Arbor MI, Michigan University Library.

Dutt, W.A. 1921. *Standing Stones of East Anglia*. Lowestoft, Flood and Sons.

Dutt, W.A. 1926. *Ancient Mark-Stones of East Anglia*. Lowestoft, Flood and Sons.

Dymond, C.W. 1877. The megalithic antiquities at Stanton Drew. *Journal of the British Archaeological Association* 33, 297–307.

Dyson, S.L. 1999. Brahmins and bureaucrats: some reflections on the history of American Classical archaeology. In A.B. Kehoe and M.B. Emmerichs (eds), *Assembling the Past: studies in the professionalization of archaeology*, Albuquerque NM, University of New Mexico Press, 103–116.

Eddy, J.A. 1974a. Popular astro-archaeology, review of G.S. Hawkins, *Beyond Stonehenge. Journal for the History of Astronomy* 5 (12), 66.

Eddy, J.A. 1974b. Astronomical alignment of the Big Horn Medicine Wheel. *Science* 184, 1034–1043.

Eddy, J.A. 1980. Review of Wood 1978. *Archaeoastronomy Supplement to the Journal for the History of Astronomy* 2, S95–S97.

Ellegård, A. 1981. Stone Age science in Britain? [and comments and reply]. *Current Anthropology* 22 (2), 99–125.

Ellegård, A. 1985. Review of Ruggles 1994b. *Archaeoastronomy Supplement to the Journal for the History of Astronomy* 9, S154–S157.

Elliot, P. and Daniels, S. 2006. The school of true, useful and universal science? Freemasonry, natural philosophy and scientific culture in eighteenth-century England. *The British Journal for the History of Science* 39 (2), 207–229.

Engleheart, G. 1930. Concerning orientation. *Antiquity* 4, 340–346.

Erdeswicke, S. 1717. *A Survey of Staffordshire.* London, E. Curll.

Escalona Ramos, A. 1940. *Cronología y anstronomía Maya-Mexica*. Mexico, Editorial 'Fides'.

Esteban, C. 2014. Struggling for interdisciplinarity: reflections of an astrophysicist working in cultural astronomy. *Culture and Cosmos* 18 (1), 5–19.

Esteban, C. and Belmonte, J.A. 2000a. Foreword. In Esteban and Belmonte (eds), 2000b, 9–10.

Esteban, C. and Belmonte, J.A. (eds) 2000b, *Astronomy and Cultural Diversity*. Tenerife, Organismo Autonomo de Museos y Centros, Cabildo de Tenerife.

Esteban, C., Belmonte, J.A. and Aparicio, A. 1994. Astronomía y calendario entre las culturas aborígenes canarias. In J.A. Belmonte (ed.), *Arqueoastronomía Hispanica: prácticas astronómicas de la Península Ibérica y los Archipiélagos Balear y Canario*. Madrid, Equipo Sirius, 183–213.

Etherington, K. 2005. *Becoming a Reflexive Researcher: using ourselves in research*. London, Jessica Kingsley.

EAA = European Association of Archaeologists. 2021. Welcome to EAA. [online] Accessed April, 2021, https://www.e-a-a.org/

Evans, R.J. 2000. *In Defence of History*. London, Granta Books.
Fabian, S.M. 1992. *Space-time of the Bororo of Brazil*. Gainesville FL, Florida University Press.
Fabian, S.M. 2001. *Patterns in the Sky, an introduction to ethnoastronomy*. Long Grove IL, Waveland Press.
Fagan, G.G. and Feder, K.L. 2006. Crusading against straw men: an alternative view of alternative archaeologies: response to Holtorf (2005). *World Archaeology* 38 (4), 718–729.
Faivre, A. and Voss, K-C. 1995. Western esotericism and the science of religions. *NUMEN* 42 (1), 48–77.
Farrah, R.W.E. 1993. The megalithic astronomy of Lundy: evidence for the remains of a solar calendar. *Archaeoastronomy Supplement to the Journal for the History of Astronomy* 18, S69–S72.
Farrer, C. 1993. Ethnoastronomy. *Archaeoastronomy and Ethnoastronomy News* 7 https:// https:// terpconnect.umd.edu/~tlaloc/archastro/ae7.html
Feder, K.L. 1984. Irrationality and popular archaeology. *American Antiquity* 49 (3), 525–541.
Figueiredo, A., Vilas-Estévez, B. and Silva, F. 2018. The planning and orientation of the Rego da Murta dolmens (Alvaiázere, Portugal). *Proceedings of the Prehistoric Society* 84, 207–224.
Fisher, V.B. 2015. Presentation of archaeoastronomy in introductions to archaeology. In Ruggles (ed.) 2015a, 251–261.
Flaubert, G. 1881. *Bouvard and Pécuchet*. Paris, Bibliotêche-Charpentier.
Fleming, A. and Johnson, M. 1990. The Theoretical Archaeology Group (TAG): origins, retrospect, prospect. *Antiquity* 64, 303–306.
Foreman, E. 1877. Archaeological frauds. *Field and Forest* 3, 111–115.
Forestry Commission Scotland. 2015. *Recumbent Stone Circles*. Edinburgh, Forestry Commission Scotland.
Forstemann. E. 1904. The Pleiades among the Mayas. *Bureau of American Ethnology Bulletin* 28, 521–524.
Fosbrook, T. D. 1822. *Encyclopaedia of Antiquities, and Elements of Archaeology, Classical and Medieval*. London.
Foucault, M. 1980. *Power/Knowledge: selected interviews and other writings, 1972-1977* (ed. C. Gordon, trans. C. Gordon, L. Marshall, J. Mepham and K. Soper). New York, Pantheon Books.
Foucault, M. 2002. *The Order of Things*. London, Routledge Classics.
Fountain, J.W. and Sinclair, R.M. 2005. Introduction. In J.W. Fountain and R.M. Sinclair (eds), *Current Studies in Archaeoastronomy: Conversations Across Time and Space*. Durham NC, Carolina Academic Press.
Fox, C. 1923. *The Archaeology of the Cambridge Region*. Cambridge, Cambridge University Press.
Frank, R.M. 1996. Hunting the European sky bears: when bears ruled the Earth and guarded the gate of Heaven. In Koleva and Kolev (eds) 1996, 116–142.
Fraser, J. 1923. Some antiquities in Harray parish. *Proceedings of the Orkney Antiquarian Society* 1, 31–37.
Fraser, J. 1924. Antiquities of Sandwick parish. *Proceedings of the Orkney Antiquarian Society* 2, 22–29.
Frazer, J.G. 1995 [1890]. *The Golden Bough*. London, Papermac.
Freeman, P.R. 1976. A Bayesian analysis of the Megalithic Yard, followed by discussion of Dr Freeman's paper. *Journal of the Royal Statistical Society* A139 (1), 20–55.
Freeman, P.R. and Elmore, W. 1979. A test for the significance of astronomical alignments *Archaeoastronomy Supplement to the Journal for the History of Astronomy* 1, S86–S96.
French, P.J. 1987. *John Dee: the World of an Elizabethan Magus*. London, Routledge.
Frere, J. 1800. Letter. *Archaeologia* 13, 204–205.
Frincu, M. and Frincu, S. (eds). 2019. *Astronomia străbunilor*. Szeged, JatePress.
Fussner, F.S. 2010. *The Historical Revolution: English historical writing and thought 1580-1640* (revised edition). London, Routledge.
G. M. 1935. Obituary of Alfred Watkins. *Transactions of the Woolhope Naturalists Field Club*, 165–167.
Gaffney, V. 2020. When not to look at the sky? *Journal of Skyscape Archaeology* 6 (2), 265–267.

Gaffney, V., Fitch, S., Ramsey, E., Yorston R., Ch'ng, E., Baldwin,E., Bates, R., Gaffney, C., Ruggles, C.,Sparrow, T., McMillan, A., Cowley, D., Fraser, S., Murray, C., Murray, H., Hopla, E. and Howard, A. 2013. Time and a place, A luni-solar time-reckoner from 8th millennium BC Scotland. *Internet Archaeology* 34. [online] Accessed July, 2013, intarch.ac.uk/journal/issue34/gaffney_index.html

Gaillard, F. 1888. Les alignements de menhirs dans le Morbihan et leur definition. *Bulletins de la Société d'Anthropologie de Paris* 11, 434–437.

Gaillard, F. 1897. *L'astronomie préhistorique.* Paris, Les Sciences Populaires.

Gardner, T., Westra, A., Wood, A. and Vogelaar, C. 2017. Stone and social circles, taskscapes and landscape survey at Yadlee Stone Circle. In U. Rajala and P. Mills (eds), *Forms of Dwelling, 20 years of Taskscapes in Archaeology.* Oxford, Oxbow Books, 151–170.

Gates, J. 1986. Measures and tests of alignment. *Biometrika* 73 (3), 731–734.

Gathercole, P. 1994. Introduction. In P. Gathercole and D. Lowenthal (eds), *The Politics of the Past*, London, Routledge, 1–4.

Gautschy, R. 2020. Thoughts triggered by 'Skyscapes in the Academy: is there a future?'. *Journal of Skyscape Archaeology* 6 (1), 98–100.

Geertz, C. 1973. *The Interpretation of Cultures, Selected Essays.* London, Fontana Press.

Geertz, C. 1974. 'From the native's point of view', on the nature of anthropological understanding. *Bulletin of the American Academy of Arts and Sciences* 28 (1), 26–45.

Geertz, C. 1976. Toward an ethnography of the disciplines. Unpublished speech, held in Folder 9, Box 222 of the Geertz papers held at the Special Collections Research Center of the University of Chicago Library, 1–33.

Geoffrey of Monmouth. 1966 [1136]. *Historia Regum Britanniae* (trans. L. Thorpe 1966). Harmondsworth, Penguin Books.

Gingerich, O. 1980. Review of *Rings of Stone* by Aubrey Burl. *Archaeoastronomy Supplement to the Journal for the History of Astronomy* 2, S103– S104.

Glastonbury Festival. 2017. History 1971. [online] Accessed February 2017, www.glastonburyfestivals.co.uk/history/history-1971/

González-García, A.C. 2016. Review of F. Silva and N. Campion (eds), *Skyscapes: the role and importance of the sky in archaeology. European Journal of Archaeology* 19 (2), 1–5.

González-García, A.C. and Belmonte, J.A. 2010. Statistical analysis of megalithic tomb orientations in the Iberian Peninsula and neighbouring regions. *Journal for the History of Astronomy* 41 (2), 225–238.

González-García, A.C and Costa-Ferrer, L. 2011. The diachronic study of orientations, Mérida, a case study. In Ruggles (ed.) 2011a, 374–381.

González-Ruibal, A., González, P.A. and Criado-Boada, F. 2018. Authority *vs* power, capitalism, archaeology and the populist challenge *Antiquity* 92, 525–527.

Goode, M. 2003. Dryasdust antiquarianism and soppy masculinity: the Waverley Novels and the gender of history. *Representations* 82 (1), 52–86.

Goodrick, G.T. 1998. VRML, virtual reality and visualisation: the best tool for the job. In V. Gaffney and P. van Leusen (eds), *CAA97: Archaeology in the age of the Internet.* Oxford, British Archaeological Report S750, 247–254.

Goodrick-Clarke, N. 2011. Stonehenge to the Sphinx: esoteric theory and practice in twentieth-century astroarchaeology. In N. Campion and L. Greene (eds), *Astrologies: plurality and diversity in the history of astrology.* Lampeter, Sophia Centre Press, 151–184.

Goodrum, M.R. 2002. The meaning of Ceraunia: archaeology, natural history and the interpretation of prehistoric stone artefacts in the eighteenth century. *The British Journal for the History of Science* 35 (3), 255–269.

Goodrum, M.R. 2009. The creation of societies for the study of prehistory and their role in the formation of prehistoric archaeology as a discipline, 1867–1929. *Bulletin of the History of Archaeology* 19 (2), 27–35.

Gordon, A. 1726. *Itinerarium Septentrionale: or, a journey thro most of the counties of Scotland, and those in the north of England.* London, G. Strahan.
Gordon, E.O. 1914. *Prehistoric London: its mounds and circles.* London, Elliot Stock.
Gordon, J. F. S. 1880. *The Book of the Chronicles of Keith, Grange, Ruthven, Cairney and Botriphnie.* Glasgow, Robert Forrester.
Gough, R. 1768. *British Topography.* London, Payne & Son.
Gough, R. 1770. An historical account of the origin and establishment of the Society of Antiquaries. *Archaeologia* 1, i–xxxix.
Gowland, W. 1902. 16 Recent excavations at Stonehenge: abstract of the discussion of Mr W. Gowland's paper on Stonehenge read at a Special Meeting of the Anthropological Institute, January 13th, 1902, by W.A. Gowland. *Man* 2, 22–26.
Grebe Vicuña, E.M. 1998. *Indigenous Cultures of Chile, A Preliminary Study.* Santiago, Chile, Pehuén Editores.
Greenwell, W. 1894. Antiquities of the Bronze Age found in the Heathery Burn Cave, County Durham. *Archaeologia* 54 (1), 87–114.
Grensted, F.R. 1892. The orientation of ancient monuments. *Nature*, 17 March, 45, 464.
Griffith, J. 1908a. Astronomical archaeology in Wales. *Nature* 30 July, 295.
Griffith, J. 1908b. Welsh astronomical traditions. *Nature* 78, 436–437.
Griffith, J. 1908c. The Royal Commission on Welsh Monuments. *Nature* 78, 512.
Griffith, J. 1909. English earthworks and their orientation *Nature* 80, 69–72.
Grimes, W.F. 1936. The megalithic monuments of Wales. *Proceedings of the Prehistoric Society* 5, 106–139.
Grundy, G.B. 1939. The ancient highways of Somerset. *Archaeological Journal* 96 (1), 226–297.
Gullberg, S. 2020. The importance for education in archaeoastronomy and astronomy in culture. *Journal of Skyscape Archaeology* 6 (1), 101–104.
Gurshtein, A.A. 1990. From the editorial board. *Istoriko-astronomicheskiye Issledovaniya* 1990, 14–16.
Gusinde, M. 1922. Métados de investigación antropólogia adoptados por el Museo de Etnología y Antropólogia tomo II. In *Publicacaciones dela Museo de Etnología y Antropólogia.* Santiago de Chile, Museo de Etnología y Antropólogia, 183–200.
Guthe. K. 1932. The Maya lunar count. *Science* 75, 271–277.
Hadingham, E. 1985. *Early Man and the Cosmos.* Norman OK and London, University of Oklahoma Press.
Haile, B. 1947. *Starlore Among the Navajo.* Sante Fe NM, Museum of Navajo Ceremonial Art.
Halliday, H.C. 1937. Divining for water, minerals etc. *Proceedings of the Suffolk Institute of Archaeology and Natural History* 23, 31–34.
Hammersley, M. 1955. Discussion on Professor Thom's paper, 291–292 in A. Thom, A Statistical examination of the megalithic sites in Britain', *Journal of the Royal Statistical Society*, Series A (General) 118 (3), 275–295.
Hancock, G. 1992. *The Sign and the Seal: the quest for the Lost Ark of the Covenant.* New York, Crown.
Hancock, G. 1995. *Fingerprints of the Gods: a quest for the beginning and the end.* New York, Random House.
Hando, F. 1944. *The Pleasant Land of Gwent.* Newport, R.H. Johns.
Hando, F. 1958. *Out and About in Monmouthshire.* Newport, R.H. Johns.
Hanegraaff, W.J. 2013. *Western Esotericism: a guide for the perplexed.* London, Bloomsbury.
Hannah, R. 2013. Greek temple orientation: the case of the older Parthenon in Athens. *Network Nexus Journal* 15, 423–443.
Harding, J. 2013. *Cult, Religion and Pilgrimage, Archaeological Investigations at the Neolithic and Bronze Age Monument Complex of Thornborough, North Yorkshire.* York, Council for British Archaeology Research Report 174.
Harding, J. 2015. The Neolithic and Bronze Age monument complex of Thornborough, North Yorkshire, UK. In Ruggles (ed.) 2015a, 1239–1247.

Harding, J., Johnston, B. and Goodrick, G. 2006. Neolithic cosmology and the monument complex of Thornborough, North Yorkshire. *Archaeoastronomy, The Journal of Astronomy in Culture,* 20, 26–51.

Harris, O.J.T. and Cipolla, C.N. 2017. *Archaeological Theory in the New Millennium*. London and New York, Routledge.

Harrold, F.B. and Eve, R.A. (eds). 1987. *Cult Archaeology & Creationism: understanding pseudoarchaeological beliefs about the past*. Iowa City IA, University of Iowa Press.

Hartung, H. 1969. Consideraciones urbanísticas sobre los trazos de los centros ceremoniales de Tikal, Copán and Chichén-Itzá. In *Akten des XXXVIII Internationalen, Ameikandistenkongresses, Stuttgart-München*. Munich, Renner, 1121–1125.

Hartung, H.1971. *The Diece Zeremonialzentren der Maya (Mayan Ceremonial Centres). Ein Beitrag zur Untersuchung der Planungsprinzipien*. Graz: Akademische Druck-u. Verlagsanstalt.

Harvey, D.C. 2008. The history of heritage In B.J. Graham and P. Howard (eds), *The Ashgate Research Companion to Heritage and Identity*, Farnham, Ashgate, 19–36.

Hatto, A.T. 1953. 151. Stonehenge and midsummer: a new interpretation. *Man* 53, 101–106.

Hauser, K. 2009. *Bloody Old Britain*. London, Granta.

Hawkes, C.F C. 1948. International Congress of Pre- and Proto-Historic Sciences. *Proceedings of the Prehistoric Society* 14, 234.

Hawkes, C.F.C. 1951. British prehistory half-way through the century: presidential address. *Proceedings of the Prehistoric Society* 17 (1), 1–15.

Hawkes, C.F.C. 1954. Archaeological theory and method: some suggestions from the Old World. *American Anthropologist* 56, 155–168.

Hawkes, C. and Hawkes J. 1949. *Prehistoric Britain*. Harmondsworth, Penguin.

Hawkes, J. 1967. God in the machine. *Antiquity* 41, 174–180.

Hawkins, G.S. 1963. Stonehenge decoded. *Nature* 200, 306–308.

Hawkins, G.S. 1964. Stonehenge: a Neolithic computer. *Nature* 202, 1258–1261.

Hawkins, G.S. in collaboration with White, J.B. 1965a. *Stonehenge Decoded*. Garden City NY, Doubleday.

Hawkins, G.S. 1965b. Callenish, a Scottish Stonehenge. *Science* 147, 127–130.

Hawkins, G.S. 1966. *Astro-Archaeology*. Washington DC, Smithsonian Astrophysical Observatory Special Report.

Hawkins, G.S. 1967. Hoyle on Stonehenge: some comments. *Antiquity* 41, 91–92.

Hawkins, G.S. 1973. Archaeoastronomy in Pre-Columbian America. *Journal for the History of Astronomy* 4, 214.

Hawkins, G.S. 1974. Astronomical alinements in Britain, Egypt and Peru. In Hodson (ed.) 1974, 164–165.

Hawkins, G.S. 1980. Review of P. Lancaster Brown, *Megaliths and Masterminds*. *Archaeoastronomy Supplement to the Journal for the History of Astronomy* 11, S97–S99.

Hawkins, G.S. 1982. On megalithic astronomy, 218–219 in G.S. Hawkins, A. Thom, I.J. Thorpe and A. Ellegård, On megalithic astronomy. *Current Anthropology* 23 (2), 218–222.

Hayman, R. 1997. *Riddles in Stone: myths, archaeology and the Ancient Britons*. London, Hambledon Press.

Heath, R. 1999. *A Key to Stonehenge: a holistic look at the relationships between Stonehenge and the sun, moon and earth, together with the geographic siting of the monument*. Dyfed, Bluestone Press.

Heath, R. 2005. *Powerpoints*. Dyfed, Bluestone Press.

Heath, R. 2007. *Alexander Thom: cracking the Stone Age code*. Dyfed, Bluestone Press.

Heath, R. and Michell, J. 1999. *Measure of Albion: the lost science of prehistoric Britain*. Dyfed, Bluestone Press.

Heggie, D.C. 1981a. Highlights and problems of megalithic astronomy. *Archaeoastronomy* 3, S17–S37.

Heggie, D.C. (ed.). 1981b. *Megalithic Science: ancient mathematics and astronomy in north-west Europe*. London, Thames and Hudson.

Heggie, D.C. 1982a. Review of C.L.N. Ruggles and A.W.R. Whittle (eds), *Astronomy and Society in Britain during the Period 4000- 1500 BC*. Archaeoastronomy Supplement to the Journal for the History of Astronomy 4, S68–S69.

Heggie, D.C. (ed.). 1982b. *Archaeoastronomy in the Old World*. Cambridge and New York, Cambridge University Press.

Heggie, D.C. 1987a. Review of Brecher and Feirtag (eds), 1979. Archaeoastronomy Supplement to the Journal for the History of Astronomy 11 (2), S99–S101.

Heggie, D.C. 1987b. Alexander Thom. *Journal of the Royal Astronomical Society* 28, 178–182.

Heggie, D.C. 2009 [1982]. Megalithic astronomy: highlights and problems. In D.C. Heggie (ed.), *Archaeoastronomy in the Old World* (reissue). Cambridge, Cambridge University Press, 1–24.

Heinsch, J. 1979 [1933]. *The Xanten Mosaic-Cosmogram* (trans. M. Behrend). Cambridge, Ferris-Wolf.

Henare, A., Holbraad, M. and Wastell, S. (eds). 2007. Introduction. In A. Henare (ed.), *Thinking Through Things, Theorising Artefacts Ethnographically*. Oxford, Routledge, 1–31.

Henty, L. 2014. The archaeoastronomy of Tomnaverie recumbent stone circle, a comparison of methodologies. *Papers from the Institute of Archaeology* 24, 45–59.

Henty, L. 2015. Continuity or change? A microscopic scale analysis of monuments and ritual in Aberdeenshire. *Journal of Skyscape Archaeology* 1 (2), 243–275.

Henty, L. 2020a. Ludovic MacLellan Mann's place in the history of prehistoric metrology. *Scottish Archaeological Journal* 42, 52–64.

Henty, L. 2020b. Skyscape archaeology, the place of the sky in the academy. In Henty and Brown (eds) 2020, 13–34.

Henty, L. and Brown D. (eds). 2020. *Visualising Skyscapes, Material Forms of Cultural Engagement with the Heavens*. Oxford, Routledge.

Henty, L. and Silva, F. 2018. Editorial. *Journal of Skyscape Archaeolog*, 4 (2), 159–160.

Heritage Daily. 2014. Archaeo-astronomy steps out from the shadows of the past, 24 June. [online] Accessed December, 2017, www.heritagedaily.com/2014/06/archaeo- astronomy-steps-out-from-the-shadows-of-the-past/103749

HeyWhatsThat. 2021. What's heywhatsthat? [online] Accessed June 2021, www.heywhatsthat.com/faq.html

Hicks, R. 1984. Stones and henges: megalithic astronomy reviewed. In Krupp (ed.) 1984, 169–210.

Hicks, R. 1981. Archaeoastronomy and related problems, Old World approaches vs. New. In Williamson (ed.) 1981, 43–49.

Hicks, R. 1993. Beyond alignments. *Archaeoastronomy and Ethnoastronomy News* 9. [online] Accessed March 2015. terpconnect.umd.edu/~tlaloc/archastro/ae9.html

Hicks, R. 2006. Review J.W. Fountain and R.M. Sinclair (eds), *Current Studies in Archaeoastronomy, Conversations Across Time and Space ... American Anthropologist* 108 (3), 586–587.

Higginbottom, G. and Clay, R. 1999. Reassessment of sites in northwest Scotland: a new statistical approach. Archaeoastronomy Supplement to the Journal for the History of Astronomy 24, S41–S46.

Higginbottom, G., Smith, A., Simpson, K. and Clay R. 2000. Gazing at the horizon: sub-cultural differences in western Scotland? In Esteban and Belmonte (eds) 2000, 43–50.

Higgins, G. 1827. *The Celtic Druids*. London, Rowland Hunter.

Hobsbawm, E. 2012. Introduction. In E. Hobsbawm and T. Ranger (eds), *The Invention of Tradition*, Cambridge, Cambridge University Press, 1–14.

Hippisley Cox, R. 1914. *The Green Roads of England*. London, Methuen.

Hively, R.M. 1981. Review of Aveni 1983, 204– 207.

Hodder, I. (ed.). 1982. *Symbolic and Structural Archaeology*. Cambridge, Cambridge University Press.

Hodder, I. 1995. *Theory and Practice in Archaeology*. London, Routledge.

Hodder, I. 2003. Archaeological reflexivity and the 'local' voice. *Anthropological Quarterly* 76 (1), 55–69.

Hodder, I. 2004. *Theory and Practice in Archaeology* (2nd edition). London, Routledge.

Hodder, I. 2008. Multivocality and social archaeology. In J. Habu, C. Fawcett and J. Matsunaga (eds), *Evaluating Multiple Narratives: beyond nationalist, colonialist, imperialist archaeologies*, New York, Springer Science+Business Media.

Hodson, F. R. (ed.). 1974. *The Place of Astronomy in the Ancient World. Philosophical Transactions of the Royal Society* A276

Holbraad, M. and Pedersen, M.A. 2017. *The Ontological Turn, An Anthropological Exposition*. Cambridge, Cambridge University Press.

Holden, E.S. 1897. Review. *Science* NS 6, 847–850.

Holtorf, C. 2005. Beyond crusades, how (not) to engage with alternative archaeologies. *World Archaeology* 37 (4), 544–551.

Hoskin, M. 1970. Editorial foreword. *Journal for the History of Astronomy* 1, 4.

Hoskin, M. 1976. Commission 41 at Grenoble. *Journal for the History of Astronomy* 7, 216–224.

Hoskin, M. 1985. The Talayotic Culture of Menorca: a first reconnaissance. *Archaeoastronomy Supplement to the Journal for the History of Astronomy* 9, S133– S155.

Hoskin, M. 1989. The orientations of the taulas of Menorca (1): the southern taulas. *Archaeoastronomy Supplement to the Journal for the History of Astronomy* 14, S117–S136.

Hoskin, M. 1994. Review of G. Romano, *Archaeoastronomia Italiana*. *Archaeoastronomy Supplement to the Journal for the History of Astronomy* 19, S89.

Hoskin, M. 1996. *Cambridge Illustrated History of Astronomy*. Cambridge, Cambridge University Press.

Hoskin, M. 1997. Mediterranean tombs and temples and their orientations. In C. Jaschek and F. Atrio Barandela (eds), *Proceedings of the IVth SEAC Meeting 'Astronomy and Culture'*. Salamanca, Universidad de Salamanca, 19–25.

Hoskin, M. 2001. *Tombs, Temples and their Orientation*. Bognor Regis, Ocarina.

Hoskin, M. and Nùñez, J.J.N. 1991. The orientations of the burial monuments of Menorca. *Archaeoastronomy Supplement to the Journal for the History of Astronomy* 16, S15–S42.

Hoskin, M. and Pérez, T.P.I. 1998. Studies in Iberian archaeoastronomy: (4) the orientations of megalithic tombs of eastern Catalunya. *Journal for the History of Astronomy* 29 (1), 63–79.

Hoskin, M. and Zedda, M. 1997. Orientations of Sardinian dolmens. *Archaeoastronomy Supplement to the Journal for the History of Astronomy* 22, S1–S16.

Hoskin, M, Allan, E. and Gralewski, R. 1993. *The Tombe di Giganti* and temples of Nuraghic Sardinia. *Archaeoastronomy Supplement to the Journal for the History of Astronomy* 18, S1– S26.

Hoskin, M, Allan, E. and Gralewski, R. 1995. Studies in Iberian Archaeoastronomy: (3) customs and motives in Andalucia. *Archaeoastronomy Supplement to the Journal for the History of Astronomy* 20, S41–S48.

Hoskin, M., Hochsieder, P. and Knösel, D. 1990. The Orientations of the Taulas of Menorca, (2): The Remaining Taulas *Archaeoastronomy Supplement to the Journal for the History of Astronomy*, 15, S37–S48.

Hoyle, F. 1966a. Stonehenge – an eclipse predictor. *Nature* 211, 454–456.

Hoyle, F. 1966b. Speculations on Stonehenge. *Antiquity* 40, 262–276.

Hoyle, F. 1977. *On Stonehenge*. San Francisco CA, W.H. Freeman.

Hubbard, A and Hubbard, G. 1907. *Neolithic Dew-ponds and Cattleways*. London, Longmans, Green and Co.

Hudson, H. 1933. Ancient sun alignments: the meaning of artificial mounds and mark stones. *Proceedings of the Suffolk Institute of Archaeology and Natural History* 21, 120–138.

Hudson, T. 1984. California's first astronomers. In Krupp (ed.) 1984, 11–81.

Hugh-Jones, C. 1979. *From the Milk River: spatial and temporal processes in Northwest Amazonia*. Cambridge, Cambridge University Press.

Hugh-Jones, S. 1979. *The Palm and the Pleiades, Initiation and Cosmology in Northwest Amazonia*. Cambridge, Cambridge University Press.

Hutton, R. 2009a. *Blood and Mistletoe: the history of the Druids in Britain.* New Haven CO & London, Yale University Press.
Hutton, R. 2009b. Megaliths and memory. In J. Parker (ed.), *Written in Stone: the cultural reception of British prehistoric monuments.* Newcastle upon Tyne, Cambridge Scholars Publishing, 10–22.
Hutton, R. 2013. The strange history of archaeoastronomy. *Journal for the Study of Religion, Nature and Culture* 7 (4), 376–396.
Ingold, T. 1993. The temporality of landscape. *World Archaeology* 25, 125–174.
Ingold, T. 2000. *The Perception of the Environment. Essays on Livelihood, Dwelling and Skill.* London and New York, Routledge.
Ingold, T. 2010. Bringing Things to Life, Creative Entanglements in a World of Materials Realities Working Papers, 15, University of Manchester, 2010 (ESRC National Centre for Research Methods, NCRM Working Paper Series 05/10).
Innerebner, G. 1942. *Sonnenlauf und Zeitbestimmung im Leben der Urzeitvölker.* Berlin-Dahlem, Germanien 2
Innes, C. 1857–59. Opening address *Proceedings of the Society of Antiquaries for Scotland* 3 (1), 5–7.
INSAP 2018. The INSAP Conferences. [online] Accessed, August 2018, https://insap.org/
Insoll, T. 2016. Review of Silva and Campion (eds) 2015. *Journal of Skyscape Archaeology* 2 (1), 117–120.
ISAAC. 2021. Membership. [online] Accessed April 2021, https://www.archaeoastronomy.org/membership
Ivimy, J. 1974. *The Sphinx and the Megaliths.* Basingstoke, HarperCollins.
Iwaniszewski, S. 1988. El papel de astronomía en el desarollo cultural en Mesoamérica. Unpublished PhD thesis, National Autonomous University of Mexico.
Iwaniszewski, S. 1989. Exploring some anthropological theoretical foundations for archaeoastronomy. In Aveni (ed.) 1989b, 27–37.
Iwaniszewski, S. 1991. Astronomy as a cultural system Интердисциплинарни изследвания 18, 282–288.
Iwaniszewski, S. 1992a. Archaeoastronomy and ethnoastronomy in Poland: the last two decades. In Iwaniszewski (ed.) 1992b, 57–70.
Iwaniszewski, S. (ed.). 1992b. *Readings in Archaeoastronomy: proceedings of the international conference: Current Problems and Future of Archaeoastronomy. Held at the State Archaeological Museum in Warsaw 15–16 November 1990.* Warsaw, State Archaeological Museum, Department of Historical Anthropology and Institute of Archaeology, Warsaw University.
Iwaniszewski, S. 1994a. Cultural astronomy in Europe. *Archaeoastronomy and Ethnoastronomy News* 11. https://terpconnect.umd.edu/~tlaloc/archastro/ae11.html
Iwaniszewski, S. 1994b. De l'Astroarqueología a la Astromía Cultural. *Trabajos de Prehistoria* 51 (2), 5–20.
Iwaniszewski, S. 1995a. The Funnel Beaker Culture (TRB) long barrows from the Kujawy District in central Poland: first results of archaeoastronomical investigations. In Pásztor (ed.) 1995b, 33–37.
Iwaniszewski, S. 1995b. Archaeoastronomy and cultural astronomy: methodological issues. In *Atti Dei Convegni Lincei 121: Convegno Internazionale sul tema: Archaologia E Astronomia: Espererienze E Prospettive Future*, Rome, Accademia Nazionale dei Lincei. 17–26.
Iwaniszewski, S. 1996. Review of J.A. Belmonte (ed.), *Arqueoastronomía Hispánica. Supplement to the Journal for the History of Archaeoastronomy* 21, S81–S85.
Iwaniszewski, S. 1997. Neolithic uses of time and astronomy: Funnel Beakers and long barrows in Kuiavia, Poland. In C. Jaschek and F.A. Barandela (eds), *Actas del IV Congreso de la SEAC Astronomia en la Cultura.* Salamanca, Universidad de Salamanca, 173–184.
Iwaniszewski, S. 1998. The development of a regional archaeoastronomy: the case of Central-Eastern Europe. In *Archaeoastronomica, Credenze e Religioni nel Mondo Antico, (Roma, 14-15 maggio 1997)*, Rome, Accademia Nazionale dei Lince, 177–201.

Iwaniszewski, S. 1999. Archaeoastronomy in traditional areas of Eurasia: a review paper. *Archaeoastronomy, The Journal of Astronomy in Culture* 14 (2), 87–127.

Iwaniszewski, S. 2001. Time and space in social systems – further issues for theoretical archaeoastronomy In C. Ruggles, F. Prendergast and T. Ray (eds), *Astronomy, Cosmology and Landscape, Proceedings of the SEAC 98 meeting, Dublin, Ireland, September 1998*, Bognor Regis, Ocarina, 1–7.

Iwaniszewski, S. 2007. Looking through the eyes of ancestors, concepts of the archaeoastronomical record. In Zedda and Belmonte (eds) 2007, 11.

Iwaniszewski, S. 2008. Alternative archaeoastronomies – an overview. In J. Vaišknas (ed.), *Astronomy and Cosmology in Folk Traditions and Cultural Heritage.* Klaipèda, Klaipèda Press, 253–266.

Iwaniszewski, S. 2010. Ancient cosmologies, understanding ancient skywatchers and their worldviews. *Journal of Cosmology* 9, 2121–2129. [online] Accessed August 2017, journalofcosmology.com/AncientAstronomy117.html

Iwaniszewski, S. 2011. The sky as a social field. In Ruggles (ed.) 2011a, 20–37.

Iwaniszewski, S. 2015a. Concepts of space, time, and the cosmos. In Ruggles (ed.) 2015a, 3–14.

Iwaniszewski, S. 2015b. Cultural interpretation of archaeological evidence relating to astronomy. In Ruggles (ed.) 2015a, 341–352.

Jacquot, L. 1915. Persistence du culte des asters jusqu'à nos jours: Boutons à figurations astrales. *Société Préhistorique Françaises* 12, 197–198.

Jara, F. 1987. Some Arawak constellations. In *Proceedings of the First International Ethnoastronomy Conference. Indigenous Astronomical and Cosmological Tradition of the World.* Washington DC, Smithsonian Institution/University of Maryland.

Jara, F. 2015. Skyscape of an Amazonian diaspora, Arawak astronomy in historical comparative perspective. In Ruggles (ed.) 2015a, 931–944.

Jencks, C. 1996. *What is Post-modernism?* (4th edition). Chichester, Wiley Academy.

Jenkins, K. 2003. *Re-thinking History.* London & New York, Routledge.

Johnson, M. 2010. *Archaeological Theory: an introduction.* Chichester, Wiley-Blackwell.

Jones, I. 1655. *The most notable antiquity of Great Britain, vulgarly called Stone-Heng on Salisbury plain.* London. [online]. Accessed May 2013, www.joh.cam.ac.uk/library/special_collections/early_books/pix/stonehenge.htm

Jones, A. and Hicks, D. 2008. Archaeological Ontologies TAG Session and Paper Abstracts, Southampton. https://antiquity.ac.uk/sites/default/files/downloads/tag/TAG_2008_abstracts.pdf

Jones, R.P. 1939. Appendix II, Synopsis of a pamphlet by Dr. Heinsch, of Moers (Rhineland), entitled *Principles of Pre-historic Cult-Geography.* In F.C. Tyler, *The Geometrical Arrangement of Ancient Sites.* London, Simpkin Marshall, 43–44.

Jordan, P. 2001. *The Atlantis Syndrome.* Stroud, Sutton.

Journal of Skyscape Archaeology 2021. Home. [online] Accessed June 2021, https,//journal.equinoxpub.com/JSA

Kebbell, P. 2009. The changing face of British Freemasonry, 1640–1740. Unpublished PhD Thesis, University of Bristol.

Kelley, D.H. and Milone, E.F. 2005. *Exploring Ancient Skies: an encyclopedic survey of archaeoastronomy.* New York, Springer Science+Business Media.

Kelley, D.H. and Milone, E.F. 2011. *Exploring Ancient Skies: a survey of ancient and cultural astronomy* (2nd edition). New York, Springer Science+Business Media.

Kendrick, T.D. 2003 [1928]. *Druids and Druidism.* New York, Dover Publications.

Kepler, J. 1939 [1619]. *Harmonices Mundi* (trans. C.G. Wallis). Linz, Johann Planck. [online] Accessed April 2017, sacred- texts.com/astro/how/how00.htm

Kerviler, R. 1904. Les measures be longuer et les nombres 7 et 3 et les connaissances en arith métique, géométrie et astronomie chex les constuctuers de monuments mégalithiques en Armorique. *Bulletin archéologique de l'Association Bretonne* 23, 288–306.

King-Hele, D.G. 1974. Concluding remarks. In Hodson (ed.) 1974, 273–274.

Kingsborough, E.K., Lord 1830–1848. *Mexican Antiquities*. London, Robert Havell and Conaghi.

Kintigh, K.W. 1992. I wasn't going to say anything, but since you asked. *Archaeoastronomy and Ethnoastronomy News* 5 (1), 4.

Knight, C. 1991. *Blood Relations, Menstruation and the Origins of Culture*. London and New Haven CO, Yale University Press.

Koleva, V. and Kolev, D. (eds). 1996. *Astronomical Traditions in Past Cultures, Proceedings of the First Annual General Meeting of the European Society for Astronomy in Culture, Smolyan, Bulgaria, 31 August–2 September, 1993*. Sofia, Institute of Astronomy, Bulgarian Academy of Sciences, National Astronomical Observatory, Rozhen.

Konakov, N.D. 1994. Calendar symbolism of the Uralic peoples of the pre-Christian era. *Arctic Anthropology* 31 (1), 47–61.

Krishnan, A. 2009. *What are Academic Disciplines? Some observations on the disciplinarity vs. interdisciplinarity debate*. Southampton, ESRC National Centre for Research Methods, NCRM Working Paper Series, 03/09.

Krupp, E.C. (ed.). 1979. *In Search of Ancient Astronomies*. London, Chatto & Windus.

Krupp, E.C. (ed.). 1984. *Archaeoastronomy and the Roots of Science*. Boulder CO, Westview Press, AAAS Selected Symposia Series.

Lancaster Brown, P. 1976. *Megaliths, Myths and Men: an introduction to astro-archaeology*. Blandford Forum, Blandford Press.

Lang, A. 1893. Editor's introduction to the *Antiquary*. [online] Accessed April 2017, ebooks.adelaide. edu.au/s/scott/walter/antiquary/introduction2.html [link no longer active].

Latour, B. 2005. *Reassembling the Social, an Introduction to Actor-Network-Theory*. Oxford, Oxford University Press.

Lawson, A. 1817. Ancient circles of stone discovered underground in the Parish of Creich, Fifeshire *The Edinburgh Magazine and Literary Miscellany* 80, 423–427.

Lebeuf, A. 1996. The Milky Way, a part of the souls. In Koleva and Kolev (eds) 1996, 148–161.

Lenoir, R. 1956. La mentalidad megalítica *Revista Mexicana de Sociología*, 18, 507–523.

Le Roux, C.T. 2002. Standing stones in western France. In R. Joussaume, L. Laporte and C. Scarre (eds), *Origin and Development of the Megalithic Monuments of Western Europe*. France, Musée des Tumulus de Bougon.

Levine, P.J.A. 2003. *The Amateur and the Professional: antiquarians, historians and archaeologists in Victorian England 1838-1886*. Cambridge, Cambridge University Press.

Lewis, A.L. 1888. Stone circles near Aberdeen. *Journal of the Anthropological Institute of Great Britain and Ireland* 17, 44–57.

Lewis, A.L. 1892. Stone circles of Britain. *Archaeological Journal* 49, 136–154.

Lewis, A.L. 1900. The stone circles of Scotland. *The Journal of the Anthropological Institute of Great Britain and Ireland* 30, 56–73.

Lewis, A.L. 1910. Review of Lockyer's *Stonehenge*, 1909 edition. *Man* 10, 61–63.

Libby, W.F. 1955. *Radiocarbon Dating* (2nd edition). Chicago IL, Chicago University Press.

Little, D. 2019. Assemblage theory. [online] Accessed April, 2019, understandingsociety.blogspot. com/2012/11/assemblage-theory.html.

Lockyer, Sir N. 1891. On some points in the early history of astronomy. *Nature* 44, 199–202.

Lockyer, Sir N. 1894. *The Dawn of Astronomy. A Study of the Temple Worship and Mythology of Ancient Egyptians*. London, Macmillan.

Lockyer, Sir N. 1906a. *Stonehenge and Other British Stone Monuments Astronomically Considered*. London, Macmillan.
Lockyer, Sir N. 1906b. Questions for archaeologists. *Nature* 73, 280–282.
Lockyer, Sir N. 1908. On the observation of sun and stars made in some British stone circles, third note, the Aberdeenshire circles. *Proceedings of the Royal Society of London Series* A80, 285–289.
Lockyer, Sir N. 1909. *Surveying for Archaeologists*. London, Macmillan.
Lockyer, Sir N. and Penrose, F.C. 1902. An attempt to ascertain the date of the original construction of Stonehenge from its orientation. *Proceedings of the Royal Society of London* 69, 137–147.
Loomis, L.H. 1930. Geoffrey of Monmouth and Stonehenge. *Publications of the Modern Language Association* 45 (2), 400–415.
López, A.M. 2011. Ethnoastronomy as an academic field, a framework for a South American program. In Ruggles (ed.) 2011a, 38–49.
Lowenthal, D. 1985. *The Past is a Foreign Country*. Cambridge, Cambridge University Press.
Lowenthal, D. 1994. Conclusion. In P. Gathercole and D. Lowenthal (eds), *The Politics of the Past*. London, Routledge, 302–314.
Lubbock, J. 1865. *Pre-Historic Times, as illustrated by Ancient Remains and the Manners and Customs of Modern Savages*. London and Edinburgh, Williams and Norgate.
Lubbock, J. 1870. *The Origin of Civilisation and the Primitive Condition of Man*. New York, Appleton.
Lyell, C. 1835. *Principles of Geology*. Vol. 1 (4th edition). London, John Murray.
Lynch, B.D. and Lynch, T.F. 1968. The beginnings of a scientific approach to prehistoric archaeology in 17th and 18th century Britain. *Southwestern Journal of Anthropology* 24 (1), 33–65.
Lyotard, J.F. 1979. *La condition postmoderne: rapport sur la savoir*. Quebec, Collections Critique.
Lyotard, J.F. 2001. *The Postmodern Condition: a report on knowledge* (trans. G. Bennington and B. Massumi). Manchester, Manchester University Press.
MacDonald, J. 2006. New media applications and their potential for the advancement of public perceptions of archaeoastronomy and for the testing of archaeoastronomical hypotheses SEAC Conference Proceedings, Rhodes, 2006. *Mediterranean Archaeology and Archaeometry* 6 (3), 181–184.
Mackey, A.G. 1860. *A Lexicon of Freemasonry: containing a definition of all its communicable terms, notices of its history, traditions, and antiquities, and an account of all the rites and mysteries of the Ancient World*. Oxford, Brother Moss.
MacKie, E. 1971. Archaeoastronomy, *Megalithic Lunar Observatories* by Alexander Thom. *The Listener* 28 January, 120–122.
MacKie, E. 1974. Archaeological tests on supposed prehistoric astronomical sites in Scotland. In Hodson (ed.) 1974, 169–194.
MacKie, E. 1976. The Glasgow Conference on Ceremonial and Science in Prehistoric Britain. *Antiquity* 50, 136–138.
MacKie, E. 1977a. *Science and Society in Prehistoric Britain*. London, Paul Elek.
MacKie, E. 1977b. *The Megalith Builders*. Oxford, Phaidon Press.
MacKie, E. 1988. Investigating the solar calendar. In C.L.N. Ruggles (ed.), *Records in Stone: papers in memory of Alexander Thom*. Cambridge, Cambridge University Press, 206–231.
MacKie, E. 2000. *The Roundhouses, Brochs and Wheelhouses of Atlantic Scotland, c. 700 BC–AD 500: the Orkney and Shetland Isles*. Oxford, Archaeopress, British Archaeological Report 342.
MacKie, E. 2009. The prehistoric solar calendar: an out-of-fashion idea revisited with new evidence. *Time and Mind* 2 (1), 9–46.
MacLagan, C. 1881. *Chips from Old Stones*. Edinburgh, George Waterston & Sons.
MacPherson, P. 1881. Astronomy of the Australian Aborigines. *Journal & Proceedings of the Royal Society of New South Wales* 15, 71–80.
Magaña, E. 1984. Carib tribal astronomy. *Social Science Information* 23 (2), 341–368.

Magli, G. 2009. *Mysteries and Discoveries of Archaeoastronomy: from Giza to Easter Island.* New York, Springer Science+Business Media.
Magli, G. 2010. Archaeoastronomy and archaeo-topography as tools in the search for a missing Egyptian pyramid. *PalArch's Journal of Archaeology of Egypt/Egyptology* 7 (5), 1–9.
Magli, G. 2016. *Archaeoastronomy: introduction to the science of stars and stones.* Chem, Springer.
Malafouris, L. 2013. *How Things Shape the Mind, A Theory of Material Engagement.* Cambridge MA, MIT Press.
Maltwood K. 1929 *The High History of the Holy Grail.* London, The Women's Printing Society.
Malville, J.M. 2010. Cosmology in the Inca Empire, Huaca sanctuaries, state-supported pilgrimage, and astronomy. *Journal of Cosmology* 9, 2106–2120. [online] Accessed August 2018, journalofcosmology.com/AncientAstronomy116.html
Malville, J. M. 2015a. Chimney Rock and the ontology of skyscapes, how astronomy, trade and pilgrimage transformed Chimney Rock. *Journal of Skyscape Archaeology* 1 (1), 39–64.
Malville, J.M. 2015b. Preface; meaning and intent in ancient skyscapes –an Andean perspective. Silva and Campion (eds) 2015, ix–xvi.
Malville, J.M. and Holbrook, J. (eds). 2010. *Archaeoastronomy, Cosmology of Ancient Cultures. Journal of Cosmology* 9. [online] Accessed October, 2015, journalofcosmology.com/Contents9.html
Mann, L. McL. 1915. *Archaic Sculpturings. Notes on Art, Philosophy, and Religion in Britain 2000 B.C. To 900 A.D.* Scotland, William Hodge & Co.
Mann, L. McL. 1930. *Craftsmen's Measures in Prehistoric Times.* Glasgow, Mann Publishing Co.
Mann, L. McL. 1938a. *Earliest Glasgow a Temple of the Moon: An Outline of Early Science and Religion.* Glasgow, Mann Publishing Co.
Mann, L. McL. 1938b. *Ancient Measures: their Origin and Meaning.* Glasgow, Mann Publishing Co.
Mann, L. McL. 1939. *The Druid Temple Explained (newly-discovered earthwork near Glasgow).* Glasgow, Mann Publishing Co.
Marshack, A. 1964. Lunar notation on Upper Palaeolithic remains. *Science* 146, 743–745.
Marshack, A. 1991. *The Roots of Civilization.* New York, Mayer Bell.
Marshall, P. 2004. *Europe's Lost Civilisations, Uncovering the mysteries of the megaliths.* London, Headline Books.
Martin, A. 1911. L'unité de mesure chez les Néolithiques. *Bulletin de la Société Archaéologique su Finistère* 38, 116–118.
Martin, M. 1716. *Description of the Western Isles of Scotland* (2nd edition). London, A. Bell.
Martin, P.S. 1971. The revolution in archaeology. *American Antiquity* 36, 1–8.
Maton, W.G. 1800. Account of the fall of some of the stones of Stonehenge, in a letter from William George Maton, M.B. F.A.S. to Aylmer Bourke Lambert, Esq. F.R.S. and F.A.S. *Archaeologia* 13, 103–106.
Matthews, T.A. 1907. Some notes on Arbor Low and other lows in the High Peak. *Journal of the Derbyshire Archaeological and Natural History Society* 29, 103–112.
Matthews, T.A. 1911. Some further notes on the Lows in the High Peak. *Journal of the Derbyshire Archaeological and Natural History Society* 33, 87–94.
McCluskey, S.C. 2015. Analyzing light-and-shadow interactions. In Ruggles (ed.) 2015a, 427–444.
Meaden, T. (ed.). 2017. Editorial: Advances in understanding megaliths and related prehistoric lithic monuments. *Journal of Lithic Studies* 4 (4), 1–4.
Meadows, A. 1975. Ancient observatories. *Nature* 253, 395.
Meadows, A.J. 2008. *Science and Controversy: a biography of Sir Norman Lockyer, founder editor of Nature.* Basingstoke, Macmillan.
Mees, A. 2007. Die Kelten und der Mond: Neue Das Furstengrab bei Villingen-Schwennnigen – ein Kalenderwerk der Hallstattzeit. *Jahrbuch des Römisch-Germanischen Zentralmuseums* 54, 217–264.
Mejuto, J. 2020. Lessons learned from the Honduran path to an academic structure in cultural astronomy. *Journal of Skyscape Archaeology* 6 (1), 105–107.

Métraux, A. 1946. Ethnography of the Chaco. In J.H. Steward (ed.), *Handbook of South American Indians, Volume 1, The Marginal Tribes*. Washington DC, Smithsonian Institution, Bureau of American Ethnology Bulletin 143, 197–370.

Meynier, A. 1944. Champs et chemins de Bretagne. *Conférences Universitaire de Bretagne* 1942–43, 159–178.

Michel, A. 1958. *Flying Saucers and the Straight Line Mystery*. New York, S.G. Phillips.

Michell, J. 1978. *The View Over Atlantis* (new edition). London, Abacus.

Michell, J. 1989. *A Little History of Astro-Archaeology: stages in the transformation of a heresy* (2nd edition). New York, Thames & Hudson.

Michell, J. 2007. *Megalithomania* (new edition). Glastonbury, Squeeze Press.

Miller, W. 1955. Two possible astronomical pictographs found in northern Arizona. *Plateau* 27 (4), 6–13.

Milner, J. 1790. Description of several barrows opened in Dorsetshire. *Gentleman's Magazine* 60 (2), 897–901.

Mladenović, D. 2021. Roman archaeology and cultural astronomy: why do we have a dialogue breakdown? In E. Antonello (ed.), *Ex Oriente: Mithra and the others. Astronomical contents in the cults of Eastern origin in ancient Italy and Western Mediterranean*. Padova, Padova University Press, 31–48.

Moir, G. 1980. Megalithic Astronomy and Society, Newcastle Upon Tyne, 1980. *Archaeoastronomy Bulletin* 3 (2).

Moore, W. 1851. *The Gentlemen's Society at Spalding: Its Origin and Progress*. London.

Morgan, L.H. 1877. *Ancient Society or Researches in the Lines of Human Progress from Savagery through Barbarism to Civilization*. Chicago IL, Charles H. Kerry.

Morley, S.G. 1956. *The Ancient Maya* (3rd edition). Stanford CA, Stanford University Press.

Morrison, L.V. 1980. On the analysis of megalithic lunar sightlines in Scotland. *Archaeoastronomy Supplement to the Journal for the History of Astronomy* 2, S65–S89.

Morrisson, M.S. 2008. The periodical culture of the occult revival, esoteric wisdom, modernity and counter-public spheres. *Journal of Modern Literature* 31 (2), 1–22.

Moshenka, G. 2017. Alternative archaeologies. In G. Moshenka (ed.), *Key Concepts in Public Archaeology*. London, UCL Press, 127–137.

Moyano, R. 2002. Los santuarios de altura y la teoría del conflicto, una forma de entender la complejidad social y las relaciones de poder en los andes. *Revista Werken* 3, 133–145.

Muglova, P. and Stoev, A. 1996. The limits of cognition in the archaeoastronomical interpretations. In Koleva and Kolev (eds) 1996, 34–37.

Mulholland, D.J. 1983. Review of R. A. Williamson (ed.), *Archaeoastronomy in the Americas*. *Archaeoastronomy Supplement to the Journal for the History of Astronomy* 5, S73–S74.

Müller, M. 1871. *Chips From a German Workshop* Vol. 3. New York, Charles Scribner.

Muller, R. 1936. *Himmelskundliche Ortung auf Nordisch-Germanischem Boden*. Leipzig, Curt Kabitzsch.

Muller, R. 1970. *Der Himmel über dem Menschen der Steinzeit*. Berlin, Springer

Murphy, A. and Moore, R. 2008. *Island of the Setting Sun. In Search of Ireland's Ancient Astronomers*. Dublin, Liffey Press.

Murray, The Hon. Lord. 1852–54. Anniversary address. *Proceedings of the Society of Antiquaries for Scotland* 1 (2), 97–101.

Murray, H.K., Murray, J.C. and Fraser, S.M. 2009. *A Tale of the Unknown Unknowns, a Mesolithic pit alignment and a Neolithic timber hall at Warren Field, Crathes, Aberdeenshire*. Oxford, Oxbow Books.

Murray, W.B. 1998. Models of temporality in archaeoastronomy and rock art studies. *Archaeoastronomy Supplement to the Journal for the History of Astronomy* 23, S1–S6.

Murray, W.B. 2000. The contributions of the ethnosciences to archaeoastronomical research. *Archaeoastronomy* 15, 112–120.

Myatt, L.J. 1988. A megalithic winter solstice alignment at Dorrery, Caithness. *Archaeoastronomy Supplement to the Journal for the History of Astronomy* 12, S63–S68.
NASA. 2017. Global Positioning System History. [online] Accessed August, 2017, www.nasa.gov/directorates/heo/scan/communications/policy/GPS_History.html
Neitzsche, F. 2006 [1873]. *The Use and Abuse of History*. New York, Cosimo.
Nell, E.A. 2003. *Astronomical Orientations and Dimensions of Archaic and Classical Greek Temples*. MA thesis, University of Arizona.
Nell, E. and Ruggles, C.L.N. 2014. The orientations of the Giza pyramids and associated structures. *Journal for the History of Astronomy* 45 (3), 304–360.
Nelson, B. 1956. *My Trip to Mars, the Moon and Venus*. Grand Rapids MI, UFOrum: Grand Rapids Flying Saucer Club.
Newall, R.S. 1955. *Stonehenge Wiltshire (Official Guidebook)* (2nd edition). London, HMSO.
Newham, C.A. 1964. *The Enigma of Stonehenge and its Astronomical and Geometrical Significance*. Privately printed.
Newham, C.A. 1966. Stonehenge – a Neolithic observatory. *Nature* 211, 456–458.
Newham, C.A. 1972. *The Astronomical Significance of Stonehenge*. Leeds, John Blackburn.
Newham, C.A. 1982. Letter to Robert L. Merritt, published posthumously. *Archaeoastronomy Supplement to the Journal for the History of Astronomy* 4, S73–S74.
Newton, Sir I. 1687. *Philosophiæ Naturalis Principia Mathematica*. London.
Newton, Sir I. 1728. *A Short Chronicle from the First Memory of Things in Europe, to the Conquest of Persia by Alexander the Great*. London. [online] Accessed September, 2016, www.newtonproject.sussex.ac.uk/view/texts/normalized/THEM00185
Newton, Sir I. 1737. A dissertation upon the sacred cubit of the Jews and the cubits of the several nations; in which, from the dimensions of the greatest Egyptian Pyramid, as taken by Mr. John Greaves, the antient cubit of Memphis is determined. In J. Greaves, *Miscellaneous Works of Mr. John Greaves, Professor of Astronomy in the University of Oxford*. London, II, 405–433.
Nilsson, S. 1868. *The Primitive Inhabitants of Scandinavia* (trans. J. Lubbock). London, Longmans, Green and Company.
Norris, R. 1988. Megalithic observatories in Britain: real or imagined? In C.L.N. Ruggles (ed.), *Records in Stone: papers in memory of Alexander Thom*. Cambridge, Cambridge University Press, 262–276.
North, J. 1994. *The Norton History of Astronomy and Cosmology*. London, Norton.
North, J. 1996. *Stonehenge, A New Interpretation of Prehistoric Man and the Cosmos*. London, Harper Collins.
Nowakowski, J.A., Kennet, C., Gossip J. and Sheen B. 2020. Investigating archaeology and astronomy at The Hurlers, Cornwall 2013-2019. *Journal of Skyscape Archaeology* 6 (1), 53–85.
Oakeshott, M. 1933. *Experience and its Modes*. Cambridge, Cambridge University Press.
O'Donnell, I. 2019. Review of K. Ray and J. Thomas, *Neolithic Britain: The Transformation of Social Worlds*. *Journal of Skyscape Archaeology* 5 (2), 227–231.
Ogilvie, J. 1789. *The Fane of the Druids, A Poem. Book the Second; comprehending an account of the origin, progress, and establishment of society in north Britain*. London, J. Murray.
O'Kelly, M.J. and O'Kelly, C. 1982. *Newgrange: archaeology, art and legend*. London, Thames and Hudson.
O'Neill, J. 1893. *The Night of the Gods: an inquiry into cosmic and cosmogonic mythology and symbolism* vol. 1. London, Quaritch.
O'Neill, J. 1897. *The Night of the Gods: an inquiry into cosmic and cosmogonic mythology and symbolism* vol. 2. London, Quaritch.
Orlova, E.P. 1966. Kalendari narodov severa Sibiri I Dalnego Vostoka. *Sibirsky arkheologichesky sbornik* 2, 297–321.
Owen, T. and Pilbeam, E. 1992. *Ordnance Survey, Map Makers to Britain since 1791*. London, HMSO.
Pankenier, D. 2015. Astronomy and city planning in China. In Ruggles (ed.) 2015a, 2085–2093.

Papadopoulos, C. and Moyes, H. (eds) 2017. *The Oxford Handbook of Light in Archaeology.* [online] Accessed June 2021, www.oxfordhandbooks.com/view/10.1093/oxfordhb/9780198788218.001.0001/oxfordhb-9780198788218

Papathanassiou, M. and Hoskin, M. 1996. The Late-Minoan cemetery at Armenoi: a reappraisal. *Journal for the History of Astronomy* 27 (1) 86, 53–59.

Papathanassiou, M., Hoskin, M. and Papadopoulou, H. 1992. Orientations of tombs in the Late-Minoan cemetery at Armenoi, Crete. *Archaeoastronomy Supplement to the Journal for the History of Astronomy* 17, S43–S55.

Parker Pearson, M. 1998. The beginning of wisdom. *Antiquity* 72, 680–686.

Parker Pearson, M. 2013. *Stonehenge: exploring the greatest Stone Age mystery.* London, Simon & Schuster.

Parsons, T. 2007. An outline of the social system [1961]. In C. Calhoun (ed.), *Classical Sociological Theory*, Malden MA, Blackwell, 421–440.

Pásztor, E. 1993. Some remarks on the moon cult of Teutonic tribes. In Ruggles (ed.) 1993b, 98–106.

Pásztor, E. 1995a. Representation of the sun and symbols from the Bronze Age. In Pásztor (ed.) 1995b.

Pásztor, E. (ed.). 1995b. *Archaeoastronomy from Scandinavia to Sardinia.* Budapest, Roland Eötvös University.

Pásztor, E. 1999. Archaeoastronomy. [online] Accessed April 2021, https://csweb.bournemouth.ac.uk/eaa99/block2.htm#IIv

Pásztor, E. (ed.). 2007. *Archaeoastronomy in Archaeology and Ethnography. Papers from the annual meeting of SEAC (European Society for Astronomy in Culture) held in Kecskemét in Hungary in 2004.* Oxford, Archaeopress, British Archaeological Report S1647.

Pedersen, C. 2009 [1982]. The Present Position of Archaeoastronomy In D.C. Heggie (ed.), *Archaeoastronomy in the Old World* (reissue). Cambridge, Cambridge University Press.

Pennick, N. and Devereux, P. 1989. *Lines on the Landscape: leys and other linear enigmas.* London, Robert Hale.

Penprase, B.E. 2011. *The Power of Stars.* New York, Springer.

Penrose, F.C. 1893. On the results of an examination of the orientation of a number of Greek temples, with a view to connect these angles with the amplitudes of certain stars at the time these temples were founded, and an endeavour to derive there from the dates of their foundation by consideration of the changes produced upon the Right Ascension and Declination of the stars arising from the precession of the equinoxes. *Proceedings of the Royal Society of London* 53, 379–384.

Pereira, G. 2004. Persistencia y renovación, La Vía Láctea entre los Guaraníes del Chaco Boliviano. In *Etno y Arqueo-Astronomía en las Américas. Memorias del Simposio ARQ-13, Etno y Arqueoastronomía en las Américas, 51º Congreso Internacional de Americanistas.* Santiago de Chile ICA51, 299–314.

Perry, W.J. 1923. *The Children of the Sun: a study in the early history of civilisation.* London, Methuen.

Petrie, W.M.F. 1880. *Stonehenge: plans descriptions, and theories.* London, Edward Stanford.

Petrie, W.M.F. 1877. *Inductive Metrology, the recovery of ancient measures from the monuments.* London, Hargrove Saunders.

Petrie, W.M.F. 1904. *Methods and Aims of Archaeology.* London, Macmillan.

Phillips, M.S. 1996. Reconsiderations on history and antiquarianism, Arnaldo Momigliano and the historiography of eighteenth-century Britain. *Journal of the History of Ideas* 57 (2), 298.

Piggott, S. 1935. Stukeley, Avebury and the Druids. *Antiquity* 9, 22–32.

Piggott, S. 1950. *William Stukeley, an eighteenth-century antiquary.* Oxford, Clarendon Press.

Piggott, S. 1954a. The Druids and Stonehenge. *The South African Archaeological Bulletin* 9, 138–140.

Piggott, S. 1954b. *The Neolithic Cultures of the British Isles.* Cambridge, Cambridge University Press.

Piggott, S. 1959. *Approach to Archaeology.* London, A. & C. Black.

Piggott, S. 1974a. William Stukeley, doctor, divine, and antiquary. *The British Medical Journal* 3 (5933), 725–727.

Piggott, S. 1974b. Concluding remarks. In Hodson (ed.) 1974, 275–276.
Pilcher, J.R. 1969. Archaeology, palaeoecology, and ^{14}C dating of the Beaghmore Stone Circle site. *Ulster Journal of Archaeology* 32, 73–91.
Pimenta, F., Tirapicos, L. and Smith A. 2009. A Bayesian approach to the orientations of central Alentejo megalithic enclosures. *Archaeoastronomy: The Journal of Astronomy in Culture* 22, 1–20.
Pimenta, F., Ribeiro, N., Silva, F., Campion, N., Joaquinito, A. and Tirapicos, L. (eds). 2015. *SEAC 2011 Stars and Stones: voyages in archaeoastronomy and cultural astronomy*. Oxford, British Archaeological Report S2720.
Pliny the Elder. *Natural History* (trans. H. Rackham, W.H.S. Jones and D.E. Eicholz). London, Heinemann, 1949–1954. [online] Accessed August, 2018, en.wikisource.org/wiki/Natural_History_(Rackham,_Jones,_%26_Eichholz)/Book_16
Plot, R. 1686. *The Natural History of Staffordshire*. Oxford.
Pluciennik, M. 2012. Theory, fashion, culture. In J. Bintliff and M. Pearce (eds), *The Death of Archaeological Theory?* Oxford, Oxbow Books, 31–47.
Pohorecky, Z.S. 1969. Rupestral art in the Pre-Cambrian Shiled of Canada. *Akten des XXXVIII Internationalen Amerikanistenkongresses, Stuttgart-München.* Vienna, Ferdinand Berger, vol. 1, 103–108.
Polcaro, V.F. 2015. The role of cultural astronomy in bridging the Snow's "Two Cultures": some Italian experiences. In Pimenta *et al.* (eds) 2015, 318–321.
Polcaro, A. and Polcaro, V.F. 2009. Man and sky: problems and methods of archaeoastronomy *Archeologia e Calcolatori* 20, 223–245.
Pollard, J. 2005. From meaning to materiality, TAG Session and Paper Abstracts, Sheffield. [online] https://antiquity.ac.uk/sites/default/files/downloads/tag/TAG_2005_abstracts.pdf.
Pollard, J. 2017. The Uffington White Horse geoglyph as sun-horse. *Antiquity* 91, 406–420.
Ponting, G. and Ponting M. 1978. *The Standing Stones of Callenish, Isle of Lewis*. Lewis, Essprint.
Porteous, H.L. 1973. Megalithic yard or megalithic myth? *Journal for the History of Astronomy* 4 (9), 22–24.
Powell, M.J. 1995. Astronomical Indications at a bell-barrow in South Wales. *Archaeoastronomy Supplement to the Journal for the History of Astronomy* 20, S49–S46.
Pratt, E. 2015. 'It's all magical and made up, really', negotiating between academic and alternative narratives of British prehistory. *The Archaeological Review from Cambridge* 30 (2), 56–70.
Prendergast, F.T. 1991. Shadow casting phenomena at Newgrange. *Survey Ireland* November, 9–18.
Prendergast, F.T. 2000. The stone rows of the west of Ireland: a preliminary archaeoastronomical analysis. In Esteban and Belmonte (eds) 2000, 35–42.
Prendergast, F. 2015. Techniques of field survey. In Ruggles (ed.) 2015a, 389–409.
Prendergast, F., O'Sullivan, M., Williams, K. and Cooney, G. 2017. Facing the Sun. *Archaeology Ireland* 31 (4), 10–17.
Pritchard, O. 2016. Shadows, stones and solstices. *Journal of Skyscape Archaeology* 2 (2), 145–164.
Proverbio, E., Romano, G. and Aveni, A. 1987. Astronomical orientations of five megalithic tombs at Madau, near Fonni in Sardinia. *Archaeoastronomy Supplement to the Journal for the History of Astronomy* 11, S55–S65.
Ralph, E.K. and Stuckenrath, R. Jr. 1960. Carbon-14 measurements of known age samples. *Nature* 188, 185–187.
Rappenglück, B. 2015. 'The Materiality of the Sky', the 22nd Conference of the European Society of Astronomy in Culture, Valetta (Malta), 22nd–26th September, 2014. *Journal of Skyscape Archaeology* 1 (1), 138–141.
Rappenglück, M.A., Rappenglück, B., Campion, N. and Silva F. (eds). 2016. *Astronomy and Power: how worlds are structured: Proceedings of the SEAC 2010 Conference*. Oxford, British Archaeological Report S2794.
Ray, B.C. 1987. Stonehenge: a new theory. *History of Religions* 26 (3), 225–278.

Ray, K. and Thomas, J. 2018. *Neolithic Britain, The Transformation of Social Worlds*. Oxford, Oxford University Press.

Renfrew, C. 1973. *Before Civilisation*. London, Cape.

Renfrew, C. 1981. Comments. In A. Ellegård, Stone Age Science in Britain? [and comments and reply]. *Current Anthropology* 22 (22), 120–121.

Renfrew, C. 1982. *Towards an Archaeology of Mind*. Cambridge, Cambridge University Press.

Renfrew, C. and Bahn, P. 1991. *Archaeology, Theories Methods and Practice*. London, Thames and Hudson.

Renfrew, C. and Bahn, P.G. 2005. *Archaeology, the Key Concepts*. London and New York, Routledge.

Reports. 1937 = *Reports of the Joint Committee on Ancient Measures: Presented to the Glasgow Archaeological Society and The Geological Society of Glasgow*. Glasgow.

Reuter, O.S. 1921–3. *Das Rätsel der Edda und der arische Urglaube*. Hessen, Sontra

Reuter, O.S. 1934. *Germanischer Himmelskunde*. Munich, Lehrmanns.

Reyman, J.E. 1973. Comments, 436 in Baity 1973, 436.

Reyman, J.E. 1975a. *The Nature and Nurture of Archaeoastronomical Studies*.

Reyman, J.E. 1975b. The nature and nurture of archaeoastronomical studies. In Aveni (ed.) 1975, 205–215.

Reyman, J.E. 1979. Some observations on archaeology and archaeoastronomy. *Archaeoastronomy Bulletin* 2, 11R.

Ricketson, O.G. Jr. 1928. Astronomical observatories in the Maya area. *Geographical Review* 18, 215–225.

Ritchie, J. 1926. Folklore of the Aberdeenshire stone circles and standing-stones *Proceedings of the Society of Antiquaries of Scotland* 60, 304–313.

Ritchie, J.N.G. 1998. *Brochs of Scotland*. Princes Risborough, Shire.

Ritchie, J.N.G. 2009 [1982]. Archaeology and Astronomy: An Archaeological View In D.C. Heggie (ed.), *Archaeoastronomy in the Old World* (reissue). Cambridge University Press, 25–44.

Robertson, A. 1853. Notes of the discovery of stone cists at Lesmurdie, Banffshire, containing primitive urns, &c., along with human remains. *Proceedings of the Society of Antiquaries for Scotland* 1 (2), 205–211.

Rolston, W.E. 1908. Review of A. John and G. Hubbard, *Neolithic Dew-ponds and Cattle-ways*. Nature 1994 (77), 245.

Romano, G. and Traversari (eds). 1991. *Colloquio Internazionale: Archaeologia e Astronomia*. Rome, Giorgio Bretschneider, Revista di Archaeologia Supplementi 9.

Romero, J.B., Morales, O.L.G. and Sarmiento, E.S. 2019. *Archaeoastronomy, an Alternative Teaching of Pre-Columbian Astronomy in the University*. Revista Cinetífica Special Issue, 234–243.

Rowe, S. 1848. *A Perambulation of the Antient and Royal Forest of Dartmoor, and the Venville Precincts*. Plymouth and London, J.B. Rowe & Hamilton Adams.

Rowlands, H. 1723. *Mona Antique Restaurata, An Archaeological Discourse on the Antiquities, Natural and Historical, of the Isle of Anglesey. The Ancient Seat of the British Druids*. London. [online] Accessed April, 2014, https://archive.org/details/monaantiquarest00lhuygoog/page/n8/mode/2up?view=theatre [link no longer active]

Rowlands, M. 1997. The politics of identity in archaeology. In G.C. Bond and A. Gilliam (eds), *Social Construction of the Past: representation as power*. Oxford, Routledge, 129–143.

Royal Archaeological Institute. 2017. About the Royal Archaeological Institute. [online] Accessed May, 2017, www.royalarchinst.org/about

Ruggles, C. 1981a. Archaeoastronomical anomalies. *Nature* 294, 485–486.

Ruggles, C. 1981b. A critical examination of the megalithic lunar observatories. In Ruggles and Whittle (eds) 1981, 153–210.

Ruggles, C.L.N. 1982. A reassessment of the high precision megalithic lunar sightlines, 1: backsights, indicators and the archaeological status of the sightlines. *Archaeoastronomy Supplement to the Journal for the History of Astronomy* 4, S21–S40.

Ruggles, C.L.N. 1983. A reassessment of the high precision megalithic lunar sightlines, 2: foresights and the problem of selection. *Archaeoastronomy Supplement to the Journal for the History of Astronomy* 5, S1–S36.

Ruggles, C.L.N. 1984a. Megalithic astronomy: the last five years. *Vistas in Astronomy* 27, 231–289.

Ruggles, C.L.N. 1984b. *Megalithic Astronomy: a new archaeological and statistical study of 300 western Scottish sites*. Oxford, British Archaeological Report 123.

Ruggles, C.L.N. 1984c. A new study of the Aberdeenshire recumbent stone circles, 1, site data. *Archaeoastronomy Supplement to the Journal for the History of Astronomy* 6, S55–S79.

Ruggles, C.L.N. 1985a. The linear settings of Argyll and Mull. *Archaeoastronomy Supplement to the Journal for the History of Astronomy* 9, S105–S132.

Ruggles, C.L.N. 1985b. Review of E. Hadingham, *Early Man and the Cosmos. Archaeoastronomy Supplement to the Journal for the History of Astronomy* 8, S63– S65.

Ruggles, C.L.N. 1986. You can't have one without the other? I.T. and Bayesian statistics, and their possible impact in archaeology. *Science and Archaeology* 28, 8–15.

Ruggles, C.L. N. 1988. Editorial preface. *Archaeoastronomy Supplement to the Journal for the History of Astronomy* 12.

Ruggles, C.L.N. 1989. Recent developments in megalithic astronomy. In Aveni (ed.) 1989b, 13–26.

Ruggles, C. 1993a. Introduction: archaeoastronomy – the way ahead. In Ruggles (ed.) 1993b, 1–13.

Ruggles, C.L.N. (ed.). 1993b. *Archaeoastronomy in the 1990s*. Bognor Regis, Ocarina.

Ruggles, C.L.N. 1993c. Four approaches to the Borana calendar. In Ruggles (ed.) 1993b, 117–122.

Ruggles, C.L.N.1994a. The stone rows of south-west Ireland: a first reconnaissance. *Archaeoastronomy Supplement to the Journal for the History of Astronomy* 19, S1–S20.

Ruggles, C.L.N. 1994b. The European Society for Astronomy in Culture. *Archaeoastronomy Supplement to the Journal for the History of Astronomy* 19, S90.

Ruggles, C. 1995. Review of G. Romano and G. Traversari (eds) 1991. *Archaeoastronomy Supplement to the Journal for the History of Astronomy* 20, S80–S86.

Ruggles, C.L.N. 1996a. Stone rows of three or more stones in south-west Ireland. *Archaeoastronomy Supplement to the Journal for the History of Astronomy* 21, S55–S71.

Ruggles, C. 1996b. New approaches to the investigation of astronomical symbolism within the ritual landscapes of the prehistoric British Isles. In Koleva and Kolev (eds) 1996, 1–13.

Ruggles, C.L.N. 1997a. Whose equinox? *Archaeoastronomy Supplement to the Journal for the History of Astronomy* 22, S45–S50.

Ruggles, C.L.N. 1997b. Astronomy and Stonehenge. In Cunliffe and Renfrew (eds) 1997, 203–230.

Ruggles, C. 1999a. *Astronomy in Prehistoric Britain and Ireland*. New Haven CO and London, Yale University Press.

Ruggles, C. 1999b. Review of J.D. North, *Stonehenge: Neolithic Man and the Cosmos. Archaeoastronomy Supplement to the Journal for the History of Astronomy* 24, S83–S88.

Ruggles, C. 2000. The general and the specific: dealing with cultural diversity *Archaeoastronomy. The Journal of Astronomy in Culture* 15, 151–177.

Ruggles, C. 2003. Course AR3015 Sample Lecture Notes (2003). [online] Accessed February 2021, https://www.le.ac.uk/has/cr/oldrug/aa/a3015/lec3.html

Ruggles, C.L.N. 2005a. *Ancient Astronomy: an encyclopedia of cosmologies and myth*. Santa Barbara CA, ABC-CLIO.

Ruggles, C.L.N. 2005b. Archaeoastronomy. In Renfrew and Bahn 2005, 11–16.

Ruggles, C.L.N. 2009 [1982]. Megalithic astronomical sightlines: current reassessment and future directions. In D.C. Heggie (ed.), 2009. *Archaeoastronomy in the Old World* (reissue). Cambridge, Cambridge University Press, 83–105.

Ruggles C.L.N. (ed.). 2011a. *Archaeoastronomy and Ethnoastronomy, Building Bridges between Cultures: proceedings of the 278th Symposium of the International Astronomical Union and Oxford IX International*

Symposium on Archaeoastronomy, held in Lima, Peru, January 5-14, 2011. Cambridge, Cambridge University Press.

Ruggles, C.L.N. 2011b. Pushing back the frontiers or still running around in the same circles? Interpretative archaeoastronomy thirty years on. In Ruggles (ed.) 2011a, 1–18.

Ruggles, C.L.N. (ed.). 2015a. *Handbook of Archaeoastronomy and Ethnoastronomy.* New York, Springer.

Ruggles, C.L.N. 2015b. Nature and analysis of material evidence relevant to archaeoastronomy. In Ruggles (ed.) 2015a, 353–372.

Ruggles. C. 2021. DECPAK. [online] Accessed February 2021 https://www.le.ac.uk/has/cr/oldrug/aa/progs/decpak.html

Ruggles, C.L.N. and Burl, H.A.W. 1985. A new study of the Aberdeenshire recumbent stone circles, 2: interpretation. *Archaeoastronomy Supplement to the Journal for the History of Astronomy* 8, S25–S60.

Ruggles, C.L.N. and Martlew, R.D. 1989. The North Mull Project (1): excavations at Glengorm 1987–88. *Archaeoastronomy Supplement to the Journal for the History of Astronomy* 14, S137–S149.

Ruggles, C. and McCluskey, S. 1996. Towards an international organisation. *Archaeoastronomy and Ethnoastronomy News* 23. [online] Accessed March, 2015, terpconnect.umd.edu/~tlaloc/archastro/ae23.html

Ruggles, C.L.N. and Saunders, N.J. 1993a. The study of cultural astronomy. In Ruggles and Saunders (eds) 1993b, 1–31.

Ruggles, C.L.N. and Saunders, N.J. (eds).1993b. *Astronomies and Cultures: papers derived from the third 'Oxford' International Symposium on Archaeoastronomy, St Andrews, UK, September 1990.* Niwot CO, University Press of Colorado.

Ruggles, C.L.N. and Whittle, A.W.R. (eds). 1981. *Astronomy and Society in Britain During the Period 4000-1500 BC.* Oxford, British Archaeological Report 88.

Ruggles, C.L.N. Martlew, R.D. and Hinge, P.D. 1991 The North Mull Project (2): the wider astronomical potential of the sites. *Archaeoastronomy Supplement to the Journal for the History of Astronomy* 16, S51–S75.

Ruggles, C., Prendergast, F. and Ray T. 2001. Preface. In C. Ruggles, F. Prendergast and T. Ray (eds), *Astronomy, Cosmology and Landscape, Proceedings of the SEAC 98 meeting, Dublin, Ireland, September 1998.* Bognor Regis, Ocarina, vi–vii.

Ruis-Castell, P. 2011. Review of D. Aubin *et al.* (eds), The Heavens on Earth, Observatories and Astronomy in Nineteenth-Century Science. *Journal for the History of Astronomy* 42 (4), 351–352.

Russell, J.L. 1974. Cosmological teaching in the seventeenth-century Scottish universities, part 1. *Journal for the History of Astronomy* 5 (13), 122–132, 145–154.

Santillana, G. de and Dechend, H. von. 1977. *Hamlet's Mill: an essay on myth and the frame of time.* Boston MA, Godine.

Saletta, M. 2011. The archaeoastronomy of the megalithic monuments of Arles–Fontvieille, the equinox, the Pleiades and Orion. In Ruggles (ed.) 2011a, 364–373.

Salmon, N. 1731. *A New Survey of England*, London, J. Walthoe.

Salt, A. 2009. Creating collective identities through astronomy? A study of Greek temples in Sicily. Unpublished PhD thesis, University of Leicester.

Salt, A. 2015. Development of archaeoastronomy in the English-speaking world. In Ruggles (ed.) 2015a, 213–226.

Sayce, A.H. 1914. The date of Stonehenge. *The Journal of Egyptian Archaeology* 1 (1), 18–19.

Sayer, F. 2014. Politics and the development of community archaeology in the UK. *The Historic Environment* 5 (1), 55–73.

Schadla-Hall, T. 1999. Editorial, public archaeology. *European Journal of Archaeology* 2 (2), 147–158.

Schadla-Hall, T. 2004. The comforts of unreason, the importance and relevance of alternative Archaeology. In N. Merriman (ed.), *Public Archaeology*. London and New York, Routledge, 255–271.

Schaefer, B.E. 1986. Atmospheric extinction effects on stellar alignments. *Archaeoastronomy Supplement to the Journal for the History of Astronomy* 10, S32–S42.
Schaefer, B.E. 1987. Heliacal rise phenomena. *Archaeoastronomy Supplement to the Journal for the History of Astronomy* 11, S19–S33.
Schaefer, B.E. 1992. The length of the lunar month. *Archaeoastronomy Supplement to the Journal for the History of Astronomy* 17, S32–S42.
Schaefer, B.E. 1993. Confluences of astronomical spectacles *Archaeoastronomy, The Journal of Astronomy in Culture* 11 (1989–1993), 91–93.
Schaefer, B.E. 1999. Astronomy in historical studies. *Archaeoastronomy, The Journal of Astronomy in Culture* 14 (1), 89–108.
Schaefer, B.E. and Liller, W. 1990. Refraction near the horizon. *Publications of the Astronomical Society of the Pacific* 102, 796–805.
Schiavottiello, N. 2009. From survey to education, how augmented reality can contribute to the study and dissemination of archaeo-astronomy. In J.A. Rubiño-Martin, J.A. Belmonte, F. Prada and A. Alberdi (eds), *Cosmology Across Cultures*. San Francisco CA, Astronomical Society of the Pacific Conference Series, 464–467.
Schlosser, W. 1989. Astronomy in Europe between 8000 and 1200 B.C. *Astronomie et sciences humaines* 3, 79–91.
Schlosser, W. and Cierny J. 1997. *Stern und Steine: Ein praktische Astronomie der Vorzeit*. Stuttgart, Theiss.
Schmeidler, F. 1988. Obituary – Muller, Rolf 1898–1981. *Quarterly Journal of the Royal Astronomical Society* 29 (1), 89.
Schnapp, A. 2014. Introduction. In A. Schnapp, L. von Falkenhausen,P. N. Miller and T. Murray, *World Antiquarianism, Comparative Perspectives*. Los Angeles CA, Getty.
Schofield, J., Carmen J. and Belford P. 2011. *Archaeological Practice in Great Britain, A Heritage Handbook*. New York, Springer.
Science Daily. 2014. Archaeo-astronomy steps out from the shadows of the past, 23 June. [online] Accessed December, 2017, www.sciencedaily.com/releases/2014/06/140623092326.htm
Scott, D. 1990. Astronomical survey of three groups of standing stones in Strath Spey, Scotland. *Archaeoastronomy Supplement to the Journal for the History of Astronomy* 15, S56–S58.
Scott, D. 2016. The solar lunar orientations of the Orkney-Cromarty and Clava cairns. *Journal of Skyscape Archaeology* 2 (1), 45–66.
Scott, Sir W. 1816. *The Antiquary*. Edinburgh, Archibald Constable.
Scott, Sir W. 1819. *A Legend of Montrose*. Edinburgh, Archibald Constable.
Screeton, P. 1974. *Quicksilver Heritage: the mystic leys: their legacy of ancient wisdom*. London, Abacus.
SEAC 2020. Who we are [online] Accessed September 2020, http://www.archeoastronomy.org/content/who-we-are/
Serio, G.F., Hoskin, M. and Ventura, F. 1992. The orientations of the temples of Malta. *Journal for the History of Astronomy* 23 (2), 107–119.
Seymour, W.A. (ed.). 1980. *A History of the Ordnance Survey*. Folkestone, Wm. Dawson.
Shanks, M. 2017. Chorography. [online]. Accessed April, 2017, https://mshanks.com/chorography/
Shanks, M. and Hodder. I. 1997. Processual, post-processual and interpretive archaeologies. In I. Hodder, M. Shanks, A. Alexandri, V. Buchli, J. Carmen, J. Last and G. Lucas (eds), *Interpreting Archaeology: finding meaning in the past*, London, Psychology Press, 3–29.
Shanks, M. and Tilley, C. 1988. *Social Theory and Archaeology*. Albuquerque NM, University of New Mexico Press.
Shanks, M. and Tilley, C. 1992. *Reconstructing Archaeology*. London and New York, Routledge.
Sherratt, A. 1995. Reviving the grand narrative: archaeology and long-term change. *Journal of European Archaeology* 3 (1), 1–32.

Silva, F. 2013. Landscape and astronomy in megalithic Portugal, the Carregal do Sal Nucleus and Star Mountain Range. *Papers from the Institute of Archaeology* 22, 99–114.
Silva, F. 2014a. 'A tomb with a view', new methods for bridging the gap between land and sky in megalithic archaeology. *Advances in Archaeological Practice, A Journal of the Society for American Archaeology* 1 (2), 24–37.
Silva, F. 2014b. Skies ancient and modern, rethinking skyscapes, cosmology and archaeology. *Sophia Project News*, September 2014. [online] Accessed June, 2017, sophia-project.net/SophiaProjectNews/issues/2014-09.html
Silva, F. 2015a. The Role and importance of the sky in archaeology, an introduction. In Silva and Campion (eds) 2015, 1–7.
Silva, F. (ed.). 2015b. *Landscape – Seascape – Skyscape. Culture and Cosmos* Special Issue 17 (2).
Silva, F. 2016. Equinoctial full moon models and non-Gaussianity: Portuguese dolmens as a test case. In Rappenglück *et al.* (eds) 2016, 51–56.
Silva, F. 2017a. Inferring alignments I, exploring the accuracy and precision of two statistical approaches. *Journal of Skyscape Archaeology* 3 (1), 93–111.
Silva, F. 2017b. Defining skyscape. [online]. Accessed June 2020, https,//sophiacentrepress.com/defining-skyscape/
Silva, F. 2020a. On measurement, uncertainty and maximum likelihood in skyscape archaeology. In Henty and Brown (eds) 2020, 55–74.
Silva F. 2020b. A probabilistic framework and significance test for the analysis of structural orientations in skyscape archaeology. *Journal of Archaeological Science* 118, 105–138.
Silva, F. 2020c. Whither skyscape archaeology. *Journal of Skyscape Archaeology* 6 (1), 108–113.
Silva, F. 2021. skyscapeR software. [online] Accessed November, 2021, https://cran.r-project.org/web/packages/skyscapeR/index.html
Silva, F. and Campion, N. 2012. The Role and Importance of the Sky in Archaeology. TAG Liverpool 2012, Conference Programme, 17–20. [online] https://antiquity.ac.uk/sites/default/files/downloads/tag/TAG_2012_programme.pdf.
Silva, F. and Campion, N. (eds). 2015. *Skyscapes, The Role and Importance of the Sky in Archaeology*. Oxford, Oxbow Books.
Silva, F. and Henty, L. 2015. Editorial. *Journal of Skyscape Archaeology* 1 (1), 1–7.
Silva, F. and Henty, L. 2018. Editorial. *Journal of Skyscape Archaeology* 4 (1), 1–5.
Silva, F. and Henty, L. 2020a. Skyscapes in the Academy: is there a future? *Journal of Skyscape Archaeology* 6 (1), 86–87.
Silva, F. and Henty, L. 2020b. Skyscapes in the Academy: is there a future? part 2. *Journal of Skyscape Archaeology* 6 (2), 259–260.
Silva, F. and Pimenta, F. 2012. The crossover of the sun and the moon. *Journal for the History of Astronomy* 43 (2), 191–208.
Silva, F., Malville, K., Lomsdalen, T. and Ventura, F. (eds). 2016. *The Materiality of the Sky, Proceedings of the 22nd Annual SEAC Conference, 2014*. Lampeter, Sophia Centre Press.
Simpson, J.Y. 1860–62. Address on archaeology. *Proceedings of the Society of Antiquaries for Scotland* 4 (1), 5–51.
Simpson, Rev. J. 1862. Stone circles near Shap, Westmoreland. *Proceedings of the Society of Antiquaries of Scotland* 4 (2), 443–449.
Simpson, W. 1897. *The Orientation or Direction of Temples*. Bromley, G.W. Speth, published for the Quatuor Coronati Lodge
Sims, L. 2003. *Stonehenge Rediscovered*. Film produced, directed and edited by C. Hall. London, Parthenon Entertainment.
Sims, L. 2006. The solarization of the moon, manipulated knowledge at Stonehenge. *Cambridge Archaeological Journal* 2 (16), 191–207.

Sims, L. 2007a. Lighting up dark moon, ethnographic templates for testing paired alignments on the sun and the moon. In Zedda and Belmonte (eds) 2007, 309.

Sims, L. 2007b. Reconstructing the underworld, the anthropology and archaeology of otherworlds TAG York 2007 session programme. [online] https://antiquity.ac.uk/sites/default/files/downloads/tag/TAG_2007_programme.pdf

Sims, L. 2008. Integrating archaeoastronomy with landscape archaeology, Silbury Hill – a case study. *Archaeologica Baltica* 10, 220–225.

Sims, L. 2009. Entering, and returning from, the underworld, reconstituting Silbury Hill by combining a quantified landscape phenomenology with archaeoastronomy. *Journal of the Royal Anthropological Institute* NS 15 (2), 386–408.

Sims, L. 2010. Which way forward for archaeoastronomy? West Kennet Avenue as a test case. *Journal of Cosmology* 9, 2160–2171.

Sims, L. 2013. Interpretation through emergence: reconstituting the lost complexity of the late Neolithic/Early Bronze Age cosmovision by multi-disciplinary method. Unpublished PhD thesis, University of East London.

Sims, L. 2021. Returning from the underworld, the West Kennet palisades in the Avebury monument complex. *Proceedings of the Prehistoric Society*, First View [online] Accessed June 2021, https,//www.cambridge.org/core/journals/proceedings-of- the-prehistoric-society/article/abs/returning-from-the-underworld-the-west-kennet- palisades-in-the-avebury-monument-complex/89278F9B9F2AD436F2314C73C0046213

Smith, A.G. K. 2018. Horizon v0.12a. *Journal of Skyscape Archaeology* 4 (2), 272–273.

Smith, A.G.K. and Higginbottom, G. 2009. Investigating the possibility of astronomical connections at the Crathes Warren Field site Unpublished report archived in The National Monuments Record of Scotland, Edinburgh, 1–19.

Smith, G.E. 1933. *The Diffusion of Culture*. London, Watts.

Smith, J. 1771. *Choir Gaur, the Grand Orrery of the Ancient Druids, Commonly Called Stonehenge, on Salisbury Plain Astronomically Explained and, proved to be a Temple for Observing the, Motions of the Heavenly Bodies*. Salisbury, E. Easton.

Smith, M.E. 2003. Can we read cosmology in ancient Maya city Plans? Comment on Ashmore and Sabloff. *Latin American Antiquity* 14 (2), 221–228.

Smyth, C.P. 1868. *On the Antiquity of Intellectual Man from a Practical and Astronomical Point of View*. Edinburgh, Edmonston and Douglas.

Smyth, C.P. 1874. *Our Inheritance in the Great Pyramid*. London, W. Ibister and Co.

Snow, C.P. 1961. *The Two Cultures and the Scientific Revolution*. The Rede Lecture, 1959. New York, Cambridge University Press.

Snow, D.R. 1973. Comments. In Baity 1973, 438.

Somerville, B. 1912. Prehistoric monuments in the outer Hebrides and their astronomical significance. *Journal of the Royal Anthropological Institute of Great Britain and Ireland* 42, 23–52.

Somerville, B. 1923. VIII. Instances of orientation in prehistoric monuments of the British Isles. *Archaeologia* 73, 193–224.

Somerville, B. 1927. Orientation. *Antiquity*, 1 (1), 31–41.

Somerville, B. 1928. Two great dolmens of central France. *Antiquity* 2 (6), 147–160.

Spence, L. 1905. *The Mysteries of Britain or the Secret Rites and Traditions of Ancient Britain Restored*. London, Rider and Co.

Spence, L. 1949. *The Magic Arts in Celtic Britain*. New York, Dover Publications.

Spence, M. 1894. *Standing Stones and Maeshowe of Stenness*. Paisley and London, Gardner.

Spencer, H. 1864. *The Principles of Biology*. London, Williams and Norgate.

Spencer, J. H. 1889. Ancient trackways in England. *The Antiquary* 20, 94–101.

Šprajc, I. 2005. More on Mesoamerican cosmology and city plans. *Latin American Antiquity* 16 (2), 209–216.
SRPIC 2021. *Fourth Conference of the Romanian Society for Cultural Astronomy.* [online] Accessed June 2021, https://sites.google.com/view/comunicarisrpac/home-en
Stebbins, R.A. 1977. The amateur: two sociological definitions. *The Pacific Sociological Review* 20 (4), 582–606.
Stellarium. 2021. v. 0.21.1. [online] Accessed April 2021, https,//stellarium.org/
Stevens, F. 1916. *Stonehenge Today and Yesterday*. London, Sampson Low, Marston & Co.
Sticker-Jantscheff, M. 2015. Magdalenenberg: an examination of archaeological and archaeoastronomical interpretations of a Hallstatt period burial mound. *Spica* 3 (1), 19–40.
Sticker-Jantscheff, M. 2018. A new look at old temples, Augusta Raurica and its skyscape in the first and second centuries AD. *Journal of Skyscape Archaeology* 4 (1), 52–81.
Stiebing, W. 1984. *Ancient Astronauts, Cosmic Collisions: and other popular theories about man's past*. Buffalo NY, Prometheus Books.
Stone, E.H. 1922. 68. Stonehenge. Notes on the midsummer sunrise. *Man* 22, 114–118.
Stone, E.H. 1925. 40. The purpose of Stonehenge. *Man* 25, 69–72.
Stooke, P.J. 1994. Neolithic lunar maps at Knowth and Baltinglass, Ireland. *Journal for the History of Astronomy* 25 (1) 78, 39–55.
Stout, A. 2008. *Creating Prehistory*. Oxford, Blackwell.
Stout, A. 2012. Grounding faith at Glastonbury. Episodes in the Early History of Alternative Archaeology. *NUMEN* 59 (2/3), 249–269.
Stuart, J. 1853. Notices of various stone circles in the parishes of Cairney, Monymusk, and Tough, Aberdeenshire; and of Inverkeithny, Banffshire. *Proceedings of the Society of Antiquaries for Scotland* 1 (2), 141–142.
Stuart, J. 1856. *Sculptured Stones of Scotland* vol. 1. Aberdeen, Spalding Club.
Stuart, J. 1859. Note of incised marks on one of a circle of standing stones in the Island of Lewis. *Proceedings of the Society of Antiquaries for Scotland* 3 (1), 212–214.
Stuart, J. 1867. *Sculptured Stones of Scotland* vol. 2. Aberdeen, Spalding Club.
Stukeley, W. 1740. *Stonehenge, A Temple Restor'd to the British Druids.* London. [online] Accessed April 2013, www.sacred-texts.com/neu/eng/str/
Stukeley, W. 1743. *Abury, A Temple of the British Druids, with some others described.* London. [online] Accessed July 2013, www.avebury- web.co.uk/AburyWS/AburyWS.html
Stukeley, W. 1776. *Itinerarium Curiosum or, an Account of the Antiquities, and Remarkable Curiosities in Nature or Art, Observed in Travels through Great Britain.* London, Baker and Leigh.
Sturge, W.A. 1911. Presidential address. *Proceedings of the Prehistoric Society of East Anglia* 1 (1), 9–16.
Sullivan, M. 2012. *A brief history of GPS*. [online]. Accessed August, 2017, www.pcworld.com/article/2000276/a-brief-history-of-gps.html
Sweet, R. 2001. Antiquaries and antiquities in eighteenth-century England. *Eighteenth-century Studies* 34 (2), 181–206.
Symons, S. 1999. Ancient Egyptian astronomy: timekeeping and cosmography in the new kingdom Unpublished PhD thesis, University of Leicester.
Taylor, R.F. and Bar-Yosef, O. 2014. *Radiocarbon Dating, Second Edition: An Archaeological Perspective*. Walnut Creek CA, Left Coast Press.
Teasdale, W. 1900. Astronomical theories relative to Stonehenge. *Leeds Astronomical Society Journal* 1900.
Teeple, J. 1931. Maya astronomy. *Carnegie Institution of Washington Contributions to American Archaeology* 1, 29–115.
Temple, R.K.G. 1976. *The Sirius Mystery*. London, Sidgwick and Jackson.

Teudt, W. 1931. *Germanische Heiligtümer* (trans. M Behrend, in 4 web sections). [online] Accessed June, 2013, www.cantab.net/users/michael.behrend/repubs/teudt_hl/pages/main_en_1.html

The Archaeological Journal. 1908. Notices of archaeological publications. *The Archaeological Journal*, 65, 137–139.

The Ashmolean Museum. 2014. About. [online] Accessed June, 2014, www.ashmolean.org/about/historyandfuture/

The Geo Group. 2020. Finding places of power: dowsing earth energies. [online] Accessed December, 2020. www.geo.org/dowse1.htm

The Guardian. 2016. The prehistoric tombs that may have been used as 'telescopes'. 30 June. [online] Accessed December, 2017, https,//www.theguardian.com/science/2016/jun/30/the-prehistoric-tombs-that-may- have-been-used-as-telescopes

The Spalding Gentlemen's Society. 2013. History [online] Accessed May, 2013, www.spalding-gentlemens-society.org/history.html

Thom, A. 1954. The solar observatories of megalithic man. *Journal of The British Astronomical Association* 64, 396–404.

Thom, A. 1955. A statistical examination of the megalithic sites in Britain. *Journal of the Royal Statistical Society* Series A (General) 118 (3), 275–295.

Thom, A. 1958. An empirical investigation of atmospheric refraction. *Empire Empirical Review* 14, 248–262.

Thom, A. 1961a. The geometry of megalithic man. *The Mathematical Gazette* 45, 83–93.

Thom, A. 1961b. The egg-shaped standing stone rings of Britain. *Archives International d'Histoire des Sciences* 14, 291.

Thom, A. 1962. The megalithic unit of length. *Journal of the Royal Statistical Society* Series A125 (2), 243–251.

Thom, A. 1964a. The larger units of length of megalithic man. *Journal of the Royal Statistical Society* Series A127 (4), 527–523.

Thom, A. 1964b. Megalithic geometry in standing stones. *New Scientist* 21, 690–692.

Thom, A. 1964c. Observatories in ancient Britain *New Scientist* 21, 17–19.

Thom, A. 1966a Megaliths and mathematics. *Antiquity* 40, 121–128.

Thom, A. 1966b. Lunar observatories of megalithic man. *Nature* 212, 1527–1528.

Thom, A. 1967. *Megalithic Sites in Britain*. Oxford, Oxford University Press.

Thom, A. 1971. *Megalithic Lunar Observatories*. Oxford, Oxford University Press.

Thom, A. and Burl. A. 1990. *Stone Rows and Standing Stones: Britain, Ireland and Brittany*. Oxford, British Archaeological Report S560.

Thom, A. and Merritt, R.L. 1978. Some megalithic sites in Shetland. *Journal for the History of Astronomy* 9, 54–60.

Thom, A. and Thom, A.S. 1971. The astronomical significance of the large Carnac menhirs *Journal for the History of Astronomy* 2 (3), 147–160.

Thom, A. and Thom, A.S. 1972. The Carnac alignments. *Journal for the History of Astronomy* 3 (6), 11–26.

Thom, A. and Thom, A.S. 1978a. A reconsideration of the lunar sites in Britain. *Journal for the History of Astronomy* 9 (3), 170–179.

Thom, A. and Thom, A.S. 1978b. *Megalithic Remains in Britain and Brittany*. Oxford, Clarendon Press.

Thom, A. and Thom, A.S. 1979. Another lunar site in Kintyre. *Archaeoastronomy Supplement to the Journal for the History of Astronomy* 10 (1), S97–98.

Thom, A. and Thom, A.S. 1980a. *Megalithic Rings, collated with archaeological notes by A. Burl*. Oxford, British Archaeological Report 81.

Thom, A. and Thom A.S. 1980b. A new study of all megalithic lunar lines. *Archaeoastronomy Supplement to the Journal for the History of Astronomy* 11 (2), S78–S89.

Thom, A. and Thom, A.S. 1980c. Astronomical foresights used by megalithic man. *Archaeoastronomy Supplement to the Journal for the History of Astronomy*, 11 (2), S90–S94.
Thom, A. and Thom, A.S. 1983. Observation of the moon in megalithic times. *Archaeoastronomy Supplement to the Journal for the History of Astronomy* 14 (5), S57–S66.
Thom, A. and Thom, A.S. 1984. The two major megalithic observatories in Scotland. *Archaeoastronomy Supplement to the Journal for the History of Astronomy* 7, S129–S148.
Thom, A., Thom, A.S. and Foord, T.R. 1976. Avebury (1): a new assessment of the geometry and metrology of the ring. *Journal for the History of Astronomy* 7, 183–192.
Thom, A.S. 1984. Solar and lunar observatories of the megalithic astronomers. In Krupp (ed.) 1984, 83–168.
Thomas, F.W.L. 1851. Account of some of the Celtic antiquities of Orkney, including the Stones of Stenness, tumuli, Picts-houses, &c., with plans ... *Archaeologia* 34, 88–136.
Thomas, J. 1999. *Understanding the Neolithic*. London, Routledge.
Thomas, J. 2006. Phenomenology and material culture. In C. Tilley, W. Keane, S. Küchler, M. Rowlands and P. Spyer (eds), *Handbook of Material Culture*, London, Sage, 43–59.
Thomas, J. 2015. The future of archaeological thinking. *Antiquity* 89 (348), 1287–1296.
Thompson, J.E.S. 1974. Maya Astronomy. *Philosophical Transactions of the Royal Society of London* A176, 83–98.
Tichy, F. 1993. Mesoamerican geometry combined with astronomy and calendar, the way to realise orientation. In Ruggles (ed.) 1993b, 278–287.
Tilley, C. 1994. *A Phenomenology of Landscape: places, paths and monuments.* Oxford, Berg.
Tilley, C. 1996. *An Ethnography of the Neolithic*. Cambridge, Cambridge University Press.
Tilley, C. 1998. Archaeology: the loss of isolation. *Antiquity* 72, 691–693.
Toland, J. 1814. *History of the Druids with Appendix by R Huddleston*. Montrose.
Toland, J. 1815 [1726]. *A Critical History of the Celtic Religion and Learning Containing an Account of the Druids*. Edinburgh.
Tomasini, A. 1997. *The Shamanism of the Nivaklé of the Gran Chaco*. Buenos Aires, Argentine Center of American Ethnology.
Trigger, B. 1980. *Gordon Childe: revolutions in archaeology*. London, Thames and Hudson.
Trigger, B. 1998. 'The loss of innocence' in historical perspective. *Antiquity* 72, 694–698.
Trotter, A.P. 1927. Stonehenge as an astronomical implement. *Antiquity* 1, 42–53.
Tusa, S., Serio, G.F. and Hoskin, M. 1992. Orientations of the *Sesi* of Pantelleria. *Archaeoastronomy Supplement to the Journal for the History of Astronomy* 17, S15– S20.
Tyler, F.C. 1939. *The Geometrical Arrangement of Ancient Sites*. London, Simpkin Marshall.
Tylor, E.B. 1920 [1871]. *Primitive Culture*. London, John Murray.
Underwood, G. 1969. *The Pattern of the Past*. London, Museum Press.
UWTSD (The University of Wales Trinity Saint David) 2021. Cultural Astronomy and Astrology. [online] Accessed June 2021. https,//www.uwtsd.ac.uk/ma-cultural-astronomy- astrology/
Vadala, J.R. and Milbrath, S. 2016. Using virtual reality to understand astronomical knowledge and historical landscapes at Preclassic Cerros, Belize. *Journal of Skyscape Archaeology* 2 (1), 25–44.
Velikovsky, I. 1950. *Worlds in Collision*. New York, Doubleday.
Ventura, F. 2017. Beyond orientations and intentions towards motivation and meaning, an enduring challenge and a possible response. *Journal of Skyscape Archaeology* 3 (2), 176–190.
Ventura, F., Serio, G.F. and Hoskin, M. 1993. Possible Tally Stones at Mnajdra. *Journal for the History of Astronomy* 24 (3), 171–183.
Wang, Q.E. 2008. Beyond east and west, antiquarianism, evidential learning, and global trends in historical study. *Journal of World History* 19 (4), 489–519.
Wansey, H. 1809 [1796]. Account of Stonehenge. In J. Easton (ed.), *A Description of Stonehenge on Salisbury Plain*. Salisbury, J. Easton, 60–61.

Watkins, A. 1923. Cuttings. *Hereford Times*, October.
Watkins, A. 1974 [1925]. *The Old Straight Track*. London, Abacus.
Watkins, A. 1928. Arthur's Stone. *Transactions of the Woolhope Naturalists Field Club* 1928, 149–151.
Watkins, A. 1931. The proof of ancient track alignment. *Journal of the Antiquarian Association of the British Isles* 2, 65–71.
Watkins, A. 1932. *Archaic Tracks Round Cambridge*. London, Simpkin Marshall.
Watson, J. 1773. Druidical remains in or near the Parish of Halifax in Yorkshire, discovered and explained by the Rev. John Watson, M.A. F.S.A and Rector of Stockport in Cheshire. *Archaeologia* 2 (11), 353–363.
Webb, J. 1665 *Vindication of Stone-Heng Restored*. London, Bassett.
Weiss, P.L. 1990. Reflections on refraction: a source of ancient imprecision still humbles astronomers. *Science News* 138, 15, 236–237.
Weitzel, R.B. 1949. The dark phase of the moon and ancient Maya methods of solar eclipse prediction. *American Antiquity* 3, 230–233.
Welfare, A. 2008. The antiquarian tradition. In RCAHMS, *The Shadow of Bennachie: a field archaeology of Donside, Aberdeenshire*. Edinburgh, Royal Commission on the Ancient and Historical Monuments of Scotland/Society of Antiquaries of Scotland, 7–16.
Wheeler, Sir M. 1925. *Prehistoric and Roman Wales*. Oxford, Clarendon Press.
Wheeler, Sir M. 1955. *Still Digging: interleaves from an antiquary's notebook*. London, Michael Joseph.
White, M. 2017. *William Boyd Dawkins and the Victorian Science of Cave Hunting*. Barnsley, Pen and Sword.
Whitlock, G. 1994. Essay: archaeoastronomy and philosophy. *Archaeoastronomy and Ethnoastronomy News* 13. [online] Accessed March, 2015, terpconnect.umd.edu/~tlaloc/archastro/ae13.html
Willey, G.R. and Phillips, P. 1958. *Method and Theory in American Archaeology*. Chicago IL, Chicago University Press.
Williamson, R.A. (ed.). 1981. *Archaeoastronomy in the Americas*. Los Altos CA. Ballena Press/Center for Archaeoastronomy.
Williamson, R. A. 1987. Review of A. Benson and T. Hopkinson (eds), *Earth and Sky, Papers from the Northridge Conference on Archaeoastronomy*. *Archaeoastronomy Supplement to the Journal for the History of Astronomy* 11, S68.
Wilson, C. 2017. Prehistoric tombs may have doubled as star-gazing observatories. *New Scientist* 30.06.2016. [online] Accessed December 2017, https,//www.newscientist.com/article/2095597-prehistoric-tombs-may-have-doubled- as-star-gazing observatories/?utm_source=NSNS&utm_medium=SOC&utm_campaign=hoot&cmpi d=SOC%257CNSNS%257C2016-GLOBAL-hoot
Wilson, D. 1851. *The Archaeology and Prehistoric Annals of Scotland*. Scotland, Sutherland and Knox.
Wilson, D. 1851–52. Address. *Proceedings of the Society of Antiquaries for Scotland* 1 (1), 1–8.
Wilson, D. 1853. On the class of stone vessels known in Scotland as Druidical Pateræ *Proceedings of the Society of Antiquaries for Scotland* 1(2), 115–118.
Wilson, J. 1856. *The Lost Solar System of the Ancients Discovered*. London, Longman, Brown, Green, Longmans and Roberts.
Wilson, M. 2014. The British environmental movement: The development of an environmental consciousness and environmental activism, 1945–1975. Unpublished PhD thesis, University of Northumbria.
Windle, B.C.A. 1913. On certain megalithic remains immediately surrounding Lough Gur, County Limerick. *Proceedings of the Royal Irish Academy* 30, 283–306.
Winwood Reade, W. 1861. *The Veil of Isis or Mysteries of the Druids*. London, Charles J. Skeet. [online] Accessed April 2017, www.sacred-texts.com/pag/motd/motd.htm.
Witcher, R. 2018. Editorial. *Antiquity* 92, 3–6.
Wolfschmidt, G. 2008. *Prähistorische Astronomie und Ethnoastronomie*. Hamburg, Norderstedt bei Hamburg.

Wood, J. 1747. *Choir Gaure Vulgarly Called Stonehenge, on Salisbury Plain, Described, Restored, and Explained.* London, Bath and Salisbury.

Wood, J.E. 1978. *Sun, Moon and Standing Stones.* Oxford, Oxford University Press.

Zedda, M. and Belmonte, J.A. 2004. On the orientations of Sardinian nuraghes, some clues to their interpretation. *Journal for the History of Astronomy* 35 (1), 85–107.

Zedda, M.P. and Belmonte, J.A. (eds). 2007. *Lights and Shadows in Cultural Astronomy, Proceedings of the SEAC 2005, Isili, Sardinia, 28 June to 3 July*, Isili, Associazione Archeofila Sarda.

Zeilik, M. 1985. A reassessment of the Fajada Butte Solar Marker. *Archaeoastronomy Supplement to the Journal for the History of Astronomy* 16 (9), S69–S85.

Zeilik, M. 1989. Keeping the sacred and planting calendar. In Aveni (ed.) 1989b, 143–166.

Ziolkowski, M.S. and Lebeuf, A. 1991. Archaeoastronomie? *Les novelles de l'archaéologie* 44, 19–22.

Zotti, G. 2015. Visualization tools and techniques. In Ruggles (ed.) 2015a, 445–457.

Zotti, G. 2019. Review of Cultural Astronomy Beyond Paradigms. The 27th Annual Conference of the European Society of Astronomy. *Journal of Skyscape Archaeology* 5 (2), 215–220.

Zuidema, R.T. 1964. The Ceque System of Cuzco, the social organization of the capital of the Inca. *International Archives of Ethnography*, supplement to Vol. 50. Leiden, E.J. Brill.

Zuidema, R.T. 1990. *Inca Civilization in Cuzco.* Austin TX, University of Texas Press.

Glossary

Alignment

An alignment is where two or more objects are positioned in a straight line, for example in a row of upright stones. An alignment can also be found from a stone or other material artefact to a feature on the horizon, whether it is a hill or a rising or setting celestial body. Alignments to the horizon can be calculated from three known variables: **altitude**, **azimuth** and **latitude**. Because azimuth and latitude are particular to the location of the observer, to find the points at which celestial bodies rise and set it is necessary to convert azimuth to **declination**, which is a universal measurement. Therefore to test for astronomical alignments, the latitude (φ), azimuth (A) and horizon altitude (a) have to be measured and converted to declination (δ) using the standard equation:

$$\sin \delta = \sin \varphi \cdot \sin a - \cos \varphi \cdot \cos a \cdot \cos A$$

From the calculated declination it is then possible to identify which celestial body will rise or set on the horizon for any azimuth/latitude from a list of known declinations for the sun, moon, planets and stars. Archaeoastronomers can analyse the results to find if they match the declinations of the celestial bodies for any time period.

Altitude

Altitude is a measurement of the height of an object above the ground. In archaeoastronomy, horizon altitude is a measurement in degrees which represents the difference between a theoretically flat horizon of 0°, such as that seen on an open sea, and the visible **horizon**. it is another measure that needs to be taken into account when looking for an **alignment**. there are three ways to measure horizon altitude, first by using a clinometer, secondly by triangulating readings from ordnance survey maps, or thirdly if two or more measurements are obtained, altitude can be extrapolated by using photographs (Fig. G1).

Atmospheric refraction

Atmospheric refraction has the effect of bending the rays of celestial bodies downward, as viewed from a distance, and negatively affects the azimuth at which the sun can be seen to rise. This needs to be taken into account when **precision alignments** are being posited.

Azimuth

Starting from 0° **true north** an imaginary circle of 360° can be drawn around the observer's position to represent the circumference of the **horizon**. These measurements represent degrees of azimuth, so that if you are an observer facing true north you will be facing 0° of azimuth; by rotating your position you will observe 90° in the east, 180° in the south and 270° in the west.

Backsight (see Surveying for alignments)

Celestial mechanics

Celestial mechanics governs the movements of the sun, moon, planets and stars within the **celestial sphere**.

Celestial sphere

The celestial sphere (Fig. G2) is an imaginary sphere projected outwards around the earth with the earth at its centre. Its co-ordinates are **right ascension (RA)** and **declination**. From the viewpoint of a terrestrial observer the celestial sphere can be imagined as a dome projected into the sky overhead and because the earth rotates on its axis, this dome appears to rotate so it looks as if the celestial bodies themselves are moving. For example, from earth the sun is seen to rise in the east and set in the west.

Circumpolar stars

Circumpolar stars are those stars whose paths are so high above the horizon that they cannot be seen to rise or set at any time of the day or year. Whether a star is circumpolar is a function of latitude and horizon altitude. For example if the observer is standing at an elevation where the surrounding hills project higher into the sky giving for example 5° of altitude, then stars that would have been circumpolar on a horizon with 0° of altitude can be seen to rise and set at a declination that degree higher.

Crossovers

Because the moon's monthly path varies between being wider than and narrower than the solstice limits set by annual path of the sun, they cross over twice a month. This happens when the sun and the moon have the same declination though this is rarely visible. However, they can be determined empirically by observing where both objects rise or set on the horizon and noting when these points cross over (Fig. G3). Crossovers, as they are termed, occur at various times in the sun's cycle and may be significant for some cultures. For example around the times of the spring and autumn equinoxes they occur when the moon is full. Near the time of the solstices the crossovers occur at the times of the first and last crescent moon in both summer and winter (see Silva and Pimenta 2012). These crescent crossover declinations come very close to the declination values not only of the solstitial sun, but also that of the minor lunar standstill, though the range of days in which they may occur is dependent on latitude. In contrast to the lunar standstill cycle, these crossovers are annual events.

Cross-quarter days (see Sun)

Declination

The celestial sphere is divided by the celestial equator into two hemispheres, the northern and the southern; consequently the objects contained within the sphere are measured from the celestial equator to either of the celestial poles by degrees of declination. The measurement starts with 0° at the equator and ends with +90° degrees at the north celestial pole and –90° at the south celestial pole. Declination reflects the earth's terrestrial **latitude** projected onto the heavens and each degree of geocentric latitude determines at what degree of declination celestial bodies can be seen to rise or set on the **horizon** of that location. To find the value of this declination in the northern hemisphere, the latitude of the location must be subtracted from 90°. Thus, for example at Stonehenge where the latitude is 51°N the declination limit possible for rising and setting objects is +/–39° (90°–51°). Any object, such as a star, with a declination higher than +39° will describe a circle above the horizon (see **circumpolar stars**) and any object with a declination lower than –39° will not be seen at all. By contrast at a location of 57°N latitude, which is close to the latitude for the majority of the Aberdeenshire recumbent stone circles (RSCs), the limiting range of declination is +/–33° (90°–57°).

Eclipse

There are times when either the light of the sun or the reflected light of the moon is blocked out by an eclipse (Fig. G4). This occurs when, as seen from earth, the two bodies appear to be either closely aligned or opposite one another. A solar eclipse takes place when the moon passes the earth in front of the sun (Fig. G4a). Although this only happens in the new moon phase, the shadow cast on earth by the moon's body blocks out the light of the sun. A lunar eclipse occurs when the moon is full and opposite the sun. At this time the moon is behind the earth and in its shadow so no moon can be seen (Fig. G4b).

Ecliptic

The apparent annual path of the sun around the earth is called the ecliptic (see Fig. G2). The ecliptic is a great circle inclined to the plane of the equator, the angle of which reflects the earth's axial tilt in relation to the sun. This angle is known as

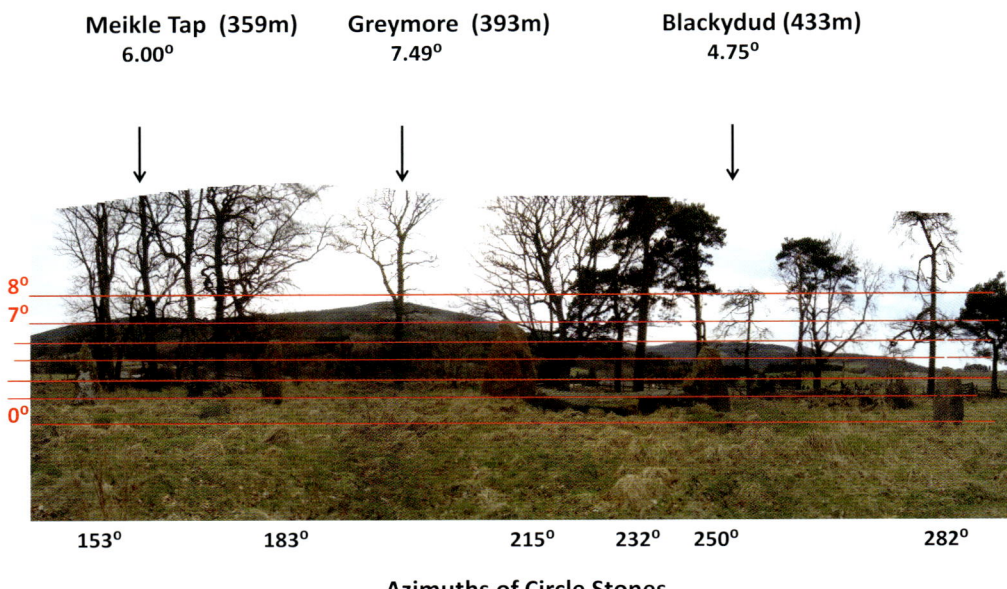

Figure G1. Annotated panorama of Sunhoney Recumbent Stone Circle showing how altitude can be measured using photographs.

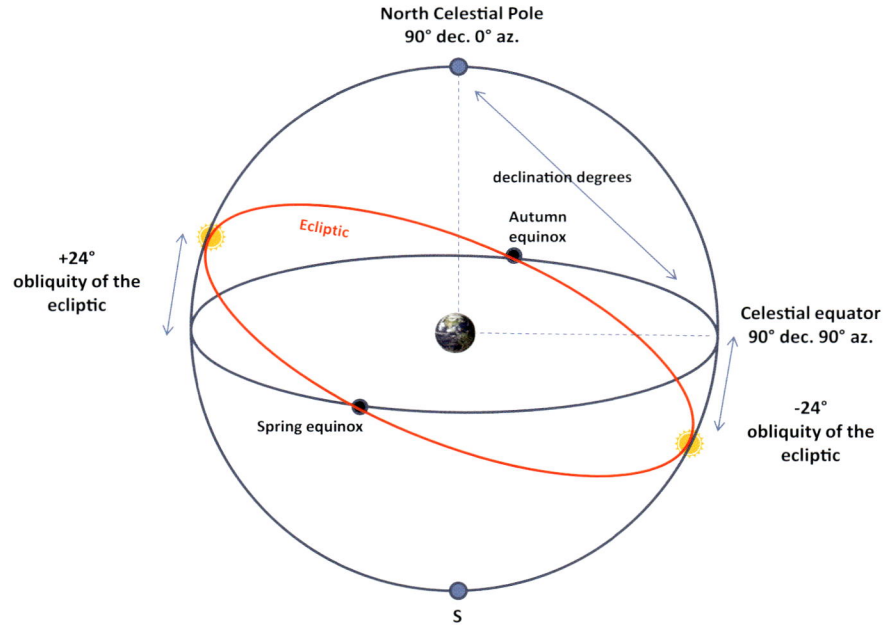

Figure G2. Schematic representation of the Celestial Sphere.

Glossary 267

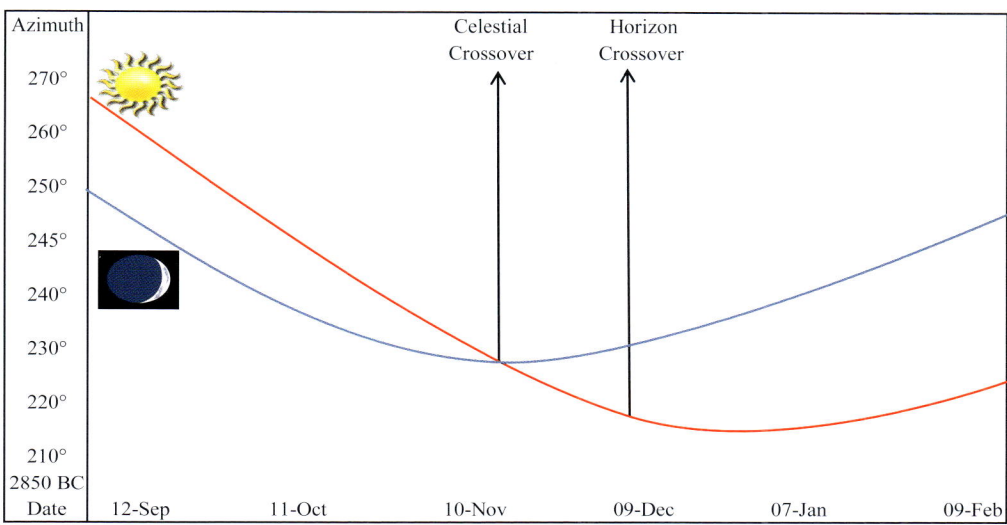

Figure G3. Passage of the sun and the moon at Tomnaverie Recumbent Stone Circle showing both celestial and horizon crossovers for 2580 BC.

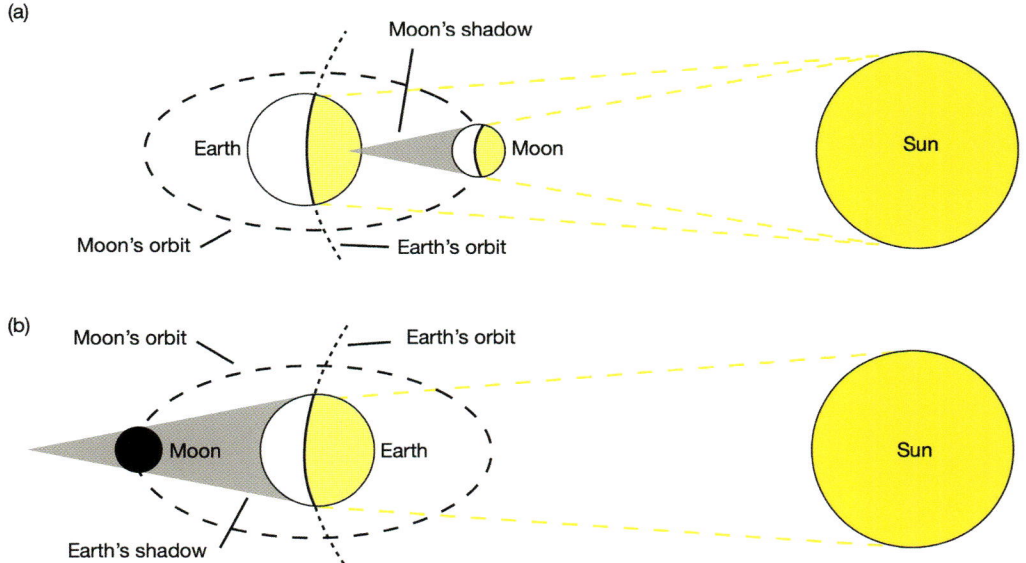

Figure G4. Diagrams of a solar eclipse (a) and a lunar eclipse (b).

the **obliquity of the ecliptic** which decreases over time because the earth slowly pivots on its axis over a period of some 26,000 years. This decrease in the angle of obliquity affects the sun's range of declination so that at 3000 BC it was +/−24.05° but today it is +/−23.4°.

Equinox (see **sun**)

Extinction angle (see **the stars' motions**)

Foresight (see **surveying for alignments**)

Horizon

The horizon is the place where the earth meets the sky and where celestial bodies are seen to rise and set. It appears as a circular plane around the observer, and positions along it can be measured in **azimuth.**

Heliacal risings and settings (see **the stars' motions**)

Latitude

Latitude is measured in +/− 90° from the equator. In the northern hemisphere the further north one travels from the equator, the higher the degree of latitude: the reverse in the southern hemisphere is that the further south one travels from the equator, the lower the latitude (0° to 90°S or -90°). Consequently latitude, like declination affects what can be seen to rise and set on the observer's horizon. For example the declination of the star Deneb Adige at 2500 BC was +36.26° which meant it could be seen to rise and set at Stonehenge but it was circumpolar (**circumpolar stars**) in Aberdeenshire.

Longitude

Lines of longitude are determined by their angular distance from the Greenwich prime meridian, a great circle, which passes through the north and south poles and the equator. The measurement starts at 0° at Greenwich and continues 180° east and west until it reaches the International Date Line, halfway around the world from the Greenwich meridian.

Magnetic north

A compass, used in the field to measure degrees of **azimuth**, responds to the earth's magnetic field so that it gives readings of magnetic north, not **true north**. All magnetic readings have to be adjusted to true north by the amount of magnetic declination, also known as magnetic variation, which differs according to both geographic location and time. For example, in Aberdeen, Scotland it was 6°30' west of true north in 1991 but has since moved eastwards by 5°12' so that in 2021 it is 1°18' west of true north.

Major lunar standstill (see **moon**)

Metonic cycle of the moon

The Metonic cycle of the moon is the time taken for the moon to return with the same phase and position relative to the earth that it previously occupied on the same day and time. This cycle takes 19 years or 235 synodic months. This is not the same as the lunar nodal cycle (standstill cycle, see **moon**) which occurs because the moon's orbit is tilted at 5.15° to the earth's axis.

Minor lunar standstill (see **moon**)

Moon

The moon reflects the light of the sun but because it orbits the earth rather than the sun, the portion which is illuminated changes over the course of a **synodic lunar month**. Unlike the sun which follows an annual path, changes in the moon's declination take place over a month (see Thom 1971, 17–25). Because of its celestial latitude of +/–5.15°, the moon's path can reach its most northerly or southerly rising or setting point that degree further than that reached by the sun at its **solstice**. The point at which the moon reaches its maximum declination is called a lunar extreme or major standstill (Fig. G5). In 3000 BC these limits were +28.3° and −30.05° (Ruggles 1999a, 57). Because the equation used to calculate declination assumes a position at the centre of the earth instead of one at the surface, a negative correction for parallax of about 0.95° needs to be applied when looking for alignments to the moon (Ruggles 1999a, 23). Over a period of 9.3 years after the major standstill the moon's limits narrow +/–5.15° within the solstice extremes until the minor lunar standstill is reached (Fig. G5). The declinations for 3000 BC, also adjusted for parallax (the adjustment necessary between the earth's centre and its surface) were +18.05° and −19.65° (Ruggles 1999a, 23, 57). From this time they commence to widen again in the direction of the major standstill declinations. The entire cycle from one major lunar standstill to the next takes 18.6 years to complete. Another factor which needs to be taken into account when looking for high precision alignments for the moon is perturbation, a slight wobble in the moon's axis of up to 9' of arc.

Obliquity of the ecliptic (see **ecliptic**)

Orientations

An orientation is a general compass direction so that a structure with an easterly orientation for example would not be precisely 90° east but close to it. In archaeoastronomy,

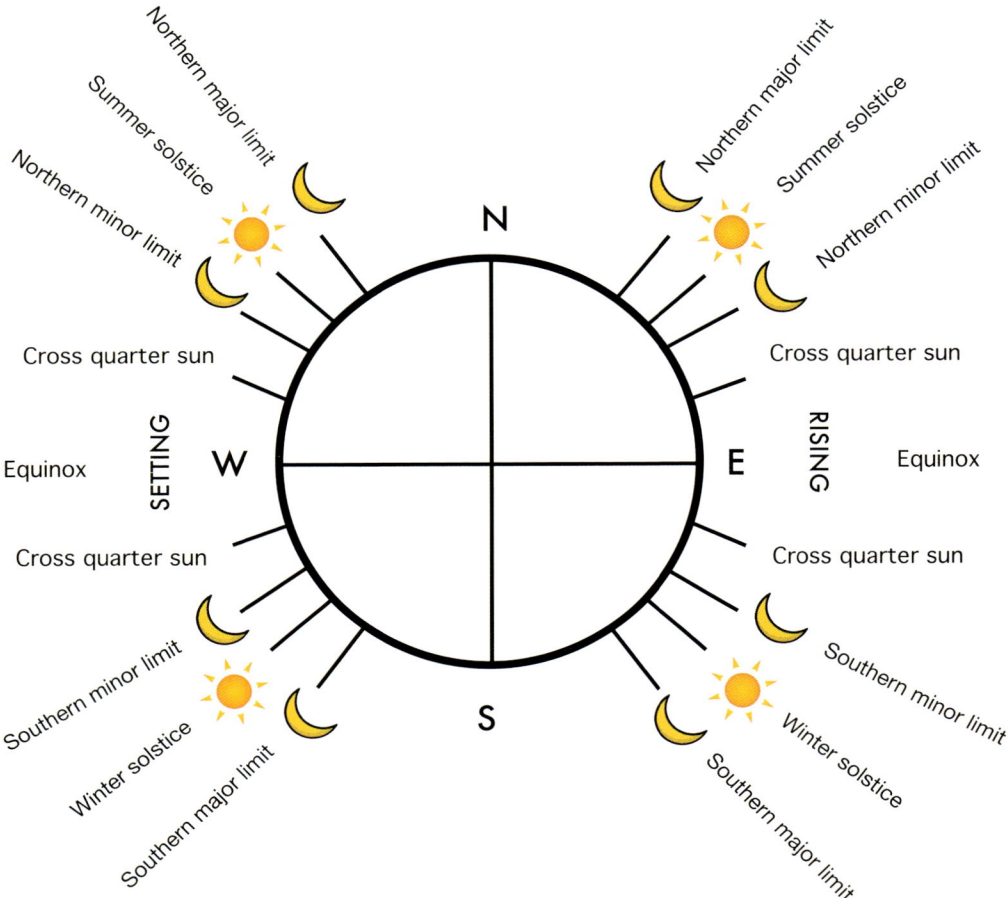

Figure G5. Schematic representation of where the sun's solstices, the sun's cross quarter days and the moon's major and minor lunar standstills appear on the horizon in Britain.

suggested orientations of stones or material artefacts use less stringent criteria than **precision alignments** and can be posited from around +/−2° of precision.

Perturbation (see **moon**)

Parallax (see **moon**)

Positional astronomy

Positional astronomy is concerned with where in the **celestial sphere**, the sun, moon, planets and stars are located.

Figure G6. Measuring the azimuths of two stones at Loanhead of Daviot Recumbent Stone Circle.

Precession of the equinoxes (see **sun**)

Precision alignments

Precision alignments refer to those alignments which are measured in arc minutes to less than 1°.

Right ascension (RA)

Right ascension is a measurement around the **celestial sphere** from 0° at the **vernal equinox** point, also known as the First Point of Aries. It reflects the earth's terrestrial latitude and is measured in hours so that 15° of RA equals 1 hour.

Solstice (see **sun**)

Sun

Because the path of the **ecliptic** crosses the equator, the sun's declination ranges between 0° at the equinoxes and +/−23.4° at the solstices, thus determining the annual seasons of spring, summer, autumn and winter. As viewed from earth, in the northern hemisphere, the sun appears to move along the ecliptic and it reaches its highest declination close to 21 June, the longest day, and its lowest declination close to 21 December, the shortest day. Around these dates when the sun is at its most northerly and/or southerly rising and setting positions it appears to rise and set at the same place on the horizon for a few days. Then times when the sun appears to stand still are referred to as **solstice**s (Fig. G5). Equally between the solstices and equinoxes are the astronomical cross-quarter days which occur around 5 February, 6 May, 7 August and 8 November when the sun's declination is around +/−16.5° (Fig. G5). As shown in Figure G2, the ecliptic cuts the equator at the points of the two **equinox**es, the vernal or spring equinox, also known as the First Point of Aries, and the autumnal equinox which, in the northern hemisphere, occur close to 21 March and 21 September respectively, when days and nights are approximately equal in length (Fig. G2). At the equinoxes the sun's declination is 0° and on a flat horizon the sun rises at 90° and sets at 270° of azimuth. The pivotal movement of the earth, noted above, causes a very gradual shift of the equinoctial points backwards along the ecliptic and this is known as the **precession of the equinoxes.**

Surveying for alignments

The archaeoastronomer surveys sites to look for astronomical alignments. Determining these involves finding a site of interest and deciding on an observation point, known as the backsight, from where measurements can be taken. From the backsight a straight virtual line can be drawn through a particular feature, such as a stone of interest, to the point, known as the foresight, where the line intersects the **horizon**. For example if the researcher stands in the centre of a stone circle, a number of virtual lines can be drawn which run from this central backsight through each stone in the circle to foresights on the visible horizon (see Fig. G6). Either a theodolite or a magnetic compass can be used but all measurements need to be adjusted to ensure that the measurements are adjusted to **true north**. In this way the position of the stones can be measured in degrees of true **azimuth**.

Synodic lunar month

A synodic lunar month refers to the 29.5 days that elapse between successive recurrences of the same phase, for example from full moon to full moon. Over a month, as seen from earth, the moon goes through different phases (first crescent, 1st–3rd quarters), as it waxes from dark moon, when it is invisible, to full moon (Fig. G7). From that point the visible portion gets smaller as it wanes to invisibility once again.

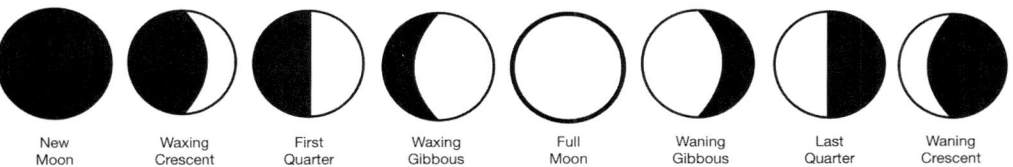

Figure G7. The moon's monthly cycle showing its different phases.

The planets

The planets, like the earth, also orbit the sun though their elliptical orbits vary in their synodic periods, which is the time taken for them to return to the same or approximately the same position relative to the sun as seen by an observer on earth. Mercury for example takes 88 days, Saturn takes 29 years while Neptune takes 165 years. Because they all occupy a narrow band approximately 9° either side of the ecliptic they have variable declination ranges. Venus orbits between the sun and the earth and is brighter in the sky than any star. When it rises in the east before the sun it is known as the morning star but cannot be seen to set as it disappears from view in the full light of the setting sun. When Venus rises in the east after the sun, the sunrise blocks out its view in the east but at this time Venus sets after the sun so it can be seen as the evening star.

The stars' motions

The fixed stars change their position only slightly over time. Because they are so far away their proper motion is very slight relative to the earth and change is only apparent over hundreds of years. Additionally, there is a 'drift in star positions' which occurs because of the **precession of the equinoxes** which causes a slow movement of the zero point, from which their positions are measured (North 1996, 7). They also vary in their proper motions, for example, between 2500 BC and 2000 BC, the declination of Denib Adige only changed by +0.22° whereas that of Capella changed by +2.72°. This makes it much more difficult to predicate stellar alignments on precise azimuths because there is always the issue of dating. The pole stars are the conspicuous fixed stars closest to the celestial poles. There was no pole star in the above period but the star closest to the north celestial pole was Thuban with a declination of +88.33° in 2500 BC. Today's pole star is Polaris which is 0.75° from the North Pole (Measurement taken from Stellarium v. 0.21.1, August 2021). First magnitude stars are the brightest stars in the sky with magnitudes between −1 and +1, and these are the stars that archaeoastronomers generally look for. Additionally, when looking for a stellar event, the extinction angle of a star has to be taken into account because atmospheric haze can render a star invisible on the horizon. Although not every star does this, some stars as well as planets go through a period of invisibility when the sun, close by, outshines them: as the sun moves along the horizon, the invisible star becomes visible again and the first or last sight of it is termed heliacal rising or heliacal setting.

True north

The earth rotates on two geographic poles, the north and the south geodetic poles, which is where the lines of **longitude** merge. Because True north is a geographic direction which points to the north geodetic pole, it varies from magnetic or compass north (**magnetic north**), and is therefore called true.

Index

Page numbers in *italics* are figures.

academic programmes/courses 161–4, 174, 177, 182, 206–8, *207*, 221–2, 225–6
Age of Enlightenment 15
alignments *see* orientation and alignments
Americas *see* New World
ancient wisdom 18, 20, 76, 95, 96, 108, 160, 176
anthropology 46, 143
antiquarianism 2, 10, 11–15, *14*, *23*, 25, 26–9, *28*, 48
 and astronomy 32–7, *36*
 background 15–18
 and esotericism 18–20
 methodology 29–32
 societies 17–18, 21–5
archaeoastronomers 209, 219–23
archaeology/archaeologists 24, 47–8, 60–4, 216–19, 225–6
 antiquarian methodology 29–32
 and archaeoastronomy 98–100, 219
 and Britain 152–5
 British 1–2
 contested space 2–7
 and convergence 208–11, 212–13, 215
 culture history approach 61–4
 EAA 187–8
 esoteric 64–5
 landscape 8, 72, 156–7, 165
 and megalithic science 115–19
 processualism 88, 90–1, 103, 152–5
 and science 67–70
archaeotopography 172–3
astro-archaeology 88–93, 98
astronomical theories 37–46, *41*, 48–9
Atkinson, Richard 89, 94, 99–100, 109, 113, 148, 164
Aubrey, John 16, 22, 29, 43
Avebury (Wiltshire) 27, 29, 44, 63, 71, 109
Aveni, Anthony 88, 126–7, *127*, 129, 130, 134, 136–7, 138–9, 141–4, 151, 178, 183, 208

Bahn, P. G. 30, 87, 213
Baity, Elizabeth 125–7
Bauval, Robert 160
Belloc, Hilaire 74–5
Belmonte, Juan Antonio 132, 170, *171*–2, 172, 173–4, 190, 192, 201, 202, 222
Bender, Barbara 3, 7, 208

Bennett, A. F. 68, 77
Boece, Hector 27, 38, 43–4
Bourdieu, P. 4, 5, 87
Bradley, Richard 211, 219
Brady, Bernadette 192, 193, 206, *207*
Braudel, Fernand 11, 18, 31, 48
Britain 113, 122, 147–52, *152*, 155–9, *158*, 164–7, 208, 224, 226
 archaeology 1–2, 152–5
 cultural astronomy 183
 and esotericism 159–60
 learning resources/courses/academic programmes 161–4, 206–8, 225–6
 see also Avebury; Calanais; Glastonbury; Isle of Mona; Maeshowe; Silbury; stone circles; Stonehenge
Burl, Aubrey 27, 97, 109, 113, 120–1, 151, 152, 156, 164

Calanais (Callenish) (Isle of Lewis) 27, 33, 43, 53, *58*, 93, 149
calendars 56, 77, 80–1, 104, 105, 109–10, 112, 136, 168, 177, 179, 213
 Stonehenge as 33, 38, 49, 56, 63, 69, 93–5
Callender, Henry 32, 33, 43
Camden, William 16, 29
Campion, Nicholas 8, 19, 85, 97, 160, 199–200, 206, *207*, 222
Carlson, John B. 127–8, 130–1, *131*, 134–5, 137, 165
Carnac (Brittany) 56, *57*, 76, 108, 110
Center for Archaeoastronomy 130–1
Central and Eastern Europe 179–82
Childe, V. Gordon 61, 62, 90, 113
Clarke, David 91, 92, 120, 154
computer technology 91–2, *92*
conferences 64, 223
 'Oxford' 115, 119, 142, 144, 147, 164, 166, 187, 189
 see also individual societies
contestation 2–7, 46–8, 190, 215–16, 224
convergence 208–11, 212–13, 224–5
Crawford, O. G. S. 61, 66, 72, 85, 86
cultural astronomy 132–3, *133*, 140, 168, 169–73, 182–4, 186, 189, 201, 204

Darvill, Timothy 165, 200, 209–10, *210*, 212, 221
Devoir, Alfred 56, *57*, 59–60, 80

diffusion theory 43, 62, 65, 90
Diodorus of Sicily 26–7, 42, 56, 223
Douglas, John 18, 19, 43, 62
dowsing 76, 82, *83*, 97
druids/druidry 20, 26–7, 33–4, 35, *36*, 40, 42–6, 47, 49, 82, 96
Duke, Edward 21, 22, 27, 35, 39–40, *41*, 44, 45, 47
Dupuis, Charles François 17, 34, 176

EAA (European Association of Archaeologists) 187–8, 223, 224, 226
earth mysteries 95–8, 111, 202, 203
Eastern Europe see Central and Eastern Europe
eclipses 93–4, 95, 104, 106, *267*
Eddy, John 88, 100, 124, 135, 138, 147–8
Egypt 39, 45, 63, 65, 95
Ellegård, A. 108, 114, 151
esoteric archaeology 64–5, 85
esotericism 2, 18–20, 81–4, 159–60, 202–3, 218
ethnoastronomy 126–7, 128–30, 204
Europe 168, 188–90
  communities 184–8, *185*
  cultural astronomy 182–4
  and Michael Hoskin 169–73, *171–2*
  studies 173–82, *178*
  see also Britain; France; Germany; Italy; Menorca

Farrer, C. 141
Flinders Petrie, William 30, 53
Foucault, Michel 15, 48–9
France 56, *57*, 59–60, 64, *76*, 108, 110, 174, 175–6
Fraser, John 54, 59, 74
Freemasonry 19–20, 22, 49

Gaillard, F. 42, 56, 175
Gardner, Grahame 76, *83*
Gautschy, Rita 177, 221
Geoffrey of Monmouth 15–16, 38
Germany 80–1, 176–7, *178*
Glastonbury 81–2, 96, 97, 202
gnomons 37, 39, 49, 52, 77
Goodrum, M. R. 16, 22, 30–1
Gordon, Sandy 12, 24
green/brown methodologies 142–5, 169, 189, 204, 205
Griffith, John 60, 65, 66, 88

Hawkes, Christopher 62–3, 65, 86, 99, 217
Hawkes, Jacquetta 8, 62, 63, 99, 113
Hawkins, Gerald 10, 88–9, *89*, 91–2, *92*, 98–100, 137, 157
Higgins, Godfrey 33, 35, *36*, 44
Hipparchus 44
historiography 7–9
horizon astronomy 32, 37, 156, 159, 191, 203

Hoskin, Michael 113, 115, 148, 158, 169–73
Hoyle, Fred 89, 93–5, 99
Hudson, Herbert 59, 64, *73*, 79
hybrid studies 79–81

INSAP (The Inspiration of Astronomical Phenomena) 187
Institute of Field Archaeologists 122
ISAAC (International Society for Archaeoastronomy and Astronomy in Culture) 168, 186–7, 189, 190, 224
Isle of Mona (Anglesey) 26–7
Iwaniszewski, Stanislaw 112, 129, 132, 135, 143–4, 173–4, 176, 179–81, 182–4, 188, 196–7, 201, 213

journals/publications 113, 122, 130, 134–6, 140, 146, 147, 148, 156–7, 181–2, 203–5, 204–5, 212, 218
  Antiquity 66, 69, 85, 86, 98, 122
  Archaeoastronomy Bulletin 130
  Astronomie et Sciences Humaines 181
  The Journal of Astronomy in Culture 140, 205
  Journal for the History of Astronomy (JHA) 113, 122, 147, 169, 188–9
  Journal of Skyscape Archaeology (JSA) 205, 212, 214, 217, 223
  Nature 51, 66, 71

Kepler, Johannes 19
Kintigh, Keith 141–2, 186, 210

landscape archaeology 8, 72, 156–7, 165
landscape lines 72–4, *73*, 84–6, 202
  esotericism and metrology 81–4, *83*
  hybrid studies 80–1
  and Romanticism 74–9, *76*
landscape phenomenology 164
Latin America 91, 124, *127*, 129, 131–3, *133*, 137, 139, 140, 141, 146, 180, 182, 224
  Nazca ceremonial site (Peru) 79, 124, *124*
Leland, John 16, 21
Lennox, Charles, 3rd Duke of Richmond 17
Lewis, A. L. 53, 55, 56
ley lines 75–9, 85, 96–7, 112, 120–1, 202, 203, 216, 218
Lockyer, Sir Norman 10, 50–1, 66, 70, 82, 85, 220–1
  and landscape lines 72, 79–80
  orientation 51–2, 53, 54–5, 59, 64, 66, 68
Lubbock, John 31, 46, 48
Lyell, Sir Charles 31, 32

MacLagan, Christine 34
Maeshowe (Orkney) 74, 156, 165
Maltwood, Katherine 81, 97, 98
Malville, Kim 157, 196, 200, 205, 206, 212

Mann, Ludovic McLellan 82–4, 109
Marshack, Alexander 95, 168, 192
meaning 1, 4, 7, 49, 123, 154, 174, 193, 198, 206, 225
measurement systems 45–6, 49, 81–4, 108–9
megalithic science 101–3, 119–22, 160, 112–15
    and New Agers 110–14
    Thom paradigm 103–10, *105, 107*
Menorca 169, *170, 171, 171–2*
methodology 6, 29–37, 173, 193–4, 196–7, 201, 220, 223
metonic cycles 27, 33, 38, 57
metrology 45–6, 49, 81–4, 108–9
Michell, John 9, 89, 97–8, 111, 120, 160
monumentalism 16, 173
monuments 26–7, 71, 82
    astronomical theories 37–42, 48–9, 223
    builders of 42–4, 49, 63, 82, 115–16, 120
    see also megalithic science
moon 26–7, 38–40, 49, 55–9, 103, 151, 192, 223
    crossovers 174–5, 192, 212
    equinoctial full moon (EFM) 175, 212
    and esotericism 18
    lunar month 272–3, *273*
    metonic cycles 27, 33, 38, 57
    standstills 57, 104, 106, 192, 198
    and Stonehenge 93–5, 99, 210
    Thom paradigm 104–6, *105*
    see also calendars; orientation and alignments

National Astronomy Meetings (NAM) 199, *200*, 204
Nazca ceremonial site (Peru) 79, 124, *124*
New Agers/New Age 2, 3, 9, 87, 95–8, *97*, 110–12, 135–6, 176, 218
New World 88, 123–8, 145–6, 182
    antiquarians 15, 24
    Center for Archaeoastronomy 130–1, *131*
    communities 130–40, *131, 133*, 145–6
    conferences 64, 133, 135, 136–40, 144, 145–6
    debates and divides 140–5
    ethnoastronomy 128–30
    'New' archaeology (processualism) 90
    orientation studies 59, 60
    publications 134–6, 140, 146
Newgrange (Ireland) 63, 156, *158*, 165, 211
Newham, C. A. 89, 94, 100, 122
Newton, Sir Isaac 15, 22, 45
Nissen, Heinrich 52, 66

observatories 32–3, 42, 121, 202
Old World 60, 123, 142–5
    see also Britain; megalithic science
ontological turn 194–7, 212
Ordnance Survey 17–18, 82
orientation and alignments 50, 67–70, 151, 192–3, *270*
    and archaeology 60–1, 86

Central and Eastern Europe 179–80
and Hawkins 88–9, *89*
and Lockyer 50–3
practice 53–60, *54, 54, 57–8*
and Thom's paradigm 109
see also landscape lines
'Oxford' conferences 115, 119, 142, 144, 147, 164, 166, 187, 189

Parker Pearson, Mike 8, 154, 167, 203, 219
Penrose, F. C. 10, 51–2, 56, 69, 72
Petrie, Sir William Flinders 30, 45–6, 61, 220
phenomenology 154, 155, 164, 197–8, 198, 212, 2001
Piggott, S. 19, 29–30, 63, 82, 89, 100
Pitt Rivers, A. Lane-Fox (General) 25, 30, 61
planetariums 39–40, 49, 132, *200*
    software 158, 169, 194, 198
Pliny the Elder 10, 27, 42
Plot, Robert 27, 32–3
Portugal 174–5
postprocessualism 147, 153–6, *155*, 159, 163, 165, 184
processualism ('New' archaeology) 88, 90–1, 103, 152–5
    see also postprocessualism
progression theory 46, 48, 62, 98
pseudoarchaeology 159–60, 203, 218
pseudoscience *see* esotericism; New Agers/New Age
Ptolemy 35

radiocarbon dating 61, 89–90, 92, 99, 121
recumbent stone circles 9, 55, 150–1, *266–7, 271*
reflexivity 8, 153, 154, 193, 196, 201
religion 34, 42, *59*, 62, 63–4, 81, 118
    see also druids/druidry; New Agers/New Age
Renfrew, Colin 30, 87, 91, 98, 100, 103, 114
Reuter, Otto 80, 81
Rollright Stones complex 97, *97*
Romanticism 18, 19, 49, 75, 78
Rowlands, Henry 24, 26, 27, 30
Royal Archaeological Institute 24, 61, 66
Ruggles, Clive 87, 113, 114, 117, 135, 144, 148, 149–52, 155–6, 157–9, 165, 167, 196, 200–1, 213, 220–1, 222
    courses in archaeoastronomy 161–4
    and cultural astronomy 183, 186, 189, 206
    Handbook of Archaeoastronomy and Ethnoastronomy 133, 204, 211
    and ISAAC 186–7
    and SEAC *150*, 186

Scott, Sir Walter 11–15, *12*, 22
SEAC (Société Européenne pour L'Astronomie dans la Culture/European Society for Astronomy in

Culture) 168, 181, 184–6, *185*, 188, 189, 190, 191, 197, 224
sidelining 216, 217–18, 219–21
Silbury 22, 29, 40, 72, 198
Silva, Fabio 198–9, *199*, 200–1, 205, *207*, 221
Simpson, J. Y. 33, 46, 47
Sims, Lionel 162–4, *163*, 192, 193, 198, 199, 206, 210, 221
skyscapes/skyscape archaeology 197–201, *199*–*200*, 208, 211–12, 221, 224–5
Sloane, Sir Hans 24
Smith, John (of Boscombe) 33, 35, 37, 38
Smyth, Charles Piazzi 39, 45
Snow, C. P. 87, 100
societies
    antiquarian 17–18, 21–5, *23*, 61, 66, 67
    modern 139, 140, 168, 177, 179, 181
        see also *individual societies*; ISAAC; SEAC
Somerville, Boyle 50, 70, 86
    landscape lines 84
    and orientation 51, 53, 55, 56–9, *58*, 68, 69
Spencer, Herbert 46, 48
Spencer, John Houghton 42
standstills 57, 104, 106, 192
Stanton Drew (Somerset) 27, *28*, 37, 38
stars 38–9, 192–3, 198
    see also moon; sun
stone circles 30
    and the druids 47, 82
    and landscape lines 74, 77, 97, *97*
    and the lunar cycle 27
    Michell on 98
    as observatories 33–4, 39
    orientation 52–3, 55–6, 60, 65, 68
    in Scotland 38, 43, 55, *83*, *107*
    and the Thom paradigm 104, 106, *107*, 108
    see also recumbent stone circles; Stonehenge
Stonehenge 49, 152, *152*, 209, 216
    and antiquarians 29
    astronomical theories 27, 38–40, 66–7
    builders 43–4
    early astronomical methodology 33–5, *36*, 37
    and Hawkins 89, 91–2, *92*, 93–5, 99–100
    landscape lines 72, 74, 76, 77
    Lockyer on 66
    and orientation 56, 165
    purpose of 63, 156
    and Ruggles 167
    Stukeley on 22, 29, 34–5, 38, 44, 45–6
    and the sun 34–5, 37, 38, 56
Straight Track Postal Portfolio Club 78, 86
Stukeley, William 10, *14*, 16–17, 19, 21, 27, *28*, 29, 30, 39–40, 71
    and Stonehenge 22, 34–5, 38, 44, 45–6
sun 192, 194
    and antiquarians 27, 32, 34, 35
    and computer technology 91, 98, 99
    and esotericism 18, 20, 81, 86
    and European cultural astronomy 174–6, 179–80
    and Hoskin 170
    and landscape lines *73*, 74, 76–7, 78, 79–80, 84
    and monuments 38–40, *41*, 42, 49, 202, 215–16
    and Stonehenge 93–5, 198
    Thom paradigm 104, *105*, 109–10, *110*
    see also orientation and alignment
surveying 29, 37, *127*, 155, 157
    and Lockyer 54–5, *54*, 64, 66, 77–8
    and Thom 104, 106

terminology 1, 5–6, 16, 21, 24, 32, 65–7, 112–15
Teudt, Wilhelm 80–1
Theoretical Archaeology Group (TAG) 114, 119, 122, *163*, 195, 199, *199*, 204, 205, *207*, 209, 210, 223, 226
theories, astronomical 37–46, *41*, 48–9
Thom, Alexander 10, 57, 86, 101–3, *102*, 113, 148, 149–51, 213
    Thom paradigm 103–11, *105*, *107*, 112, 115–16, 121, 122
Thomas, F. W. 38–9
Thompson, Sir Eric J. 125
Three Age system 31–2, 48, 62, 98
Tilley, Christopher 153–4, 165, 184
Toland, John 27, 33, 43
Tyler, F. C. 77, 78, 79, 80, 84

universal measures 83–5
universal solar religion 34
universities 4, 61, 114, 223, 225–6
    academic programmes/courses 161–4, 174, 177, 182, 206–8, *207*, 221–2

Watkins, Alfred 75–9, 85, 96, 217–18
Wheeler, Sir Mortimer 61, 72, 220
Williamson, Ray 130, 134, 138–9
Wilson, Daniel 22, 25, 32, 47, 67
Wood, John 20, 27, 38, 39